CANADA AS A SETTLER COLONY ON THE QUESTION OF PALESTINE

CANADA AS A SETTLER COLONY ON THE QUESTION OF PALESTINE

EDITED BY
JEREMY WILDEMAN & M. MUHANNAD AYYASH

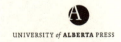
UNIVERSITY of ALBERTA PRESS

Published by

University of Alberta Press
1–16 Rutherford Library South
11204 89 Avenue NW
Edmonton, Alberta, Canada T6G 2J4
amiskwaciwâskahikan | Treaty 6 |
Métis Territory
uap.ualberta.ca | uapress@ualberta.ca

Copyright © 2023 University of Alberta Press

LIBRARY AND ARCHIVES CANADA
CATALOGUING IN PUBLICATION

Title: Canada as a settler colony on the question of Palestine / edited by Jeremy Wildeman and M. Muhannad Ayyash.
Names: Wildeman, Jeremy, editor. | Ayyash, Mark Muhannad, editor.
Description: Includes bibliographical references and index.
Identifiers: Canadiana (print) 20230444865 | Canadiana (ebook) 20230445101 | ISBN 9781772126853 (softcover) | ISBN 9781772127287 (EPUB) | ISBN 9781772127294 (PDF)
Subjects: LCSH: Canada—Foreign relations—Palestine. | LCSH: Palestine—Foreign relations—Canada. | LCSH: Settler colonialism—Palestine. | LCSH: Palestinian Arabs—Social conditions—21st century. | LCSH: Palestinian Arabs—Canada—Social conditions—21st century. | LCSH: Arab-Israeli conflict—Foreign public opinion, Canadian. | LCSH: Canada—Foreign relations—Israel. | LCSH: Israel—Foreign relations—Canada.
Classification: LCC FC244.M53 C36 2023 | DDC 327.7105694—dc23

First edition, first printing, 2023.
First printed and bound in Canada by Houghton Boston Printers, Saskatoon, Saskatchewan.
Copyediting and proofreading by Alicia Hibbert.
Map representing loss of Palestinian land by Wendy Johnson.

All rights reserved. No part of this publication may be reproduced, stored in a retrieval system, or transmitted in any form or by any means (electronic, mechanical, photocopying, recording, or otherwise) without prior written consent. Contact University of Alberta Press for further details.

University of Alberta Press supports copyright. Copyright fuels creativity, encourages diverse voices, promotes free speech, and creates a vibrant culture. Thank you for buying an authorized edition of this book and for complying with the copyright laws by not reproducing, scanning, or distributing any part of it in any form without permission. You are supporting writers and allowing University of Alberta Press to continue to publish books for every reader.

University of Alberta Press gratefully acknowledges the support received for its publishing program from the Government of Canada, the Canada Council for the Arts, and the Government of Alberta through the Alberta Media Fund.

CONTENTS

Acknowledgements VII

Foreword IX
VELDON COBURN

Introduction XIII
M. MUHANNAD AYYASH AND JEREMY WILDEMAN

I Conceptualizing Palestine–Canada Relations through the Settler-Colonial Framework

1 Hyphenation and Conciliation in the Settler Colony 3
M. MUHANNAD AYYASH

2 A Shared Settler Colonialism 17
JEREMY WILDEMAN

II Settler-Colonial Dispossession and Repression

3 Canada and the Palestinian Refugees 57
A Humanitarian License to Dispossess
RANDA FARAH AND PEIGE DESJARLAIS

4 Enforcing the Settler Contract 99
Repression of Palestine Solidarity in Canadian Colonial Multiculturalism
AZEEZAH KANJI

III Canada's Policies and the Perpetuation of Settler-Colonial Domination

5 Canada's Role in the People-to-People Programme 127
A Critical Assessment
NADIA NASER-NAJJAB

6 Aid for Peace Revisited 151
A New Paradigm for Understanding Conflict and Development
NADIA ABU-ZAHRA

IV Restricting the Public Debate on Palestine

7 Palestinian Images, Israeli Narratives 177
Radio-Canada Coverage of the 2014 War on Gaza
RACHAD ANTONIUS

8 Canada's Israel Lobby and the Palestinians 207
MIRA SUCHAROV

V Palestinian Life and Activism in Canada

9 Exclusion and Exile 231
The Identity of Working-class Palestinians in Canada
LINA ASSI AND SAMER ABDELNOUR

10 Palestinian Organizations in Ottawa 259
Understanding Communities in Practice
EMILY REGAN WILLS

11 Re-Presenting Palestine 279
Sami Hadawi and the Palestinian Revolution in Canada
MAURICE JR. LABELLE

Conclusion 307
The Struggle for a Fairer Future
JEREMY WILDEMAN

Contributors 321

ACKNOWLEDGEMENTS

THIS BOOK COULD NOT HAVE BEEN POSSIBLE without the support of various individuals and institutions. First, this book has been published with the help of a grant from the Faculty of Arts, Mount Royal University. We sincerely thank them for their much-needed support. The origins of this book began with papers submitted to a "Canada and Palestine" symposium held at the University of Ottawa in 2019. This symposium was organized by Professors Michael Lynk, Reem Bahdi, Nadia Abu-Zahra, Dr. Jeremy Wildeman, and Omar Burgan. Without the networks formed at this symposium, and the fruitful exchange of ideas, this book would not have been possible.

Thank you to Mat Buntin from the University of Alberta Press, who worked tirelessly and with such great efficiency to see this book through the review process and into production. We are forever grateful for all his wonderful work. Our thanks also go to Mahroo Rashidirostami, who pulled together the manuscript and ensured uniform style and formatting across the different chapters. We are so grateful for her invaluable contribution to this work.

Last but not least, we would like to thank the contributors of this book for their patience, dedication, willingness to review their papers, positive responses to our inquiries, and confidence in us and our collective project. Most of all, we thank them for their excellent analyses, insights, and contributions to our understanding of the Canada-Palestine relationship. Thank you all.

Finally, it has been an absolute pleasure to work with each other as editors of this collected volume. We often saw things in a similar light, which, among other things, made for efficient and productive meetings between us! Co-editing a volume is time consuming and tiring, but we managed to carry the book forward by working off each other's strengths and trusting one another with the various tasks along the way. We hope that in producing this book, we can contribute, in a small way, to the efforts of many people across Canada to realize the much and urgently needed radical transformation of Canada's position on the question of Palestine.

VIII   *Acknowledgements*

FOREWORD

YOU WOULD BE FORGIVEN FOR BELIEVING that Canadians were *genuinely* alive to the insidiousness of one of history's most destructive projects. For the most part, Canadians care little, if at all, about the ongoing devastation of settler colonialism. This might be surprising given the enormous strides that Indigenous peoples across Canada have made in the last decade to raise the profile of settler colonialism within the public consciousness. A Truth commission, as well as numerous high-profile inquiries, have thrust the subject into the broader public consciousness. The Idle No More movement, entailing countless demonstrations of resistance, has similarly registered with settler society and the settler state. Many allies in decolonization have come out of the shadows of public institutions, such as the media and formal public education systems, that were designed to produce their ignorance of our colonization. The publicity of Indigenous resistance in Canada—our public, "in-your-face" presence—made our subjugation and plight impossible to ignore. But the Canadian education in settler colonialism remains woefully deficient.

Perhaps nowhere in the world are the voraciously eliminatory impulses of settler colonialism more evident than in Palestine. Yet this odious project fails to register with the general Canadian public. Many of us from Indigenous nations within Canada recognize the breakneck pace of the very worst excesses of settler colonialism being visited upon our Palestinian brethren. We see the forced expulsion of Palestinians from their homes, their communities razed, and their territory seized for Israeli settlement—often accompanied with violence by settler state authorities. We see the humanity of Palestinians suspended by terror and its unremitting threat of arbitrary exercise. As Indigenous peoples, we recognize our history in Palestine's present.

I sit here, on my own Anishinaabe ancestral territory, reflecting on the Palestinian future. I cannot avoid the conclusion that Canada's history of settler colonialism has formed a model for the political situation in Palestine. As an Algonquin, my nation is mere years away from concluding a modern treaty with the settler state in the Province of Ontario. An Agreement-in-Principle was ratified in 2016, a document that will likely evolve into the final treaty, but with few minor changes. When negotiations with the Crown began in the early 1990s, the Algonquin Anishinaabeg Nation territory in Ontario held unceded and unmodified title to 36,000 square kilometres. After thirty years of negotiations, we will be left with 1.3 per cent of our territory, a mere 475 square kilometres. This arrangement comes after several hundred years of colonial occupation of our territory and the unrestrained settlement of our land. In the mid-nineteenth century, our nation was broken up and forcibly displaced. Colonial authorities left us with a small parcel of land. As a citizen of the Algonquins of Pikwàkanagàn, my reserve at Golden Lake, Ontario remains a mere 6.9 square kilometres. There is not much left, and, from my view, this could be the future for Palestinians.

This book arrives in a cultural moment that claims to be attuned to the atrocities of settler colonialism but in a politically myopic culture. While Canadians awake to the settler colonialism carried out by the state at home against Indigenous nations here, they are largely unaware that their government is deeply implicated in a contemporaneous process in Palestine. It is true that the tensions in Palestine receive very little public attention in Canada. But this outcome—the general ignorance of what has been unfolding in Palestine—is not the result of some innocent brand of Canadian inexperience. As we learn in this book, there are forces at work that sustain the hegemony of Israeli superiority in the Middle East. And, as the contributions demonstrate, actors from segments of Canadian civil society form part of the colonial scaffolding not just here at home, but also in support of Canada's international partners undertaking their own colonizing endeavours. None of this should surprise keen observers of Indigenous colonial politics in

x   *Foreword*

Canada. But like our domestic disciplinary focus of study on Indigenous peoples, there are ardent denialists of Palestinian persecution at the hands of the settler state.

The contributions in this book contend with Canada's naive popular culture and its haughty unworldliness. Canada's sense of itself is not one of international strongman. Rather, Canadians cultivate and exude a smug sense of self-satisfaction of being champions for human rights and brokers of peace on the world stage. But Canada's foreign policy vis-à-vis Israel should put the lie to this popular fiction. Awakening to its own violent origins— a birth marked with brutality against the people and political institutions of Indigenous nations—should give us pause to question Canada's relationship to Israeli settler colonialism of Palestine. And this is the point of *Canada as a Settler Colony on the Question of Palestine*. Canada is a settler colony at home, as well as abroad. Each chapter deftly moves the audience through a coherent argument that will leave the reader with no alternative conclusion.

VELDON COBURN
Assistant Professor of Political Science
University of Ottawa

INTRODUCTION

M. MUHANNAD AYYASH AND JEREMY WILDEMAN

THIS BOOK EXPLORES CANADA–PALESTINE RELATIONS through a settler-colonial lens. The field of settler colonial studies addresses a specific subset of colonialism, where an invasive settler society is constructed on land inhabited by an Indigenous society, or societies. It is a violent process of replacement and erasure, a struggle where the colonizer seeks to systematically defeat and then dominate, annihilate, and replace the Indigenous population. The colonizer's aim in settler colonialism is to become the overwhelming numerical majority on the land, wherein the settlers come to develop an identity distinct from the colonial métropole they originated from and begin to claim that they are themselves the Indigenous peoples of the recently colonized lands. Prominent settler states include, but are not limited to, Canada, Australia, New Zealand, the United Sates, and Israel. Settler colonialism also describes the territoriality of large swathes of the Swedish state, Morocco, and the Russian Federation. Settler colonialism has also been attempted and defeated in diverse states such as Algeria, South Africa, Kenya, and Zimbabwe.

Given the dominance today of world affairs by states that engaged in settler colonialism, including hegemonic powers like the United States, it is difficult to analyze global affairs without taking consideration of settler

XIII

colonialism. The field of settler colonial studies is itself decades old, and Indigenous scholars have long laid the groundwork and critiques of settler colonialism. Yet, despite the importance of the processes it describes, its general—though not yet widespread—acceptance in the Western academy is relatively nascent, popularized in particular from the late 1990s onward by Patrick Wolfe, Lorenzo Veracini, and the journal *Settler Colonial Studies*. The case of Palestine is itself foundational to the field of settler colonial studies. Palestinian scholars like Fayez Sayegh[1] and Edward Said[2] have for decades situated the Israeli project within the framework of colonialism and settler colonialism. The British-born journalist and writer Rosemary Sayigh,[3] and the French Marxist scholar Maxime Rodinson,[4] also advanced a settler-colonial framework in the 1960s and 1970s. Over the past two decades, scholars in the field of Palestine Studies like Nur Masalha, Joseph Massad, Ilan Pappé, Nahla Abdo, Emile Badarin, Rashid Khalidi, and Noura Erakat (among others) have effectively anatomized Israel's relationship with Palestine within a colonial and settler-colonial framework, to the point that settler colonialism is now the intellectually dominant framework used to describe the Palestinian reality.[5]

Settler colonialism is one of the greatest oppressions and a crime against humanity. So, it may be a small wonder that centres of knowledge production in states that have attempted or benefitted from settler colonialism have historically denied, ignored, and rendered inadmissible settler-colonial conceptual framings. In a process Masalha has referred to in Palestine as "memoricide," they have actively ignored the perspectives and experiences of Indigenous victims of settler colonialism.[6] Indeed, the Western academy was founded in the age of European imperialism and global colonialism, and has long attempted to bar and silence subaltern voices that reflected and humanized colonized populations' experiences. Yet, scholars like C.L.R. James, Frantz Fanon, and Aimé Césaire, among many others, would not be silenced, revealing in their canonical texts the true character, logic, and features of brutal colonial systems and worldviews.[7] This tradition continues today on Turtle Island (which European colonizers named North America), where scholars of Indigenous studies have been at the forefront of the development of our understanding of settler-colonial states and decolonial alternatives.[8] This has left a profound—though not yet widely accepted—impact on the Canadian academy, in fields like Canadian studies, with scholars like Glen Coulthard, Waziyatawin, Adam J. Barker, and James Daschuk delineating Canada's inherent settler coloniality.[9]

Despite settler colonialism having come to play a significant role in the analysis of Canada in fields like Indigenous and Canadian studies, and of Israel and Palestine in Palestine studies, and though Canada's position on the Palestinian question has come under critical scholarship elsewhere, using settler colonialism as the analytical framework for understanding Canada's relationship with Palestine has largely not been a focal point of critical analysis. Meanwhile, the settler-colonial lens is still mostly not accepted within more conservative academic traditions like Canadian foreign policy and international relations. This has an undoubted impact on how scholars have analyzed the Middle East, where so little scholarship has historically been conducted on a region where Canada has, at times, been a major actor. In turn, the region itself has had a profound impact on Canadian politics and Canada's place in the world.

In 1947, Canada and leading Canadians played an important role in the partition of Palestine at the United Nations. This notable international role contributed to the idea of Canada being a "Middle Power" in global politics and to Canada's Under-Secretary of State of External Affairs, Lester B Pearson, being dubbed a Canadian Balfour by Israelis for his efforts.[10] That plan for partition, pursued most assiduously by Europeans in a United Nations then dominated by European states, gave a majority of the best land to a minority population of recent colonizers, and was considered deeply unfair by indigenous Palestinian Arabs.[11] In 1956, Canada helped end a stand-off over the Suez Canal and a grave crisis in global affairs, after Britain and France invaded Egypt, with Israel's help, to try to overthrow a newly decolonized Egyptian government that dared to nationalize a canal controlled by British and French interests. Canada and its then Secretary of State for External Affairs, Lester B. Pearson, worked with the United Nations to create the world's first peacekeeping force, also creating the conditions for British and French withdrawal, and earning Canada broad acclaim.

In another case, Canada's one-time Liberal MP (1999–2015) and Minister of Justice (2003–2006), Irwin Cotler, is understood to have played a notable role in the 1970s as an intermediary between the Israeli and Egyptian governments, two countries that had been in various states of war or "low-level" armed conflict, since Israel's establishment in Palestine in 1948. A

Introduction XV

law professor at the time, Cotler's actions may have contributed to the 1978 Camp David Peace Accords,[12] the first such deal between Israel and an Arab state, which would lead to Israel returning the Sinai to Egypt. These Accords explicitly put off finding a resolution to the Palestine question, even though Camp David was considered by the sponsor of the process, the United States Carter Administration, to be a first step toward a regional peace plan. This would be one of a long list of "peace" Accords and negotiations that would exclude Palestinians from the table, such as the 2020 Abraham Accords, where leading world powers attempt to force Palestinians to accept whatever fate is determined for them, like partition at the United Nations in 1947.

All of these incidents would profoundly affect Canada's standing in the international community at a time when the settler society was developing its own identity, separate from its British colonial métropole.[13] At a time when the Canadian state was assaulting Indigenous communities and forcibly abducting children from their parents in acts of cultural genocide, most infamously in Residential Schools or through adoption by settler families, Canada entered into a Golden Age of foreign policy, taking on the persona of a "peacemonger," human rights defender, and advocate for the downtrodden. This progressive personification of Canada in the international community provided a sense of distinct Canadian-ness most settlers identify with to this day.

There is also the impact of the Middle East, and specifically Palestine, on Canadian governance, which includes a 1979 election when Prime Minister-elect Joe Clark's new Progressive Conservative government immediately entered into a diplomatic crisis after coming to power, caused by a campaign pledge to move the Canadian Embassy to Israel, from Tel Aviv to Jerusalem.[14] That would have made Canada the first Western country to do so, after Israel occupied Palestinian territory in a 1967 war, which included military occupation of Gaza, the West Bank, East Jerusalem, as well as the Egyptian Sinai and the Syrian Golan Heights. The diplomatic fallout against Canada within the Arab world included threats to Canadian business and diplomacy, and this caused disarray in the Clark Progressive Conservative government. This led to its quick backtracking on the Jerusalem Embassy pledge, and almost certainly contributed to the Clark minority government's demise just nine months later. This allowed Pierre Elliot Trudeau to lead his Liberal Party back to power in 1980 for a fourth term, and in 1982 it repatriated Canada's constitution from the British Parliament, fundamentally changing how the Canadian settler state and society are organized.

After the 1979 Jerusalem Embassy crisis, a small but concerted flourishing of Canadian scholarly interest in Canada's foreign policy relationship with the Middle East took hold. This includes, in particular, Tareq Y. Ismael's 1985 edited volume looking at Canada's foreign policy in the Arab World, with critical contributions made by influential scholars like Peyton Lyon.[15] This work intersected with a 1980 report by the Special Envoy appointed by the Clark government to the Middle East, Robert L Stanfield, who had been tasked with finding ways to improve Canada's standing in the region.[16] The next flurry of interest came with scholarship on Canada's role as a mediator facilitating Israeli-Palestinian peace talks within the context of the Middle East Peace Process (MEPP). This scholarship culminated in a 2007 edited volume by Paul Heinbecker and Bessma Momani, which, while containing strands of scholarship that are critical of Canada's approach to the Middle East, was mostly written in a Canadian academic tradition that had become confident in the idea that Canada was mostly a fair-minded actor working toward peace, development, and an equitable outcome for all parties in the Middle East.[17] Both traditions of scholarship of Canada in the Middle East, written respectively in the early to mid-1980s, and then in the late-1980s to the mid-2000s, focused on the centrality of Palestine and Israel to building regional peace and the pursuit of Canadian interests. Neither adopted explicitly colonial lenses when analyzing a region that had been defined by struggles of decolonization since the end of World War II. Heinbecker and Momani, in particular, embraced the Canadian definition of Canada as a middle power that is a helpful and peace-making fixer on the world stage.

A mid-2000s shift in Canada's foreign policy stance toward an overt and ardent pro-Israel position, pursued by successive Paul Martin Liberal, Stephen Harper Conservative, and Justin Trudeau Liberal governments, has contributed to a process of questioning the traditional perception of Canada delineated in scholarship like Heinbecker and Momani's. This spurred a late 2000s to mid-2010s flourishing of critical scholarship, like that of Husseini, Lynk, Abu-Laban and Bakan, Seligman, and Engler.[18] This took place during the invigoration of the settler-colonial paradigm in the Western academy, which rendered untenable traditional myths like Canada being an exceptional middle power without the colonizing or imperial tradition of other

Introduction XVII

European societies. Still, other than exceptions like Mike Krebs and Dana M. Olwan,[19] who directly describe the Palestinian and Indigenous struggle as one and the same; or works by Scott Morgensen, and Michael Jackman and Nishant Upadhyay,[20] connecting Canadian and Israeli colonization through a queer settler-colonial lens; the use of a settler-colonial theoretical framework to understand the Canada-Palestine relationship has been under-explored. This book directly addresses that gap.

Analyzing Canada–Palestine Relations through a Settler-Colonial Lens

So, what does it mean to use the settler-colonial framework for understanding Canada-Palestine relations? For starters, though most of our chapters utilize a settler-colonial lens, we do not believe that every engagement with this question needs to utilize concepts from the field of settler-colonial studies. We believe that our collection shows how some analysis can reveal settler-colonial dynamics without using a specific settler-colonial paradigm. We understand that in disciplines like sociology, political science, and history, not everyone will be familiar with or comfortable using settler colonialism as a framework of analysis. Though the question of why that is the case is important and deserves urgent attention, we cannot address it here. Suffice it to say, we believe that this book offers an invitation for those previously unfamiliar and uncomfortable with the settler-colonial paradigm to (re) consider how it can be useful in illuminating the complex social and political realities of Canada's position on the Palestinian question.

In presenting this fresh look at the relationship between Canada and Palestine, the book is divided into five sections. The first section (1) sets the analytical framework for the book, providing an introductory window into how we ought to approach the study of settler colonialism across different contexts, highlighting their connections without at the same time losing sight of the differences. The four sections thereafter speak to a different dimension of the question of how Canada's settler colonialism shapes and guides its position on Palestine: (2) dispossession and repression, (3) the entrenchment and expansion of settler-colonial domination, (4) the erasure of the narrative of the colonized from public discourse, and finally (5) the activism and resistance of the colonized.

After introducing the settler-colonial paradigm in the first section, the focus of the book's second section is on the foundational violence of settler colonialism, which concerns the dispossession of Indigenous peoples from

XVIII   *Introduction*

their lands. Settler colonialism is, first and foremost, defined by the elimination of the Indigenous peoples of the land and their replacement with settlers from elsewhere. Though there are a variety of methods, scopes, and scales in which elimination and replacement take place (genocide, forced assimilation, expulsion, transfer, and so on), settler colonialism in all contexts seeks to establish total settler state control and authority over the colonized land and the people, eliminating Indigenous sovereignty.[21] This foundation is always concealed in the self-narration of the settler-colonial state, as dispossession is secured and expanded through the continuous repression of the colonized. Repression serves to silence and erase Indigenous revelation and illumination of the character, logics, and structures of settler-colonial violences, which are ever continuous. This repression of the narrative of the colonized serves to maintain the settler-colonial state's proclaimed self-image as a liberal, advanced, and civilized modern nation-state.

The dispossession of the colonized is not restricted to a particular event, as the often-repeated truism shows. Rather, settler colonies are not events but structures. By their structure, settler colonies tend to always be concerned with securing and expanding their settler-colonial conquest. Therefore, the book examines in the third section how Canadian policies entrench and expand the settler-colonial foundation of dispossession, ensuring that the dispossessed remain colonized and their aspirations for freedom and sovereignty denied. We often find that settler colonies accomplish this "secure and expand" drive through ideological and material misdirection and concealment. Instead of victims who are resisting settler-colonial aggression, the colonized are cast as violent belligerents who need to be taught by the colonizers and their allies how to adopt "civilized" and "peaceful" mores, attitudes, and institutions. This conceals settler-colonial realities and misdirects public attention away from the necessary task of naming and transforming settler-colonial systems of power and domination.

This leads us into the fourth section, where we can observe how public discourse in the media and politics is structured so that the narrative and explanatory paradigm of the indigenous Palestinians is erased. For decades, since at least Aimé Césaire, anti-colonial theory has shown how the colonized are posited as a subject that is incapable of understanding, explaining, and aspiring to change their reality. This feature of colonial modernity is alive and well today and can be seen in how Palestinians are regularly

Introduction   XIX

excluded from entering public discourse as subjects who can narrate their own story. Palestinians are sometimes posited as suffering subjects deserving of Euro-American pity, and often as violent and hateful subjects deserving of Euro-American ire and righteous violence, but not often as thinking and knowing subjects who yearn for a free life.

But these structures of power are not able to crush and silence Palestinian resistance, and in the fifth section of the book, we are invited into a ground-level view of the complexity and diversity of Palestinian life in Canada as Palestinians navigate their quest for freedom and decolonial liberation across two settler colonies. Though settler colonialism is a structure of domination that seeks to eliminate Indigenous peoples, it never accomplishes this goal definitively or totally due to the resistance of the colonized. Indigenous peoples always remain and resist, providing an alternative path to the destruction and violence of settler colonialism. Scholars, activists, and policy analysts must turn to these experiences in order to better understand settler colonialism and properly follow a decolonial path that transforms our settler-colonial worlds.

The Book's Chapters

The first section, "Conceptualizing Palestine-Canada Relations through the Settler Colonial Framework," establishes the analytical approach of the book. Chapter one, by M. Muhannad Ayyash, outlines some of the stakes at play in conceiving Canada as primarily a settler colonial state, rather than a liberal, democratic, and multicultural one. Ayyash argues that Palestinians should direct their energies towards a conciliation, not between their Palestinian and Canadian identities, but towards Indigenous communities on Turtle Island. When we begin to see Canada's position on Palestine as emergent from Canada's settler colonial foundations and structures, then it becomes clear that a decolonial path in Palestine must also mean a decolonial path on Turtle Island. The second chapter by Jeremy Wildeman elucidates precisely how Canada's settler colonial foundations and structures guide, shape, and direct Canada's position on the question of Palestine. Wildeman argues that it is, more or less, logical and predictable that Canada would actively participate in the settler colonial dispossession of Palestinians, replicating its own settler colonial dispossession of Indigenous peoples on Turtle Island. Wildeman's chapter places in parallel the two cases of dispossession and illustrates the many commonalities that they share. These commonalities can only be explained properly when we utilize a settler colonial framework.

The second section, "Settler Colonial Dispossession and Repression," examines two specific ways in which Canada participates in the dispossession of Palestinians. Chapter three, by Randa Farah and Peige Desjarlais, considers Canada's relationship with the large diaspora of Palestinian refugees, which Canada helped to create in 1947. This chapter argues that Canada's history as a settler-colonial state and its structural position as an imperial power is the framework of analysis that best explains its role and policies on the Palestinian question, particularly towards Palestinian refugees. This contrasts directly with the aforementioned mythical characterization of Canada as a peacemaker driven by its humanitarian impulses, and a Canadian commitment to the precepts of international law. As with Wildeman, Farah and Desjarlais consider it natural for Canada to support Israel in the exploitation of Palestinians when considering Canada and Israel's shared settler coloniality.

The fourth chapter, by Azeezah Kanji, examines how Canada represses Palestinian solidarity activism through the language of multiculturalism and liberal anti-racism. Kanji's analysis of three specific cases (the Al-Quds Day Rally, the Ontario government's exclusion of organizations critical of Zionist policies, and Prime Minister Justin Trudeau's criticism of the Boycott, Divestment, and Sanctions [BDS] campaign) shows how Canada's use of liberal multiculturalism to repress Palestine solidarity activism should not surprise us given that Canada has also used liberal multiculturalism to divert attention away from the critical issues of Indigenous sovereignty, lands, and the right to exist as Indigenous peoples. Likewise, the repression of Palestinian solidarity work is basically concerned with the effort to hide and conceal, and therefore perpetuate, the dispossession of Palestinians.

The third section, "Canada's Policies and the Perpetuation of Settler Colonial Domination," takes a critical look at specific government policies that perpetuate and enable Israel's settler colonial domination over the Palestinians. Chapter five, by Nadia Naser-Najjab, analyses Canada's contribution to second-track People-to-People programming, a peace-building exercise established for Israelis and Palestinians within the Oslo peace framework. Far from contributing to peace by bringing Palestinians and Israelis together to challenge psychological barriers, prejudices and

Introduction   XXI

stereotypes against each other, Naser-Najjab found the programming systematically distorted the underlying causes and objective dimensions of the Israeli-Palestinian relationship by constructing the illusion of two relatively equal sides being at war with each other while diverting attention away from the ongoing colonization of Palestinian land, dispossession and violence. In this way, Canada and other Western donors contributed to the ongoing colonization of Palestine through a convenient obscuring and denial of settler colonial realities beneath a rhetorical framework of peacebuilding and understanding.

In chapter six, Nadia Abu-Zahra uses a Canadian case study to explore how international donors divert much-needed Palestinian aid funding into programming that is contingent on Israelis and Palestinians being brought together to "overcome their differences." Abu-Zahra delineates how aid-for-peace programming operates oblivious to the realities of settler colonialism, as if the controlling relationship does not exist, while only superficially addressing its symptoms. In the process, donors like Canada end up treating Palestinians as though they are the primary impediment to peace, rather than being the occupied survivors of ongoing violence. By funding these programs, Canada contributes to an enabling environment for Israel to intensify its colonialism while masking the true nature of its rule, supporting Israel at maintaining an ongoing colonial project that includes the annexation of Palestinian land, expanding its settlements, and growing its economy, all at a direct cost to Palestinian land, lives, and livelihoods. By contrast, if Canada were to challenge this abusive reality and foster conditions for a just peace, it would need to undertake a radical departure from its current support for Israel's settler colonial control over the Palestinians, and instead engage in allyship with the Palestinians and all those who strive for justice and healthy relations. Such a transformation would require recognizing and seeking to end Israel's colonial relationship of control to build healthy ones instead.

In the fourth section, "Restricting the Public Debate on Palestine," the book explores how media and politics in Canada determine what counts as legitimate public discourse on the question of Palestine. Though these two chapters do not use a settler colonial paradigm as an analytical framework, they both reveal how Canada's close relationship and allyship with Israel operates in the critical spheres of media and politics to suppress the Palestinian anti-colonial narrative. In chapter seven, by Rachad Antonius, we observe how Radio-Canada, the French sector of the Canadian Broadcasting Corporation (CBC), de-contextualizes Palestinian suffering by not allowing Palestinian explanatory paradigms to reach the surface of public discourse. Though stories about Palestinian suffering are covered, they are rarely, if ever, accompanied by a Palestinian explanation of why they are suffering, the nature of the Palestine question, and so on. In short, they are never accompanied by the narrative of the colonized, which explains Israeli violence as colonial violence and their resistance as anti-colonial. The explanatory paradigms circulated in the Canadian media landscape simply repeat the Israeli paradigm and narrative, which paints the distorted picture of Israeli violence as a self-defence response to the violence of the political Islamist fundamentalism of Hamas. This kind of coverage thus ensures that Israeli policies and practices can proceed without major hindrance and with public and policy support from Canada.

Mira Sucharov, in chapter eight, highlights how the Israel lobby advocates for pro-Israel positions within Canadian politics. Dominant and mainstream lobby organizations, notably The Centre for Israel and Jewish Affairs (CIJA), have succeeded in convincing Canadian politicians that the Jewish community in Canada is united in its staunch support for Israel, and that the Jewish community as a united whole expects Canadian political parties to take strong positions against Palestinian solidarity and activism, such as the BDS campaign. Though the influence of the Israel lobby is substantial, Sucharov argues that there is daylight between Canada and Israel, and that Canadian leverage on Israel is still a possible goal for other political lobby groups. Sucharov also believes that Canada can take and has attempted to take a fairminded approach to the Palestinian-Israeli issue, even though this has yet to materialize in tangible ways.

The fifth and final section, "Palestinian Life and Activism in Canada," gives us a view into how Palestinians go about struggling for the Palestinian cause in Canada. Lina Assi and Samer Abdelnour show us in chapter nine how working-class Palestinians navigate the politicization of their Palestinian identity. Using their interviews with working-class Palestinians, they employ an inductive analysis to show how Palestinians in Canada must face the oppressive intersectional structures of class and national identity in their struggle for a just and dignified life as Palestinians. The chapter skillfully opens a window onto the complex existence of Palestinians in Canada as a fundamentally stateless people who yearn for their right to return

Introduction XXIII

to their lands. In chapter ten, Emily Regan Wills investigates Palestinian organizing in Ottawa. She highlights how different organizations allow individuals to identify as Palestinians in diverse ways, not all of which are political. Attuned to the diversity that exists within the Palestinian community, Wills deploys a concept of "community in practice" to highlight how organizations, regardless of their stated intentions and the nature of their activities, create lived experiences for individuals who participate in those organization's events. Basically, participation in community in practice instantiates diverse versions and lived experiences of a larger Palestinian identity. Cultural events, fundraising for charity, social networking, physical activity or celebration all come to serve the function of constructing a tangible sense of community in practice, and in the process, they communicate to Canadians the richness and diversity of Palestinian culture and practice. It is from this rich well of Palestinian identity, which is neither overdetermined nor homogenous, that Palestinians maintain their presence in Canada as Palestinians, and despite their overpoliticization, continue to exist across the spectrum of social, political, and cultural spheres.

Finally, chapter eleven, by Maurice Jr. Labelle, tells us the remarkable story of the intellectual and Palestinian advocate, Sami Hadawi, who never tired of pushing the Palestinian cause in Canada, despite the innumerable obstacles he faced, including threats of violence. Perhaps we can all take some inspiration from Hadawi and persist in our efforts to show ordinary people across Canada/Turtle Island the justness of the Palestinian cause. Like Hadawi, we ought to be sober and critical in our assessment of where matters stand for Palestine today, and how Canada continues to be part of the problem. Like Hadawi, we ought simultaneously to remain hopeful that we can make a change. Scholars, activists, policy makers, policy analysts, and all communities concerned with peace and justice have to believe that we can create a critical mass of support, forcing a real reckoning with Canada's policies and positions, both on Turtle Island and in Palestine, setting the country on the road to decolonization so that Palestinians and Indigenous peoples across Turtle Island can finally enjoy freedom, peace, sovereignty, and justice, not in some distant future, but now at this moment.

Notes

1. Sayegh, "Zionist Colonialism in Palestine (1965)."
2. Said, "Zionism from the Standpoint of its Victims"; Said, *The Politics of Dispossession.*

3. Sayigh, *The Palestinians: From Peasants to Revolutionaries*.

4. Rodinson, *Israel: A Settler Colonial State?*

5. Masalha, *Expulsion of the Palestinians*; Masalha, "Settler-Colonialism"; Masalha, *The Palestine Nakba*; Joseph Massad, "Peace Is War"; Pappé, *Ethnic Cleansing of Palestine*; Pappé, "International Law and Settler Colonialism"; Abdo, *Captive Revolution*; Badarin, "Settler-Colonialist Management of Entrances"; Erakat and Radi, eds., "Gaza in Context"; Khalidi, *The Hundred Years' War on Palestine*.

6. Masalha, "Settler-Colonialism."

7. James, *The Black Jacobins*; Césaire and Kelley, *Discourse on Colonialism*; Fanon, *The Wretched of the Earth*.

8. Glenn, "Settler Colonialism as Structure"; Konishi, "First Nations Scholars," 290.

9. Coulthard, *Red Skin, White Masks*; Waziyatawin, "Malice Enough in Their Hearts"; Barker, "'A Direct Act of Resurgence"; Daschuk, *Clearing the Plains*.

10. Holmes, *The Shaping of Peace*.

11. Yusuf, "The Partition of Palestine," 43.

12. Bard, "Irwin Cotler Sparked Egypt-Israel Peace."

13. Until 1947, there were not even Canadian citizens per se. Rather, "Canadians" were simply British subjects living in Canada. On January 1, 1947, the Canadian Citizenship Act came into effect and "Canadian citizens" came into being. The first twenty-seven included then–Prime Minister William Lyon MacKenzie King and a Palestinian Naif Hanna Azar. First Nations would remain "wards of the state," unable to vote in federal elections until 1960, and still unable to vote in some provincial elections by 1960.

14. Flicker, "Next Year in Jerusalem."

15. Ismael, *Canada and the Arab World*.

16. The 1980 Stanfield Report was even featured in Ismael's 1985 book. Stanfield, *Final Report*.

17. Heinbecker and Momani, eds., *Canada and the Middle East in Theory and Practice*.

18. Husseini, "A 'Middle Power' in Action"; Lynk, "A Fierce Attachment"; Abu-Laban and Bakan, "After 9/11: Canada, the Israel/Palestine Conflict"; Seligman, "Canada's Israel Policy under Justin Trudeau"; Engler, *Canada and Israel: Building Apartheid*.

19. Krebs and Olwan, "'From Jerusalem to the Grand River."

20. Morgensen, "Queer Settler Colonialism in Canada and Israel"; Jackman and Upadhyay, "Pinkwatching Israel, Whitewashing Canada."

21. Barakat, "Writing/Righting Palestine Studies"; Coulthard, *Red Skin, White Masks*; Kauanui, *Hawaiian Blood*; Kauanui, "A Structure, not an Event"; Pateman and Mills, *Contract and Domination*; Simpson, *Mohawk Interruptus*; Simpson, "The State is a Man"; Veracini, *Settler Colonialism*; Wolfe, *Settler Colonialism and the Transformation of Anthropology*; Wolfe, "Settler Colonialism and the Elimination of the Native."

References

Abdo, Nahla. *Captive Revolution: Palestinian Women's Anti-Colonial Struggle within the Israeli Prison System*. London: Pluto Press, 2014.

Abu-Laban, Yasmeen, and Abigail B. Bakan. "After 9/11: Canada, the Israel/Palestine Conflict, and the Surveillance of Public Discourse." *Canadian Journal of Law & Society / La Revue Canadienne Droit et Société* 27, no. 3 (December 2012): 319–39.

Badarin, Emile. "Settler-Colonialist Management of Entrances to the Native Urban Space in Palestine." *Settler Colonial Studies* 5, no. 3 (2015): 226–35.

Barakat, Rana. "Writing/Righting Palestine Studies: Settler Colonialism, Indigenous Sovereignty and Resisting the Ghost(s) of History." *Settler Colonial Studies* 8, no. 3 (2018): 349–63.

Bard, Mitchell. "Irwin Cotler Sparked Egypt-Israel Peace with a Slip of Paper, Here's How." *Jewish News Syndicate*, May 25, 2022. https://www.jns.org/irwin-cotler-sparked-egypt-israel-peace-with-a-slip-of-paper-heres-how/.

Barker, Adam J. "'A Direct Act of Resurgence, a Direct Act of Sovereignty': Reflections on Idle No More, Indigenous Activism, and Canadian Settler Colonialism." *Globalizations* 12, no. 1 (2015): 43–65.

Coulthard, Glen. *Red Skin, White Masks: Rejecting the Colonial Politics of Recognition.* Minneapolis: University of Minnesota Press, 2014.

Daschuk, James W. *Clearing the Plains: Disease, Politics of Starvation, and the Loss of Aboriginal Life.* Regina, SK: University of Regina Press, 2013.

Engler, Yves. *Canada and Israel: Building Apartheid.* Fernwood Publishing, 2010.

Erakat, Noura, and Tareq Radi, eds. "Gaza in Context: War and Settler Colonialism." *JadMAG*, 4, no. 1 (2016).

Flicker, Charles. "Next Year in Jerusalem: Joe Clark and the Jerusalem Embassy Affair." *International Journal* 58, no. 1 (2002): 115–38.

Glenn, Evelyn Nakano. "Settler Colonialism as Structure: A Framework for Comparative Studies of U.S. Race and Gender Formation." *Sociology of Race and Ethnicity* 1, no. 1 (January 1, 2015): 52–72.

Heinbecker, Paul, and Bessma Momani, eds. *Canada and the Middle East in Theory and Practice.* Waterloo, ON: Wilfrid Laurier University Press, 2007.

Holmes, John W. *The Shaping of Peace: Canada and the Search for World Order, 1943–1957, Vol. II.* Toronto: University of Toronto Press, 1982.

Husseini, Hassan. "A 'Middle Power' in Action: Canada and the Partition of Palestine." *Arab Studies Quarterly* 30, no. 3 (2008): 41–55.

Ismael, Tareq Y. *Canada and the Arab World.* Edmonton: University of Alberta Press, 1985.

Jackman, Michael Connors, and Nishant Upadhyay. "Pinkwatching Israel, Whitewashing Canada: Queer (Settler) Politics and Indigenous Colonization in Canada." *Women's Studies Quarterly* 42, no. 3/4 (Fall/Winter 2014): 195–210.

James, C.L.R. *The Black Jacobins: Toussaint L'Ouverture and the San Domingo Revolution.* Second Revised Edition. New York: Vintage Books, 1989 [1938].

Kauanui, J. Kēhaulani. *Hawaiian Blood: Colonialism and the Politics of Sovereignty and Indigeneity.* Durham, NC: Duke University Press, 2008.

Kauanui, J. Kēhaulani. "'A Structure, not an Event': Settler Colonialism and Enduring Indigeneity." *Lateral: Journal of the Cultural Studies Association* 5, no. 1 (Spring: 2016).

http://csalateral.org/wp/issue/5-1/forum-alt-humanitiessettler-colonialism-enduring-indigeneity-kauanui.

Khalidi, Rashid. *The Hundred Years' War on Palestine: A History of Settler Colonialism and Resistance, 1917–2017*. New York: Metropolitan Books, 2020.

Konishi, Shino. "First Nations Scholars, Settler Colonial Studies, and Indigenous History." *Australian Historical Studies* 50, no. 3 (July 3, 2019): 285–304.

Krebs, Mike, and Dana M. Olwan. "'From Jerusalem to the Grand River, Our Struggles Are One': Challenging Canadian and Israeli Settler Colonialism." *Settler Colonial Studies* 2, no. 2 (January 1, 2012): 138–64.

Lynk, Michael. "A Fierce Attachment: Canada, Israel, Palestine and the Harper Years." *The Harper Decade*, August 25, 2015. http://www.theharperdecade.com/blog/2015/8/21/a-fierce-attachment-canada-israel-palestine-and-the-harper-years.

Masalha, Nur. *Expulsion of the Palestinians: The Concept of "Transfer" in Zionist Political Thought, 1882–1948*. Beirut: Institute for Palestine Studies, 2012.

Masalha, Nur. "Settler-Colonialism, Memoricide and Indigenous Toponymic Memory: The Appropriation of Palestinian Place Names by the Israeli State." *Journal of Holy Land and Palestine Studies* 14, no. 1 (May 1, 2015): 3–57.

Masalha, Nur. *The Palestine Nakba: Decolonising History, Narrating the Subaltern, Reclaiming Memory*. London: Zed Books, 2012.

Massad, Joseph. "Peace Is War: After the Oslo Accords." *Al Jazeera*, November 3, 2013. http://www.aljazeera.com/indepth/opinion/2013/10/peace-war-after-oslo-accords-20131031124827574136.html.

Morgensen, Scott Lauria. "Queer Settler Colonialism in Canada and Israel: Articulating Two-Spirit and Palestinian Queer Critiques." *Settler Colonial Studies* 2, no. 2 (January 1, 2012): 167–90.

Pappé, Ilan. *Ethnic Cleansing of Palestine*. Oneworld Publications, 2006.

Pappé, Ilan. "International Law and Settler Colonialism in Historical Palestine." *Omran* 10, no. 38 (2021): 155–71.

Pateman, Carole, and Mills, Charles W. *Contract and Domination*. Malden, MA: Polity Press, 2007.

Rodinson, Maxime. *Israel: A Settler Colonial State?* New York: Pathfinder Press, 1973.

Said, Edward. "Zionism from the Standpoint of its Victims." *Social Text* 1 (Winter 1979): 7–58.

Said, Edward. *The Politics of Dispossession: The Struggle for Palestinian Self-Determination, 1969–1994*. New York: Vintage Books, 1995.

Sayegh, Fayez. "Zionist Colonialism in Palestine (1965)." *Settler Colonial Studies* 2, no. 1 ([1965] 2012): 206–25.

Sayigh, Rosemary. *The Palestinians: From Peasants to Revolutionaries*. New York: Zed Books, ([1979] 2007).

Seligman, Steven. "Canada's Israel Policy under Justin Trudeau: Rejecting or Reinforcing the Legacy of Stephen Harper?" *American Review of Canadian Studies* 48, no. 1 (January 2, 2018): 80–95.

Simpson, Audra. *Mohawk Interruptus: Political Life across the Borders of Settler States.* Durham, NC: Duke University Press, 2014.

Simpson, Audra. "The State is a Man: Theresa Spence, Loretta Saunders and the Gender of Settler Sovereignty." *Theory and Event* 19, no. 4 (2016).

Stanfield, Robert L. *Final Report of the Special Representative of the Government of Canada Respecting the Middle East and North Africa.* Ottawa: Government of Canada, 1980.

Veracini, Lorenzo. *Settler Colonialism: A Theoretical Overview.* New York: Palgrave Macmillan, 2010.

Yusuf, Muhsin. "The Partition of Palestine (1947)—An Arab Perspective." *Palestine–Israel Journal of Politics, Economics, and Culture* 9, no. 4 (November 30, 2002): 39–49.

Waziyatawin. "Malice Enough in Their Hearts and Courage Enough in Ours: Reflections on US Indigenous and Palestinian Experiences under Occupation." *Settler Colonial Studies* 2, no. 1 (2012): 172–89.

Wolfe, Patrick. *Settler Colonialism and the Transformation of Anthropology: The Politics and Poetics of an Ethnographic Event.* London & New York: Cassell, 1999.

Wolfe, Patrick. "Settler Colonialism and the Elimination of the Native." *Journal of Genocide Research* 8, no. 4 (2006): 387–409.

I

CONCEPTUALIZING PALESTINE-CANADA RELATIONS THROUGH THE SETTLER-COLONIAL FRAMEWORK

1

HYPHENATION AND CONCILIATION IN THE SETTLER COLONY

M. MUHANNAD AYYASH

IN A NUMBER OF HIS INTERVIEWS AND WRITINGS, Edward Said captured well the difficulty of living and working in the United States as a Palestinian American.[1] Outside of mainstream public discourse, not many academics and critical intellectuals take seriously the claim that the United States is a "neutral arbiter" in the Palestinian-Israeli struggle.[2] Since at least the 1940s, the United States has staunchly supported Israel and has actively participated in the dispossession of Palestinians and the erasure of Palestine. For a scholar who is committed to justice for Palestinians, Said faced numerous obstacles in American academia and politics, from marginalization in mainstream public discourse to the burning of his office. The difficulty of Said's path, though, does not only concern such obstacles and threats, but also springs from the fact that Said felt and experienced a real and tangible connection to his American identity and to American social and political life.

Without this connection, he would not have dealt with the complex tensions and dynamics of hyphenation: he would not have exhibited an exiling kind of thinking and writing.[3] He was not only a Palestinian struggling for the Palestinian cause in the United States, but he was also connected to his American identity and the ideals that America conjured for him (freedom of expression, academic freedom, and so on). Even though the American side stood in opposition to the Palestinian side, Said attempted to translate the Palestinian side to the American side and vice versa. He saw his intellectual efforts as a bridge that could bring together these two sides in order to advance the cause of justice. In his scathing critiques of the imperialism and violence that is embedded in American culture and politics, Said thus pursued an immanent critique that sought to improve both the United States and Palestine.

Much like Said, many Palestinian Canadians face these difficulties of hyphenation within a context that is openly hostile to one side of the hyphenation. Though not nearly as powerful and influential as the United States on this issue, the Canadian state has stood and continues to stand in the path of Palestinian freedom. As the chapters in this book illustrate, Canada is far from a neutral arbiter, which is visible in the politics of the state and society (Lina Assi and Samer Abdelnour, Mira Sucharov, Jeremy Wildeman), media coverage (Rachad Antonius, Maurice Jr. Labelle), and in Canadian policy (Nadia Naser-Najjab, Nadia Abu-Zahra, Randa Farah and Peige Desjarlais, Azeezah Kanji). Standing against grandiose-sounding state discourse, the chapters offer an evidence-based account of social and political life for Palestinian Canadians and deeply challenge Canada's projected self-image of a nation-state that is based on, and that continuously strives towards, universal values of justice, freedom, equality, and human rights. Following in the footsteps of Said's immanent critique, the analyses are a call for Canada to actually live up to these ideals that it proclaims to stand for.

Taken as a whole, this book's chapters deconstruct and critique Canada's self-proclaimed image as peacemaker, peacekeeper, multicultural, and anti-racist, emphasizing instead the settler-colonial character of Canada and how that shapes its position on Palestine. As Kanji, Farah and Desjarlais, Abu-Zahra, Naser-Najjab, Wildeman, and others in the collection allude to, Canada's failure to live up to that projected self-image is not new and has been made abundantly clear by Indigenous peoples ever since the emergence of the Canadian state. There are two reasons why this is important: (1) it situates Canada's failures within its proper historical context: this is not a new or recent failure in the history of Canada, but rather these failures are part and parcel of the Canadian state; and (2) it allows us to see that what Palestinian Canadians implore the Canadian state to live up to is not necessarily a set of purely settler Canadian ideals, but rather are ideals that have been formed in the Indigenous-settler hybridity that underpins the Canadian state. Towards the end of this chapter, I will make the case, though only in a preliminary fashion, that much of what Palestinian Canadians are attempting to push the Canadian state towards, namely collective freedom and well-being, indeed follows Indigenous knowledges, values, ideals, and principles.

Canada's Justification of Settler-Colonial Violence

The Canadian state has failed to properly and substantively deal with and address the racism and violence of settler colonialism in Canada. Violence against Indigenous women, child welfare policies, policing and the criminal justice system, education and health policies, the unequal distribution of government resources, and the resource extraction industries' violation of Indigenous rights and sovereignty are all ongoing settler-colonial institutions, processes, policies, and practices that are built on and themselves perpetuate the dispossession of Indigenous peoples. One of the dynamics that underpins all of these systemic settler-colonial violences is the way in which liberal humanist ideology conceals and hides these very violences, thus ensuring their perpetuation.[4]

In a similar way, the Canadian state has fallen short of dealing with settler-colonial violences on the international stage, as can be seen in the case of Palestine. While the specific types of violence that Palestinians face are different from the types that Indigenous peoples in Canada face, both sets of violences are settler colonial in the sense that their foundation and ultimate goal is the erasure and expulsion of Indigenous peoples and the eradication of Indigenous sovereignty.[5] There are two concepts that stand out in the liberal-humanist ideology's enablement of settler-colonial violence in the case of Palestine: "democracy" and "Western values."

The statement that Canada supports Israel because Israel is "the only democracy in the Middle East" has been repeated ad nauseum across the last few decades. Sucharov shows in her chapter how this talking point (among others) has permeated Canadian foreign policy discourse. This discourse proclaims a desire for a "negotiated settlement" in the form of a two-state solution and thus seems to be concerned with the rights and freedom of

Palestinians. However, it is not backed by any concrete political action that would lead to the realization of the two-state solution, much less freedom and rights. Numerous studies, including the chapters in this book, have clearly demonstrated that Israel is far from democratic (in the sense of full and equal representation, rights, inclusion, and protections) in its treatment of approximately 1.6 million Palestinians as second-class citizens,[6] and in its clearly non-democratic, militarily established and enforced, brutal settler colonial and apartheid systems of rule over approximately 5 million Palestinians in East Jerusalem, the West Bank, and Gaza. But I do not want to repeat these deconstructions and critiques here and focus instead on the operation of such ideologies.

The main reason "democracy" is constantly evoked in this context is the same reason it is evoked when discussing Indigenous–settler relations in Canada. The settler colonial state cannot admit the violences that created it in the first place, and the violences that ensure its continuation. But since it cannot completely hide these brutal violences either, it must create ideological manoeuvers to reframe them in its favour. The evocation of democracy is ultimately an effort to paint the state's violence as necessary for the defence of what is inarguably a common good: democracy. Since the state's actions are presented as the defenders and carriers of democracy, its violences come to be seen as measured acts whose primary purpose is the defence and spread of democracy in the supposedly enlightened march of civilization for the betterment of all humankind. This is basically an attempt to align the settler-colonial state with the "good," and thus render the eliminatory and genocidal violences of settler colonialism a kind of "righteous" violence.

The second feature of Canada's justification of and for settler-colonial violence is the evocation of shared "Western values." This evocation is effective in its operation precisely because it is so broad and opaque: it has been used to denote gender equality, respect for diverse expressions of sexuality and sexual identity, tolerance for cultural diversity, law and order, blind justice, scientific and cultural literacy, the Judeo-Christian tradition, and even democracy (to name just a few). Of course, all of these items have been deconstructed and critiqued, but again, it is the operation that I want to highlight here. Regardless of which specific value is being conjured, assuming anything specific is being conjured at all, the desired effect is always the same: Canada's staunch alliance with Israel is due to something greater than

6   *Hyphenation and Conciliation in the Settler Colony*

self-interest, something that is deemed undeniably "good" and "just"—"the values of Western civilization."

The shallowness and weakness of this concept notwithstanding,[7] "Western civilization" does serve to create the appearance of an alliance between the forces of the good against the forces of evil, destruction, backwardness, and irrationality. This kind of battle between good versus evil can be seen in the framing of the 2014 war on Gaza that is examined in Antonius's chapter. Within this narrative of good versus evil, settler-colonial violences that in fact expel, oppress, displace, maim, and kill become framed as defensive actions that promote and protect civilization. Wildeman's chapter also provides many examples of this discursive manoeuver in Canadian and Israeli framing of Israeli violence, such as the media coverage of "Operation Defensive Shield."

While these two features of settler-colonial ideology have been deconstructed in critical scholarly work, we cannot underestimate their effectiveness in the political and social spheres of the settler colony. These are ideas that are deeply entrenched in settler-colonial societies, and they have proven themselves capable of surviving for many years despite numerous efforts to pull back the ideological curtain and show the violences that are behind them. Regardless, pulling the curtain remains an important task, and one that Palestinian Canadians have engaged in throughout the history of their struggle and activism in Canada and beyond.

The Path Towards Conciliation

In order for the settler colony to justify its brutality and violence, it must be able to paint itself as an entity that stands over and above narrow self-interest. My point here is not that such a task towards universality is impossible or always undesirable. Political and social movements, such as the Haitian Revolution, the early 2010s Arab Uprisings, and the struggle of the Mohawks of Kahnawà:ke can, and do, reach for universal goals and aspirations that transcend narrow self-interest.[8] How movements and political institutions measure up to that quest is what is in question here. The Canadian state has so completely failed in addressing its settler coloniality that we must question whether or not it is accurate to use the terminology of "failure" here. It is more accurate, as many Indigenous scholars have done, to posit settler-colonial violences as embedded and integral to the foundation and functioning of the Canadian state.[9]

This is why many Indigenous scholars and activists have argued that it is not appropriate to discuss *re*conciliation in Canada, but rather simply conciliation.[10] Similarly, the Canadian state has not been (re)conciliatory towards Palestine, as chapters by Naser-Najjab and Abu-Zahra show. Instead of reconciliation, it is more appropriate to speak about a conciliation with the Palestinians, which would involve a radical transformation of Canadian policy that has almost always been in total support of Israeli settler colonialism.

What connects Canada and Israel is partly explained by the desire of Canadian politicians to win the vote of the mainstream Jewish community in Canada (Sucharov), but it also concerns imperial and settler-colonial strategic interests (Kanji, Farah & Desjarlais). Their shared values are not the substantive contents of equality, freedom, democracy, law and justice, and so on, but rather the strategic utility of these concepts: to hide and conceal settler-colonial violence, and the construction of a shared identity and interests among settler states. Sucharov suggests that it will be difficult for Jewish Canadians, Palestinian Canadians, and others fighting for Palestinian rights to enter the political lobbying game and make an impact in and through it. This means for me that only *pressure* from grassroots effort can be utilized at this particular historical moment.

Palestinian Canadians, as well as their non-Palestinian allies, have been fighting through grassroots activism over the last few decades.[11] Despite all the setbacks, frustrations, and oppositions that Palestinian Canadians face, they are still committed to the Canadian part of their identity, as chapters by Wills and Labelle illustrate. In their effort to conciliate their hyphenated identities, Palestinian Canadians are constantly trying to make legible to other Canadians the plight of Palestine and the Palestinians, which is a testament to their enduring belief that change is possible: that Canada, and more importantly, Canadians, can be moved towards a just and conciliatory position on the issue of Palestine. Regardless of whether they wish to organize politically, culturally, or both, Palestinians are keenly aware that their identity as Palestinians is always already political and necessitates the work of, and struggle for, conciliation.

This struggle takes on varied forms and must deal with many obstacles. For example, in their study, Assi and Abdelnour illustrate the intersectionality of oppression that working-class Palestinian refugees face in Canada. In the various narratives they present us, we can garner the sort of jagged experiences of working-class Palestinians in Canada. Their experiences in the workplace cannot be seamless, their Palestinian-ness cannot go unnoticed or untouched. It is always open for interrogation, questioning, suspicion, disapproval, but rarely, if ever, support. This is what makes it jagged: their Palestinian-ness is always either unnerving or potentially unnerving for their fellow workers, managers, and customers. This creates a condition where Palestinian-Canadians always discover the inevitability of their having to struggle, and they become aware that they have little choice on the matter: their very identity pushes them towards the struggle and necessitates their activism. This activism is not always organized or explicitly formulated. It simply becomes a case of Palestinian existence as that which necessitates resistance.

This is the condition of people who are threatened with elimination, disappearance, and marginalization: it is certainly (if not primarily) about physical survival, and it is also about political and social survival, where the struggle emerges as a matter of necessity. For Palestinian Canadians, we find the prevalence of a dynamic where people are being pulled in different directions by hyphenation because wholeness and a seamless harmony in one's identity become difficult, if not impossible, to achieve. The tension is inevitable, and it thus creates the impetus toward conciliation between the different elements that constitute a hyphenated existence. This conciliation does not mean a betrayal of one element in favour of another, and it certainly does not mean a kind of compromise that effectively defeats the elements facing elimination and repression. Rather, conciliation concerns an attempt to create a space where the threatened elements can be nurtured and released in their full potentiality, not to simply augment the more powerful elements or come to belong to them, but to radically transform the more powerful elements.

To put it in more concrete terms: despite all of the obstacles of racism and classism within Canada, despite Canada's refusal to accept the Palestinian part of their identity as belonging to the "nations of civilization" (i.e., "Western civilization"), despite Canada's role in preventing Palestinian freedom, these communities retain their commitment to the ideals to which the Canadian state claims to live by. Critical to their commitment to Canada is the commitment to Palestine as an ideal for *liberation*, as Assi and Abdelnour convincingly argue. It is precisely this liberation that gives substance, depth, and a decolonial trajectory to the ideals of democracy, justice, law, equality, and human rights. Moreover, I would argue that these so-called "Canadian values," when they are rooted in collective freedom, liberation, and well-being, are never settler Canadian, but rather spring from Indigenous knowledges and worldviews as well as the hybridity of what Said would call "contrapuntal" settler-Indigenous exchanges—the interconnectedness and intertwinements of multiple historical trajectories, cultures, ideas, beliefs, and values.

The Canadian state often prides itself on its orientation towards the collective good, as opposed to an individualistic society that operates on the logic of social Darwinism (which, generally speaking, Canadians often associate with the United States). We can observe this in how the state constantly congratulates itself for policies like universal healthcare. Putting aside the necessary deconstructions of that mythology, it is important to underscore what scholars like John Ralston Saul[12] have argued, that this orientation towards the collective good does not emanate from liberalism or other British and French political ideologies, but is rather born in the space of intermixture between settler and Indigenous ideologies and worldviews. Specifically, the presence of Indigenous ways of knowing, being, and doing, as well as Indigenous systems of governance and law in the political system in Canada, is much more significant than conventional Eurocentric nationalist narratives would lead us to believe. There is already embedded in Canadian social and political life certain Indigenous ideals that we need to acknowledge, promote, and nurture; as opposed to the current approach of denial, repression and elimination.[13] The emphasis on collective freedom and well-being, as opposed to a focus on individual citizenship rights and capitalist ownership of property, is one of those core ideals. Among numerous other examples, it can be seen in the ideas and practices of Idle No More,[14] and in the Dene Nation resistance that is examined and theorized by Glen Coulthard.[15] This ideal springs from the alternative political orders of Indigenous peoples and their opposition to the instrumental rationality of the modern settler-colonial state.[16] Instead of an effort to assimilate and come to belong to the settler nation-state, this ideal places in the forefront the collective right of Indigenous peoples to build, develop, and live in their sovereign systems of politics, law and society.[17] Across their different experiences, histories, and visions for what politics, society, and the law ought to look like, this ideal's impetus and drive towards collective liberation and

Indigenous sovereignty is precisely what is shared between the Palestinian and Indigenous decolonial struggles in Canada.

Palestinian Canadians have much to learn from the struggle of Indigenous peoples in Canada, and we have the moral and political obligation to stand shoulder-to-shoulder with Indigenous peoples in this struggle.[18] Certainly, some Palestinian Canadians are already on this path,[19] but we need to expand and build on these efforts. This is a path that we must take where collective freedom and well-being acts as our guide in discovering, learning, and articulating our similar condition and our hope for a liberated future. Therefore, in addition to pressuring the Canadian state towards conciliation with Palestine, Palestinian Canadians need to also build a path of conciliation with Indigenous peoples. The latter should indeed be prioritized and emphasized over the former.

I am not a representative of the diverse Palestinian Canadian community, nor do I speak on behalf of it. All I can do is speak from my own positionality as someone born and raised in Palestine before immigrating to Canada at the age of fourteen. Most people assume that the major challenge that I must face in my experience as an immigrant is racism. And while I certainly have experienced and continue to experience my fair share of racism, this was never my greatest challenge in Canada. Racism is not new to me. I grew up under occupation in an environment saturated with settler-colonial violence and racism. I grew up being constantly told that I was barbaric, irrational, unintelligent, uncivilized, "lesser than." And I knew how to deal with that, how to reject this racism and oppose it on an interpersonal level. This is not, of course, to downplay or minimize interpersonal racism, much less institutional racism which is much more difficult to oppose and remove; but my point here is that by the time I immigrated to Canada, I more or less knew what I needed to do to fight it. There was a path that I was familiar with, and therefore could follow, even if at times, unsuccessfully. I cannot say the same for the main challenge that I faced as a Palestinian Canadian: the recognition of my new positionality in Canada as a settler.[20]

This positionality deeply challenged how I made sense of the world as a native under the violent colonial occupation of a settler. While I came from a violent context of settler colonialism, I now, as a settler in Canada, had to shift my entire universe of meaning. How do I make sense of myself in this country? I knew, intuitively, that like Palestinians, Indigenous peoples were racialized as "lesser than," that we have faced and continue to face elimination and erasure, and that we were beaten but not defeated people, but I did not know any of the history of Indigenous peoples in Canada. More troubling for me than my lack of knowledge in my first few years, though, was my knowing that in this context, I am not positioned on the side of the beaten but still resilient—I am now positioned, even though not fully and against my will, on the side of the "conquerors." I must admit, this was all too much for me to deal with, and I simply avoided the question for as long as I could. It gnawed at me, and I was never satisfied with this approach, but I could not look into a mirror that revealed a settler, even if an unwitting one.

It was not until my master's program in Ottawa that I began to meet Indigenous students and interact with them in classes and conferences. These interactions were often sporadic, but this slow movement did eventually accumulate—spurred forward by certain key interactions and by Idle No More—and led me to slowly face that mirror and begin my work on facing and challenging the reflection. As a university professor in Calgary, I have become much more engaged with Indigenous students, faculty, activists, and community members. These interactions have pushed me towards a path of conciliation, forcing me to ask difficult questions about my settler existence in Canada. This path is its own end. I have no desire to reach an "endpoint" and then move on from it. I still have much to learn, and my transformation on this path is certainly not yet finished.

Just like Palestine itself, and just like Indigenous communities in Canada, Palestinian Canadians will not simply collapse and disappear under the weight of suppression, repression, and oppression. So long as the dispossessed and colonized are threatened with erasure and elimination, they will persist and fight for what is right and just. And it is this very fight that creates something worth fighting for. It is this very fight that keeps the decolonial trajectories on Turtle Island in reach of the lofty ideals from which the majority of people on Turtle Island and beyond find inspiration and aspiration.

Notes

1. Said, *Out of Place*; Said, *Reflections on Exile*; Said, *Power, Politics, and Culture*.
2. For example, see Khalidi, *Brokers of Deceit*.
3. Ayyash, "Edward Said: Writing in Exile."
4. A. Simpson, "The State is a Man."

5. Massad, *The Persistence of the Palestinian Question*; Wolfe, *Traces of History*; Veracini, "Israel-Palestine through a Settler-Colonial Studies Lens."

6. As Lana Tatour convincingly argues, the citizenship regime enforced upon the Palestinians who remained in what became Israel in 1948 is ultimately a system of settler-colonial domination. Tatour, "Citizenship as Domination."

7. There are numerous postcolonial critiques of this concept, from Aimé Césaire's *Discourse on Colonialism* to Gurminder K. Bhambra's *Rethinking Modernity: Postcolonialism and the Sociological Imagination*.

8. The aspiration for freedom in these examples is universal in the sense that it speaks to and shapes people's desires and aspirations in contexts that are different from the ones in which these movements sprung. For the Haitian Revolution's aspiration for freedom from slavery, see the classic works of Cooper, *Slavery and the French and Haitian Revolutionists: L'attitude de la France a l'egard de l'esclavage pendant la revolution* and James, *The Black Jacobins: Toussaint L'Ouverture and the San Domingo Revolution*. For the Arab Uprisings' aspiration for a decolonial freedom from the postcolonial condition, see Dabashi, *The Arab Spring: The End of Postcolonialism*. For the politics of refusal of the Mohawks of Kahnawà:ke and their struggle for Indigenous sovereignty that challenges the Eurocentric model of state sovereignty, see A. Simpson, *Mohawk Interruptus: Political Life across the Borders of Settler States*.

9. Coulthard, *Red Skin, White Masks*.

10. For example, see Sterritt, "What does Reconciliation Mean to Indigenous People?" Also see this study from a non-Indigenous scholar whose work stresses the need for a conciliation that is based on genocide recognition, MacDonald, *The Sleeping Giant Awakens: Genocide, Indian Residential Schools, and the Challenge of Conciliation*.

11. See Wills, Wildeman, Bueckert, and Abu-Zahra, *Advocating for Palestine*.

12. Saul, *A Fair Country*.

13. For example, see Borrows, *Law's Indigenous Ethics*.

14. The Kino-nda-niimi Collective, eds., *The Winter We Danced*.

15. Coulthard, *Red Skin, White Masks*.

16. Coulthard, *Red Skin, White Masks*; A. Simpson, "The State is a Man"; L. Simpson, *As We Have Always Done*.

17. L. Simpson, "Land as Pedagogy."

18. Salaita, *Inter/nationalism: Decolonizing Native America and Palestine*.

19. For example, see Kawas, "Solidarity between Palestinians and Indigenous Activists has Deep Roots."

20. I cannot delve into the important academic debate on migration in a settler-colonial context here, and whether we should call racialized people who are forced to migrate into white settler colonies, "settlers." Suffice it to say, the position of "settler" for racialized communities forced to migrate from one settler-colonial context to another is not the same as white settlement (see Saranillio, "Why Asian Settler Colonialism Matters: A Thought Piece on Critiques, Debates, and Indigenous Difference"). For a critical discussion on some of the dynamics involved in the intersection between

decolonial politics, conciliation, and diasporic people of colour living in white settler colonies from the perspective of transnational feminist thought and praxis, see Patel, Moussa, and Upadhyay, "Complicities, Connections, & Struggles."

References

Ayyash, Mark Muhannad. "Edward Said: Writing in Exile." *Comparative Studies of South Asia, Africa and the Middle East* 30, no. 1 (2010): 107–18.

Bhambra, Gurminder K. *Rethinking Modernity: Postcolonialism and the Sociological Imagination*. New York: Palgrave Macmillan, 2007.

Borrows, John. *Law's Indigenous Ethics*. Toronto: University of Toronto Press, 2019.

Césaire, Aimé. *Discourse on Colonialism*. Translated by J. Pinkham. New York: Monthly Review Press, [1955] 2000.

Cooper, Anna Julia. *Slavery and the French and Haitian Revolutionists: L'Attitude de la France a l'Egard de l'Esclavage Pendant la Revolution*. Edited and translated by Frances R. Keller, second edition. Lanham, MD: Rowman & Littlefield Publishers, [1925] 2006.

Coulthard, Glen. *Red Skin, White Masks: Rejecting the Colonial Politics of Recognition*. Minneapolis: University of Minnesota Press, 2014.

Dabashi, Hamid. *The Arab Spring: The End of Postcolonialism*. New York: Zed Books, 2012.

James, C.L.R. *The Black Jacobins: Toussaint L'Ouverture and the San Domingo Revolution*. Second Revised Edition. New York: Vintage Books, [1938] 1989.

Kawas, Marion. "Solidarity between Palestinians and Indigenous Activists has Deep Roots." *The Palestine Chronicle*, February 18, 2020: https://www.palestinechronicle.com/solidarity-between-palestinians-and-indigenous-activists-has-deep-roots/.

Khalidi, Rashid. *Brokers of Deceit: How the US has Undermined Peace in the Middle East*. Boston: Beacon Press, 2013.

Kino-nda-niimi Collective, eds. *The Winter We Danced: Voices from the Past, the Future, and the Idle No More Movement*. Winnipeg: ARP Books, 2014.

MacDonald, David B. *The Sleeping Giant Awakens: Genocide, Indian Residential Schools, and the Challenge of Conciliation*. Toronto: Toronto University Press, 2019

Massad, Joseph A. *The Persistence of the Palestinian Question: Essays on Zionism and the Palestinians*. London & New York: Routledge, 2006.

Patel, Shaista, Ghaida Moussa, and Nishant Upadhyay. "Complicities, Connections, & Struggles: Critical Transnational Feminist Analysis of Settler Colonialism." *Feral Feminisms* 4 (Summer 2015): https://feralfeminisms.com/wp-content/uploads/2015/12/ff_intro_issue4.pdf.

Said, Edward. *Out of Place: A Memoir*. New York: Vintage, 2000.

Said, Edward. *Reflections on Exile and Other Essays*. Cambridge, MA: Harvard University Press, 2002.

Said, Edward. *Power, Politics, and Culture: Interviews with Edward W. Said*, edited by Gauri Viswanathan. New York: Vintage, 2002.

Salaita, Steven. *Inter/nationalism: Decolonizing Native America and Palestine*. Minneapolis: University of Minnesota Press, 2016.

Saranillio, Dean Itsuji. "Why Asian Settler Colonialism Matters: A Thought Piece on Critiques, Debates, and Indigenous Difference." *Settler Colonial Studies* 3, no. 3–4 (2013): 280–94.

Saul, John Ralston. *A Fair Country: Telling Truths About Canada*. Toronto: Penguin Canada, 2008.

Simpson, Audra. *Mohawk Interruptus: Political Life across the Borders of Settler States*. Durham, NC: Duke University Press, 2014.

Simpson, Audra. "The State is a Man: Theresa Spence, Loretta Saunders and the Gender of Settler Sovereignty." *Theory and Event* 19, no. 4 (2016).

Simpson, Leanne Betasamosake. "Land as Pedagogy: Nishnaabeg Intelligence and Rebellious Transformation." *Decolonization: Indigeneity, Education & Society* 3, no. 3 (2014): 1–25.

Simpson, Leanne Betasamosake. *As We Have Always Done: Indigenous Freedom Through Radical Resistance*. Minneapolis: University of Minnesota Press, 2017.

Sterritt, Angela. "What does Reconciliation Mean to Indigenous People?" *CBC News*, January 3, 2019. https://www.cbc.ca/news/canada/british-columbia/reconciliation-doesn-t-exist-yet-say-indigenous-leaders-1.4963594.

Tatour, Lana. "Citizenship as Domination: Settler Colonialism and the Making of Palestinian Citizenship in Israel." *Arab Studies Journal* XXVII, no. 2 (2019): 8–39.

Veracini, Lorenzo. "Israel-Palestine through a Settler-Colonial Studies Lens." *Interventions* 21, no. 4 (2018): 568–81.

Wills, Emily Regan, Jeremy Wildeman, Michael Bueckert, and Nadia Abu-Zahra, eds. *Advocating for Palestine in Canada: Histories, Movements, Action*. Halifax: Fernwood Publishing, 2022.

Wolfe, Patrick. *Traces of History: Elementary Structures of Race*. London & New York: Verso, 2016.

A SHARED SETTLER COLONIALISM

2

JEREMY WILDEMAN

Introduction

In the summer of 2016, a 22-year-old Cree man, Colten Boushie, was shot in the head and killed at close range by a 56-year-old white farmer, Gerard Stanley, on the Stanley farmstead near the rural Canadian community of Biggar.[1] The killing took place in a Treaty 6 region of the province of Saskatchewan, in Canada, where I was raised, and where a legacy of European colonization, settlement building and violence toward the Indigenous First Nations remains a defining characteristic of everyday life.[2] Halfway around the world, such violence is part of everyday life for indigenous Palestinians, too, colonized by another state established by European settlers, also by and within the British Empire. There, the extra-judicial murder of Palestinians is not uncommon, such as the tragedy to befall sixteen-year-old Mohammed Abu Khdeir, who was kidnapped and murdered by two Israeli teenagers and an Israeli man in 2014. In a particularly gruesome case, Mohammed was abducted near a mosque, beaten and then burned to death in a forest outside Jerusalem.[3] In 2015, a Jewish settler fire-bombed a Palestinian home with a Molotov cocktail in the West Bank village of Duma, near Nablus, killing 18-month-old Ali Dawabsheh and his parents, before spray-painting "Revenge" and "Long Live King Messiah" on the walls of their home.[4] Ali's four-year-old brother Ahmad survived with significant burns to his body. In 2019, seven-year-old Tariq Zabania from Hebron (Al-Khalil in Arabic) was killed when an Israeli Jewish settler ran his car over him.[5] All cases are indicative of a devaluing of the Other, their lives and their cultures, within ongoing processes of settler colonial dispossession applied to remove one society and replace it with another.

A Shared Colonial Foundation

Canada and Israel are European settler colonies established within the late British Empire. They share much in common, including a commitment to liberal democratic institutions, a belief in capitalist economic organizing principals and a sense of connectedness to a perceived Western civilization. They also share a history, and present, of exclusion, oppression, and violence toward the original inhabitants of the land they built their states on. That process of state-building began inside a system of European imperialism where settler colonization was premised on the total destruction and replacement of established societies with new European ones. There, after an initial extermination or expulsion of a majority of the Indigenous peoples, their lands were (and are) demographically swamped with settlers from a founding imperial métropole (i.e., the United Kingdom) and/or a variety of other non-Indigenous locales (i.e., other regions of Europe).[6] It is a shared legacy that underscores both Canada's and Israel's institutional predisposition toward supplanting indigenous populations.[7]

Settler colonialism destroys and replaces the old, without leaving room for assimilation of the native inhabitant. The violence used to shape, control, and remove Indigenous peoples includes everyday forms of humiliation, exclusion, and racial segregation. Some of it is carried out informally, and some of it is sanctioned officially under law.[8] Behind the official and de facto borders erected by a settler state, the Indigenous native will mostly not live as a citizen or live as a deeply unequal one. Yet, the settler state will argue that it is justified in controlling them because of their inherent backwardness and uncivilized nature. Attempts made to "educate and give culture to" Indigenous people, even extreme ones like the Residential School system in

Canada,[9] will also almost never lead to their acceptance as equals by a settler state. Ultimately the end goal is to turn the settlers into the indigenous people of the land and to cease being settlers,[10] while the Indigenous native becomes the foreigner and guest.

As part of this process of displacement, extermination and replacement, the government of a settler state routinely and specifically denies public goods from Indigenous natives. This happens while their own settlers agitate for and attain individual rights. Thus, a characteristic of these settler societies is an exclusionary racial identity, where the benefits of participation in the new society are (particularly in the first decades of colonization) denied to the Indigenous peoples, even while the settlers themselves demand equality and self-government.[11] Those colonists are also always considered civilized, imbued with the rights and obligations of their peers in the imperial métropole, while the original inhabitants are labelled child-like, uncivilized, incapable, immature, irrational, and lacking in basic competencies. This un-civilized-ness is then used as a justification to withhold rights from Indigenous peoples and to force them through destructive projects of social engineering, which are typically described in enlightenment developmental terms or civilizing phraseology. Denying the rights of Indigenous peoples, rights that are being offered to colonists, reflects an underlying belief by the colonizers that their own rights, and even democracy, rest upon Indigenous subordination and dispossession. This denial produces a potent mix of "intra-racial egalitarianism" and "inter-racial exclusion,"[12] characterized by the oppressor's hatred of the oppressed.[13] It also explains how a settler colonial state can be simultaneously liberal, democratic, and capitalist, while being predisposed toward a violent illiberalism, authoritarianism, and the denial of basic goods to a significant part of its population. Thus, in revolutionary United States, the expansion of liberty was conceived of simultaneously with the expansion of slavery and further Indigenous displacement, in their own settlement enterprise.[14]

Krebs and Olwan write that the defining aspect of Canadian and Israeli settler colonialism is the displacement of Indigenous people from their land, and theft of that land and all its possible resources for the use and benefit of the settler population.[15] The Indigenous peoples are ultimately segregated from the new state and forced onto small and less coveted territories, which are scattered and cut off from one another. In the case of Canada, this was done through the establishment of a reserve system,[16] comprised of small,

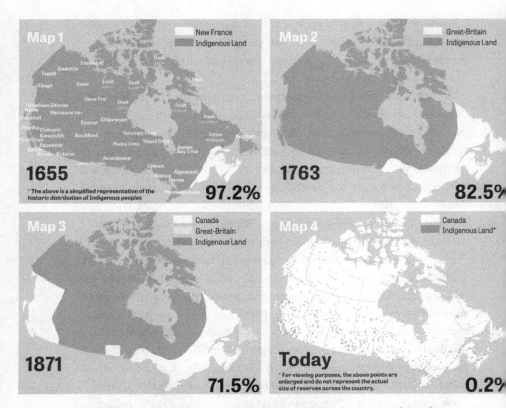

FIGURE 2.2: Maps of Indigenous dispossession in the establishment of Canada. (*Illustration from* CJPME *Foundation, "Indigenous Dispossession Map," 2020. Used with permission from the* CJPME *Foundation*).

"unwanted," and discontiguous lands upon which those Indigenous peoples were forced to live. In the case of the Palestinians in the Occupied Palestinian Territory (OPT), a similar cross-stitching of "bantustans" of discontiguous communities surrounded by Israeli-only settler infrastructure has been developing in the West Bank and East Jerusalem, while hundreds of thousands of Palestinians are trapped in the tiny, besieged Gaza Strip on the Mediterranean. Figures 2.2 and 2.3 reveal how these settler colonial realities compare for the Indigenous peoples of Turtle Island and Palestinians.

Ultimately "Land is Life" for settler-colonial projects, and land is the primary good sought out by the colonizers.[17] The indigenous people are, in this equation, considered quite dispensable,[18] and, as described above, even considered a threat to the settler society being built. In the case of Israel, it

20   *A Shared Settler Colonialism*

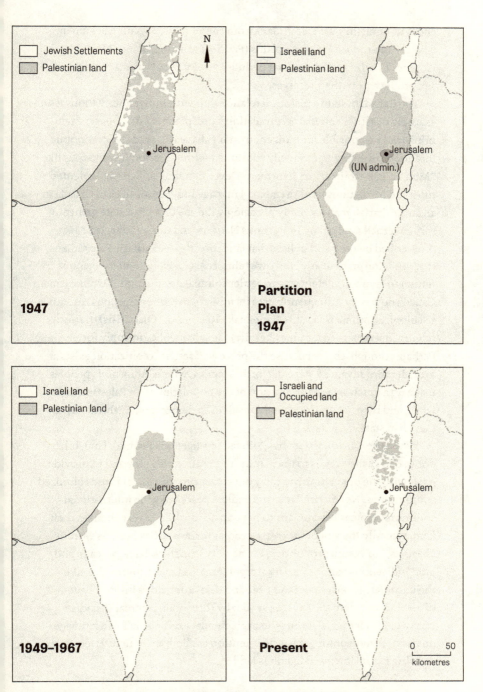

FIGURE 2.3: Maps of Palestinian dispossession in the establishment of Israel. *(Used with permission.)*

chose not only to clear Palestinians from the land but boycott Palestinian labour and produce.[19] On the plains (Prairies) of Turtle Island (North America), Canada chose for long periods to deny First Nations the right to sell produce from their reserves.

The Canadian state's historical relationship with Indigenous nations is an example of settler colonial accumulation by dispossession.[20] Government ministries responsible for Indigenous affairs have betrayed their economic intentions by being traditionally subsumed within economic ministries like "Mines and Resources" or "Northern Development," which implemented rules and regulations used to (micro-) manage Indigenous lives in Canada in an authoritarian manner. Only grudgingly did the Canadian state grant any self-governed land to any Indigenous Nations, and unlike Israel (in Areas A described below), still polices that land directly. As with the Palestinians, that grudging grant of any land owes almost exclusively to an Indigenous refusal to give completely way to settler colonial domination.[21] Unlike Israel, Canada now only infrequently uses its military to curb Indigenous resistance to colonization, such as at the Kanesatake Resistance (Oka Crisis) in 1990, relying first on armed (at times heavily) Canadian police to apply force.[22] Perhaps, though, that is because the process of settler colonization exists at a much more advanced stage in North America, where Indigenous peoples make up a much smaller proportion of the population than Palestinians in Israel, and may not any longer be considered a demographic "threat" by the Canadian state at a federal level.[23]

When the Canadian state has "offered" Indigenous people's land, it has done so in such a way as to undermine their self-sufficiency and to provide itself with the opportunity to carry out closer surveillance of those colonized communities. Not dissimilar to the endless peace talks the international community forces Palestinians to participate in while Israel colonizes their land, typically the aim of the treaty process in Canada has been, as Gordon observes, "to absorb serious political activity into the safer legal realm and bind Indigenous nations into legal arguments and manoeuvring," while the Canadian government buys time and delays decisions inside a system of resolution where the laws are set out by the settler-colonial Canadian state itself.[24] Like Israel, even when agreements exist, Canada often reneges on them, demonstrating it has no intention to allow them to interfere with ongoing expansion on Indigenous land.[25]

Settler Colonial Commonalities

Saskatchewan is a western Prairie province of Canada. It encompasses 588,239 square kilometres,[26] and was formed in 1905 on land comprising parts of Treaty 2 (1871), Treaty 4 (1874), Treaty 5 (1875), Treaty 6 (1876 and 1889), Treaty 8 (1899), and Treaty 10 (1906), signed between Canada/ the British Empire and various Indigenous nations. According to the 2016 Census, Saskatchewan's population stood at 1,098,352 people,[27] with the Aboriginal per cent of the population comprising 175,015 people.[28] This makes Saskatchewan a Canadian region with one of the highest percentages of Indigenous versus non-Indigenous populations. The average age of the Indigenous population is young, at 28.2 years, compared with 40.6 years for the non-Indigenous population.[29]

The OPT was conquered by Israel in 1967 and comprises three main geographical units: Gaza, the West Bank, and East Jerusalem. Gaza is a coastal region with an area of just 365 square kilometres.[30] It has a youthful population of 2,047,969,[31] where 41.3 per cent are aged 0 to 14 years and 28.5 per cent are aged 15 to 29 years.[32] Nearly three-quarters of that population, or 1,460,000 people, are registered as refugees from what is now Israel.[33] The West Bank is landlocked and has an area of 5,660 square kilometres.[34] It is also a youthful population of 3,053,183,[35] where 31.6 per cent are aged 0 to 14 years and 28.8 per cent aged 15 to 29 years.[36] Some 858,758 are registered as refugees.[37] The Jerusalem governorate has a population of 461,666 inhabitants,[38] in the overall West Bank population. However, East Jerusalem (the primary component part) has been cut off from the West Bank (and Gaza) by Israel's massive and fortified Separation Barrier and Israeli settlements.[39] Though living on the coast, Palestinians in Gaza have extremely limited access to the Mediterranean and exist under a siege-like Israeli–Egyptian joint blockade, which has been in place since around the mid-2000s.

The West Bank is divided into three areas (A, B, and C), which are under different jurisdictions, as defined by the 1995 Oslo II Accord between Israel and the Palestinians. Area A includes leading Palestinian urban centres and comprises just 18 per cent of the West Bank. It is left mostly to Palestinian security and civil control. Area B covers small towns and near-urban areas, making up 21 per cent of the West Bank. It is under Israeli security but Palestinian civil control. Area C accounts for 61 per cent of the West Bank, is under Israeli security and civil control, and has mostly been allocated for the Israeli military and settlements. As a result, an estimated 325,500 Israeli citizens living in settlements and outposts may outnumber the 180,000 to 300,000 Palestinians still living in Area C.[40] Overall, there are now in excess of 600,000 Israeli settlers in the West Bank and East Jerusalem.[41] All such settlement building on occupied territory is considered illegal under international law,[42] in a post-war international legal system that was designed specifically to prevent the acquisition of territory by force.

Treaties and Dispossession

Both Canada and Israel have used treaties and accords as tools for managing and controlling the Indigenous peoples upon whose land they built their states. The British and Canadian governments used treaties to construct a narrative that they had taken sovereign control over those lands on Turtle Island (North America) through diplomacy and "consent" in *most* of what now constitutes Canada.[43] There, Indigenous nations were forced onto small parcels of land, called "reservations," while their former lands were swamped with (mostly) European settlers. In the case of Israel and the OPT, the framework for spatial management and control over the Palestinian population was really established diplomatically during the Peace Process, with the Oslo I (1993) and II (1995) Accords, and the Paris Protocol (1994). Those have acted as guideposts where Israel picks and chooses what aspects of the agreements it will respect, while establishing a complex system of control over every aspect of OPT life.[44] Palestinians are forced onto the tiny West Bank "bantustans," the besieged Gaza Strip, or pushed to emigrate abroad, while their homes are demolished and land swamped by Israeli settlers. That includes many settlers from Eastern Europe, which bears similarities to a very eastern European immigration pattern in Saskatchewan.

For Canadian officials, reserves had more benefits than just clearing land to make way for European colonization; they facilitated control over Indigenous treaty populations.[45] Once the Indigenous peoples were settled on reserves and made dependent on Government of Canada supplied rations for sustenance, the government could counter protests and defuse resistance simply by withholding food. On the Prairies, the government could be unapologetic in its use of starvation tactics to force reluctant Indigenous Nations into treaties and onto reservations.[46] Likewise, the government could disrupt political organizing by community chiefs by refusing to supply inter-community council gatherings.[47] As it was, in the early decades of settler-colonization Indigenous communities were already suffering famine

24   *A Shared Settler Colonialism*

and outbreaks of scarlet fever, tied to malnutrition, as their own food sources and economic system broke down with the disappearance of the once vast bison herds. Prime Minister John A. Macdonald and his Conservative Party were particularly willing to use food to pacify and dominate plains First Nations to facilitate colonization.[48]

In a similar way, the isolation of OPT Palestinians into Gaza, East Jerusalem, and West Bank bantustans has made controlling them easier. Unlike Canada, Israel benefits from support by the international community in its colonization efforts, where states from around the world (but particularly in the West) have been willing to pay for many of Israel's colonial costs through a combination of humanitarian and development aid that sustains the Palestinians, at a profit to Israel, while also funding Palestinian Authority (PA) security forces to operate in concert with Israel to curb Palestinian resistance.[49] Israel has even enlisted the support of Arab regimes it was once at war with, like Egypt in their joint blockade of Gaza, which has created a man-made humanitarian crisis.[50]

Canada and Israel have a history of using agreements and periods of negotiating as a time to entrench colonial enterprises, seizing further indigenous land and resources.[51] Negotiations are deeply asymmetrical and always favour the colonial aggressor if they take place while indigenous communities are suffering under occupation from violence, restrictions on freedom of movement, barriers to trade, economic strangulation and/or they are being prevented access to food and natural resources. Just like Canada would withhold food resources from Indigenous nations to force political settlements upon them, in its decades of colonization of the OPT, Israel has withheld resources it is obligated to transfer to the Palestinians, as a means to put pressure on Palestinians, too.[52] At times the Canadian and United States governments have applied the same tactics against the Palestinians, in support of Israel, by withholding humanitarian aid in order to push the Palestinians toward accepting specific political outcomes.[53]

In contemporary Canada, treaties with Indigenous nations are now considered fundamental components of its constitution, "analogous to the terms of union under which provinces joined Confederation."[54] The 1996 *Royal Commission on Aboriginal Peoples* further stated, "the fulfilment of the spirit and intent of the treaties is also considered a fundamental test of the honour of the Crown and of Canada," such that, "their non-fulfilment casts a shadow over Canada's place of respect in the family of nations."[55] The

Commission concluded that it is indisputable, too, that the, "existing treaties have been honoured by governments more in the breach than in the observance, and this might give Aboriginal parties reason to pause and reconsider the wisdom of using this process."[56] Any refusal to negotiate or adhere to treaties in good faith is an affront to the normative liberal ideals of international law and represents a "barbarism" where no laws of war exist to protect civilians.[57] Breach more than in observance best describes Israel's approach to the accords within the Peace Process.

Dominating and "Civilizing"

The Canadian settler state generally assumed the pre-industrial culture of Indigenous Nations was, "anachronistic and, for practical and humanitarian reasons, they should be 'civilized,' 'Christianised' and 'schooled in the art of agriculture."[58] "Indian-ness" was equated with immorality.[59] This presupposed an argument that the Indigenous peoples should be ruled as wards of the state, until they were fundamentally reformed through a programme of modernization to the point where they could live naturally in peace with the more civilized European settlers. Not coincidentally, the period of wardship would leave Canada even more free to seize additional territory and resources, while side-stepping its treaty obligations. In an extreme iteration of liberal modernizing of the "savage," the Canadian state established a policy of "aggressive assimilation" where it took away (abducted) 150,000 First Nation, Inuit, and Métis children from their parents to be taught at church-run, government-funded industrial schools (Residential Schools) where they were educated to adopt Christianity and speak English or French,[60] in what amounted to an act of cultural genocide.[61] At least 2,800 of those children are known to have died,[62] with other estimates ranging 4,118 to 6,509,[63] in an environment where physical and sexual abuse was rife.

Similarly, a perception held among the public, educated elite and many Middle East observers in the West, is that Israel is a civilized and modern liberal democracy, which is unfortunately situated in a hostile neighbourhood of illiberal, less-civilized, and militaristic Arab Muslims.[64] Thus, Canadian Prime Minister Stephen Harper would infamously describe Israel as a, "light of freedom and democracy in what is otherwise a region of darkness."[65] The Trump Administration's chief architect for Middle East peace, Jared Kushner, argued in 2020 that Palestinians are not capable of governing themselves,[66] in spite of leading global institutions—the World Bank,

International Monetary Fund and United Nations—declaring a decade earlier that Palestinian institutions were strong enough to manage their own state.[67] That includes, after significant contributions to state-building by countries like Canada, such as Liberal Prime Minister Paul Martin's "all of government" approach to providing assistance to Palestinians. There Canadian departments and institutions were directly engaged with strengthening Palestinian ones in key sectors like justice and border administration.[68] Such programmes were situated with an overall development scheme intended to civilize and "catch the Palestinians up to Israel," by imbuing them with liberal-democratic and capitalist institutions found in Israel and the West, thereby naturally abandoning their inherently despotic and militaristic ways. This would leave Israel with a Palestinian partner "willing" and able to embrace peace with it. Kushner's comments implied that the Palestinians had still not been modernized enough, however, after decades and billions of dollars in international development interventions, meaning Palestinians had best remain wards of Israel and of the international community. Such an argument is convenient for an ongoing programme of Israeli settler colonization that Kushner has himself donated to.[69]

Law and National Security

Colonization relies on the asymmetrical application of force. During colonial expansion, military forts were among the first structures built on Indigenous territories, with jails following soon after. On the Prairies, the enforcers of the treaties and Indigenous wardship were the federal North-West Mounted Police, predecessors of the Royal Canadian Mounted Police (RCMP). The military nature of the Canadian presence on the Prairies was underscored by the fact that, until after 1879, the Mounted Police were, for instance, responsible for the day-to-day administration of Indian affairs in the Treaty 7 region.[70] For a moment, the force had been regarded as something of a saviour to the Indigenous population, providing the latter with some form of security from growing communities of European settlers.[71] Once the police were brought under the mandate of the Department of Indian Affairs in October 1884, however, they transformed into just ambivalent agents of Indigenous subjugation.[72] In the OPT, the Israeli Defence Forces (IDF) enforce Israeli rule and the settler-colonial project. Israeli human rights organization B'Tselem has described the IDF's role as military support for state-backed settler violence,[73] protecting Israeli settlers who are engaged in violence against Palestinians.

Settler colonization is carried out within a structure of laws and order, such as the conceptual underpinning of "peace, order and good government" (or POGG) found in Canada's 1867 Constitution Act,[74] and which many liberal Canadians consider an exemplar to export in global governance.[75] While Canadian and Israeli settlers may argue for the benefits of a liberal legal system for themselves, they do the opposite for the indigenous people they rule. In Canada, that has included what Dhamoon and Abu Laban have described as a racialized "Othering," which has constructed the Indigenous subject as an, "outlaw who posed an internal danger to Canadian law and order, even though it was the land and security of Indigenous people and nationhood that was under threat."[76] In Saskatchewan, this contributed to an ethos held by non-Indigenous settlers that "we" must control "them" (the Indigenous) lest they hurt "us."[77]

Even though the legal system is already structured to sanctify racialized dispossession, these settler states will routinely suspend the law in the face of legitimate, violent, or non-violent resistance.[78] In 2012, the non-violent "Idle No More" movement emerged in Saskatchewan in response to various pieces of Canadian government legislation that eroded environmental protections, and Indigenous land and treaty rights.[79] The Indigenous movement articulates radical politics of decolonization to assert their rights, and to pressure Canada to honour existing treaties and share resources on an equal nation-to-nation basis.[80] That presents a direct threat to the Canadian state's claim to sovereignty over all the land. The movement was interpreted by Canadian authorities to be both criminal and a national security threat,[81] and was categorized as criminal and extremist.[82] It was thus monitored by Canadian security agencies like the RCMP, Department of National Defence, Canadian Security Intelligence Service, and Public Safety Canada.[83]

In 2005, the non-violent Boycott, Divestment, Sanctions (BDS) movement was launched by 170 Palestinian unions, refugee networks, women's organizations, professional associations, popular resistance committees and other Palestinian civil society bodies.[84] It calls on the international community to force Israel to respect the fundamental rights it has denied Palestinians and to comply with international law.[85] The movement styles itself around the, "simple principle that Palestinians are entitled to the same rights as the rest of humanity,"[86] draws inspiration from the successful anti-apartheid campaign against South Africa, and has only grown over time. Like the Canadian government's reaction to Idle No More, Israel views BDS as a security threat that is both strategic and existential by nature.[87] In response, the Government of Israel has expended significant capital and diplomatic energy to have the movement labelled as anti-Semitic and to criminalize it worldwide.[88] This has contributed to the ongoing campaign to criminalize and delegitimize criticisms of Israel across the world, including notably in Canada.[89]

Movement

The structures of control over colonized people are by nature pervasive. Waziyatawin observes that, "even when we are not in prison we do not have to see physical walls or barriers because we know that if we violate the invisible borders we will join the ranks of the incarcerated or dead."[90] Some of the more severe measures of oppression include restrictions on indigenous freedom of movement. They can be visibly present at any time, such as in the form of physical barriers or armed colonial security, or more ephemeral and less visible by nature, such as the requirement to apply for and carry permits to travel freely on their own land. On the Prairies, this appeared in the form of a Pass System put into place during the 1885 Northwest Resistance in what was then the District of Saskatchewan.[91] Initially described as a temporary security measure,[92] it was considered a useful means by government authorities to monitor Indigenous people who might potentially participate in, or support, rebellion. Under the system, any Indigenous person who wanted to leave their community had to have a pass approved by the reserve's Indian agent, who was imbued with a power similar to judges. That pass would stipulate the leave's purpose and duration, and the holder would have to carry it on them at all times,[93] even though it ran contrary to treaty promises against restrictions on movement.[94] Since Indigenous peoples were not considered citizens of Canada until 1960, that made official legal means of resistance to the Pass System very difficult,[95] and the "temporary" measure remained in place for generations, until at least the 1940s.[96]

Restrictions on Indigenous freedom of movement is the norm for Palestinians. An extensive system of permits, checkpoints, and a Separation Barrier restrict and regulate Palestinian movement.[97] Israeli policies of closure limit the ability of Palestinians to enter Israel or move freely inside the OPT. Palestinians require permits to visit East Jerusalem, to move

JEREMY WILDEMAN   29

between Gaza and the West Bank, to travel outside the country and to work in Israel. Attaining those permits is never guaranteed, not simple, and in periods of tension, can be extremely difficult to attain. This system of control directly contravenes the Paris Protocol and Oslo promise to allow Palestinian workers to freely enter the Israeli job market, as part of the agreements officially tying their economies together. Since October 2003, Israel has also enforced a permit system in what is described as the "seam zone," consisting of areas severed from the West Bank by the Separation Barrier. This separates landowners from their own land. Under this system, Palestinian farmers must apply for permits for access to their orchards and fields, and they are required to renew those permits repeatedly. Entire communities in Area A, like the city of Qalqilya, are surrounded by fortifications and barriers, and can be shut by closing gates and imprisoning the inhabitants inside. These measures of closure are justified in the name of security and were instituted right after the Peace Process got underway in 1993.[98] They conveniently undermine Palestinian competition to Israeli business and labour, too.[99]

The Economics of Exploitation

Indigenous reserves, dominated by the Government of Canada, and Palestinian bantustans, dominated by the Government of Israel, are economically non-viable, easily exploitable, and facilitate totalitarian control to the colonizer. In general, people can only exist on them with external cash and resource flows, particularly because of the lack of a hinterland, colonial de-development and due to their discontiguous nature. For Palestinians, that has been an impetus behind approximately $US 40 billion (at least) in official development assistance (ODA) since the Oslo I Accord was signed in 1993.[100] Those funds have been used to purchase resources predominantly from Israeli suppliers and include sums spent on foreign aid personnel from donor countries. Canada has itself provided development and humanitarian assistance to the West Bank and Gaza, and United Nations Relief and Works Agency for Palestine Refugees in the Near East (UNRWA), reaching up to $CA 1,170.27 billion from the 1996/97 to 2018/19 fiscal years.[101] In 2019, the Government of Canada noted it had spent $CA 16.8 billion on investments for Indigenous peoples over three previous budget years.[102]

In what became the province of Saskatchewan, Indigenous nations suffered a humanitarian disaster in the late 1870s when they were beset by the collapse of the bison herds that their economies were structured around.

30 *A Shared Settler Colonialism*

For nations in desperate situations, it is difficult to refuse the assistance-domination trap. Up to 1877, with very few exceptions agreements between the Canadian state and Indigenous nations were reached from positions of mutual strength. Before the end of the decade, the balance changed irrevocably with the disappearance of the bison. Without the herds, Indigenous nations could not maintain their freedom.[103]

Meanwhile, government-supplied rations had become a means of coercing Indigenous nations into submitting to treaties that isolated them onto reserves.[104] Those reserves often lacked adequate resources for self-sufficiency, particularly for the long-standing Indigenous way of life. Regardless, the Government of Canada was obliged to provide food and other support in return for the treaty agreements. Cree negotiators had even, for instance, succeeded at including famine relief in the text of Treaty 6.[105] In general, Canadian officials either ignored their obligations or used food to suppress a population who, less than a decade earlier, had controlled the plains.[106]

The reserve system presented a tremendous tool not only for colonization and control, but also business opportunities for private companies supplying food, which was all too often provided at a low or substandard quality. In 1878, one of the first years of widespread hunger, I.G. Baker and Company shipped $2.5 million worth of goods from Fort Benton, Montana, paid for by the Government of Canada.[107] Over the years, many millions of dollars would be spent on similar procurements, and tons of food and other goods stockpiled in government warehouses. This happened while suffering proliferated among the increasingly malnourished and sick reserve populations.[108] As the demand for food increased due to the ongoing collapse of the Indigenous way of life and their forced relocation onto reserves, officials would often choose to invest in more security rather than increase the flow of food.[109] Half-hearted relief measures during the famine of 1878 to 1880, and afterward, kept people in a constant state of hunger, illustrating the, "moral and legal failures of the Crown's treaty commitment to provide assistance in the case of a widespread famine on the plains."[110] Canadian officials, meanwhile, made personal wealth off the financial flows,[111] and resources would be procured from settlers off reserve, seeing the reservation system structured economically to benefit ongoing settler colonization on the plains.

Palestinians have long been in a desperate economic situation and caught in the assistance-domination trap. Their conditions deteriorated steadily throughout the Peace Process, leading to a dystopian humanitarian collapse in Gaza that affects nearly 40 per cent of the OPT population. Some 54 per cent of Palestinians in Gaza are food insecure and 75 per cent are recipients of aid, while 90 per cent of the water from the Gaza aquifer is undrinkable.[112] Much like the Indigenous loss of the plains bison herds, over the course of the Peace Process OPT Palestinians have seen the share of agriculture as a proportion of their economy decline precipitously from 12 per cent to just 4 per cent between 1994 and 2015,[113] with Israel rapidly colonizing their hinterland. Nothing is more important to a nation's security than access to food sources. Agriculture had once been the backbone of the Palestinian economy.

As a result of broad economic decline, Palestinians came at many points to depend on foreign aid for survival. Whereas in 1991 the private sector comprised as much as 80 per cent of gross domestic product (GDP), in 2009 foreign aid comprised the largest part of the economy at 49 per cent of GDP.[114] As result of that aid dependency, most Palestinian economic growth has occurred in public sector services over the past two decades,[115] despite billions of dollars in ODA inflows. Donors like Canada were putting money into an economic system where Israel had long structured the OPT economy solely to its own benefit.[116] That includes a history of undermining competitive Palestinian industries and labour, while Israeli producers benefit from market access to the OPT that is tariff-free, non-competitive and from which Palestinian goods are often prevented entry to Israel.[117] Roy referred to this as the, "deliberate, systematic deconstruction of an indigenous economy by a dominant power."[118] ODA funds thus have sustained the PA and paid Palestinian salaries, but have in turn been used to purchase basic goods that mostly arrive into the OPT from Israeli suppliers. Thus, ODA for Palestinians further enriches Israel,[119] with up to 72 per cent ending up in the (wealthy) Israeli economy.[120]

Similar to what took place with Indigenous nations when they were particularly vulnerable on the plains and in need of assistance, donors have often chosen to reinforce security spending to maintain control over Palestinians. Since the Second Intifada concluded in 2006 and the Western-backed Fatah faction carried out a coup to take control of the PA in 2007,[121] Western donors have invested in Palestinian security forces that are expected to work in coordination with Israeli security. Those Palestinian security forces are trained by European, American, and Canadian

32   *A Shared Settler Colonialism*

personnel, and routinely engage in the arrest and torture of peaceful critics and opponents.[122] The effect is to benefit Israel from a strategic perspective by reducing the direct exposure of its troops to Palestinians in Area A, while helping Israel to maintain control over the OPT, and without Israel bearing the financial costs of outsourcing security to the Palestinians. This is incredibly beneficial for Israel, and so even while the United States Trump Administration was drastically slashing funding for health and education services for Palestinians, including all United States support for Palestinian refugees through UNRWA, it was continuing to set aside funding for PA security forces.[123] Canada similarly kept investing in Palestinian security forces when under the Harper Conservative Government, it held back UNRWA funding in the 2011/12, 2013/14, 2014/15 and 2015/16 fiscal years.[124]

In fact, the Harper government focused its Palestinian aid spending on capacity building and the PA judicial system. Within judicial reform, Canada's main initiatives were to provide assistance by training judges, building courthouses, improving PA forensics and strengthening the PA's prosecution (though not defence) services. The official hope was that this would inculcate rule of law among the Palestinians, leading to a better environment for business investment and thereby reducing poverty. Further, at the level of the Canadian government and irrespective of the party in power, there appears to have consistently been a belief that the Palestinians had much to learn from Israel and that Israel could be a positive force in the development of a liberal democratic Palestinian state. Thus, one Canadian aid interviewee I spoke with said the Harper Conservative government had tried to encourage collaboration in a Palestinian justice project with Israel, based on the idea that Israel could help develop the Palestinian judiciary. The interviewee was being asked to have Israelis teach Palestinians about human rights when Israelis were the ones systematically meting violence out against Palestinians and erasing Palestinian society, supported by an Israeli judicial system that legally enforces settler colonialism and denies Palestinians equality under the law.[125]

Silencing and Bigotry

Sterzuk describes growing up on the Prairies and learning how the land had been devoid of any meaningful human civilization prior to European contact.[126] This author confirms having the same learning experience

FIGURE 2.1: Tombstone in Battleford, Saskatchewan, marking the mass grave of the "Battleford Eight," who were hung in the largest mass execution in Canadian history, November 27, 1885, following the Métis Resistance. *(Photograph by Saskg, "The Tombstone of the Battleford Eight," 2017. Creative Commons Attribution-Share Alike 4.0 International.)*

growing up in Treaty 6 / the Battlefords region of Saskatchewan.[127] This belief is shared in a similar phrase from the Zionist ideology that underlines Israeli state-building, where it conceives of historical Palestine as, "a land without a people for a people without a land"; like a vacant territory waiting for settlers, with Palestinian residents who are not attached to it by any historical or cultural ties.[128] Neither phrase could be further from the truth. Indeed, for this reason, one of Zionism's founding fathers, Theodor Herzl, referred to Israeli state building more as the destruction of something old and replacement of it with something completely new, "If I wish to substitute a new building for an old one, I must demolish before I construct."[129]

Only through discrimination is that possible because the previous inhabitants of a region must be dehumanized, "de-civilized," and their existence ultimately denied, in order to establish the moral logic necessary to justify the destruction that will take place. Once this has been accomplished, any and all acts of horror can be inflicted upon a colonized people without recourse, because by that point the narrative of the oppressed becomes unheard and irrelevant.[130] So, although the killing of Europeans was widely publicized in the press and remains a fixation of historians of the 1885 Mètis Resistance, the murder of Indigenous people during that period received scant attention.[131] This, despite the mass execution of eight Cree men after the Resistance by the Government of Canada being the largest ever public hanging it has carried out, whose gravestone is shown in figure 2.1.[132] That lack of valuation of Indigenous life remains characteristic of contemporary Canada where, for instance, a crisis of missing and murdered Indigenous women has long been underplayed.[133]

Studies suggest Indigenous populations in Canada are widely underrepresented in mainstream media.[134] Limited media coverage can undermine public and stakeholder interest in addressing issues faced by many Indigenous communities. One study assessed news coverage of their water security issues from 2000 to 2015. Its results point to limited coverage when compared to media coverage of non-Indigenous water issues.[135] That lack of concern for Indigenous access to safe water probably comes as more than irony in a Canada whose very existence has been predicated on seizing resources from Indigenous people, given Canada's established track record of not adequately fulfilling its treaty obligations to supply Indigenous communities. Canada's settler-colonial proclivity leans toward erasure of the Indigenous native through the denial of goods.

As Sami Hadawi found for Palestinians in Canadian media,[136] having media coverage can be as problematic as no media coverage. In 2002, Maslin examined the portrayal of Indigenous peoples in two major Saskatchewan daily newspapers, the *Leader Post*, and the *Star Phoenix*. Their study revealed that the newspapers regularly portrayed Indigenous subjects as problematic: either in the sense of having problems or of causing them for non-Indigenous people.[137] It found approximately 70 per cent of the newspaper articles characterized Indigenous peoples in "negative" or "stereotypical" categories.[138] It also found that positive portrayals of Indigenous people came with underlying negative connotations. So, when an individual was portrayed as successful, such as a "cultural icon," "good Indian," or "athlete," their success was positioned as atypical, and the individual was described as exceptional for overcoming the inherent deficiencies of their own nature.[139]

That is because a rule of settler colonialism is that indigenous peoples will never be accepted as equals, as a group, to the settlers. While the assimilation of the colonized may be a putative goal, it cannot actually be achieved by reason of racism, while political and cultural autonomy is denied to the colonized for the same racist reasons.[140] That racism is essential in maintaining a status quo of ongoing denial and of segregation, whether done crudely or wrapped in a liberal veneer, that benefits settler society.

Maslin further found the newspapers portrayed politically active Indigenous peoples as unreasonable and demanding.[141] They also found the newspapers adopted an insidious "us/them dichotomy" that appeared to communicate that any gains made by Indigenous peoples take or divert away money or privileges from other Canadians.[142] That is again consistent with a settler colonial society's proclivity to deny goods to a colonized people, and where the struggle over land and its associated resources is treated as a zero-sum struggle for both colonizer and colonized alike.[143] Meanwhile, Kanji has observed that Indigenous land and water defenders resisting their ongoing dispossession are described as "radicals," both unreasonable and demanding, while Canada is portrayed as an innocent "hostage" to Indigenous activism.[144]

Palestinians have a similar experience with the media. Recent analysis of nearly 100,000 news headlines in the American press about the Israel and Palestine conflict, over the past five decades, found the Israeli point of view was featured much more prominently than the Palestinian one.[145] It also found references to key terminology describing Palestinian conditions, such as refugees or the occupation, have been steadily omitted.[146] In 2005, a study of the Canadian print media's coverage of the Second Intifada looked at three major print newspapers, *The Globe and Mail*, the *National Post* and the *Toronto Star*,[147] at a time when print media was a significant source of news. The study analyzed their coverage of Israeli and Palestinian deaths, looking at the headlines and first paragraphs of articles for two separate one-year periods: September 29, 2000 to September 28, 2001, and January 1, 2004 to December 31, 2004. It found the media adopted a strongly pro-Israel editorial position, had a tendency to over-report Israeli deaths relative to Palestinian ones, and under-reported and downplayed the deaths of Palestinian children— to the point of near omission in the *National Post*. Ad-hoc observations during the researchers' data collection indicated Palestinians were generally more likely to be described as combatants than Israelis, despite the fact that a

36   *A Shared Settler Colonialism*

greater percentage of Palestinian civilians had been victims of conflict than Israeli civilians.[148]

An examination of Israeli media coverage during the Second Intifada found the actions of Jewish Israelis were consistently presented as defensive and necessary in response to the actions by provocative Palestinians.[149] This justified and legitimized Jewish Israelis' actions while delegitimizing those of Palestinians.[150] Analysis of Israeli media coverage of "Operation Defensive Shield," the biggest Israeli military operation during the Second Intifada, indicated a desperate Israeli need to suppress, to dismiss, and to fend off guilt.[151] The analysis found guilt could be suppressed by counterblaming, saying, "the other side is guilty and therefore I am not"; and by disqualifying judging authorities as without a right to judge.[152] Other tactics within Israeli media coverage included explaining away aggressions by blurring intention ("I did not mean to do that, it happened by mistake"), and by recourse to a claim about coercion ("I was forced to do what I did").[153] The analysis also found guilt could be bluntly pushed aside in an act of defiance ("I know exactly what I did, but I don't care").[154]

In 2007, Rinnawi found Palestinian citizens of Israel were typically presented as a threat to the Jewish social order, while West Bank and Gaza Palestinians tended to be depicted as terrorists.[155] Even in sport, Shor and Yonay find Israeli Palestinian soccer players are consistently policed and silenced by the Jewish-dominated media discourse, effectively blocking one of the few channels of expression for the Arab public in Israel.[156] They describe this as being done by an Israeli media that is by and large intolerant towards views that challenge its nationalistic fundamentals, causing it to both rebuff Palestinian players' political statements and to refuse to sympathize or engage with Palestinians in a serious dialogue.[157]

Green writes that systemic racism is embedded in the Canadian political culture in the service first of colonialism and, subsequently, in the maintenance of settler and white privilege.[158] Such discrimination has deadly consequences. In Saskatoon in the 1990s, police engaged in a lethal practice, dubbed "Starlight Tours," of driving and dumping Indigenous persons on the outskirts of the city in the Winter, in the middle of the night,[159] including at temperatures reaching minus 30 Celsius (not accounting for the additional effects of windchill). That was the last life experience of Neil Stonechild, a Saulteaux teen, who was found frozen in a field on the outskirts of Saskatoon on November 29, 1990. Just seventeen at the time, he was found face-down in a light jacket in jeans with just one shoe.[160] The case was closed despite visible injuries to Stonechild's body and the lack of serious investigation reflected the, "persistent devaluation of Aboriginal life," that Razack observes Canadian law both produces and sustains.[161] The police never even returned Stonechild's personal belongings to the family, and the offending officers were only *dismissed* in 2004, after a public inquiry.[162] Their dismissal came after two more men died, but a third survived, helping to identify the Saskatoon police services as the culprit of the killings.

Conclusion

A failure in Saskatchewan to deal with racism perpetuates endless and damaging social stresses.[163] The Starlight Tour killings and inability of the Saskatoon Police Force to address them properly are the manifestation of pervasive, systemic, and structural racism.[164] That racism is grounded in a history of state-backed dispossession of Indigenous peoples in Treaty 6. The killings are an example of the invisible boundaries Waziyatawin warned can result in Indigenous death when transgressed.[165] Colton Boushie had not even been born when Neil Stonechild died, but in a similar way the legal system in Saskatchewan appeared to favour the non-Indigenous narrative. Gerald Stanley was charged but ultimately acquitted of second-degree murder when a white-only jury in Battleford, Saskatchewan delivered a not guilty verdict. No Indigenous persons were invited to the jury.[166]

For Palestinians, justice is equally hard to attain. Mohammed Abu Khdeir's murder was so extreme that Israel labelled it an act of terrorism,[167] a category usually reserved for Palestinians, and his killers were sentenced for their actions. The ringleader, Yosef Haim Ben, was handed a life sentence plus twenty years in jail in spite of a plea of insanity.[168] His then teenaged accomplices were also sentenced, with the older of the two given twenty-eight years in prison and the second twenty-one years.[169] The killers had said soon after their arrest that the murder was an act of revenge for three Jewish teenagers who had been kidnapped and killed while hitchhiking in the OPT,[170] an act which Antonius describes in his chapter as an excuse used for Israel's third major military assault and utter devastation of Gaza in 2014. An Israeli court also convicted the Jewish settler, Amiram Ben-Uliel, guilty of racially motivated murder in the 2015 arson attack that killed Ali Dawabsheh and his parents.[171] Justice has yet to be found for Tariq Zabania if it is ever

38   *A Shared Settler Colonialism*

found. For countless Palestinians, injustice has long been the norm.[172]

In *Malice Enough in Their Hearts and Courage Enough in Ours*, Waziyatawin writes how, "colonization ought to be one of the most easily recognized forms of oppression in the world."[173] Yet, it is not, and colonizing powers work so steadfastly to rationalize and justify their crimes against humanity, "that it eventually becomes normalized, acceptable, and even righteous."[174] Defeating racism and addressing the malice in their oppressors' hearts will be necessary to change this. With great courage, Palestinians and Indigenous nations continue to protest, resist, and strive for a better world for themselves, their families, and the communities around them.

Notes

1. Quenneville, "What Happened on Gerald Stanley's Farm."
2. This author places themself positionally as non-Indigenous, raised mostly in Treaty 6 but also Treaty 4 areas within Saskatchewan, in communities that were both non-Indigenous and where Indigenous peoples were almost never seen. In particular, the Treaty 6 community he lived in, called Unity, exhibited incredible hostility to Indigenous peoples. The author never knew about the Treaty numbers until late in adulthood, which is common among non-Indigenous inhabitants. The rural community of Biggar is very proximate to Unity, and there is frequent travel between the rural settlements.
3. Beaumont, "Israeli Teenagers Jailed."
4. *Al Jazeera*, "Jewish Settler Convicted in Arson Attack."
5. IMEMC News, "Seven-Year-Old Palestinian Child Killed."
6. Veracini, "The Other Shift," 27.
7. Wolfe, "Purchase by Other Means," 134.
8. Bell, "The Dream Machine," 22.
9. CBC News, "A History of Residential Schools in Canada."
10. Wolfe, *Settler Colonialism and the Transformation of Anthropology*, 2–3; Veracini, *Settler Colonialism*, 5.
11. Veracini, *Settler Colonialism*, 3.
12. Bell, "The Dream Machine," 20–21.
13. Memmi, *The Colonizer and the Colonized*, 23.
14. Rana, *The Two Faces of American Freedom*, 22.
15. Krebs and Olwan, "'From Jerusalem to the Grand River.'"
16. Krebs and Olwan, 144.
17. Wolfe, *Settler Colonialism and the Transformation of Anthropology*, 3.
18. Veracini, *Settler Colonialism*, 17.

19. Wolfe, "Purchase by Other Means," 152.

20. Gordon, "Canada, Empire and Indigenous People in the Americas, 52.

21. Barker, "A Direct Act of Resurgence, a Direct Act of Sovereignty," 44.

22. Nikiforuk, "From the Archives."

23. Veracini, *Settler Colonialism*, 5.

24. Gordon, "Canada, Empire and Indigenous People in the Americas," 60.

25. Gordon, 61–62.

26. Statistics Canada, "Province of Saskatchewan."

27. Saskatchewan Bureau of Statistics, "Saskatchewan Population Report—2016 Census of Canada."

28. Statistics Canada, "Aboriginal Peoples—Province of Saskatchewan."

29. Statistics Canada, "Aboriginal Peoples—Province of Saskatchewan."

30. Palestinian Central Bureau of Statistics (PCBS), "Indicators."

31. PCBS, "Estimated Population in Palestine."

32. PCBS, "Indicators."

33. United Nations Relief and Works Agency for Palestine Refugees (UNRWA),"UNRWA in Figures 2018—Occupied Palestinian Territory."

34. PCBS, "Indicators."

35. PCBS, "Estimated Population in Palestine."

36. PCBS, "Indicators."

37. UNRWA, "Where We Work—West Bank."

38. PCBS, "Estimated Population in Palestine."

39. "East Jerusalem."

40. B'Tselem, "Area C."

41. PCBS, "Number of Settlers in the Settlements and Palestinian Population in the West Bank by Governorate, 2017."

42. "Israel's Settlements Have No Legal Validity, Constitute Flagrant Violation of International Law, Security Council Reaffirms—Resolution 2334 (2016)—Occupied Palestinian Territory," ReliefWeb, December 23, 2016, https://reliefweb.int/report/occupied-palestinian-territoryisrael-s-settlements-have-no-legal-validity-constitute.

43. In some areas, like the majority of British Columbia, colonization and the establishment of reserves took place with very few treaties.

44. Weizman, *Hollow Land*.

45. Daschuk, *Clearing the Plains*, 133.

46. Daschuk, 127.

47. Daschuk, 143.

48. Daschuk, 108.

49. Tartir and Wildeman, "Persistent Failure"; Hever, *The Political Economy of Israel's Occupation*; Hever, "How Much International Aid"; Turner, "International Aid in the Absence of Palestinian Sovereignty"; Monaghan, "Security Development and the Palestinian Authority"; Tartir, "The Palestinian Authority Security Forces."

50. United Nations Conference on Trade and Development (UNCTAD), "Gaza Could Become Uninhabitable."
51. Krebs and Olwan, "'From Jerusalem to the Grand River," 148.
52. Sherwood, "Israel Seizes $120m in Palestinian Tax Revenue."
53. Csillag, "Canada Redirecting Palestinian Aid from UNRWA"; Amr, "In One Move, Trump Eliminated United States Funding"; Landau and Tibon, "Nikki Haley: U.S. to Withhold Funding."
54. Royal Commission on Aboriginal Peoples, "Restructuring the Relationship," 16, 18.
55. Royal Commission on Aboriginal Peoples, 16.
56. Royal Commission on Aboriginal Peoples, 3.
57. Moses, "Empire, Colony, Genocide."
58. Barron, "The Indian Pass System," 26.
59. Barron, 32.
60. CBC News, "A History of Residential Schools in Canada."
61. The Truth and Reconciliation Commission of Canada wrote, "Physical genocide is the mass killing of the members of a targeted group, and biological genocide is the destruction of the group's reproductive capacity. Cultural genocide is the destruction of those structures and practices that allow the group to continue as a group. States that engage in cultural genocide set out to destroy the political and social institutions of the targeted group. Land is seized, and populations are forcibly transferred and their movement is restricted. Languages are banned. Spiritual leaders are persecuted, spiritual practices are forbidden, and objects of spiritual value are confiscated and destroyed. And most significantly to the issue at hand, families are disrupted to prevent the transmission of cultural values and identity from one generation to the next. In its dealing with Aboriginal people, Canada did all these things." Truth and Reconcilliation Commission of Canada, *Honouring the Truth, Reconciling for the Future*.
62. Maimann and Doherty, "Thousands of Indigenous Children Died."
63. Deer, "Why It's Difficult."
64. Read Kanji's chapter in this book (chapter 4).
65. JTA, "What Makes Canada's PM One of Israel's Staunchest Supporters?"
66. AFP, "Kushner: Palestinians Not yet Capable of Governing Themselves."
67. Bronner, "Bid for State of Palestine."
68. This initiative seemed to have stopped with the election of the Hamas government in 2006 and was not taken up by the Harper government. Bell et al., "Practitioners' Perspectives on Canada," 12.
69. JTA, "Kushner Did Not Disclose."
70. Daschuk, *Clearing the Plains*, 106.
71. Daschuk, 127.
72. Daschuk, 127.
73. B'Tselem, "State-Backed Settler Violence."
74. "Constitution Act, 1867," 91.

75. Geddes, "POGG's the Word in Washington," 20.

76. Dhamoon and Abu-Laban, "Dangerous (Internal) Foreigners," 176.

77. Green, "From Stonechild to Social Cohesion," 524.

78. Lloyd, "Settler Colonialism and the State of Exception," 71.

79. Crosby and Monaghan, "Settler Colonialism and the Policing of Idle No More," 42.

80. Crosby and Monaghan, 42.

81. Crosby and Monaghan, 37.

82. Crosby and Monaghan, 50.

83. Crosby and Monaghan, 44.

84. "What Is BDS?"

85. "What Is BDS?"

86. "What Is BDS?"

87. Thrall, "BDS: How a Controversial Non-Violent Movement."

88. Baroud and Rubeo, "Israel's $72m 'War Chest' to Fight BDS."

89. Zine, Bird, and Matthews, "Criticizing Israel Is Not Antisemitic"; Bahdi, "New Human Rights Order"; Goldberg, "It's Not About Antisemitism. It's About Free Speech."

90. Waziyatawin, "Malice Enough in Their Hearts," 175.

91. The Resistance was centred largely on communities and geographic locations near where Boushie would be killed 131 years later. This includes the then capital of the Northwest Territories, Battleford, which today is still the major community in the region when combined with North Battleford to collectively form "the Battlefords."

92. CBC Radio, "The Pass System."

93. CBC Radio; Barron, "The Indian Pass System in the Canadian West," 25.

94. Barron, "The Indian Pass System in the Canadian West," 27.

95. CBC Radio, "The Pass System."

96. It is hard to find records of this dark chapter of Canadian history, and that may be indicative of a government desire to forget and erase the deeply illiberal past. Williams, *The Pass System*.

97. Krebs and Olwan, "From Jerusalem to the Grand River," 148.

98. Halper, *An Israeli in Palestine*; United Nations Development Program (UNDP), "Human Development Report 2009/10"; Office for the Coordination of Humanitarian Affairs (OCHA), "Fragmented Lives: Humanitarian Overview 2012."

99. Israel has even used "security reasons" to deny frequency allocation to Palestinian telecommunication providers, in spite of the Oslo process guaranteeing Palestinians the right to a separate and independent telecommunication networks. That allowed Israeli telecommunications companies with much lower costs to move into Palestinian market share, as an example of de-development sabotaging a Palestinian industry to benefit an Israeli one. Wade, "Organised Hypocrisy on a Monumental Scale."

100. Organisation for Economic Co-Operation and Development (OECD), "West Bank and Gaza Strip."

101. Government of Canada, "Statistical Report on International Assistance," modified June 23, 2023, https://www.international.gc.ca/transparency-transparence/international-assistance-report-stat-rapport-aide-internationale/index.aspx?lang=eng.

102. Indigenous and Northern Affairs Canada, "Archived—Budget 2019 Highlights."

103. Daschuk, *Clearing the Plains,* 99.

104. Daschuk, 114.

105. Government of Canada, *Treaty Texts: Treaty No. 6.*

106. Daschuk, *Clearing the Plains,* 124.

107. Daschuk, 129–30.

108. Daschuk, 128.

109. Daschuk, 108.

110. Daschuk, 101.

111. Daschuk.

112. OCHA, "Humanitarian Situation in the Gaza Strip Fast Facts."

113. Ahern, "West Bank and Gaza."

114. Tartir, *The Role of International Aid in Development.*

115. Ahern, "West Bank and Gaza," 7.

116. Roy, "The Gaza Strip: A Case of Economic De-Development."

117. The 1994 Paris Protocol formalized an existing union of Israel and the OPT into a single economic zone with a common currency. It also created an external border where Israel collects import taxes on goods destined for the OPT, before then transferring those taxes, at its own discretion, to the PA. Under the protocol, Israel should also transfer to the PA any Value Added Taxes (VAT) collected on goods and services sold in Israel that are meant for OPT consumption. Israel regularly breaks its own obligations under the Protocol, including withholding of VAT funds to put pressure on the PA to accede to certain political outcomes.

118. Roy, *The Gaza Strip: The Political Economy of De-Development,* 4.

119. Hever, *The Political Economy of Israel's Occupation.*

120. Hever, "How Much International Aid," 1.

121. Rose, "The Gaza Bombshell."

122. "Palestine: Authorities Crush Dissent"; Monaghan, "Security Development and the Palestinian Authority"; Tartir, "How US Security Aid to PA."

123. "Two Authorities, One Way, Zero Dissent," 20.

124. Though, unlike the Trump administration, the Harper government in Canada still gave large sums of money to development and humanitarian assistance.

125. Coordinator Kim even laughed at the notion. Kim (August 7, 2014) 29min13s to 30min22s .

126. Sterzuk, *The Struggle for Legitimacy,* 68.

127. Sterzuk describes how many settlers who first came to Saskatchewan were not from the Franco-British métropoles of the Canadian state, but rather from places in Eastern Europe whose ways of life were seen by British-Canadians as something less civilized.

Thus, schools were used against these "off-white" settlers in a similar, albeit much less violent, manner as for Indigenous peoples, as a tool of racial assimilation. Many anglicized their family names and eschewed their former cultures and languages. Like Sterzuk, this author identifies with that background, as someone with Ukrainian heritage. In ways, those Eastern European Saskatchewanites' condition bears similarity to the way Jews from the Middle East and North Africa, known as the Mizrahi, have been treated by the European Ashkenazi Jews who took leadership in building Israel. The Ashkenazi have been ever suspicious of Mizrahi Orientalism in a settler state specifically dedicated to the destructive erasure of an Oriental Palestinian society and its replacement with a new Occidental Israeli one. Mizrahi have been considered "second class" suffering discrimination in areas like housing, education, and income; though they remain well ahead in the class hierarchy with where Palestinians sit. Thus, in Labelle's chapter, Sami Hadawi wrote to the Toronto Star about Palestinians in Israel with Israeli-citizenship being "third class" citizens. Mizrahi activist Tom Megaher considers their mutual suppression a reason to find common ground with the Palestinians. Sterzuk, 69; Megaher, "Mizrahi or Ashkenazi Jews."

128. Masalha, *A Land without a People.*

129. Herzl, *The Jewish State*, 51.

130. As a youth, this author was exposed to an environment of constant verbal abuse of Indigenous peoples, particularly racist jokes, derogatory use of the word "squaw" and comments about the only good "Indian" being a dead one.

131. Daschuk, *Clearing the Plains*, 155–56.

132. Held on November 27, 1885 in Battleford, today the location of a National Heritage Site, the court proceedings were conducted in English, with no translation or legal representation allowed for the warriors, in a legal system they did not know and was not their own. Doug Cuthand, "Cuthand: Public Hanging Led to Years of Repression." Saskg, English: The Gravesite of the Battleford Eight in Battleford, Saskatchewan, Canada. This Is the Gravesite of the Largest Mass Hanging in the History of Canada Which Occurred on November 27, 1885 in the Wake of the Riel Resistance.

133. Gilchrist, "'Newsworthy' Victims?"

134. Journalists for Human Rights, "Buried Voices: Media Coverage of Aboriginal Issues in Ontario."

135. Lam et al., "How Does the Media Portray Drinking Water,"282.

136. See Labelle's chapter (chapter 11).

137. Maslin, "Social Construction of Aboriginal Peoples."

138. Maslin, 87.

139. Maslin, 85.

140. Green, "From Stonechild to Social Cohesion," 512.

141. Maslin, "Social Construction of Aboriginal Peoples," 88.

142. Maslin, 88.

143. Wolfe, "Settler Colonialism and the Elimination of the Native," 387.

144. Kanji, "A How-To Guide for the Settler Colonial Present."

145. Siddiqui and Zaheer, "50 Years of Occupation."

146. Siddiqui and Zaheer.

147. NECEF, "Media Bias in the Israeli/Palestinian Conflict."

148. NECEF, 58.

149. Both Sucharov (chapter 8) and Labelle (chapter 11) describe a similar viewpoint in the Jewish community in Canada.

150. Rinnawi, "De-Legitimization of Media Mechanisms," 164.

151. Dor, *The Suppression of Guilt the Israeli Media*, 3.

152. Dor, 3.

153. Dor, 3.

154. Dor, 3.

155. Rinnawi, "De-Legitimization of Media Mechanisms," 160.

156. Shor and Yonay, "Play and Shut up."

157. Shor and Yonay, 243.

158. Green, "From Stonechild to Social Cohesion," 513.

159. Green, 507.

160. Stewart, "Remembering Neil Stonechild."

161. Razack, "It Happened More Than Once."

162. Stewart, "Remembering Neil Stonechild."

163. Green, "From Stonechild to Social Cohesion," 511.

164. Green, 520.

165. Waziyatawin, "Malice Enough in Their Hearts and Courage Enough in Ours," 175.

166. Hubbard, *Nîpawistamâsowin*.

167. Beaumont, "Israeli Teenagers Jailed for Murder of Palestinian Boy."

168. AFP and TOI staff, "Israeli Man Handed Life in Prison for Grisly Murder of East Jerusalem Teen," May 3, 2016, http://www.timesofisrael.com/jewish-killer-of-east-jerusalem-teen-handed-life-in-prison/.

169. Beaumont, "Israeli Teenagers Jailed for Murder of Palestinian Boy."

170. The Associated Press, "3 Missing Israeli Teens Found Dead near Hebron," *CBC*, June 30, 2014, https://www.cbc.ca/news/world/3-missing-israeli-teens-found-dead-near-hebron-1.2692115.

171. *Al Jazeera*, "Jewish Settler Convicted in Arson Attack That Killed Palestinians."

172. See Zertal and Eldar, *Lords of the Land*.

173. Waziyatawin, "Malice Enough in Their Hearts and Courage Enough in Ours," 172.

174. Waziyatawin, 172.

References

Al Jazeera. "Jewish Settler Convicted in Arson Attack That Killed Palestinians." May 28, 2020. https://www.aljazeera.com/news/2020/5/18/jewish-settler-convicted-in-arson-attack-that-killed-palestinians.

Aboriginal Affairs and Northern Development Canada. "Pre-1975 Treaties in Saskatchewan." Map. Government of Canada. February 2014. https://www.

aadnc-aandc.gc.ca/DAM/DAM-INTER-HQ-AI/STAGING/texte-text/mprm_
treaties_th-ht_sk_1371839727539_eng.pdf.

AFP. "Kushner: Palestinians Not yet Capable of Governing Themselves." *Middle East Eye*,
June 3, 2019. http://www.middleeasteye.net/news/kushner-palestinians-not-yet-
capable-governing-themselves.

AFP, and TOI Staff. "Israeli Man Handed Life in Prison for Grisly Murder of East Jerusalem
Teen," *Times of Israel,* May 3, 2016. http://www.timesofisrael.com/jewish-killer-of-
east-jerusalem-teen-handed-life-in-prison/.

Ahern, Mark Eugene. "West Bank and Gaza—Economic Monitoring Report to the Ad Hoc
Liaison Committee." The World Bank, May 4, 2017. http://documents.worldbank.
org/curated/en/878481496148097124/West-Bank-and-Gaza-Economic-Monitoring-
Report-to-the-Ad-Hoc-Liaison-Committee.

Amr, Hady. "In One Move, Trump Eliminated US Funding for UNRWA and the US Role as
Mideast Peacemaker." *Brookings* (blog), September 7, 2018. https://www.brookings.
edu/blog/order-from-chaos/2018/09/07/in-one-move-trump-eliminated-us-funding-
for-unrwa-and-the-us-role-as-mideast-peacemaker/.

Assadi, Mohammed. "Palestinian Institutions Ready for Statehood: U.N." *Reuters*, April 12,
2011. https://ca.reuters.com/article/us-palestinians-israel-idUSTRE73B3IX20110412.

Badarin, Emile. "Settler-Colonialist Management of Entrances to the Native Urban Space in
Palestine." *Settler Colonial Studies* 5, no. 3 (2015): 226–35.

Bahdi, Reem. "New Human Rights Order Risks Restricting Criticism of Israel." *The
Conversation*, November 15, 2020. http://theconversation.com/
new-human-rights-order-risks-restricting-criticism-of-israel-149796.

Barclay, Ahmad, Hani Asfour, and Reem Farah. "Shrinking Palestine, Expanding Israel."
VisualizingPalestine, 2017. https://visualizingpalestine.org/visuals/
http-visualizingpalestine-org-visuals-shrinking-palestine-static.

Barker, Adam J. "'A Direct Act of Resurgence, a Direct Act of Sovereignty': Reflections on
Idle No More, Indigenous Activism, and Canadian Settler Colonialism." *Globalizations*
12, no. 1 (2015): 43–65.

Baroud, Ramzy, and Romana Rubeo. "Israel's $72m 'War Chest' to Fight BDS Arrives in
Europe." *Al Jazeera*, November 14, 2018. https://www.aljazeera.com/opinions/
2018/11/14/israels-72m-war-chest-to-fight-bds-arrives-in-europe/.

Barron, F. Laurie. "The Indian Pass System in the Canadian West, 1882–1935." *Prairie Forum*
13, no. 1 (1988): 25–42.

BDS Movement. "What Is BDS?" April 25, 2016. https://bdsmovement.net/what-is-bds.

Beaumont, Peter. "Israeli Teenagers Jailed for Murder of Palestinian Boy." *The Guardian*,
February 4, 2016. https://www.theguardian.com/world/2016/feb/04/
two-israelis-given-lengthy-sentences-for-of-palestinian-teenager.

Bell, Duncan. "The Dream Machine: On Liberalism and Empire." In *Remaking the World:
Essays on Liberalism and Empire.* Princeton, NJ: Princeton University Press, 2016.
http://www.academia.edu/12999578/_The_Dream_Machine_On_Liberalism_and_
Empire_.

Bell, Michael, Michael Molloy, David Sultan, and Sallama Shaker. "Practitioners' Perspectives on Canada–Middle East Relations." In *Canada and the Middle East in Theory and Practice*, edited by Paul Heinbecker and Bessma Momani, 7–24. Waterloo, ON: Wilfrid Laurier University Press, 2007.

Bronner, Ethan. "Bid for State of Palestine Gets Support from I.M.F." *The New York Times*, April 7, 2011. https://www.nytimes.com/2011/04/07/world/middleeast/07palestinians.html.

B'Tselem. "Area C." Accessed September 10, 2019. https://www.btselem.org/topic/area_c.

B'Tselem. "State-Backed Settler Violence." Accessed November 6, 2020. https://www.btselem.org/topic/settler_violence.

CBC News. "A History of Residential Schools in Canada." *CBC*, May 16, 2008. http://www.cbc.ca/1.702280.

CBC Radio. "The Pass System: Another Dark Secret in Canadian History." *CBC*, November 27, 2015. https://www.cbc.ca/radio/unreserved/exploring-the-past-present-and-future-of-life-in-indigenous-canada-1.3336594/the-pass-system-another-dark-secret-in-canadian-history-1.3338520.

Constitution Act, 1867, Pub. L. No. 30 and 31 Victoria, c. 3 (U.K.) (1867). https://laws-lois.justice.gc.ca/eng/Const/.

Crosby, Andrew, and Jeffrey Monaghan. "Settler Colonialism and the Policing of Idle No More." *Social Justice* 43, no. 2 (144) (2016): 37–57.

Csillag, Ron. "Canada Redirecting Palestinian Aid from UNRWA." *Jewish Telegraphic Agency*, January 15, 2010. https://www.jta.org/2010/01/14/israel/canada-redirecting-palestinian-aid-from-unrwa.

Cuthand, Doug. "Cuthand: Public Hanging Led to Years of Repression for First Nations." *The Star Phoenix*, December 1, 2018. https://thestarphoenix.com/opinion/columnists/cuthand-public-hanging-led-to-years-of-repression-for-first-nations.

Daschuk, James W. *Clearing the Plains: Disease, Politics of Starvation, and the Loss of Aboriginal Life*. Regina, SK: University of Regina Press, 2013.

Deer, Ka'nhehsí:io. "Why It's Difficult to Put a Number on How Many Children Died at Residential Schools." *CBC News*, September 29, 2021. https://www.cbc.ca/news/indigenous/residential-school-children-deaths-numbers-1.6182456.

Dhamoon, Rita, and Yasmeen Abu-Laban. "Dangerous (Internal) Foreigners and Nation-Building: The Case of Canada." *International Political Science Review* 30, no. 2 (March 1, 2009): 163–83.

Dor, Daniel. *The Suppression of Guilt the Israeli Media and the Reoccupation of the West Bank*. London: Pluto Press, 2005.

Geddes, John. "POGG's the Word in Washington. (Paul Martin's Foreign Policy Statement Echoes Michael Ignatieff's Lecture Titled, 'Peace, Order and Good Government')." *Maclean's*, 117, no. 19 (2004): 20.

Gilchrist, Kristen. "'Newsworthy' Victims? Exploring Differences in Canadian Local Press Coverage of Missing/Murdered Aboriginal and White Women." *Feminist Media Studies* 10, no. 4 (2010): 373–90.

Goldberg, Amos. "It's Not About Antisemitism. It's About Free Speech." *Canadian Jewish Record*, November 18, 2020. https://canadianjewishrecord.ca/2020/11/18/its-not-about-antisemitism-its-about-free-speech/.

Gordon, Todd. "Canada, Empire and Indigenous People in the Americas." *Socialist Studies / Études Socialistes* 2, no. 1 (January 2, 2009): 47–75. http://socialiststudies.com/article/view/23795.

Government of Canada. "Statistical Report on International Assistance." Modified June 23, 2023. https://www.international.gc.ca/transparency-transparence/international-assistance-report-stat-rapport-aide-internationale/index.aspx?lang=eng.

Government of Canada. *Treaty Texts: Treaty No. 6*. Ottawa: Queen's Printer and Controller of Stationery, 1964. https://www.rcaanc-cirnac.gc.ca/eng/1100100028710/1581292569426.

Green, Joyce. "From Stonechild to Social Cohesion: Anti-Racist Challenges for Saskatchewan." *Canadian Journal of Political Science / Revue Canadienne de Science Politique* 39, no. 3 (2006): 507–27.

Halper, Jeff. *An Israeli in Palestine: Resisting Dispossession, Redeeming Israel*. London; Ann Arbor, MI: Pluto Press, 2008.

Herzl, Theodor. *The Jewish State*. Rockville, MD: Wildside Press, 2008.

Hever, Shir. *The Political Economy of Israel's Occupation: Repression Beyond Exploitation*. London: Pluto Press, 2010.

Hever, Shir. "How Much International Aid to the Palestinians Ends up in the Israeli Economy?" *Aid Watch*, September 2015. http://www.aidwatch.ps/sites/default/files/resource-field_media/InternationalAidToPalestiniansFeedsTheIsraeliEconomy.pdf.

Hubbard, Tasha, dir. *Nîpawistamâsowin: We Will Stand Up*, 2019. https://www.nfb.ca/film/nipawistamasowin-we-will-stand-up/.

IMEMC News. "Seven-Year-Old Palestinian Child Killed by Israeli Settler in Hit-and-Run." *International Middle East Media Center*, July 16, 2019. https://imemc.org/article/seven-year-old-palestinian-child-killed-by-israeli-settler-in-hit-and-run/.

Indigenous and Northern Affairs Canada. "Pre-1975 Treaties Map in Canada." Government of Canada, July 2016. https://www.aadnc-aandc.gc.ca/DAM/DAM-INTER-HQ-AI/STAGING/texte-text/mprm_treaties_th-ht_canada_1371839430039_eng.pdf.

Indigenous and Northern Affairs Canada. "Archived—Budget 2019 Highlights: Indigenous and Northern Investments." Government of Canada, March 27, 2019. https://www.aadnc-aandc.gc.ca/eng/1553716166204/1553716201560.

"Israel's Settlements Have No Legal Validity, Constitute Flagrant Violation of International Law, Security Council Reaffirms—Resolution 2334 (2016)—Occupied Palestinian Territory." *ReliefWeb*, December 23, 2016. https://reliefweb.int/report/occupied-palestinian-territory/israel-s-settlements-have-no-legal-validity-constitute.

Journalists for Human Rights. "Buried Voices: Changing Tones: Media Coverage of Aboriginal Issues in Ontario," February 19, 2016. https://www.jhr.ca/wp-content/uploads/2016/10/JHR-IRP-Report-v3online.pdf.

JTA. "What Makes Canada's PM One of Israel's Staunchest Supporters?—Jewish World Features." *Haaretz*, January 18, 2014. http://www.haaretz.com/jewish-world/jewish-world-features/1.569292.

JTA. "Kushner Did Not Disclose His Foundation Funded Settlement Projects." *Times of Israel*, December 4, 2017. https://www.timesofisrael.com/kushner-did-not-disclose-his-foundation-funded-west-bank-projects/.

Kanji, Azeezah. "A How-To Guide for the Settler Colonial Present: From Canada to Palestine to Kashmir." Yellowhead Institute, August 5, 2020. https://yellowheadinstitute.org/2020/08/05/marking-the-settler-colonial-present-from-canada-to-palestine-to-kashmir/.

Krebs, Mike, and Dana M. Olwan. "'From Jerusalem to the Grand River, Our Struggles Are One': Challenging Canadian and Israeli Settler Colonialism." *Settler Colonial Studies* 2, no. 2 (January 1, 2012): 138–64.

Lam, Steven, Ashlee Cunsolo, Alexandra Sawatzky, James Ford, and Sherilee L. Harper. "How Does the Media Portray Drinking Water Security in Indigenous Communities in Canada? An Analysis of Canadian Newspaper Coverage from 2000–2015." *BMC Public Health* 17, no. 1 (March 27, 2017): 282.

Landau, Noa, and Amir Tibon. "Nikki Haley: U.S. to Withhold Funding for UN Agency for Palestinian Refugees Until They Join Peace Process." *Haaretz*, January 2, 2018. https://www.haaretz.com/us-news/1.832685?utm_source=dlvr.it&utm_medium=twitter.

Lloyd, David. "Settler Colonialism and the State of Exception: The Example of Palestine/Israel." *Settler Colonial Studies* 2, no. 1 (January 1, 2012): 59–80.

Maimann, Kevin, and Brennan Doherty. "Thousands of Indigenous Children Died in Canadian Residential Schools. Now We Know Some of Their Names." *Toronto Star*, September 30, 2019. https://www.thestar.com/edmonton/2019/09/30/thousands-of-indigenous-children-died-in-canadian-residential-schools-now-we-know-some-of-their-names.html.

Masalha, Nur. *A Land without a People: Israel, Transfer and the Palestinians 1949–96.* London: Faber and Faber, 1997.

Maslin, Crystal L. "Social Construction of Aboriginal Peoples in the Saskatchewan Print Media." Master's thesis, University of Saskatchewan, 2002. https://harvest.usask.ca/handle/10388/etd-06202008-130404.

Megaher, Tom. "Mizrahi or Ashkenazi Jews: Israel's Regime of Separation." *Middle East Eye*, July 18, 2016. http://www.middleeasteye.net/opinion/mizrahi-or-ashkenazi-jews-israels-regime-separation.

Memmi, Albert. *The Colonizer and the Colonized.* Milton, Abingdon: Routledge, 2013.

Monaghan, Jeffrey. "Security Development and the Palestinian Authority: An Examination of the 'Canadian Factor." *Conflict, Security & Development* 16, no. 2 (March 3, 2016): 125–43.

Moses, Dirk. "Empire, Colony, Genocide: Keywords and Intellectual History." In *Empire Colony Genocide: Conquest, Occupation, and Subaltern Resistance in World History*, edited by Dirk Moses, 3–54. New York: Berghahn Books, 2008. http://www.dirkmoses.com/uploads/7/3/8/2/7382125/moses_empire_colony_genocide.pdf.

Near East Cultural and Education Foundation (NECEF). "Media Bias in the Israeli/Palestinian Conflict: Canadian Print Media Coverage of Israeli and Palestinian Deaths." Toronto: NECEF, 2004.

Nikiforuk, Andrew. "From the Archives: When Indigenous Assert Rights, Canada Sends Militarized Police." *The Tyee*. January 17, 2019. https://thetyee.ca/Analysis/2019/01/17/Indigenous-Rights-Canada-Militarized-Police/.

Office for the Coordination of Humanitarian Affairs occupied Paletsinian territory (OCHA oPt). "East Jerusalem." United Nations Office for the Coordination of Humanitarian Affairs. Accessed September 10, 2019. https://www.ochaopt.org/ location/east-jerusalem.

OCHA oPt. "Fragmented Lives: Humanitarian Overview 2012." United Nations Office for the Coordination of Humanitarian Affairs, 2013. http://www.ochaopt.org/documents/ocha_opt_fragmented_lives_annual_report_2013_english_web.pdf.

OCHA oPt. "Humanitarian Situation in the Gaza Strip Fast Facts—OCHA Factsheet." United Nations: The Question of Palestine. Accessed November 18, 2020. https://www.un.org/unispal/humanitarian-situation-in-the-gaza-strip-fast-facts-ocha-factsheet/.

OCHA oPt. "Gaza Strip: Access and Movement." United Nations Office for the Coordination of Humanitarian Affairs, October 2020. https://www.ochaopt.org/content/gaza-strip-access-and-movement-october-2020.

OCHA oPt. "West Bank Access Restrictions." United Nations Office for the Coordination of Humanitarian Affairs, June 2020. https://www.ochaopt.org/content/west-bank-access-restrictions-june-2020.

Organisation for Economic Co-Operation and Development (OECD). "West Bank and Gaza Strip—All Donors Total—Disbursements—All Types of Aid." Database. OECD Query Wizard for International Development Statistics. Accessed May 25, 2016. http://stats.oecd.org/qwids/.

"Palestine: Authorities Crush Dissent." *Human Rights Watch*, October 23, 2018. https://www.hrw.org/news/2018/10/23/palestine-authorities-crush-dissent.

Palestinian Central Bureau of Statistics (PCBS). "Estimated Population in Palestine Mid-Year by Governorate, 1997–2021." Database. State of Palestine—Palestinian Central Bureau of Statistics. Accessed November 13, 2020. http://pcbs.gov.ps/Portals/_Rainbow/Documents/%D8%A7%D9%84%D9%85%D8%AD%D8%A7%D9%81%D8%B8%D8%A7%D8%AA%20%D8%A7%D9%86%D8%AC%D9%84%D9%8A%D8%B2%D9%8A%2097-2017.html.

PCBS. "Indicators." Database. State of Palestine—Palestinian Central Bureau of Statistics. Accessed November 13, 2020. http://pcbs.gov.ps/site/lang__en/881/default.aspx#HouseHold.

PCBS. "Number of Settlers in the Settlements and Palestinian Population in the West Bank by Governorate, 2017." Database. State of Palestine—Palestinian Central Bureau of Statistics. Accessed November 13, 2020. http://www.pcbs.gov.ps/Portals/_Rainbow/Documents/SETT4E-2017.html.

Quenneville, Guy. "What Happened on Gerald Stanley's Farm the Day Colten Boushie Was Shot, as Told by Witnesses." *CBC*, February 6, 2018. https://www.cbc.ca/news/canada/saskatoon/what-happened-stanley-farm-boushie-shot-witnesses-colten-gerald-1.4520214.

Rana, Aziz. *The Two Faces of American Freedom*. Cambridge, MA: Harvard University Press, 2011.

Razack, Sherene. "'It Happened More Than Once': Freezing Deaths in Saskatchewan." *Canadian Journal of Women and the Law* 26, no. 1 (January 1, 2014): 51–80.

Rinnawi, Khalil. "De-Legitimization of Media Mechanisms: Israeli Press Coverage of the Al Aqsa Intifada." *International Communication Gazette* 69, no. 2 (April 1, 2007): 149–78.

Rose, David. "The Gaza Bombshell." *Vanity Fair*, April 1, 2008. http://www.vanityfair.com/politics/features/2008/04/gaza200804.

Roy, Sara. "The Gaza Strip: A Case of Economic De-Development." *Journal of Palestine Studies* 17, no. 1 (October 1987): 56–88.

Roy, Sara. *The Gaza Strip: The Political Economy of De-Development*. Washington, DC: Institute for Palestine Studies, 1995.

Royal Commission on Aboriginal Peoples. "Restructuring the Relationship." In *Report of the Royal Commission on Aboriginal Peoples*, 2: 1063, 1996. https://www.bac-lac.gc.ca/eng/discover/aboriginal-heritage/royal-commission-aboriginal-peoples/Pages/final-report.aspx.

Saskatchewan Bureau of Statistics. "Saskatchewan Population Report—2016 Census of Canada." Saskatchewan Ministry of Finance. Accessed June 4, 2022. https://pubsaskdev.blob.core.windows.net/pubsask-prod/100723/100723-Saskatchewan_Population_Report_for_the_2016_Census.pdf.

Sherwood, Harriet. "Israel Seizes $120m in Palestinian Tax Revenue over UN Statehood Vote." *The Guardian*, December 3, 2012. http://www.theguardian.com/world/2012/dec/02/israel-palestinian-tax-revenue-un-vote.

Shor, Eran, and Yuval Yonay. "'Play and Shut up': The Silencing of Palestinian Athletes in Israeli Media." *Ethnic and Racial Studies* 34, no. 2 (2011): 229–47.

Siddiqui, Usaid, and Owais A. Zaheer. "50 Years of Occupation: A Sentiment and N-Gram Analysis of US Mainstream Media Coverage of the Israeli Occupation of Palestine." 416Labs, 2018. https://static1.squarespace.com/static/558067a3e4b0cb2f81614c38/t/5c36665d70a6add06a0ad567/1547069024045/416_LABS_50_Years_of_Occupation.pdf.

Statistics Canada. "Aboriginal Peoples—Province of Saskatchewan." Government of Canada. Focus on Geography Series, 2016 Census, 2017. https://www12.statcan.gc.ca/census-recensement/2016/as-sa/fogs-spg/Facts-PR-Eng.cfm?TOPIC=9&LANG=Eng&GK=PR&GC=47.

Statistics Canada. "Province of Saskatchewan." Government of Canada. Focus on Geography Series, 2011 Census, 2012. https://www12.statcan.gc.ca/census-recensement/2011/as-sa/fogs-spg/Facts-pr-eng.cfm?Lang=Eng&GK=PR&GC=47.

Sterzuk, Andrea. *The Struggle for Legitimacy: Indigenized Englishes in Settler Schools*. Bristol: Multilingual Matters, 2011.

Stewart, Michelle. "Remembering Neil Stonechild and Exposing Systemic Racism in Policing." *The Conversation*, December 5, 2019. http://theconversation.com/remembering-neil-stonechild-and-exposing-systemic-racism-in-policing-128436.

Tamari, Salim. "What the Uprising Means." *Middle East Report* no. 152 (May 1, 1988): 24–30.

Tartir, Alaa. *The Role of International Aid in Development: The Case of Palestine 1994–2008*. London: Lambert Academic Publishing, 2011.

Tartir, Alaa. "How US Security Aid to PA Sustains Israel's Occupation." *Al Jazeera*, December 2, 2016. http://www.aljazeera.com/indepth/features/2016/11/security-aid-pa-sustains-israel-occupation-161103120213593.html.

Tartir, Alaa. "The Palestinian Authority Security Forces: Whose Security?" Al-Shabaka, May 16, 2017. https://al-shabaka.org/briefs/palestinian-authority-security-forces-whose-security/.

Tartir, Alaa, and Jeremy Wildeman. "Persistent Failure: World Bank Policies for the Occupied Palestinian Territories." Al-Shabaka, October 9, 2012. https://al-shabaka.org/briefs/persistent-failure-world-bank-policies-occupied-palestinian-territories/.

The Associated Press. "3 Missing Israeli Teens Found Dead near Hebron." *CBC*, June 30, 2014. https://www.cbc.ca/news/world/3-missing-israeli-teens-found-dead-near-hebron-1.2692115.

Thrall, Nathan. "BDS: How a Controversial Non-Violent Movement Has Transformed the Israeli-Palestinian Debate." *The Guardian*, August 14, 2018. https://www.theguardian.com/news/2018/aug/14/bds-boycott-divestment-sanctions-movement-transformed-israeli-palestinian-debate.

Truth and Reconciliation Commission of Canada. *Honouring the Truth, Reconciling for the Future: Summary of the Final Report of the Truth and Reconciliation Commission of Canada*, 2015. http://epe.lac-bac.gc.ca/100/201/301/weekly_acquisition_lists/2015/w15-24-F-E.html/collections/collection_2015/trc/IR4-7-2015-eng.pdf.

Turner, Mandy. "Completing the Circle: Peacebuilding as Colonial Practice in the Occupied Palestinian Territory." *International Peacekeeping* 19 no. 4 (2012): 492–507.

Turner, Mandy. "International Aid in the Absence of Palestinian Sovereignty: Notes towards a Strategy in the Aftermath of the Trump 'Peace Plan.'" *Jadaliyya*, February 19, 2020. https://www.jadaliyya.com/Details/40706.

"Two Authorities, One Way, Zero Dissent Arbitrary Arrest and Torture Under the Palestinian Authority and Hamas." *Human Rights Watch*, 2018. https://www.hrw.org/report/2018/10/23/two-authorities-one-way-zero-dissent/arbitrary-arrest-and-torture-under.

United Nations Conference on Trade and Development (UNCTAD). "Gaza Could Become Uninhabitable in Less than Five Years in Wake of 2014 Conflict and Ongoing De-Development, According to New UNCTAD Report." Press Release, September 1, 2015. http://unctad.org/en/Pages/PressRelease.aspx?OriginalVersionID=260.

United Nations Development Program (UNDP). "Human Development Report 2009/10: Occupied Palestinian Territory." Jerusalem, Palestine: United Nations Development Programme, 2010. http://hdr.undp.org/sites/default/files/nhdr_palestine_en_2009-10.pdf.

United Nations Relief and Works Agency for Palestine Refugees (UNRWA). "UNRWA in Figures 2018—Occupied Palestinian Territory." January 8, 2019. https://reliefweb.int/report/occupied-palestinian-territory/unrwa-figures-2018-enar.

UNRWA. "Where We Work—West Bank." United Nations Relief and Works Agency for Palestine Refugees in the Near East, December 31, 2019. https://www.unrwa.org/where-we-work/west-bank.

Veracini, Lorenzo. *Settler Colonialism: A Theoretical Overview*. Basingstoke: Palgrave Macmillan, 2010.

Veracini, Lorenzo. "The Other Shift: Settler Colonialism, Israel, and the Occupation." *Journal of Palestine Studies* 42 no. 2 (April 1, 2013): 26–42.

Wade, Robert. "Organised Hypocrisy on a Monumental Scale." *London Review of Books*, October 24, 2014. http://www.lrb.co.uk/2014/10/24/robert-wade/organised-hypocrisy-on-a-monumental-scale.

Waziyatawin. "Malice Enough in Their Hearts and Courage Enough in Ours: Reflections on US Indigenous and Palestinian Experiences under Occupation." *Settler Colonial Studies* 2 no. 1 (2012): 172–89.

Weizman, Eyal. *Hollow Land: Israel's Architecture of Occupation*. London: Verso, 2007.

Wells, Jennifer. "A Warrior, a Soldier and a Photographer—Remembering the Oka Crisis." *Toronto Star*, August 22, 2015. https://www.thestar.com/news/insight/2015/08/22/a-warrior-a-soldier-and-a-photographer-remembering-the-oka-crisis.html.

Williams, Alex, dir. *The Pass System: Life Under Segregation. In Canada*. Tamarack Productions, 2015. http://thepasssystem.ca/.

Wolfe, Patrick. *Settler Colonialism and the Transformation of Anthropology the Politics and Poetics of an Ethnographic Event*. London, New York: Cassell, 1999.

Wolfe, Patrick. "Settler Colonialism and the Elimination of the Native." *Journal of Genocide Research* 8 no. 4 (2006): 387–409.

Wolfe, Patrick. "Purchase by Other Means: The Palestine Nakba and Zionism's Conquest of Economics." *Settler Colonial Studies* 2 no. 1 (January 1, 2012): 133–71.

Zertal, I., and Eldar, A. *Lords of the Land: The War Over Israel's Settlements in the Occupied Territories, 1967–2007* Translated by V. Eden.. New York: Nation Books, 2007.

Zine, Jasmin, Greg Bird, and Sara Matthews. "Criticizing Israel Is Not Antisemitic—It's Academic Freedom." *The Conversation*, November 15, 2020. http://theconversation.com/criticizing-israel-is-not-antisemitic-its-academic-freedom-148864.

II

SETTLER-COLONIAL DISPOSSESSION AND REPRESSION

3

CANADA AND THE PALESTINIAN REFUGEES

A Humanitarian License to Dispossess

RANDA FARAH AND PEIGE DESJARLAIS

Introduction

We argue that Canada's history as a settler-colonial state and its structural position as an imperial power is a framework of analyses that better explains its role and policies in the Palestinian question, particularly its policies towards Palestinian refugees, the latter being the main topic of this chapter. Canada's complicity in exploitation and domination in an unequal global order is obfuscated by its reputation as a neutral peacemaker driven by humanitarian impulses. Notwithstanding exceptional political moments when it supported Palestinian rights, the fundamental stance that guided successive Canadian governments aligns with the Israeli position. Biblical narratives spread by Christian Zionists further galvanized support for Zionism even prior to the establishment of the Israeli state. Both Canada and Israel call for the "rehabilitation" of Palestinian refugees in host Arab countries, and/or resettlement in third countries without the option for an undiminished right to return to their ancestral homeland and to reclaim confiscated land and property. Canada's position contravenes international law, which unambiguously affirms the Palestinian right of return, and is similarly inconsistent with the international community's predilection to promote voluntary repatriation as the privileged durable solution for refugees in the world.[1] Upon the "clearing" of Arab Palestine of its indigenous inhabitants by Zionist paramilitary organizations to build a Jewish state in 1948, the uprooted inhabitants were not allowed to return.

Patrick Wolfe persuasively argues that settler colonialism's primary motive is access to territory, territoriality being settler colonialism's "irreducible element"; his insight on colonialism applies to the Zionist movement and Israel's insatiable expansion on Palestinian territory.[2] Wolfe argued settler colonizers destroy native society to replace it and they have come to stay.[3] Israel and Canada have compelling historical parallels arising from their settler-colonial histories, interests and structures.[4] The difference is that in Israel's case, its territoriality remains "unbounded" and indefinite,[5] as it continues to expand on Palestinian land and to uproot the native population. In countries like Canada and Australia, all land had been colonized and therefore the frontier had closed—literally— when they reached the ocean.[6] Canada and Israel also share a public discourse that boasts of democratic values, but in reality, this barely camouflages their darker colonial and undemocratic practices mainly applied towards the indigenous populations they colonized. We contend that this colonial history and framework are crucial in explaining why successive Canadian governments have supported Israel.

The refugee right of return, upheld in United Nations General Assembly Resolution (UNGAR) 194 (III) in 1948, is a right that by then has been already established in various bodies of law, and which the Resolution simply affirmed.[7] Because the right of return challenges Israel's Zionist underpinnings based on Jewish exclusivity, the continued operation of the United Nations Relief and Works Agency for Palestine Refugees (UNRWA) has been increasingly unsettling to the Israeli state. The Agency was established in 1949 by Western powers to provide humanitarian services to Palestinian refugees, although the other undeclared purpose was to prevent their return, by facilitating their integration and/or resettlement outside Mandatory Palestine through humanitarian aid and development projects. However, for Palestinians, UNRWA became a symbol that reminded the world of the unfulfilled refugee right of return and the 1948

Palestinian Nakba (catastrophe). It is therefore unsurprising that Israel and its supporters, attempt to clip UNRWA's wings to diminish its effectiveness, most recently by drastically reducing its funding.[8] Some Israeli officials even campaign in the US and Europe to dismantle UNRWA as part of Israel's war against the Palestinian right to self-determination and the right of return.[9] On their part, Palestinians have refused to vanish as a distinct national population in the Arab world as Israel had hoped. Since 1948, they have insisted on their collective right to self-determination and the refugees' right of return. The Great March of Return, the slogan for non-violent border demonstrations held every Friday in Gaza that lasted from March 2018 to December 2019, exemplified the Palestinian unwavering yearning to return to their homeland. During these marches, over two hundred Palestinians were killed and many more injured by the Israeli military.[10]

Israel has consistently rejected the Palestinian right of return and, worse, it denies any moral responsibility for creating the refugee problem,[11] claiming return threatens its "Jewish character"[12] and its "right to self-determination."[13] Among the unsustainable Israeli arguments against the right of return is that the refugee problem was created in an era when "population exchanges" were promoted by states as "acceptable" solutions to ethnic conflicts. Israeli officials argued (and still argue) that since Jewish refugees from Arab states were "absorbed" into Israel, Palestinians should be absorbed by Arab states.[14] These fallacious arguments and ideas are attempts to obfuscate the unequal colonizer (Zionists) and colonized (Palestinians) relationship, to conceal the fact that Israel has been waging a campaign of ethnic cleansing since 1948, and to deny Palestinians their rights enshrined in international law.

In his book *The Politics of Denial* (2003), Masalha drew on Israeli archives to show that even prior to the establishment of the Jewish state, the question that deeply troubled Zionist leaders was how to "dissolve" the Palestinian refugees through expulsion to and eventual integration in the Arab world. For example, in 1941, Ben-Gurion advocated for a campaign in England and the United States to influence Arab countries, "to 'collaborate' with the Jewish Yishuv in implementing the transfer of Palestinians in return for economic gains."[15] Between 1948 and the late 1980s, there were approximately twenty official Israeli plans dealing with the 1948 refugees and later those of 1967, followed by no less than a dozen plans to deal with the refugee camps in the occupied West Bank and the Gaza Strip.[16] Masalha argues that the Zionist-Israeli cornerstones of denial was to suggest first that Arab governments incited Palestinians to leave, and secondly that they did not "absorb" them.

The claim that Arab governments incited Palestinians to abandon their land has been thoroughly refuted in the relevant literature. Here is Benny Morris, a Zionist Israeli historian on the topic,

> *I have found no contemporary evidence to show that either the leaders of the Arab states or the Mufti ordered or directly encouraged the mass exodus during April. It may be worth noting that for decades the policy of the Palestinian Arab leaders had been to hold fast to the soil of Palestine and to resist the eviction and displacement of the Arab communities.*[17]

During a visit to the United States in 1989, former Israeli Prime Minister Yitzhak Shamir proposed that Israel would contribute expertise and ideas to resettlement projects, to be funded by the United States, Arab countries, and the international community. In addition to rejecting any form of restitution to refugee property, Israel countered all attempts to work out a policy on compensation by linking it to a settlement of abandoned Jewish property in Arab states.[18] The latter proposal is based on an apocryphal narrative that deserves to be disabused of its inappopsite equivalences.

In 1948, pre-planned Zionist ethnic cleansing campaigns resulted in the occupation of 78 per cent of Mandatory Palestine. The crushing defeat of the Palestinians was made possible by British imperial patronage, infamously articulated in the Balfour Declaration (1917).[19] Economically, for example, the British Mandatory authorities in Palestine granted Jewish entrepreneurs monopolistic concessions and industrial protectionism, and implemented discriminatory labour policies that favoured the Jewish population. Britain also gave Jewish settlers "state land and land not required for public purposes," upon which to establish Jewish colonies.[20] Following the Second World War, the Zionist leaders turned to the United States as the emerging new power, where they began to mobilize for political, military, and financial support.[21]

The colonial expansion on Palestinian land was accompanied by the destruction and depopulation of hundreds of Palestinian villages and several urban centers. Most of the land was confiscated, although over 95 per cent was the individual or collective property of the expelled inhabitants of Palestine.[22] Again some 200,000 Palestinians were uprooted in 1967,[23] when Israel occupied the remaining 22 per cent of Palestinian land; around half were made refugees for the second time. However, ethnic cleansing through low-key and smaller-scale displacement of individuals, families, and communities in Palestine has continued from 1948 until today. The recent and continuous attempt to uproot Palestinian families in Sheikh Jarrah in Jerusalem and displace and destroy villages in al-Naqab (Negev) are among many examples of ongoing ethnic cleansing.[24] Framing Zionism and Israeli expansion in Mandatory Palestine as anything other than settler colonialism obscures the history and the realities on the ground.

However, Israeli officials trumpet other models around the world to justify state policies, including the "population exchange model," which early on had impressed Vladimir Jabotinsky, a prominent Zionist-Revisionist leader and intellectual father within the Jewish/Israeli right-wing nationalist movement. Indeed, Jabotinsky had copied a diagram from a study on the agreement showing how Greece became "ethnically homogeneous" stating the Arabs in Palestine "will have to make room for the Jews" and leave,[25] presumably just as in the Greek example. Masalha, quoted earlier, observed that an Israeli exchange model was proposed to exchange Palestinian property with abandoned Jewish property in Arab countries.

However, the population exchange between Greece and Turkey, agreed upon in the Treaty of Lausanne in 1923, was signed by two sovereign states, not by colonizers without a metropole and a colonized indigenous population. The population exchange, or as Lord Curzon described it, the "unmixing" of peoples, was purported to lead to international order and peace. In hindsight, we know that "unmixing" leads to segregation, racialization, and injurious ideas about the "pure" race. The imprint of the 1923 population exchange remains with us today. It severed the physical ties of millions of Muslims and Greek Orthodox from their way of life and social ties. It was a ruinous historical event that forced people to attempt to rebuild their shattered lives elsewhere and has fundamentally contributed to the character of each of the two countries to this day—including a predilection towards monoculturalism and ongoing mutual hostility. According to Igsiz, this is segregative biopolitics which relies on a racialized human taxonomy refracted in spatial redistribution policies.[26] Life histories recounting the experiences of uprootings, exposed the suffering and destruction hidden beneath grandiose statements about "peace."[27] Far from peace, it is possible to argue that the 1923 Treaty created legal precedence for the 1974 Turkish occupation of Cyprus, which led to decades of conflict. Giirsoy similarly argued that forcing almost 2 million people out of their homes in Greece and Turkey at an early stage of their nation-building contributed to the establishment of authoritarian regimes, which otherwise may have followed a different political trajectory during the interwar years.[28]

Although human suffering is shared in all cases of displacement, framing the Zionist colonization of Palestine as a case of "population exchange" or using the 1923 Treaty as historical or legal precedent is nothing less than historical casuistry. A more precise analogy is colonial settlement in Canada, which resulted in the uprooting of Indigenous people, land confiscation, and attempts to erase their cultures and histories.[29] Nonetheless, the Greco-Turkish model was adopted as early as 1936 by the British Royal Commission, which was dispatched to Palestine to propose solutions during a time when Palestinian resistance to British Zionist collaboration had escalated.[30] The main recommendation then was to partition Palestine and segregate populations. However, Palestinians have categorically and consistently rejected any such solutions, and there was no party capable of coercing an exchange of population as happened in the Greco-Turkish case.[31] Moreover, during the Ottoman and British Mandate periods, Jews were not expelled or persecuted in the Arab and Muslim world as they were for centuries in Europe; indeed, the Palestinians had no "conflict" with the Jews as Jews; rather, Palestinian discontent was with the British colonial authorities and a Zionist movement that aimed to create a "Jewish state" in their homeland.

Any attempt to dislocate the Palestinian refugee issue which is exclusively a Zionist/Israeli responsibility by relocating it or merging it with a generic question about the history of the expulsion of Jews from Arab countries (and thus render Palestinian refugee rights as contingent and negotiable) is political chicanery, aimed at mystifying the obvious fact that Palestinians are not involved and are not a party to decisions made by Arab states regarding their respective populations.[32] Furthermore, in most cases, Jews who were nationals in Arab countries were expelled as a reaction to the colonization of Palestine and during or following the 1948 Nakba, having lived and flourished in the Arab region for centuries. Thus, the aim of Arab states in deporting Jews,

62   *Canada and the Palestinian Refugees*

though unjustifiable, was not in exchange with Libyan or Egyptian Arabs. However, Palestinians cannot be held responsible for what happened to Jews in sovereign Arab states. If individual Jews have claims in their original Arab countries, they are entitled to directly address their respective states. Palestinians are not a party in this relationship.

One may add here that Zionism was an indirect cause for creating another refugee population, namely the dislocation of Arab Jews, both geographically and culturally. The Zionist movement and the Israeli state, upon its creation, launched campaigns urging Jews from around the world to settle the lands that were confiscated and emptied of their Palestinian inhabitants. The purpose of such campaigns—which live on in programs such as "Birth Right"—is to guarantee a Jewish majority at all times. Among those who arrived to the newly created "Jewish state" were Jews from Arab and/or Muslim countries, whose Arab heritage has been the target of eradication, including their Arabic language.[33] In Zionist discourse, a Jew could no longer be an Arab, and the term *Judeo-Christian tradition* all but erased the Judeo-Islamic history, which was a fundamentally different and largely positive experience.[34]

Israeli legal advocates such as Ruth Lapidoth (2001), claim that Israel fought a "war of independence" and has a right to self-determination. Self-determination was a principle, later a right adopted by UN GAR 1514 (XV) of December 14, 1960. Not by any figment of the imagination or legal juggling, however, is it possible to suggest that establishing a settler-colonial state on the ruins of another society may be called a *right* to self-determination. On the contrary, it is Israel which has prevented the fulfillment of Palestinian self-determination through expulsion and de-nationalization. Had it not been for the support of Western imperial powers, including Canada, for the idea and establishment of a *Jewish* state, there would not have been a Palestinian Nakba.

In summary, Israeli perversions of historical facts are meant to unburden Israel of its responsibility for the Palestinian Nakba and for creating the Palestinian refugee problem.[35] Despite Israel's glaring and pervasive violations of international law, confirmed recently by Amnesty International under the title "Israel's Apartheid Against the Palestinians: A cruel system of domination and a Crime Against Humanity,"[36] and in the numerous reports by UN Rapporteurs,[37] Canada acts as if gripped with impussience when it comes to Israel, and did not deviate from its support of Zionism before or after the creation of the Jewish state. Along with the United States and most of Western Europe, Canada treats Israel as exceptional and above the law. In the public domain, government officials generally reiterate Israeli propaganda and falsifications, as even a cursory glance at the Canadian government websites reveals. For example, under "Support for Israel and its Security" the government states,

Israel's right to live in peace with its neighbours within secure bound-aries and recognizes Israel's right to assure its own security, as witnessed by our support during the 2006 conflict with Hezbollah and our ongoing support for Israel's fight against terror.[38]

This is a sample of how Canada echoes the official Israeli line mimicking its propaganda statements that aim to publicly inject the idea that Israel's actions are justified and merely defensive. In official statements and through mainstream media, the Canadian government omits context, not explaining to Canadians, for example and in relation to the aforementioned quote, that Israel was for two decades an illegal occupier of South Lebanon, until it was forced to withdraw in 2000. During its occupation, it killed, maimed, and imprisoned people, and destroyed much of its infrastructure. It was the Israeli constant shelling and later occupation of South Lebanon in the early 1980s that led to the emergence of the Lebanese Hezbollah party as a measure of self-defence. Likewise, omitting context suggests to Canadians that when Israel bombards the Palestinians, for example when it turns Gaza to rubble through massive "carpet bombing," this is because Israel is "defending" itself, not because it is a belligerent and illegal occupier that has placed some two million people under siege, and had reduced Gaza into a dystopia and a humanitarian disaster. Such decontextualized statements are regularly disseminated by Israeli officials, and Canadian officials simply replicate them with minor edits. This is not surprising considering Zionism's deep roots in Canada, a history researched and traced by Freeman-Maloy,

In 1927, Shmaryahu Levin, a leading orator for the World Zionist Organisation (WZO), remarked upon the easy reception of Zionist appeals in Canada and South Africa. He. . .relayed his observations to Menachem Ussishkin of the WZO's Jewish National Fund (JNF). "There

64　　*Canada and the Palestinian Refugees*

are two small countries", wrote Levin, "which stand in our front ranks: Canada and South Africa. Would that God had been more merciful, and. . .scattered us in more countries like these two." [39]

Ultimately, Canadian policies that parrot the Israeli official line with minor modifications prolong Palestinian suffering, and intentionally or not, support ongoing Israeli colonial settlement. By ignoring international law when it comes to Palestinian rights, Canada is supporting a state based on Jewish exclusivity and privilege, apartheid, and blatant racism buttressed by Israel's legal edifice. Canada's unapologetic embrace of the Israeli state has only tightened in recent years. On April 26, 2023, Justin Trudeau, Canada's Prime Minister published a statement to congratulate Israel on its 75th "Independence Day" (without even a mention of the Palestinian Nakba, the direct consequence of the former). What was even more deplorable in the statement was the unabashed support of the International Holocaust Remembers Alliance's (IHRA) definition of antisemitism, widely rejected, including by many Canadian Jews.[40] Many of the examples the IHRA definition uses equate anti-semitism with criticism of Israeli state policies, a pernicious way to silence any voice that speaks against Israel's crimes agains the Palestinians. But Justin Trudeau praises it,

As we mark Israel Independence Day, the Government of Canada reaffirms its commitment to speaking out and fighting antisemitism and hatred in all their forms . . . including through the work of the Special Envoy on Preserving Holocaust Remembrance and Combatting Antisemitism, the Honourable Irwin Cotler. We will continue to support and promote the International Holocaust Remembrance Alliance's definition of antisemitism, which we adopted in 2019 as part of Canada's Anti-Racism Strategy. [41]

The above is an overall context, albeit brief, for what follows as we trace Canada's historical relationship to the Palestinian question. Canada has further enabled massive Israeli violations implicitly and often explicitly by tolerating Israel's ongoing ethnic cleansing instead of condemning Israel's defiance and breaches of international law.

Disavowal: "Neutrality" in Historical and Political Context

In his political memoir Navigating a New World, well-known Canadian politician and academic Lloyd Axworthy reaffirmed the national mythology through which Canadians have come to know themselves: as a peacekeeping nation, innocent of racism and uninvolved in imperialism or colonial violence.[42] Speaking to the way he envisions Canada's special role in this "new world" of global interconnection, Axworthy expresses a nostalgic admiration for the age of European conquest,

> What was true in the fifteenth century holds equally true today. Culture, technology, attitude and governance endow certain groups or communities with the talent to be navigators in the age of globalization, just as they did in the age of wind and sail. My argument, often stated in this book, is that Canadians possess qualities suited to this role. We have the right stuff to be explorers, agents of change.[43]

What does it mean for a man known for his progressive and liberal politics, primarily through his promotion of the concept of "human security,"[44] to model foreign policy on the brutal subjugation of several continents? What does this narrative of innate cultural superiority justify and conceal, and what kind of practices does it authorize? How is the myth of the benevolent peacekeeper nation invoked in relation to Canada's "neutral" role in the "Palestine Question"?

Answering these questions, we argue that Canada's claimed "neutrality" in relation to Palestinian refugees can only be understood by examining the way the idea of neutrality and legality is tied to larger national mythologies which work to disavow the violence, both internal and external, that goes into making the settler nation. The concept of neutrality, along with humanitarianism, peacebuilding, and development, has become intrinsic to the Canadian national narrative and provides a veneer of legitimacy for the operation of imperial power.

Exalted Nations: Settler Colonialism on Two Continents

While in many ways analytically distinct, Canadian and Zionist settlers share a "community of language and ideology,"[45] based on the idea that the landscape was empty and the indigenous inhabitants were impediments to civilization.[46] Notwithstanding the specificity of Israeli and Canadian settler nationalism, each emerged through an "eviction-driven" model of indigenous displacement in Palestine-Israel and Canada-Turtle Island, and an exclusionary national expansion has shaped both spaces.[47]

A growing number of scholars have argued that both Canada[48] and Israel[49] must be understood as instances of settler colonialism.[50] Canada, as a white European settler state and a former British dominion, was founded on the "dispossession and near extermination" of Indigenous peoples of Turtle Island[51] by European settlers.[52] This destruction is both physical and, in the words of Taiaike Alfred and Jeff Corntassel,[53] based on attempts to, "eradicate their existence as peoples through erasure of the histories and geographies that provide that foundation for Indigenous cultural identities and sense of self."[54] Dispossession is also foundational to the Israeli state, which, like other settler-colonial societies sees control of land as, "a zero-sum contest against the Indigenous population,"[55] waged through ethnic cleansing,[56] massacres, aerial and maritime bombardment, invasion, land theft, siege, and discriminatory laws and legal systems.[57] Canada's support for Zionism has been predicated on the idea that Jewish colonization in Palestine would act as a civilizing force in the "backward" Orient.[58] Canadian identification with Zionist settlers was rooted in a shared idea: land slated for colonization was treated as *terra nullius*, "empty" or "uninhabited" of people deserving of political and national rights, rendering it open to colonial settlement.[59] This manifestly racialized story of the civilization of pre-modern spaces by European settlers works to secure a position for both Canada and Israel on the civilized side of what W.E.B. DuBois calls the "colour line,"[60] granting themselves the rights to sovereignty, self-determination, and protection under international law denied the Indigenous inhabitants dispossessed in the making of both settler states.

The idea of a Jewish homeland in Palestine as both the fulfillment of biblical prophecy and a civilizing mission in the Orient was clearly articulated in British colonial discourse adopted by Canada's Christian communities beginning in the mid-19th century, even before the advent of modern political Zionism.[61] When the Canadian Federation of Zionist Societies held a convention in Toronto in 1906, it was addressed by the Mayor, prominent academics, and a member of federal parliament, with the lieutenant-governor of Canada proclaiming that Zionism, "is a cause which must prevail, for the gift of Palestine to your nation by the Almighty is absolute."[62] Similar proclamations were expressed by many other officials and well-known figures, including the Solicitor General (and soon to be Prime Minister) Arthur Meighan,[63] while Mackenzie-King declared the ideals of Zionism to be "in consonance" with that of "Englishmen."[64] As David Bercuson details in his book *Canada and the Birth of Israel*, the Zionist cause also enjoyed support among political leaders of the then socialist-leaning Co-operative Commonwealth Federation (CCF), precursor to the modern left-leaning New Democratic Party (NDP).[65]

It is not only in relation to Zionism and the question of Palestine that Canada's national narrative as a neutral peacekeeper does not stand up to critical scrutiny. Much of the basis for this national mythology is the fact that it served in nearly every UN-mandated peacekeeping mission up until the mid-1990s.[66] However, a historical glance at Canadian foreign policy reveals that in fact, prior to the Second World War, Canada saw itself as a partner in Britain's global "civilizing project."[67] This included sending troops to South Africa during the 1899 Boer war to both defend British imperial interests,[68] and display Canada's own imperial strength and ambitions.[69] Aligning itself with British and later American imperialism was a way to establish a role for itself in the international system.[70]

Moreover, Canada's participation in NATO missions during the Cold War dwarfed its peacekeeping contributions,[71] and it has consistently been among the top fifteen weapons exporters in the world.[72] It also engages in trade and diplomatic ties with states notorious for systematic human rights violations. At the United Nations, Canada remained one of the seven most reliable supporters of the Apartheid state in South Africa until 1984.[73] While symbolically condemning Apartheid practices, Canada continued to trade with South Africa and voted against or abstained on United Nations resolutions which called for economic sanctions or recognized resistance groups like the African National Congress (ANC).[74] As recently as 2016, Canada announced a $15 billion sale of light armoured vehicles to Saudi Arabia,[75] continuing a historical bipartisan pattern of selling arms to states with dismal human rights records.[76] In terms of military operations, Canada participated in the 1991 United States–led Gulf War and supported the sanctions regime against Iraq during the 1990s,[77] which led to mass starvation and deaths from preventable diseases.[78] Canadian Forces also took part in the NATO bombardment of Serbia and Kosovo,[79] as well as sending troops to Afghanistan,[80] where Canadian soldiers were implicated in torture.[81] Despite this long history of involvement in imperial violence, Canadian

68 *Canada and the Palestinian Refugees*

peacekeepers deployed to Somalia in 1993 shot two Somali men in the back and tortured to death sixteen-year-old Shidane Abukar Arone,[82] these acts were constructed in the public sphere as the betrayal of Canada's history of innocence by a few "bad apples." More recently, in 2011 Canadian warplanes dropped 240 laser-guided bombs on Libya in the NATO-led mission[83] that has contributed to Libya's near dissolution, whose rich resources are now being fought over by foreign powers.

The national narrative casts Canada as playing a special role in international affairs by spreading its "values" through peacekeeping and other interventions, particularly through Lloyd Axworthy's promotion of the notion of the "responsibility to protect" (R2P).[84] R2P works, "to normalize and codify a role for Canada in international affairs"[85] by conditioning state sovereignty on the protection of human rights, including states' own citizens.[86] Thus far, it has been used primarily to justify mostly United States–led military interventions in the Global South or former Communist bloc, and has wrought death and destruction. Canada's deep investments in narratives of innocence, and the ample evidence of the reality of Canada's settler-colonial structure and role in a larger imperial chain, serve as the contextual backdrop in which to examine Canada's supposedly neutral role in relation to Palestine-Israel and the Palestinian refugees.

Canada's Role in Partition and its Early Position on the Right of Return

Canada played a key role in the creation of Israel through the United Nations Special Committee on Palestine (UNSCOP) and the UN subcommittee that authored the Partition Plan affirmed by the UN General Assembly (Husseini 2008). While Supreme Court Justice Ivan C. Rand promoted partition as a solution to UNSCOP committee members who travelled to Palestine in 1947, Lester B. Pearson, in his role as Under-Secretary of State for External Affairs, played a significant part in mobilizing support for partition in the UN subcommittee and at the General Assembly.[87] Earlier works on the subject of Canada's role in the Partition Plan for Palestine by Bercuson, Kay, and Tauber[88] largely maintain that Canada's position was based on pragmatic and legal considerations. A careful examination of Canadian discourse at the time of partition reveals instead a mix of personal, internal, and external factors that influenced views on partition—including Anglo-American discord (as Britain tried to disentangle itself from the "Palestine problem"), Cold War rivalries,[89] guilt over the Holocaust,[90] the idea of common "Judeo-Christian values" and the Orientalist outlook of major decision-makers.[91]

Pearson himself espoused a neo-imperialist logic when he described a future Jewish state as, "an outpost, if you will, of the West in the Middle East," which could act as a buffer against Soviet influence in the region.[92] In turn, Ivan C. Rand described Israel as, "an anchorage in the Middle East for ethical values and civilizing influence of the West."[93] This Canadian view closely mimicked both Herzl's famous 1896 declaration that a Jewish state will stand as a, "portion of a rampart of Europe against Asia, an outpost of civilization as opposed to barbarism"[94] and the discourse of Canadian Christian Zionists in the decades following Confederation. This Zionist Eurocentrism was reiterated over a century later by Netanyahu in 2009, during his UN speech, when he said that the struggle against fanaticism "pits civilization against barbarism, the 21st century against the 9th century, those who sanctify life against those who glorify death."[95]

That Canada's role in partition is recorded as a pragmatic consideration of the law, or a decision made "with heavy hearts,"[96] speaks to the way that Zionist narratives and the consequent "sheer blotting out from history"[97] of the Arab inhabitants of Palestine has become so normalized in the Canadian public sphere that upholding this status quo could be seen as "neutral." Adherents to the view of Canada as a neutral player in the Palestine refugee question cite Canada's support for United Nations General Assembly (UNGA) Resolution 194 (III) of 1948,[98] which affirms both the right of Palestinian refugees to return to their homes at "the earliest practicable date" and to receive compensation for "loss or damage to property."[99] Cited as further evidence of benevolence is Canada's vote for UNGA Resolution 302 (IV), establishing the United Nations Relief Works Agency (UNRWA), and its continued financial support for the organization throughout the 1950s and 1960s, when Canada acted as the fourth largest contributor of material support to the Palestinian refugees,[100] giving between one-half and three-quarters of a million dollars per year.[101]

However, neither a largely symbolic nod to the refugees' right of return nor consistent (with some exceptions) financial support for UNRWA is incompatible with Canada's imperial foreign policy in general, or its unwavering support for Zionism and Israel in particular. In fact, an examination of the discourse of political leaders during the decades following the expulsion of Palestinians reveals a consistent effort to promote resettlement of the

Palestinian refugees in neighbouring Arab countries as *the* durable solution to the refugee crisis.

As early as 1952, Canada, in its capacity as a member of the Ad-Hoc Political Committee of the UNGA essentially repudiated its own support for return as a political right. In a co-authored draft resolution foreshadowing its position during the Oslo peace process, Canada agreed that previous UN resolutions should not be taken as a basis for negotiation between Israel and the Palestinians, describing these resolutions as "an obstacle to peace."[102] Generous funding of UNRWA is actually consistent with the end goal of resettlement. As Al Husseini and Bocco,[103] and Farah,[104] point out, for Western donors UNRWA was largely envisioned as a temporary organization which would serve to integrate Palestinians into host societies, mostly in Arab countries bordering historic Palestine.

Resettlement as the preferred option for resolving the Palestinian refugee crisis can be gleaned in what Jan Raska,[105] refers to as a "forgotten experiment," when a small number of (carefully selected and screened) Palestinian refugees were admitted to Canada in 1955. An examination of the internal communications between Canadian policymakers at the time of the refugee admission reveals two main motivating factors for resettling Palestinians in Canada. The first reason was to encourage other countries to also implement resettlement schemes, and the second was to ease the tension posed to "regional stability" by the presence of many Palestinian refugees close to the borders of the nascent Israeli state.[106] In an internal memorandum, Under-Secretary Léger argued that "before any positive step can be taken [to resolve the refugee crisis] the Arabs must accept two facts: that Israel has come to stay and that, except for a very few, most of the refugees will be resettled in Arab lands...no opportunity should be lost to persuade them to move in that direction."[107]

In response to Finance Minister Harris' declaration in the House of Commons in 1955 that the refugee problem should be solved by way of "rehabilitation," Social Credit MP for Wetaskiwin Ray Thomas stated that, "it is about time they were forced to get out and make their own way somehow. It should be made perfectly clear to them that any further rehabilitation grants for the refugees will be used for rehabilitation only and not for maintenance within the camps."[108] The media's framing of the refugees largely mirrored this cross-party consensus, with a Toronto Star editorial in 1955 bemoaning the "inefficiency" of the Arab who, nonetheless, needs, "food, clothing, and shelter like other people," while promoting, "the resettlement of the Palestinian Arab refugees now huddled on Israel's borders."[109] The options offered (and still offered) to Palestinian refugees were either resettlement outside of historic Palestine, or the continuation of their status as perpetual and conditional recipients of aid.

In a confidential letter from Under Secretary of State Léger to the Deputy Minister of Finance, it is stated to be in Canada's interest, "that the refugees be resettled as soon as possible since the only practical alternative is for members of the United Nations, including Canada, to continue to share in the cost of maintaining them indefinitely."[110] This historical policy clearly pushed for aid and resettlement for Palestinians refugees, aligning perfectly with Israel's position. In fact, while crafting a press release on the admission of Palestinian refugees to Canada, Israel's Foreign Minister Moshe Sharett told Secretary of State for Internal Affairs Pearson, "how impossible it would be for Israel to take back a large number of refugees and, apart from the security problem, there was simply no place where they could be resettled."[111] Seen as encouraging other countries to resettle Palestinian refugees and therefore neutralizing the "threat to regional security" posed by the refugees' existence,[112] the resettlement scheme was conceived as consistent with both Canadian and Israeli interests.

The characterization of Palestinian refugees as a burden and unworthy of full rights is also evident in the lead up to the 1956 Suez Crisis, when Israel, Britain, and France invaded Egypt over access to the Suez Canal, and when the relationship between Canada, Israel, and Egypt featured prominently in foreign policy discussions in the Canadian House of Commons. Liberal Member of Parliament Donald Carrick echoed the Israeli official position by dismissing any international or Israeli responsibility for the Palestinian refugee problem, blaming instead the Grand Mufti, claiming he ordered the refugees to leave "to disrupt the Israeli economy."[113] He complains that despite Israel's noble efforts to compensate the refugees by facilitating their assimilation into other Arab countries, these countries have not co-operated with Israel as, "it is quite clear that the purpose of the Arab governments is to drive the Israelis into the sea."[114] His solution is to provide unlimited arms to Israel, which he describes as, "an outpost and a source of security... an arsenal for the democracies of the free world in the Middle East."[115]

Pearson also explicitly pushed for resettlement. Urging Israel to allow "some token repatriation," he states that, "it is clear that so large a number [of Palestinian refugees] cannot return to their former land," as, "resettle-ment...seems to be the only answer."[116] Two members of parliament from the Co-operative Commonwealth Federation (CCF) (the precursor to the New Democratic Party) agreed with Pearson's analysis, with one CCF MP, Alistair Stewart going so far as accusing Arab states of "indoctrinating the refugees with hatred" essentially blaming the refugees for their own plight, while Social Credit MP A.B. Patterson similarly pushed for the repatria-tion of, "a limited number of refugees" on humanitarian grounds, with the rest being the responsibility of Arab states.[117] The attitude towards the refugees continued with the election of Diefenbaker, a former member of the pre-statehood Canadian Palestine Committee (an organization dedi-cated to establishing a Jewish majority state in Palestine),[118] and recipient of the Canada-Israel Friendship award,[119] to the position of Prime Minister in 1958. Under Prime Minster Pearson in 1963, the Undersecretary of External Affairs Norman Robertson prepared a memo to the External Affairs Minister to coincide with the annual Canadian Jewish Congress-United Zionist Congress brief. The memo stated that Canada's traditional policy on refu-gees, "should involve both repatriation and substantial resettlement."[120] While the inclusion of repatriation is somewhat of an improvement on earlier statements, the qualifier "substantial resettlement," coupled with Pearson's earlier statement on "token repatriation," clarifies that Canadian leaders do not interpret repatriation as a right, but as a public statement that would mask its real position and through which it could continue to claim a neutral position when necessary.

This fundamental denial of refugee return as a *right* shrouded with a discourse about its impracticability continued to shape Canadian discourse following the second major expulsion of Palestinians in 1967. During the June 8, 1967 discussion in the House of Commons, Prime Minister Pearson states that, "a real opportunity has never been given to these refugees to decide if they could or would be willing to locate in other countries, and perhaps sufficient effort has never been made to get at least some of them back to their homes in Israel."[121] While admitting that there are "other causes" for the refugee crisis, Pearson insists that the main cause is the refugees' refusal to resettle as they are "waiting for Israel to disappear" so they can reclaim their homes and properties.[122] As leader of the opposi-tion, Diefenbaker takes the opportunity to affirm "Israel's right to live,"[123] while accusing Egyptian president Nasser of genocide against Israel.[124] The

NDP-CCF, described by Kay,[125] as the most consistently pro-Israel of all the parties, agrees with the Prime Minister, condemning the actions of the Arab governments and the PLO.[126]

The House of Commons debates in 1967 similarly reveal just how deeply the aforementioned narratives had been entrenched into Canadian political discourse. In his assessment of the relationship between Canada and Israel from 1958–1968, Kay notes the continuity in policy despite changes in government, characterizing this period as, "the diplomacy of impartiality."[127] Humanitarianism is another convenient façade enabling Canada to strengthen its friendship with the Israeli state, while concurrently claiming it is aiding Palestinian refugees.

From Madrid to Oslo: Is Canada *Aid*-ing Away Refugee Rights?

With an emphasis on humanitarian contributions instead of repatriation by most Western powers, including Canada, and the refugees' insistence on their right to repatriation, humanitarianism itself transmuted into *the* Palestinian refugees' permanent-temporary solution. In a valuable study on aid in the 1967 Palestinian-occupied territories, Wildeman proposed that de-contextualized aid, which does not address the root cause, led to a situation where Israel uses aid dollars to subsidize the cost of the occupation under the rubric of the "peace process."[128] Wildeman's insight may be extended to aid provided to Palestinian refugees. By not addressing the root cause and holding Israel accountable for the ethnic cleansing of Palestine, Canadian humanitarianism, prolongs the status of the uprooted Palestinians as refugees or beneficiaries of aid.

In 1991 Canada attended the multilateral peace conference on the Israel-Palestine "conflict" in Madrid, where five working groups were established. Among them was the Refugee Working Group (RWG), which held its first meeting in Ottawa in July 1992.[129] According to Robinson, the Canadian gavel holder of the RWG from 1995 to 2000, one of the reasons that Canada accepted the invitation was that it thought it best to be "inside the tent" if there were decisions made regarding *resettlement*;[130] a clue that these negotiations were not about to discuss the right of return. Confident of Canada's sympathetic attitude towards Israel, David Levy, Israel's foreign minister at the time, told the United States he would only agree to the refugee group if Canada chaired it. In fact, according to Palestinian participants in the negotiations, in one of the meetings the Canadian gavel holder at the time referred

74   *Canada and the Palestinian Refugees*

to the right of return as a "myth" and was forced to retract under pressure.[131] Whereas Canada was mindful that UNGAR 194 (III) was Israel's red flag, and thus was ready to discuss "living conditions," it was the Palestinian negotiators who strove to keep the right of return on the agenda.[132] According to Robinson, Canada reaped the benefits of participation in the Oslo "peace" process,[133] even while Palestinian refugees' conditions and rights were never addressed. Domestically, Canada's role helped to perpetuate its reputation that it has an even-handed policy in the Middle East. On the international level, its profile was raised by chairing one of the five working groups.[134] Yet, as gavel holder, Canada missed an opportunity to speak directly to the need to implement the Palestinian right of return as the only just and durable solution. Instead, Canada submitted to Israel's "red flags" hiding behind humanitarian solutions and refugee "living conditions."

The bilateral negotiations that followed Madrid led to the Declaration of Principles (DOP) and the Oslo Accords first signed surreptitiously in Oslo between the PLO and Israel in 1993. This was a radical break in the national consensus that led to further divisions in the Palestinian political map. A few months after Mahmoud Abbas, representing Yasser Arafat, the PLO's Chariman at the time, signed the Accord, ten Palestinian factions met in Damascus and formed an "Alliance of Palestinian Forces" that opposed the Oslo Accords.[135] The Oslo agreements, Arafat had hoped, would lead to a two-state solution, whereby the Palestinian state would emerge on the West Bank and Gaza, which, nonetheless, constituted only 22 per cent of historical Palestine. As for the refugees, they were dismissed altogether, and their fate deferred to final status negotiations that never materialized. Refugees were particularly dismayed that UNGAR 194 (III) was not included in any of the signed agreements, which made them feel betrayed by their own leadership.[136] On its part, Israel made it clear that no right of return to areas colonized in 1948 areas would be negotiated and pushed for an agenda to "rehabilitate" and integrate refugees wherever they may be.

As Dr. Haydar 'Abd al-Shafi, a founding member of the Palestine National Council and head of the Palestinian negotiating team at Madrid cogently argued, by signing the Oslo agreements, Palestinians have helped confer legitimacy on what Israel has established illegally.[137] As 'Abd al-Shafi predicted, the "Peace Process" turned out to be an active Jewish illegal settlement process. Canada officially supports the two-state solution within the now-defunct Oslo "peace" process. However, Canadian officials have little to say regarding Israel's ongoing usurpation of Palestinian Arab land for colonial Jewish settlement, the territorial base upon which the Palestinian state was supposed to emerge. Canada also turns a blind eye to Israel's brutal military rule imposed on the indigenous inhabitants. On the contrary, Canadian officials twaste no opportunity to praise Israel's "democracy." Canada also rarely, if ever, criticizes Israel for passing over sixty-five laws that discriminate against its Palestinian Arab citizens,[138] or worse, its self-definition as a Jewish state, which legalizes a long-held practice whereby Jews are considered a privileged population in almost all aspects of life, contrary to all democratic principles.[139] Flagrant violations amidst the deafening silence of states like Canada continued, and in October of 2021, Israel clamped down on several humanitarian and human rights organizations labelling them as "terrorist" groups. These include: Al-Haq, a human rights group founded in 1979; the Addameer rights group; Defence for Children International-Palestine; the Bisan Center for Research and Development; the Union of Palestinian Women's Committees; and the Union of Agricultural Work Committees.[140] It is worth mentioning here that during the Harper years, the Canadian government through the International Development Research Center (IDRC) terminated two large grants meant to study the effects of systematic discrimination against Palestinian citizens of Israel. The funds had been allocated to Mada al-Carmel, a Haifa-based Arab Center for Applied Social Research, which aimed to examine the limitations imposed on Arab political participation in Israel; and in the second research project, the effects of Israeli colonial policies on the political and economic realities of Palestinian women inside Israel.[141] This is but one example that shows how Israel and Canada stifle organizations that promote social justice in Palestine. In 2009, the Canadian International Development Agency (CIDA) decided to terminate funding for KAIROS: Canadian Ecumenical Justice Initiatives. The decision was explained on the basis that the KAIROS proposal "did not fit CIDA priorities."[142] The funding was initially approved at every level of CIDA, then a handwritten "not" (approved) by the then International Cooperation Minister Bev Oda, ended a thirty-five-year funding relationship with KAIROS. The case exposed the pressures by pro-Israel Canadian officials against any civil society organization that supports the Palestinians or questions Israeli policies.[143]

However, it is the Palestinian refugees' right of return that remains the fundamental key issue in the Palestinian national question. A closer examination of the now redundant Oslo-based solution reveals that it de facto prevents half the nation, the refugees and the exiles, from the right of return and their right to self-determination. In effect, the idea, albeit illusory, of an Oslo-produced statelet "dethroned" the nation.[144] The combination of unprecedented expansion of Jewish settlements and a growing list of discriminatory laws,[145] in all of Mandatory Palestine, produced a de facto and de jure Apartheid situation.[146] This renders public pronouncements about a two-state solution more of a fairy tale endlessly reiterated, now across generations, even as Jewish settlements have swallowed most of the area that was supposed to be part of the Palestinian statelet on 22 per cent of British Mandatory Palestine.

Attempts at introducing the refugee issue in negotiations, however, persisted. For example, what became known as the "Ottawa process" (first meeting in 1997) was an informal Canadian initiative to discuss issues considered "taboo" in previous forums.[147] A workshop was held specifically to deal with the 1948 refugees' right of return. The other workshops were compensation, repatriation, the future of UNRWA, interim measures and linkages with other final status issues. However, as Rempel noted, Israel once again succeeded in sweeping the right of return off the table, forcing the participants to deal with compensation instead.[148] Despite Israeli pressure, Palestinian participants and others at the compensation workshop pointed out that in UN Resolution 194 (III), both the right of return *and* compensation have been clearly recognized: one is not a substitute for the other. Another key point was raised by Palestinian participants stating that refugees are free to reject any deal negotiated by the PLO that does not meet the parameters set forth in Resolution 194 (III).[149] In contrast, Israeli representatives insisted that any bilateral agreement with the PLO/PA should extinguish all further claims.

The Palestinian insistence on the right of return was something Canadian officials, including Lloyd Axworthy, experienced firsthand when visiting refugee camps in the region beginning in 1997. The officials on missions heard directly from refugees, and from the press in Lebanon, where Canada was presented as engaged in, "a secret plan to settle the refugees in Lebanon."[150] The Canadian representatives in the Mission heard it loud and clear from refugees who explained that UNRWA's work was critical for them, that they were very skeptical regarding the so-called "peace process," and demanded the implementation of UN resolution 194 (III), which affirms their right of return.[151] According to Robinson, Canada was at least able to direct the question away from return or no return, to something more concrete, such as "compensation regimes."[152] However, we have been arguing exactly the opposite: the Palestinian exile is a protracted and bitter journey. Instead of resorting back to rehabilitation schemes, or humanitarian services, it is time to insist on the refugees' political and legal rights within the framework of international law. This is the only path that leads to a durable and just solution.

UNRWA: The Illusions of Humanitarian "Neutrality"

When the United Nations Relief and Works Agency (UNRWA) was established in 1949, its purpose was to "dissolve" the refugee problem through large-scale "works projects," as the word "Works" in UNRWA's name indicates, and integrate them into host countries.[153] According to the Advisory Commission Chairman at the time, John Blandford Jr., these works projects with the help of the Agency would form, "the antithesis of camp life and idleness."[154]

Over the years, however, UNRWA has morphed into a vital lifeline that assists refugees in eking out a basic livelihood and due to its longevity stands as an established institution that had retained the collective memory of the Palestinian refugees since their Nakba. Today, in the context of Palestinian political fragmentation and Israeli settlement expansion, UNRWA looms like a last frontier—a surviving vestige of Palestinian national history. In this context, Joe Biden, who assumed office in January 2021, did not reverse what his Republican predecessor had done and restore funding to UNRWA. Although some funding resumed, the Framework for Cooperation between the UNRWA and the US for 2021–2022,[155] was an alarming development. Signed in July 2021 by US officials and UNRWA's Commissioner General, the agreement, which was strongly opposed by Palestinians, stipulated that the US will not make any contributions to UNRWA, unless the latter ensured that no part of the funds is used, "to assist any refugee receiving military training as a member of the so-called Palestinian Liberation Army or any other guerrilla organization or has participated in any terrorist act."[156] The conditions imposed in the Framework linked funding to the "neutrality" of UNRWA staff as well as the refugee-beneficiaries. Furthermore, the Framework allowed the US to interfere in UNRWA schools, where the history or map of Palestine, or teaching about the right of

78   *Canada and the Palestinian Refugees*

return for example, would be considered a violation of "neutrality" and thus a breach of the Framework. With an arrogant tone that reflects its power and authority, the US demanded regular, frequent, and close monitoring of the Agency, and the reporting back to relevant US Department of State officials. Indeed, the Framework is an attempt to reduce UNRWA into a compliant spy organization, while simultaneously using it as a mechanism to erode Palestinian political rights, especially the right of return.

It is therefore not far-fetched to argue that next on the United States and Israel's list of removal orders are UNRWA and, by extension, UNGAR 194 (III). A glance at the recent history affirms this proposal. In January 2018, the United States withheld $65 million of its contributions to UNRWA, which Sarah Roy described as a "potential calamity."[157] The cuts were so drastic that it even provoked Peter Lerner, the former Israeli army spokesperson, to state that by weakening UNWRA, the Palestinians will be even more susceptible to what he called "extremism and violence."[158] In 2010, former Prime Minister Stephen Harper's Conservative government had also cut aid to UNRWA. Although funding was restored in 2016 by the Liberals,[159] when it comes to supporting Israel, there are no fundamental differences among Canadian political parties, or even Canada with the United States. The differences are superficial, a point that becomes clearer in the following section when we examine the conditions attached to Canada's Liberal Party funding of UNRWA.

Some may be surprised to know that the UNRWA is one of the most monitored United Nations organizations, and yet it is consistently accused by Israeli officials of encouraging terrorism and of prolonging the refugee problem. The slandering campaigns reach Canadians through Israeli lobby groups such as B'nai Brith Canada, or the Conservative Party and pro-Israel individuals and groups.[160] An example of such messaging is an article published in 2016 by B'nai Brith which stated it was outraged that Canada committed $25 million in funding to UNRWA, an organization, "previously criticized for its ties to the Hamas terrorist organization."[161] Quoting Michael Mostyn, it continued to claim that, "UNRWA...can be clearly construed as collaborating with Hamas."[162] But these are preposterous claims. Due to international pressure and closer monitoring of the Agency, it is exceptionally diligent in ensuring it maintains its humanitarian mandate and insists on its "neutral" policy. For example, when a bomb was found in an UNRWA school in Gaza, a rare and unique incident, the Agency "strongly and unequivocally" condemned the group or groups that were responsible for this, "flagrant violation of the inviolability of its premises under international law."[163] It then launched a comprehensive investigation into the circumstances surrounding this incident.[164]

We must point out here, albeit briefly, that while mainstream Canadian media energetically reports Israeli views, it almost never reports on Israel's systematic and daily violations of international law, rendering it almost impossible for ordinary Canadians to become aware of Palestinian realities and suffering under the Israeli occupation.[165] Although there is growing awareness, slow though it may be regarding Palestinian history and realities,[166] in general most Canadians do not have access to news that inform them of Israeli state terrorism, such as the bombing of UNRWA schools, camps, ambulances, personnel, and other sites of humanitarian operations.[167] The Gaza incident is an example: Israel has a history of dropping thousands of bombs on the overpopulated Gaza Strip, killing and injuring Palestinians in the thousands, not to mention the large-scale destruction of homes and buildings. Yet, what became a central media issue in Canada is whether UNRWA has ties with "terrorism."

The authors of articles that slander UNRWA demand that Canada's funding should be accompanied by stricter monitoring mechanisms. Such demands are imbued with disdain and sarcasm, deflecting attention from the root causes that led to the creation of UNRWA and its prolonged lifespan. Instead, they position UNRWA, a humanitarian agency, as if *it* is the problem, not the *illegal Israeli occupation*. The latter is maintained by a mighty nuclear power, and has been pressing heavily and brutally on Palestinians for decades, especially in the West Bank and Gaza, turning the basic act of living an ordinary life into a Promethean exercise for mere existence.[168]

Similarly, Ron Csillag, Staff Reporter for Canadian Jewish News stated that UNRWA, "has long been accused of diverting funds to Hamas and supporting terrorism through its educational programs."[169] He quoted B'nai Brith claiming that, "it is absolutely critical that Canada and other donor countries perform due diligence to ensure the removal of these anti-Semitic and inciting materials."[170]And, quoting Shimon Koffler Fogel, CEO of the Centre for Israel and Jewish Affairs, falsifications about UNRWA continued when Csillag wrote it has, "consistently demonstrated its inability to provide aid without also promoting anti-Semitism."[171] Predictably, a

80   *Canada and the Palestinian Refugees*

recommendation followed, "That's why, Fogel said, the previous government cut aid, and why the current government has imposed 'serious safeguards,' such as anti-terror and employee screening provisions."[172]

Instead of cutbacks in UNRWA funding, the Justin Trudeau Liberal government responded to Israeli demands while appearing consistent with its humanitarian reputation by renewing funding upon coming to power. However, that being said, the Trudeau government did not veer too far away from Harper's position a decade earlier by exaggerating public statements about conditional funding to UNRWA, and funding "neutrality training." This increased monitoring usually translates into a sweeping list of prohibitions, such as the removal of any material that enables Palestinian refugees to pose as anything other than "beneficiaries" of humanitarian aid, and not as Palestinian nationals with a history and political identity. Thus, "neutrality" in this context means withdrawing any materials that teach Palestinian refugees about their history of expulsion, or maps of pre-1948 featuring their villages and towns of origin in UNRWA-run programs and facilities.[173] Therefore, much-needed Canadian funding is diverted from starving families, education and health services, and instead, a significant sum goes to train and monitor "politicized neutrality." This quote from the Government of Canada website is instructive,

> *Through this funding, Canada is also continuing its support for unrwa's ongoing efforts to promote neutrality in its operations and among its staff... Neutrality is a core obligation and value of United Nations staff...The funding will contribute to UNRWA's neutrality activities, including: regular inspections of the agency's facilities by specially trained UNRWA officers who can identify, report and take action on violations of neutrality; training for UNRWA staff on neutrality, including in social media, and for senior staff on how to carry out effective installation inspections; promotion of students' knowledge and skills reflecting UN values...and; UNRWA's development, distribution and use of additional educational materials, part of the agency's approach to enable teachers to promote neutrality.[174]*

If neutrality is truly Canada's concern, which is a central tenet to not doing harm in a conflict situation,[175] one may raise questions as to why the Canadian government does not publish a similar list of conditions to closely monitor how Israel uses Canadian support, whether financial, military, or otherwise. This would be necessary to protect Palestinians living under a military occupation that causes daily Palestinian suffering. It is difficult not to conclude that Canada seems to have increasingly become more pro-Israeli than the United States,[176] and might be Israel's "best friend," as the following quote shows,

> *Canada has always been a friend of the Jewish state, but in recent years— especially since the Harper government came to power in 2006— Ottawa has redefined what it means to be staunchly pro-Israel. Indeed, in the Middle East conflict, no other nation, not even the United States, has been so unstintingly supportive of the policies of Israel's government as the Great White North.*[177]

The article goes on to list some of Canada's acts of friendship, including the Harper government's vote in 2012 against Palestinian statehood at the UN. Even in this voting ritual at the United Nations, a public site where Canada displays its "balanced policy" on the Middle East, there seems to be a shift. In 2017, among thirty-five countries, Canada abstained on a UN resolution against Trump's decision to recognize Jerusalem as Israel's capital—and this by a Liberal government, which officially declares it does not recognize Israel's unilateral annexation of Jerusalem.[178] Under international law, East Jerusalem is an occupied territory, and thus by abstaining, Canada is declaring Israel's illegal occupation as negotiable, rather than a clear violation of international law.

Conclusion

The rejection of the Palestinian right of return by Israel and its "close friends" like Canada is often justified as a threat to the "Jewish character" of the state. Israel is indeed one of the few ethno-theocracies in the region, a fact recently reinforced by the July 19, 2018 decision to approve the "Jewish Nation-State Basic Law" that constitutionally enshrines Jewish supremacy and the identity of the nation-state as that of the Jewish people, not that of its citizens.[179] This is inconsistent with the core of a democratic system which Canada claims to uphold domestically and internationally.

In November 2019, Canada went along with the international consensus and backed the right of Palestinian self-determination at the United Nations General Assembly Resolution.[180] It did not take long before Trudeau declared that endorsing Palestinian self-determination is not a shift in Canadian policy, and that Canada is against singling out Israel for criticism on the international stage.[181] Many other assurances followed, such as when on January 16, 2020, the Canadian Ambassador to Israel Deborah Lyons welcomed over thirty Canadian "lone soldiers" serving in the Israeli Defence Forces (IDF) to her residence in Tel Aviv to celebrate Canadian citizens in the Israeli military.[182]

However, could one expect a principled stand from countries such as Canada, who bear so many similarities to that of Israel, as settler-colonial states? We see a historical consistency between how the Canadian state treats Indigenous people under its declared jurisdiction, and its stand on Palestinian refugees. Thus, it will be important for the Canadian government to confront the past, take responsibility for the ongoing suffering inflicted on Indigenous nations of Turle Island-Canada, and seek just and therefore durable solutions at home and for the Palestinians. All unjust "pragmatic" solutions envisioned for the Palestinian question have thus far failed; a lasting peace will only be achieved by fulfilling the right of return and the fulfilment of the collective right to self-determination.

In 2021, we saw thousands of Palestinians protesting in the streets of Gaza, in cities in the West Bank, including in the Sheikh Jarrah neighbour-hood, in and near al-Aqsa mosque in Jerusalem, as well as in Haifa, and the Galilee area, that is, across the political geography of historical Palestine. These recent protests are a response to Israel's escalating repression of Palestinians, and the expansion of Jewish settlements on their expropriated land. However, popular protests that transcend political divisions against Israel's prolonged occupation and its apartheid policies demonstrate clearly and loudly that decades of colonization has failed to abate the Palestinian will to return and to struggle for their right to self-determination in their homeland.

Notes

1. Chimni, "The Geopolitics of Refugee Studies," 352; Dumper, "Future Prospects for the Palestinian Refugees," 567.
2. Wolfe, "Settler Colonialism and the Elimination of the Native," 388.
3. Wolfe, 388.

4. See also Wildeman's chapter in this book (chapter 2).

5. Hughes, "Unbounded Territoriality."

6. Hughes, 217.

7. See Boling, *The 1948 Palestinian Refugees,* especially chapter 4, "The Right of Return in the Humanitarian Law" in which she draws on legal scholarship to argue that the General Assembly was not creating a new right when it affirmed the right of return of Palestinians, stating instead that the operative paragraph concerning the rights of the 1948 refugees endorsed a generally recognized principle and provided a means for implementing that principle. She refers for example to both the Hague Regulations annexed to the 1907 Hague Convention (IV) Respecting the Laws and Customs of War on Land, which are universally recognized, including by Israel, to have achieved customary status by 1939) and the 1949 Geneva Civilians Convention (Fourth Geneva Convention) to which Israel is a signatory, providing for the right of return of displaced persons to their homes following the cessation of hostilities. Thus, the right of return exists as a binding norm of humanitarian law, and Israel is under a corresponding positive obligation to ensure its implementation.

8. For example, in January 2018, $300 million in funding was cut by the US. See UN Meetings Coverage and Press Releases at: https://press.un.org/en/2018/gaspd684.doc.htm.

9. Schwartz, "Dismantle UNRWA."

10. Erekat, "The Sovereign Right to Kill."

11. Peters and Gal, "Israel, UNRWA, and the Palestinian Refugee Issue," 589.

12. Gazit, "Solving the Refugee Problem: A Prerequisite for Peace."

13. Lapidoth, "Legal Aspects of the Palestinian 'Refugee Question.'"

14. Zilbershats, Yaffa and Goren-Amitai, "Return of Palestinian Refugees to the State of Israel," 9.

15. Masalha, *The Politics of Denial*, 19.

16. Masalha, 91.

17. Morris, *The Birth of the Palestinian Refugee Problem*, 66.

18. Masalha, *The Politics of Denial*, 245.

19. On November 2, 1917, Lord James Balfour, British Foreign Secretary at the time, sent a letter to Lord Rothschild, a British Zionist leader in London, pledging support for the establishment in Palestine of a "national home for the Jewish people." There are several legal, political and moral violations inherent in the Balfour Declaration. The most important of these violations is that Britain did not have the legal authority to grant another people the land of a third people. This was done without reference to the indigenous population, who have been seeking sovereignty and self-determination. When this promise was made Britain had not yet even been officially granted Mandatory authority by the League of Nations.

20. Farsoun and Zacharia, *Palestine and the Palestinians*, 80–82.

21. Farsoun and Zacharia, 109.

22. Khalidi, ed., *All That Remains*; Abu-Sitta, "The Feasibility of the Right of Return"; Sa'di and Abu-Lughod, eds., *Nakba*; Pappé, *The Ethnic Cleansing of Palestine.*

23. Badil Resource Center, "Denial of Palestinian Use and Access to Land."

24. See Adalah The Legal Center for Arab Minority Rights in Israel, "Israel Announces Massive Forced Transfer of Bedouin Citizens in Negev."

25. Rubin, "Vladimir Jabotinsky and Population Transfers."

26. Iğsız, *Humanism in Ruins*, 4–14.

27. Leyla Neyzi for example recorded the oral history of a woman who witnessed the occupation and burning of Smyrna (Izmir) and the lesser-known burning of Manisa. Neyzi, "Remembering Smyrna/Izmir."

28. Giirsoy, "The Effects of the Population Exchange," 95.

29. Krebs and Olwan, "From Jerusalem to the Grand River." On Indigenous displacement and attempts at resurgence see Alfred, Taiaiake, and Corntassel. "Being Indigenous."

30. One of the best studies on the 1936–1939 Revolt is Kanafani, *The 1936–1939 Revolt in Palestine.*

31. Katz, "Transfer of Population as a Solution to International Disputes," 55.

32. This idea is an Orientalist view that perceives the Arab world as a homogeneous "other" space, where all its people are shackled in the same unchanging traditions, history, religious orders, and ideology.

33. According to Selma James, a leading American-Jewish writer, feminist and social activist, Yiddish was the language of the Ashkenazi working class, and the Zionists sought to wipe out that tradition as well. See Global Women's Strike, "International Resistance to Zionism—Selma James," YouTube video, 7:33, July 31, 2008, https:// www.youtube.com/watch?v=MuCNLc9olqA&t=74s.

34. Shohat, "The Invention of Judeo-Arabic."

35. This obliteration of a critical rupture in Palestine's history was equally invisible in the Oslo Accords where the basic working assumption is that the "conflict" begins in the 1967 war, not the 1948 colonial war and ethnic cleansing operations.

36. See Amnesty International, "Israel's Apartheid against Palestinians."

37. See also the annual reports by numerous UN Rapporteurs, the most recent by Michael Lynk, the Special Rapporteur on Human Rights in the Palestinian Territories Occupied in 1967.

38. See Government of Canada, "Canadian Policy on Key Issues in the Israeli-Palestinian Conflict," last modified March 19, 2019, https://www.international.gc.ca/world-monde/international_relations-relations_internationales/mena-moan/israeli-palistinian_policy-politique_israelo-palestinien.aspx?lang=eng.

39. Freeman-Maloy, "Remembering Balfour," 10.

40. Naiman, "IJV-Vancouver Letter to Mayor Ken Sim: Don't Adopy the Divisive IHRA."

41. Prime Minister's Office, "Statement by the Prime Minister on Israel Indepedence Day."

42. Razack, "From the 'Clean Snows of Petawawa,'" 128.

43. Jefferess, "Responsibility, Nostalgia, and the Mythology of Canada as a Peacekeeper," 721.

44. Jefferess, 720.

45. Said, "The Idea of Palestine in the West."

46. See Wildeman's chapter in this volume (chapter 2).

47. Nadeau and Sears, "The Palestine Test," 20.

48. Coulthard, *Red Skin, White Masks*; Simpson, *Mohawk Interruptus*; Mackay, "Tricky Myths"; Smith, "Indigeneity, Settler Colonialism, White Supremacy"; Barker, "The Contemporary Reality of Canadian Imperialism."

49. Salamanca, "Past Is Present"; Lloyd, "Settler Colonialism and the State of Exception."

50. Veracini, *Settler Colonialism*; Morgensen, "Theorising Gender, Sexuality and Settler Colonialism."

51. Turtle Island is a word used by Indigenous Peoples to refer to North America and is connected to the Haudenosaunee creation story. The drawing of colonial borders in North America fractured many Indigenous nations.

52. Razack, "When Place Becomes Race."

53. Alfred and Corntassel. "Being Indigenous: Resurgences against Contemporary Colonialism," 98.

54. Alfred and Corntassel.

55. Salamanca, "Past is Present," 1.

56. Pappé, *The Ethnic Cleansing of Palestine*.

57. Salamanca, "Past is Present," 2.

58. Said, *Orientalism*.

59. Masalha, *The Politics of Denial*.

60. Razack, *Dark Threats & White Knights*, 10.

61. Brown, "Divergent Paths."

62. Brown, 157.

63. Engler, *Canada and Israel*, 4.

64. Bercuson, *Canada and the Birth of Israel*, 13.

65. Bercuson.

66. Jefferess, "Responsibility, Nostalgia, and the Mythology," 710.

67. Teigrob, "Which Kind of Imperialism?" 403; McKercher, *Canada and the World Since 1867*.

68. Page, "The Boer War and Canadian Imperialism."

69. Page, 14.

70. Klassen, "Canada and the New Imperialism," 175; Shipley, "The New Canadian Imperialism," 4.

71. Jefferess, "Responsibility, Nostalgia, and the Mythology," 714.

72. Jefferess, 714.

73. Stultz, "The Apartheid Issue at the General Assembly," 26.

74. Platt, "The Determinants of Canada's South African Policy."

75. Juneau, *Canada and Saudi Arabia*.

76. Vucetic, "A Nation of Feminist Arms Dealers," 505.
77. Jefferess, "Responsibility, Nostalgia, and the Mythology," 710.
78. Simons, *The Scourging of Iraq*; John Mueller and Karl Mueller, "Sanctions of Mass Destruction."
79. Jefferess, "Responsibility, Nostalgia, and the Mythology," 710.
80. Dua, Razack, and Warner, "Race, Racism, and Empire," 6.
81. Shipley, "The New Canadian Imperialism," 47.
82. Razack, *Dark Threats & White Knights*.
83. CBC News, "Canada drops 240 Bombs in Libya Air Campaign."
84. Jefferess, "Responsibility, Nostalgia, and the Mythology," 720.
85. Chapnick, "The Canadian Middle Power Myth," 205.
86. Zahar, "Talking One Talk, Walking Another," 48.
87. Brynen, "Canada's Role in the Israeli-Palestine," 84.
88. Bercuson, *Canada and the Birth of Israel*; Kay, *Diplomacy of Prudence*; Tauber, *Personal Policy Making*.
89. Husseini, "A "Middle Power" in Action."
90. Bercuson, *Canada and the Birth of Israel*, 74.
91. Husseini, "A 'Middle Power' in Action."
92. Husseini, 48.
93. Husseini, 51.
94. Herzl, 1896
95. See Fingerhut, "Netanyahu's UN Speech."
96. Bercuson, *Canada and the Birth of Israel*, 130.
97. Said, "The Idea of Palestine in the West."
98. Brynen, *Canada's Role in the Israeli-Palestine Peace Process*, 204.
99. Brynen, "Much Ado About Nothing," 283.
100. Raska, "Forgotten Experiment," 449.
101. Jacoby, "Canadian Peacebulding in the Middle East," 84; Goldberg and Shames, "The 'Good-Natured Bastard,'" 205.
102. Tomeh, "When the UN Dropped the Palestinian Question," 21.
103. Al Husseini and Bocco, "The Status of the Palestinian Refugees in the Near East," 266.
104. Farah, "UNRWA: Through the Eyes of Its Palestinian Employees"; Farah, "Keeping an Eye on UNRWA."
105. Raska, "Forgotten Experiment: Canada's Resettlement of Palestinian Refugees, 1955–1956."
106. Raska, 462.
107. Raska, 451.
108. Raska, 452.
109. Raska, 454.
110. Raska, 455.
111. Raska, 461.
112. Raska, 462.

113. Parliament of Canada, "House of Commons. Debates Archives: 22nd Parliament, 3rd Session."

114. Parliament of Canada, 760.

115. Parliament of Canada, 762.

116. Goldberg and Shames, "The 'Good-Natured Bastard,'" 206.

117. Goldberg and Shames, 206

118. Kay, *The Diplomacy of Impartiality*, 18.

119. Kay, 29.

120. Kay, 47.

121. Parliament of Canada, "House of Common Debates: 27th Parliament, 2nd Session," June, 1967–7 July, 1967, http://parl.canadiana.ca/view/oop.debates_ HOC2702_02/113?r=0&s=1, 1295.

122. Parliament of Canada, 1296.

123. Parliament of Canada, 1297.

124. Parliament of Canada, 1298.

125. Kay, *The Diplomacy of Impartiality*, 65.

126. Kay, 60.

127. Kay.

128. Wildeman, "Why Aid Projects Are Doomed to Fail."

129. Jaradat-Gassner, "Political Negotiations on the Palestinian Refugee Question," 7.

130. Robinson, "Canada's Credibility as an Actor in the Middle East Peace Process," 697.

131. Zureik, "Palestinian Refugees and Peace," 14.

132. Jaradat-Gassner, "Political Negotiations on the Palestinian Refugee Question."

133. Robinson. "Canada's Credibility as an Actor in the Middle East Peace Process."

134. Robinson, 702.

135. Strindberg, "The Damascus-Based Alliance of Palestinian Forces."

136. Farah, "Palestinian Refugees."

137. Abd al-Shafi, "The Oslo Agreement." 14–15.

138. See Adalah The Legal Centre for Arab Minority Rights in Israel, "The Discriminatory Laws Data Base."

139. Iraqi, "The Redundancy of Israel's 'Jewish Nation-State Law.'"

140. *Al-Jazeera*, "Outcry as Israel Labels Palestinian Rights Groups 'Terrorists.'"

141. Chaleshtoori, "Canadian Funding for the Only Palestinian Research Center in Israel Cut."

142. CBC, "TIMELINE: Oda and the Kairos Funding."

143. Wildeman, "Undermining the Democratic Process."

144. Farah, "Palestinian Refugees."

145. On discriminatory Israeli laws, see Adalah: The Legal Center for Arab Minority Rights in Israel.

146. Even former United States President Jimmy Carter described the situation in the Occupied Palestinian Territories as Apartheid and titled his book *Palestine: Peace Not*

Apartheid (New York: Simon & Schuster Paperbacks, 2007), this is at a time when the situation for Palestinians were not as repressive and segregated as they are today.

147. Rempel, "The Ottawa Process."

148. Rempel, 37.

149. Rempel, 41.

150. Robinson, "Canada's Credibility as an Actor in the Middle East Peace Process," 712.

151. Robinson, 713.

152. Robinson, 717.

153. Bartholomeusz, "The Mandate of UNRWA at Sixty," 471.

154. Schiff, *Refugees Unto the Third Generation*, 29.

155. US Department of State, "The Framework for Cooperation between the United Nations Relief and Works Agency."

156. US Department of State.

157. Roy, "Trump's Move to Slash Aid."

158. Lerner, "Less American Aid to Palestinians Means More Violence Against Israelis."

159. Wyld, "Liberals Restore Funding to Controversial Palestinian Aid Agency."

160. Woodley, "Refugee Kids Deserve Our Help Not Your Awful Rhetoric."

161. See B'nai Brith Canada, "B'nai Brith Condemns Canadian Government's Decision to Fund UNRWA."

162. B'nai Brith Canada.

163. United Nations Relief and Works Agency for Palestine Refugees (UNRWA), "UNRWA Condemns Placement of Rockets."

164. See also Factsheet by Canadians for Justice and Peace in the Middle East (CJPME) refuting this accusation. "Attacks on Canada's Funding of UNRWA."

165. See Antonius' chapter in this book (chapter 7).

166. However, it is encouraging that a growing number of Canadian grassroots and community organizations (including Jewish organizations) and churches have become more vocal in advocating for Palestinian rights. For example, in 2016 and in disagreement with B'nai Brith article, religious figures including the Bishop of Hamilton and President of the Canadian Conference of Catholic Bishops (CCCB) requested the reestablishment of Canada's financial contributions to UNRWA. "Joint ecumenical letter to Government of Canada concerning UNRWA," Canadian Conference of Catholic Bishops, October 11, 2016, https://www.cccb.ca/letter/joint-ecumenical-letter-government-canada-concerning-unrwa/.

167. There are many examples of Israeli assaults on UNRWA, see for example the report "The Most Destructive Assault." Or, Abunimah, "UN Finds Israel Killed Dozens at Gaza Schools."

168. Hass, "Palestinians Are Fighting for Their Lives."

169. Csillag, "Canada Won't Rule Out Changing UNRWA Funding."

170. Csillag.

171. Csillag.

172. Csillag.

173. This information is based on many years conducting research on Palestinian refugees and interviewing UNRWA staff in Amman, Jordan, both at Headquarters and in camps. I have been consistently informed of growing pressure to remove materials that are related to Palestinian pre-1948 history and maps, the Nakba, flags and so on. Meanwhile, Canada's efforts at "erasure" of Palestinian national history through the school system it is contributing funds to, runs parallel to Canada's history of erasure of Indigenous national histories at Canadian residential schools, described in Wildeman's chapter in this volume (chapter 2).

174. Global Affairs Canada, "Backgrounder- Canada's Support for Palestinian Refugees."

175. Anderson, *Do No Harm.*

176. Lynk, "Closer to Power Than Justice."

177. Ahern, "Canada and Israel—Best Friends Forever?"

178. CBC News, "Canada Calls for Calm."

179. See Adalah: The Legal Centre for Arab Minority Rights in Israel, "Israel's Jewish Nation-State Law."

180. Kent, "Canada Again Votes at UN to Back Palestinian Self-Determination."

181. *National Post*, "Trudeau Says Canada's UN Vote."

182. Jackson, "Canada Citizens Fighting for Israel."

References

Abu-Sitta, Salman H. "The Feasibility of the Right of Return." Palestinian Refugee Research Net. Accessed May 10, 2019. https://prrn.mcgill.ca/research/papers/abusitta.htm.

Adalah. "Israel announces massive forced transfer of Bedouin citizens in Negev," January 30, 2019. Accessed May 7, 2022. https://www.adalah.org/en/content/view/9677.

Adalah. "Al-Araqeeb." Accessed May 7, 2022. https://www.adalah.org/en/tag/index/643.

Ahern, Raphael. "Canada and Israel—Best Friends Forever?" *The Times of Israel*, May 19, 2013. https://www.timesofisrael.com/canada-and-israel-best-friends-forever/.

Al Husseini, J., and R. Bocco. "The Status of the Palestinian Refugees in the Near East: The Right of Return and UNRWA in Perspective." *Refugee Survey Quarterly* 28, no. 2–3 (2009): 260–85.

Al-Shafi, Haydar 'Abd. "The Oslo Agreement. An Interview with Haydar 'Abd Al-Shafi." *Journal of Palestine Studies* 23, no. 1 (October 1, 1993): 14–19.

Alfred, Taiaiake, and Jeff Corntassel. "Being Indigenous: Resurgence Against Contemporary Colonialism." *Government and Opposition* 40, no. 4 (2005): 597–614.

Al-Jazeera. "Outcry as Israel Labels Palestinian Rights Groups 'Terrorists.'" October 23, 2021. Accessed October 25, 2021. https://www.aljazeera.com/news/2021/10/22/israel-palestinian-human-rights-groups-terrorism.

Amjad, Iraqi. "The Redundancy of Israel's 'Jewish Nation-State Law.'" *+972 Magazine*, July 12, 2017. Accessed October 25, 2021. https://www.972mag.com/the-redundancy-of-israels-jewish-nation-state-law/.

Amnesty International. "Israel's Apartheid against Palestinians: A Cruel System of Domination and a Crime Against Humanity." February 1, 2022. https://www.

amnesty.ca/news/israels-apartheid-against-palestinians-a-cruel-system-of-domination-and-a-crime-against-humanity/.

Anderson, Mary B. *Do No Harm: How Aid Can Support Peace—or War*. Boulder, CO: Lynne Rienner Publishers, 1999.

BADIL Resource Center. "Denial of Palestinian Use and Access to Land: Summary of Israeli Laws and Policies." Accessed May 7, 2022. Bethlehem: BADIL Resource Center for Palestinian and Refugee Rights, 2022. https://www.badil.org/publications/12947.html.

Barker, Adam J. "The Contemporary Reality of Canadian Imperialism: Settler Colonialism and the Hybrid Colonial State." *American Indian Quarterly* 33, no. 3 (2009): 325–51.

Bartholomeusz, Lance. "The Mandate of UNRWA at Sixty." *Refugee Survey Quarterly* 28, no. 2–3 (2010): 452–74.

Bercuson, David. *Canada and the Birth of Israel*. Toronto: University of Toronto Press, 1985.

Boling, Gail. "The 1948 Palestinian Refugees and the Individual Right of Return: An International Law Analysis." Bethlehem: BADIL Resource Center for Palestinian Residency and Refugee Rights, 2007.

Brown, Michael. "Divergent Paths: Early Zionism in Canada and the United States." *Jewish Social Studies* 44, no. 2 (1982): 149–68.

Brynen, Rex. "Canada's Role in the Israeli-Palestine Peace Process." In *Canada and the Middle East: In Theory and in Practice*, edited by Paul Heinbecker, 73–89. Guelph, ON: Wilfred Laurier University Press, 2007.

Brynen, Rex. "Much Ado About Nothing: The Refugee Working Group and the Perils of Multicultural Quasi-Negotiation." *International Negotiation* 2, no. 2 (1997): 279–302.

Canadians for Justice and Peace in the Middle East (CJPME). "Factsheet: Attacks on Canada's Funding for UNRWA." Accessed January 18, 2020. https://www.cjpme.org/fs_202.

CBC. "TIMELINE: Oda and the Kairos Funding." News release. March 18, 2011. Accessed January 18, 2020. https://www.cbc.ca/news/politics/timeline-oda-and-the-kairos-funding-1.1027221.

CBC News. "'Canada Calls for Calm' While Abstaining from UN Vote to Nullify U.S. Move on Jerusalem." December 21, 2017. https://www.cbc.ca/news/politics/canada-jerusalem-un-1.4460257.

Chaleshtoori, Shadi. "Canadian Funding for the Only Palestinian Research Center in Israel Cut." *The Bullet*. Accessed January 18, 2020. https://socialistproject.ca/2010/04/b340/.

Chapnick, Adam. "The Canadian Middle Power Myth." *International Journal* 55, no. 2 (2000): 188–206.

Chimni, B.S. "The Geopolitics of Refugee Studies: A View from the South." *Journal of Refugee Studies* 11, no. 4 (1998): 350–74.

Coulthard, Glen. *Red Skin, White Masks: Rejecting the Colonial Politics of Recognition*. Minneapolis: University of Minnesota Press, 2014.

Csillag, Ron. "Canada Won't Rule Out Changing UNRWA Funding, in Wake of Trump's Cut." *The Canadian Jewish News*. January 19, 2018. Accessed January 18, 2020.

https://www.cjnews.com/news/canada/canada-wont-rule-changing-unrwa-funding-wake-trumps-cut.

Dua, Enakshi, Narda Razack, and Jody Nyasha Warner. "Race, Racism, and Empire: Reflections on Canada." *Social Justice* 32, no. 4 (2005): 1–10.

Dumper, M. "Future Prospects for the Palestinian Refugees." *Refugee Survey Quarterly* 28, no. 2–3 (2009): 561–87. https://academic.oup.com/rsq/article/28/2-3/561/1584650.

Engler, Yves. *Canada and Israel: Building Apartheid.* Vancouver: RED Publishing, 2010.

Erakat, Noura. "The Sovereign Right to Kill: A Critical Appraisal of Israel's Shoot to Kill Policy in Gaza." *International Criminal Law Review* 19, no. 5 (2019): 783–818.

Farah, Randa. "Palestinian Refugees: Dethroning the Nation at the Crowning of the 'Statelet'?" *Interventions* 8, no. 2 (2006): 228–52.

Farah, Randa. "UNRWA: Through the Eyes of Its Palestinian Employees." *Refugee Survey Quarterly* 28, no. 2–3 (2010): 389–411.

Farah, Randa. "Keeping an Eye on UNRWA." Al-Shabaka, January 25, 2012. Accessed May 10, 2019. http://al-shabaka.org/policy-brief/refugee-issues/keeping-eye-unrwa.

Farsoun, Samih, and Christina E. Zacharia. *Palestine and the Palestinians: A Social and Political History.* Oxford: Westview Press, 1998.

Freeman-Maloy D. "Remembering Balfour: empire, race and propaganda." *Race & Class* 59, no. 3 (2018): 3–19.

Gazit, Shlomo. "Solving the Refugee Problem: A Prerequisite for Peace." *Palestine-Israel Journal of Politics, Economics, and Culture* 11, no. 3 (1995): 65–70. http://pij.org/articles/600.

Giirsoy, Yaprak. "The Effects of the Population Exchange on the Greek and Turkish Political Regimes in the 1930s." *East European Quarterly* XLII, no. 2 (2008): 95–128.

Goldberg, David, and Tilly Shames. "The 'Good-Natured Bastard': Canada and the Middle East Refugee Question." *Israel Affairs* 10, no. 1–2 (2004): 203–20.

Government of Canada. "Canadian Policy on Key Issues in the Israeli-Palestinian Conflict," Last modified March 19, 2019. https://international.gc.ca/world-monde/international_relations-relations_internationales/mena-moan/israeli-palistinian_policy-politique_israelo-palestinien.aspx?lang=eng.

Hass, Amira. "Palestinians Are Fighting for Their Lives; Israel Is Fighting for the Occupation." *Haaretz*, October 7, 2015. Accessed January 22, 2020. https://www.haaretz.com/opinion/.premium-the-purpose-of-the-escalation-1.5406088.

Herzl, Theodor. *The Jewish State.* Accessed May 2, 2023. New York: Dover Publications, 2008[1896]. https://www.gutenberg.org/files/25282/25282-h/25282-h.htm.

Hughes, Sara Salazar. "Unbounded territoriality: territorial control, settler colonialism, and Israel/Palestine." *Settler Colonial Studies* 10, no. 2 (2020): 216–33.

Husseini, Hassan. "A "Middle Power" in Action: Canada and the Partition of Palestine." *Arab Studies Quarterly* 30, no. 3 (2008): 41–55.

Iğsiz, Asli. *Humanism in Ruins: Entangled Legacies of the Greek-Turkish Population Exchange.* Standford: Stanford University Press, 2018.

Jackson, Miriam. "Canada Citizens Fighting for Israel Given Warm Reception by Embassy." *The Union Journal*, January 17, 2020. https://theunionjournal.com/canada-citizens-fighting-for-israel-given-warm-reception-by-embassy-middle-east-monitor-7/.

Jacoby, Tami A. "Canadian Peacebuilding in the Middle East: Case Study of the Canada Fund in Israel/Palestine and Jordan." *Canadian Foreign Policy* 8, no. 1 (2000): 83–91.

Jaradat-Gassner, Ingrid.. "Political Negotiations on the Palestinian Refugee Question: Interview with Salim Tamari." *Middle East Report* no. 201 (1996): 7–9. https://www.jstor.org/stable/3012760.

Jefferess, David. "Responsibility, Nostalgia, and the Mythology of Canada as a Peacekeeper." *University of Toronto Quarterly* 78, no. 2 (2009): 709–27. doi:10.1353/utq.0.0564.

Juneau, Thomas. *Canada and Saudi Arabia: A Deeply Flawed but Necessary Partnership.* Calgary: Canadian Global Affairs Institute, 2016.

Kanafani, Ghassan. *The 1936–1939 Revolt in Palestine.* Committee of Democratic Palestine. Accessed May 7, 2022. https://www.marxists.org/archive/kanafani/1972/revolt.htm.

Katz, Yossi. "Transfer of Population as a Solution to International Disputes." *Political Geography* 11, no. 1 (1992): 55–72. doi:10.1016/0962-6298(92)90019-P.

Kay, Zachariah. *Diplomacy of Prudence: Canada and Israel, 1948–1958.* Montreal: McGill-Queen's University Press, 1996.

Kay, Zachariah. *The Diplomacy of Impartiality.* Waterloo, ON: Wilfred Laurier University Press, 2010.

Kent, Melissa. "Canada Again Votes at UN to Back Palestinian Self-Determination." *CBC News*, December 18, 2019. Accessed January 22, 2020. https://www.cbc.ca/news/world/palestine-israel-canada-un-1.5401124.

Khalidi, Walid, ed. *All That Remains: The Palestinian Villages Occupied and Depopulated by Israel in 1948.* Washington, DC: Institute for Palestine Studies, 1992.

Klassen, Jerome. "Canada and the New Imperialism: The Economics of a Secondary Power." *Studies in Political Economy* 83, no. 1 (2009): 163–90.

Krebs, Mike, and Dana M. Olwan. "'From Jerusalem to the Grand River, Our Struggles Are One': Challenging Canadian and Israeli Settler Colonialism." *Settler Colonial Studies* 2, no. 2 (2012): 138–64.

Lapidoth, Ruth. "Legal Aspects of the Palestinian Refugee Question." Jerusalem Center for Public Affairs, *Jerusalem Letter / Viewpoints* no. 485, September 1, 2002. Accessed January 22, 2020. http://www.jcpa.org/jl/vp485.htm.

Lerner, Peter. "Less American Aid to Palestinians Means More Violence Against Israelis." *Haaretz*, January 4, 2018, Opinion. https://www.haaretz.com/opinion/less-american-aid-to-palestinians-means-more-violence-against-israelis-1.5630442.

Lloyd, David. "Settler Colonialism and the State of Exception: The Example of Palestine/Israel." *Settler Colonial Studies* 2, no. 1 (2012): 59–80.

Lynk, Michael. "Closer to Power Than Justice: International Law and the Israeli-Palestinian Conflict: Keynote Speech." Ottawa, Ontario, Canada, February 19, 2019.

Mackey, Eva. "Tricky Myths: Settler Pasts and Landscapes of Innocence." In *Settling and Unsettling Memories: Essays in Canadian Public History*, edited by Peter Hodgins, 310–39. Toronto: University of Toronto Press, 2012.

Masalha, Nur. *The Politics of Denial: Israel and the Palestinian Refugee Problem*. London: Pluto Press, 2003.

McKercher, Asa. *Canada and the World Since 1867*. London: Bloomsbury Publishing, 2019.

Morgensen, Scott L. "Theorising Gender, Sexuality and Settler Colonialism: An Introduction." *Settler Colonial Studies* 2, no. 2 (2012): 2–22. doi:10.1080/2201 473X.2012.10648839.

Morris, Benny. *The Birth of the Palestinian Refugee Problem, 1947–1949*. Cambridge: Cambridge University Press, 1988.

Mueller, John, and Karl Mueller. "Sanctions of Mass Destruction." *Foreign Affairs* 78, no. 3 (1999): 43–53.

Nadeau, Mary-Jo, and Alan Sears. "The Palestine Test: Countering the Silencing Campaign." *Studies in Political Economy* 85, no. 1 (2010): 7–33.

Naiman, Neil. "IJV-Vancouver Letter to Mayor Ken Sim: Don't Adopt the Divisive IHRA." *Independent Jewish Voices*, November 8, 2023. Accessed May 2, 2023. https://www. ijvcanada.org/no-ihra-vancouver/.

National Post. "Trudeau Says Canada's UN Vote on Palestinian Self-Determination Not a Shift in Policy on Israel." December 9, 2019. Accessed January 22, 2020. https:// nationalpost.com/news/trudeau-says-un-vote-not-a-shift-in-canadas-steadfast-support-israel.

Page, Robert. "The Boer War and Canadian Imperialism." *Canadian Historical Association*, Historical Booklet no. 44 (1987): 1–25. Accessed May 10, 2019. https://cha-shc.ca/_ uploads/5c38abb4e8d8a.pdf.

Pappé, Ilan. *The Ethnic Cleansing of Palestine*. Oxford: Oneworld Publications, 2006.

Parliament of Canada. "House of Common Debates: 27th Parliament, 2nd Session." June 6, 1967–7 July, 1967. http://parl.canadiana.ca/view/oop.debates_HOC2702_02/ 113?r=0&s=1.

Parliament of Canada. "House of Commons. Debates Archives: 22nd Parliament, 3rd Session." January 10, 1956–August 14, 1956. http://parl.canadiana.ca/view/oop. debates_HOC2203_01/763?r=0&s=1.

Peters, J., and O. Gal. "Israel, UNRWA, and the Palestinian Refugee Issue." *Refugee Survey Quarterly* 28, no. 2–3 (2009): 588–606. doi:10.1093/rsq/hdp035.

Platt, Elizabeth R. "The Determinants of Canada's South African Policy (1968 to 1984)." Master's thesis, McMaster University, 1986. Accessed May 10, 2019. https:// macsphere.mcmaster.ca/bitstream/11375/13220/1/fulltext.pdf.

Prime Minister's Office. "Statement by the Prime Minister on Israel Independence Day." April 26, 2023. Accessed May 2, 2023. https://pm.gc.ca/en/news/ statements/2023/04/26/statement-prime-minister-israel-independence-day.

Raska, Jan. "Forgotten Experiment: Canada's Resettlement of Palestinian Refugees, 1955–1956." *Histoire Sociale/Social History* 48, no. 97 (2015): 445–73. doi:10.1353/his.2015.0034.

Razack, Sherene H. "From the 'Clean Snows of Petawawa': The Violence of Canadian Peacekeepers in Somalia." *Cultural Anthropology* 15, no. 1 (2000): 127–63.

Razack, Sherene H. *Dark Threats & White Knights: The Somalia Affair, Peacekeeping, and the New Imperialism.* Toronto: University of Toronto Press, 2004.

Razack, Sherene H. "When Place Becomes Race." In *Race and Racialization: Essential Readings*, edited by Tania Das Gupta, 74–82. Toronto: Canadian Scholars' Press, 2007.

Rempel, Terry. "The Ottawa Process: Workshop on Compensation and Palestinian Refugees." *Journal of Palestine Studies* 29, no. 1 (1999): 36–49.

Robinson, Andrew. "Canada's Credibility as an Actor in the Middle East Peace Process: The Refugee Working Group, 1992–2000." *International Journal* 66, no. 3 (2011): 695–718.

Roy, Sara. "Trump's Move to Slash Aid for Palestinian Refugees Will Lead to Tragedy." *Institute for Palestine Studies*, January 25, 2018. https://www.palestine-studies.org/en/node/232095.

Rubin, Gil S. "Vladimir Jabotinsky and Population Transfers Between Eastern Europe and Palestine" *The Historical Journal* 62, no. 2: 495–517.

Sa'di, Ahmad H., and Lila Abu-Lughod, eds. *Nakba: Palestine, 1948, and the Claims of Memory.* New York: Columbia University Press, 2007.

Said, Edward. "The Idea of Palestine in the West." MERIP *Reports* 70 (1978): 3–11. Accessed May 10, 2019. https://www.jstor.org/stable/3011576?seq=1#page_scan_tab_contents.

Said, Edward W. *Orientalism.* New York: Vintage Books, 1979.

Salamanca, Omar J. "Past Is Present: Settler Colonialism in Palestine." *Settler Colonial Studies* 2, no. 1 (2012): 1–8.

Schiff, Benjamin N. *Refugees Unto the Third Generation: UN Aid to Palestinians.* Contemporary Issues in the Middle East. Syracuse, NY: Syracuse University Press, 1995.

Schwartz, Adi. "Dismantle UNRWA." The Begin-Sadat Center for Strategic Studies, July 14, 2017. Accessed May 1, 2023. https://besacenter.org/dismantle-unrwa/#:~:text=EXECUTIVE%20SUMMARY%3A%20In%20a%20surprising,decades%2Dold%20policy%20as%20well.

Shipley, Tyler. "The New Canadian Imperialism and the Military Coup in Honduras." *Latin American Perspectives* 40, no. 5 (2013): 44–61.

Shohat, Ella. "The Invention of Judeo-Arabic: Nation, Partition, and the Linguistic Imaginary." *Interventions: International Journal of Postcolonial Studies* 19, no. 2 (2017): 153–200.

Simons, Geoff. *The Scourging of Iraq: Sanctions, Law and Natural Justice.* London: Palgrave Macmillan, 1998.

Simpson, Audra. *Mohawk Interruptus: Political Life Across the Border of Settler States*. Durham, NC: Duke University Press, 2014.

Smith, Andrea. "Indigeneity, Settler Colonialism, White Supremacy." In *Racial Formation in the Twenty-First Century*, edited by Daniel M. HoSang, 66–90. Berkeley: University of California Press, 2012.

Strindberg, Anders. "The Damascus-Based Alliance of Palestinian Forces: A Primer." *Journal of Palestine Studies* 29, no. 3 (April 1, 2000): 60–76.

Stultz, Newell M. "The Apartheid Issue at the General Assembly: Stalemate or Gathering Storm?" *African Affairs* 86, no. 342 (1987): 25–45.

Tauber, Eliezer. *Personal Policy Making: Canada's Role in the Adoption of the Partition Plan*. Westport: Greenwood Press, 2002.

Teigrob, Robert. " "Which Kind of Imperialism?": Early Cold War Decolonization and Canada–US Relations." *Canadian Review of American Studies* 37, no. 3 (2007): 403–30.

Tomeh, George J. "When the UN Dropped the Palestinian Question." *Journal of Palestine Studies* 4, no. 1 (1974): 15–30.

US Department of State. "The Framework for Cooperation between the United Nations Relief and Works Agency for Palestine Refugees in the Near East and the United States of America 2021–2022." Accessed October 25, 2021. https://www.state.gov/wp-content/uploads/2021/07/2021-2022-US-UNRWA-Framework-Signed.pdf.

United Nations Relief and Works Agency for Palestine Refugees (UNRWA). "UNRWA Condemns Placement of Rockets, for a Second Time, in One of Its Schools: Agency Demands Full Respect for the Sanctity of Its Premises in Gaza." News release. July 22, 2014. Accessed January 18, 2020. https://www.unrwa.org/newsroom/press-releases/unrwa-condemns-placement-rockets-second-time-one-its-schools.

Veracini, Lorenzo. *Settler Colonialism: A Theoretical Overview*. Cambridge Imperial and Post-Colonial Studies Series. Basingstoke: Palgrave Macmillan, 2010.

Vucetic, Srdjan. "A Nation of Feminist Arms Dealers? Canada and Military Exports." *International Journal* 72, no. 4 (2017): 503–19.

Wildeman, Jeremy. "Undermining the Democratic Process: The Canadian Government Suppression of Palestinian Development Aid Projects," *The Canadian Journal for Middle East Studies* 2, no. 1 (August 24, 2017).

Wildeman, Jeremy. "Why Aid Projects Are Doomed to Fail." *The Electronic Intifada*, September 6, 2012. Accessed May 10, 2019. https://electronicintifada.net/content/why-aid-projects-palestine-are-doomed-fail/11642.

Wolfe, Patrick. "Settler Colonialism and the Elimination of the Native." *Journal of Genocide Research* 8, no. 4 (2006): 387–409.

Woodley, Thomas. "Refugee Kids Deserve Our Help Not Your Awful Rhetoric." *Huffington Post*, September 1, 2017. https://www.huffpost.com/archive/ca/entry/palestinian-refugee-kids-deserve-our-help-not-your-awful-rhetoric_a_23189838.

Wyld, Adrian. "Liberals Restore Funding to Controversial Palestinian Aid Agency." *The Globe and Mail*. Accessed November 16, 2016. https://www.theglobeandmail.com/

news/politics/liberals-restore-funding-to-controversial-palestinian-aid-agency/article32877755/.

Zahar, Marie-Joelle. "Talking One Talk, Walking Another: Norm Entrepreneurship and Canada's Foreign Policy in the Middle East." In *Canada and the Middle East: In Theory and Practice*, edited by Paul Heinbecker and Bessma Momani, 45–72. Waterloo, ON: Wilfrid Laurier University Press, 2007.

Zilbershats, Yaffa, and Nimra Goren-Amitai. "Return of Palestinian Refugees to the State of Israel." Translated from Hebrew. Accessed May 10, 2019. http://din-online.info/pdf/mz7.pdf.

Zureik, Elia. "Palestinian Refugees and Peace." *Journal of Palestine Studies* 24, no. 1 (1994): 5–17.

4

ENFORCING THE SETTLER CONTRACT

Repression of Palestine Solidarity in Canadian Colonial Multiculturalism

AZEEZAH KANJI

Introduction

Increasingly it is becoming commonplace to understand the political, economic, militaristic, diplomatic, and legal[1] forms of mutual support and engagement between Canada, the United States, and Israel as modes of settler solidarity: cooperation between states constituted through settler-colonial violence against Indigenous nations.[2] This framing also informs and infuses critical (re-)conceptualizations and practices of solidarity, from Turtle Island to Palestine, between those contesting and seeking to decolonize settler-colonial polities. It is a recognition that activism in Canada for Palestinian rights does not occur from a place of innocence, but rather from one that continues to be produced and permeated by the same genres of settler-colonial violence being enacted against the Palestinian people.[3]

99

Settler colonialism, as Patrick Wolfe observed in an oft-quoted aphorism, is a "structure, not an event."[4] In other words, settler colonialism is not an instance of violent erasure located in a past that has been transcended, but a structure requiring perpetual reproduction, maintenance, and stabilization through ongoing investment in processes of dispossession, sovereign exertion, and control—accompanied by attempts to naturalize these processes so as to render them invisible, and therefore unassailable. In *Red Skin, White Masks*, Glen Coulthard pointed to the multiple vectors of power comprising the matrix of settler-colonial statehood: "capitalism, patriarchy, white supremacy, and the totalizing character of state power interact with one another to form the constellation of power relations that sustain colonial patterns of behaviour, structures, and relationships."[5] As Coulthard argues, "colonialism, as a structure of domination predicated on [Indigenous] dispossession, is not 'a thing,' but rather the sum effect of the diversity of interlocking oppressive social relations that constitute it."[6]

Canada and Israel are collaborators across borders in multiple modalities of governmental power central to the perpetuation of settler-colonial rule in both states, including surveillance, securitization, policing, incarceration, militarization, and border control.[7] At the same time, the Canadian state is vigilant in punishing those who challenge these transnational collusions of settler power by advocating against Israel's colonization of Palestinian lands, people, and sovereignty. Official political recriminations of the Boycott, Divestment, Sanctions (BDS) campaign pressuring Israel to comply with international law, alongside private policing of Palestine solidarity activism diffused through academic and other institutions, combine to create a climate of repression and punishment.[8]

Previous analyses have remarked on the apparently oxymoronic fact that the language of multiculturalism and liberal anti-racism has frequently been deployed in these efforts to repress activism against Israel's racist colonial policies.[9] In the Canadian context, Rafeef Ziadeh has documented how exercises of punishment, subjugation, and marginalization against Palestine solidarity activists—institutional attacks against Israeli Apartheid Week; the defunding of Arab/Palestinian ethnocultural organizations, development organizations, and research bodies deemed impermissibly pro-Palestinian; and the campaign to ban Queers Against Israeli Apartheid from marching in Pride Toronto—have been rationalized by appeals to multiculturalist logic: accusations of anti-semitism, calls for balance and dialogue, and representations of Palestine solidary activists as "extremists" juxtaposed against voices of "moderation."[10] James Cairns' and Susan Ferguson's analysis of the Canadian Parliamentary Coalition to Combat Antisemitism likewise revealed that invocations of human rights, liberalism, and pluralism were pervasive in submissions to the Coalition castigating criticisms of Israel's anti-Palestinian policies as anti-semitic.[11]

As Neve Gordon and Nicola Perugini incisively demonstrated in *The Human Right to Dominate*, Israel's regular appeals to international human rights discourse to justify its project of colonial domination do not represent a perversion of human rights' essential nature, so much as an exploitation of deeply embedded structural tensions and ambiguities arising from human rights' state-centric formulation and colonial genealogy.[12] Along similar lines, I want to consider here how the amenability of liberal multiculturalist discourse to suppression of Palestine solidarity is not accidental, but rather a product of Canadian multiculturalism's colonial foundations: its development as a tool to manage difference within a white supremacist colonial framework, through the reconfiguration of racial hierarchies as manifestations of cultural diversity disconnected from matters of land, sovereignty, and coloniality.[13]

As Wolfe noted in *Traces of History*, settler colonial structures are sustained through tactics that may appear superficially distinct, or even antithetical, but are united by an underlying logic of elimination and subjugation.[14] And so, colonial formations of power have been advanced and entrenched both through exercises of extrusion *and* exercises of assimilation,[15] through exclusion from the law *and* forceful inclusion in the law,[16] through political denial *and* conditional forms of political recognition.[17] Far from signifying weakness, the methodological flexibility of settler colonialism is a source of its strength, durability, and resilience. It is not surprising, then, that liberal state multiculturalism and anti-racism would also serve as accessories (in the dual senses of aid and adornment) to settler colonialism's racial project.

In what follows, I explore the entanglement of Canadian multiculturalism with intertwined colonial discourses of anti-Indigeneity, Orientalism, and anti-semitism, and the implications of this entanglement as it played out in three recent instances involving governmental attacks on Palestine solidarity in the name of multiculturalism/anti-racism: Toronto City Council's efforts to ban the annual Al-Quds Day Rally; the Ontario Anti-Racism

Directorate's exclusion of organizations critical of Zionist policies; and Prime Minister Justin Trudeau's criticism of BDS in an official apology for Canada's rejection of a ship of Jewish refugees, the MS St Louis, during World War II. Erasure of the Canadian state's involvement in interpenetrating forms of colonial and imperial violence against Indigenous peoples, from Turtle Island to Palestine,[18] undergirds and circumscribes multiculturalism's liberatory possibilities. The repression of Palestine solidarity activism in Canada serves as a productive site for surveying multiculturalism's colonial horizons.

Orientalism, Anti-Semitism, Settler Colonialism

In *Orientalism*, Edward Said suggested that Islamophobia was a "secret sharer" of anti-semitism,[19] and indeed, the figures of the "Jew" and "Arab/Muslim" (variously configured at different points in time also as Moor, Saracen, and Turk) have been intimately connected in the proto-racist discourses involved in the long-durée production of Christian European identity.[20] Centuries of European Christian polemic depicted, "the Jew [as] the theological (and internal) enemy" and, "the Muslim [as] the political (and external) enemy," as Gil Anidjar explicated in *The Jew, the Arab: A History of the Enemy*.[21] Medieval European authors often portrayed Islam as a perverse reincarnation of the "law of Moses,"[22] and a common stock of stereotypes was applied to dehumanize and demonize Jewish and Muslim populations.[23] Due to the association and conflation of Jew and Muslim, calls for Crusades on Muslim-held lands frequently led to pogroms against Jewish communities within Europe.[24] In 1215, the Catholic Church's Fourth Lateran Council imposed the same clothing restrictions on Jews and Muslims, "as if the two infidel races were halves of a single body of Semitic aliens," in the words of Geraldine Heng.[25]

Conspiracy theories of anti-Christian collaboration between Muslims and Jews were recurrent in medieval Europe: Jewish communities were accused, for example, of aiding Muslim troops against the Christian Visigoths in Spain in the eighth century, working with the Fatimid Empire to destroy the Holy Sepulchre in Jerusalem in the eleventh century, and plotting with the Muslim king of Granada in the fourteenth century to infect Christendom with leprosy.[26] "The accusation that Jews or Muslims wish to dominate the world is ironic," observed Ivan Kalmar and Tariq Ramadan, "given that

102   *Enforcing the Settler Contract*

historically it was *Christianity* that first used to worship of the One God as the justification for building a world-wide empire."[27]

In the extension of this empire-building project to the "New World," the figures of the "Jew" and the "Muslim" served as key points of reference and comparison in Europeans' development of colonial relationships with the Indigenous peoples of the Americas.[28] The temporal coincidence of the final Christian *conquista* of the Muslim caliphate in Al-Andalus with the fall of Granada—leading to the forced conversion, inquisition, and ultimately expulsion of Jewish and Muslim communities from what would become European Spain—and Christopher Columbus's "discovery" of the "New World," both in 1492, was not coincidental. Rather, these two events, both foundational in the construction of colonial modernity, were causally connected (Columbus having received royal assent for his mission from Ferdinand and Isabella following their triumph in Al-Andalus) and inaugurated the relational racialization of populations abjected by European domination on both sides of the Atlantic.[29]

Practices of epistemicide, religious surveillance and persecution, sexual demonization, and legal rationalization developed in European interactions with Muslim and Jewish populations were transferred to and adapted for the Americas—for example, the concept of *limpieza de sangre* (purity of blood), and myths of sexual and gender deviance.[30] The doctrine of *terra nullius* underlying European assertion of sovereignty over Indigenous land in the Americas—upon which Canadian state sovereignty still rests despite formal Supreme Court repudiations of the doctrine, as John Borrows has pointed out[31]—was originally rooted in an eleventh-century papal edict permitting the seizure of the lands and sovereignty of non-Christian peoples in the Crusades.[32] However, the figure of the "New World" Indigenous Other was not simply superimposed onto the pre-existing template of the "Old World" religious others (the Jew and the Muslim), but also distinguished from them. The casting out of the Indigenous of the Americas from the ambit of humanity, with their depiction as "people without religion" in contrast to Jews and Muslims as "people with the wrong religion," permitted the development of new modes of racial and genocidal violence, which then travelled to other sites of European colonial encounter.[33]

The two halves of the "single body of Semitic aliens" were split with the induction of the "Jewish nation" into the imperial project through the colonization of Palestine; as Justin Trudeau remarked in his MS St Louis apology, discussed below, "It would take new leadership, a new world order, *and the creation of the State of Israel*, a homeland for the Jewish people, for Canada to amend its laws and begin to dismantle the policies that had legitimized and propagated anti-Semitism."[34] This indicates the truth in Enrique Dussel's observation that the route to recognition of full ontological humanity in the paradigm of colonial modernity lies through embodiment of the *ego conquiro* (the conquering self), the condition precedent of the Cartesian *ego cogito* (who thinks, therefore he is).[35]

The burden of the demonic trace of anti-semitism originally shared by the Muslim/Arab and the Jew is now borne by the Muslim/Arab alone, and the umbilical connection between the two rendered a "secret." "Islamism, and for the less sophisticated or politically correct, Islam itself, is now the abject...of the demonizing aspects of Semitism, of which the Jews have more or less managed to free themselves," as Ivan Kalmar notes. "Anti-Islamism is the new anti-Semitism."[36]

Multicultural Occlusions

Canada's colonial structure continues to be reproduced through a multiplicity of incommensurable but relational racializing practices, which locate their subjects in distinct, and sometimes competing or conflicting, positions with respect to the settler state.[37] For example, conceptualizations and methods of "counter-terrorism" pioneered by Israel in its colonial project, and adopted by Western liberal democracies against Muslim populations domestically and internationally,[38] have also been wielded against Indigenous anti-colonial land and water defenders,[39] even while anti-Islamophobia activists in Canada have often been complicit in the erasure of Indigenous sovereignty, orienting their activism around claiming belonging in and rights from the settler state.[40]

Multiculturalism, as both rhetorical posture and policy, has the effect of abstracting racialized communities from the "different histories,"[41] lying behind the distinct regimes of differentiation through which they have been constituted: the "specific ways that mark out and reproduce the unequal relationships into which Europeans have co-opted these populations,"[42] some of which have been elaborated in the previous section. The reconfiguration of racial hierarchies as commensurable cultural differences—disconnected from particular material histories of expropriation, exploitation, elimination, and militarization—erases the fundamental differences in positionality between Indigenous nations and non-Indigenous racialized communities, as well as among various non-Indigenous racialized communities.[43] In this framing, the Canadian state appears as the neutral vertical mediator of horizontal cultural diversity, obscuring the state's own existential dependence on Indigenous dispossession and perpetuation of racial differentiation beneath the veneer of formal citizenal equality.[44] Multiculturalism, then, serves to rearticulate the state's constitutive "racial" and "settler contracts"[45] in a putatively post-racial idiom.

The utility of multiculturalist and liberal anti-racist discourses for settler-colonial projects was evident in three recent examples of Palestine solidarity suppression in Canada.

The Campaign Against Al-Quds Day

In September 2017, Toronto City Councillor James Pasternak put forward an inquiry regarding the feasibility of preventing "hate rallies" from congregating on city or provincial property in Toronto.[46] The question of hate rallies gathering in the city was, ostensibly, a subject of legitimate concern, with Toronto serving as a breeding ground for white supremacist, neo-Nazi, anti-immigrant, and anti-Muslim groups, such as the Soldiers of Odin, PEGIDA Canada (Patriotic Europeans Against the Islamization of the Occident), the Worldwide Coalition Against Islam, and the Jewish Defence League.[47] However, it was clear from Pasternak's inquiry that the primary source of his consternation was not these specimens of the far right, but rather Palestine solidarity activism. The title of his inquiry referred exclusively and specifically to the annual Al-Quds Day Rally as an example of the type of "hate rallies" he was seeking to prohibit.

Pasternak's efforts against Al-Quds Day represent the extension of his personal crusade against Palestine solidarity activism. In 2012, Pasternak played a central role in City Council efforts to bar the group Queers Against Israeli Apartheid from participation in the Pride Parade, on threat of denial of funding for Pride Toronto; "we don't want world conflicts here [in Toronto]," he averred, "people come here to avoid world conflicts."[48] In the text of his 2017 inquiry, Pasternak described the Al-Quds Day event in Toronto as an "anti-Semitic" and "hate-infested rally," before proceeding to also mention the potential "threat" posed by, "white supremacist and neo-Nazi rallies...similar to those in the United States," being hosted in the city.[49] Thus, his framing inverted reality to render activism for Palestine the primary source of actualized hate, and white supremacy a secondary, and as yet only prospective and unrealized, danger.

Racial animus was depicted as central to Palestine solidarity, while white supremacy was represented as a phenomenon confined to the fringes of Canadian society, an exogenous import from the United States. This functioned to simultaneously obscure the foundational investment of the Canadian state in anti-Indigenous, anti-Black, anti-Muslim, and anti-Arab racial logic,[50] the long history of white supremacist groups functioning openly and often at the center of Canadian politics,[51] and the fact that Toronto itself continues to be a site of colonial violence against Indigenous peoples and erasure of sovereign Indigenous presence.[52]

At the Council hearings on Pasternak's motion, the National Director of the anti-Muslim hate group Jewish Defence League Canada was permitted to expound at length on how "crowds are incited to hate Jews" at Al-Quds Day events, without being asked to adduce any substantiation.[53] This was in stark contrast to the treatment of a community activist recounting the findings of human rights organizations regarding Israel's colonial policies, who was precipitately cut off and had her speaking time curtailed by the chair of the meeting, Toronto Mayor John Tory.[54] Tory's was an overt act of silencing against the background invisibilization of Canadian settler colonialism. The motion to refer the inquiry for further consultation passed 8 to 2.[55]

Ontario Progressive Conservative Party leader Doug Ford endorsed the effort to eradicate Al-Quds Day in his first official pronouncement as the Premier of Ontario, proclaiming his government's commitment to ensuring that, "events like Al-Quds Day, which calls for the killing of an entire civilian population in Israel, are no longer part of the landscape in Ontario."[56] He did this even while reversing and refusing to implement measures mitigating the impact of genocidal policies on Indigenous communities in the province,[57] including by debilitation of the Ontario Anti-Racism Directorate.[58]

Anti-Zionism in the Antinomies of the Anti-Racism Directorate

The Ontario Anti-Racism Directorate (ARD) was established in February 2016 under the auspices of the Liberal provincial government headed by Premier Kathleen Wynne, with the mission of, "lead[ing] the government's anti-racism initiatives to build a more inclusive society, and work[ing] to identify, address and prevent systemic racism in government policy,

106   *Enforcing the Settler Contract*

legislation, programs and services."[59] Its mandated activities included collection of data in several areas of governmental activity implicated in systemic racism (health, education, child welfare, and criminal justice), research and education projects, and consultation with committees composed of members from communities affected by the forms of racism lying at the center of the Directorate's focus (anti-Indigenous, anti-Black, Islamophobic, and anti-Semitic).[60]

The institution of the ARD was a result of sustained advocacy by anti-racism organizations,[61] and its effective dismantling by the Progressive Conservative government that succeeded the Liberals has been condemned as seriously detrimental to efforts to address systemic racism in the province.[62] Precisely because the ARD in its previous incarnation was hailed as being at the vanguard of governmental approaches to rectification of systemic racism, scrutiny of its restrictions and contradictions is valuable for appraising the critical limits of anti-racism initiatives promulgated by the settler-colonial state.

The Directorate's approach to understanding and addressing the problem of systemic racism was laid out in *A Better Way Forward: Ontario's 3-Year Anti-Racism Strategic Plan*.[63] The Plan identified the specific material histories behind the forms of systemic racism with which it is concerned: "histories of slavery, colonization and institutions of our past continue to shape the present and create a further gap between racialized and Indigenous people and others";[64] and purported to distinguish the ARD's "anti-racist" approach from that of multiculturalism: "anti-racism [...is] different from other approaches that focus on multiculturalism or diversity because it acknowledges that systemic racism exists and actively confronts the unequal power dynamic between groups and the structures that sustain it."[65]

Despite this critique of multiculturalist logic, however, the ARD remained trapped within many of the same colonial strictures that delimit liberal state multiculturalism, and so reproduced similar antinomies. Most salient was the failure to problematize the settler foundations of the Canadian state itself, which was positioned in the Directorate's Strategic Plan as a *solution* to systemic racism—"government has a leading role to play in eliminating systemic racism"[66]—rather than conceiving of government as a *manifestation* of settler colonialism. Thus, it was a formulation that paradoxically bolstered racially constituted settler sovereignty in the claimed service of anti-racism, foreclosing decolonial trajectories of action.

AZEEZAH KANJI 107

In *A Better Way Forward*'s colonial dead-end, contemporary racism appeared largely as a residue of the past—"history that goes back hundreds of years resulted in systemic racism that impacts Indigenous and racialized people today, and change won't happen overnight"[67] —thereby masking the state's continued investment in maintaining the "colonial present,"[68] with colonial and imperial actions directed against racialized communities. Policies actively perpetuating the dispossession and elimination of Indigenous nations—for example, the provincial government's long-standing refusal to remediate the mercury poisoning at Grassy Narrows,[69] and the appropriation of unceded Indigenous territories for the construction of Enbridge's Line 9 pipeline[70]—were completely elided in the Strategic Plan's account of colonialism's current reverberations.

The ARD's conceptualization of anti-Muslim racism was similarly disso-ciated from state policies committed to the securitization, military invasion, and occupation of Muslim populations. Instead, the problem was reduced to the perpetration of "hate crimes" and "Islamophobic behaviour"[71] by private individuals, devoid of actual context: a focus that persisted despite repeated critique by members of the Directorate's anti-Islamophobia subcommittee. Instead, Islamophobia was construed primarily as an issue of interpersonal rather than structural violence, analogous and comparable to anti-semi-tism (although implicitly of lesser magnitude by that metric, since Jewish communities are the more frequent target of reported hate crimes according to Statistics Canada data[72]). Indeed, Islamophobia and anti-semitism were consistently paired in ARD analysis documents[73] and discussions as commensurable phenomena: incidents of private aggression committed by non-state actors against groups defined by religious identity.

In this framework, forms of state-sponsored violence against Muslims and Arabs, including the Canadian and Ontario governments' complicity with and subsidization of Israel's colonial policies,[74] were rendered illeg-ible as subjects of anti-racist concern; there was no space to address the issue on the Islamophobia subcommittee, and efforts to raise it were received with silence. Civil society solidarity with Palestine, then, figured in the Directorate's field of vision not as an exercise of resistance to racism, since colonial racism against Palestinians was not simply unacknowledged but *unacknowledgeable*. On the contrary, such solidarity was vulnerable to being interpreted as a source of anti-Jewish racism itself. This danger was both signalled and compounded by the ARD anti-semitism subcommittee's

108   *Enforcing the Settler Contract*

intransigent refusal to include Jewish organizations critical of the conflation of anti-Zionism with anti-semitism, such as Independent Jewish Voices and the United Jewish Peoples' Order, even while Israel advocacy and Zionist groups were accorded copious representation.[75]

At a town hall in Ottawa in January 2018, then-Premier of Ontario Kathleen Wynne cited the work of the ARD as a response to the threat of anti-semitism allegedly posed by Palestine solidarity movements such as BDS on university campuses,[76] echoing her previous denunciation of BDS as a, "position that promotes or encourages anti-Semitism," while on a provincial government business mission to Israel in May 2016.[77]

No Country for BDS

Like former Liberal Premier Wynne, Liberal Prime Minister Justin Trudeau has issued repeated condemnations of the BDS movement,[78] including in an official apology made in November 2018 for the 1939 MS St Louis incident, when the Canadian government turned away a boat of Jewish refugees fleeing the Nazi Holocaust.[79] The refoulement of the MS St Louis occurred against a backdrop of widespread and institutionalized anti-semitism and racism, including immigration policies enforcing the exclusion and marginalization of a wide spectrum of "non-preferred [i.e., non-white] races,"[80] as a manifestation of the leading role government has played in establishing and reinforcing systemic racism in Canada.[81]

Immigration and refugee policies have been a central component of settler-colonial state formations—advancing the desiderata of populating the territory with white settlers through historically racist selection criteria,[82] while simultaneously displaying the state's control over borders carved out on Indigenous land,[83] in a paradigmatic display of colonial sovereignty. The site of the MS St Louis's rejection, Halifax Harbour, is also a site of ongoing colonial erasure: Halifax is the unceded Mikmaw territory of Kjipuktuk, the Great Harbour,[84] and Halifax Harbour itself the location of an Indigenous community, Turtle Grove, that was "erased"[85] by the 1917 Explosion. Turtle Grove remained in ruins and uninhabitable more than a century later, even while the surrounding settler communities were rebuilt shortly after the disaster.[86]

In *Exalted Subjects: Studies in the Making of Race and Nation in Canada*, Sunera Thobani showed how Canadian national identity has been forged through exaltation of "the 'preferred race' settler," differentiated from both "the Aboriginal, marked for physical and cultural extinction," and "the 'non-preferred race' immigrant, marked as stranger and sojourner, an unwelcome intruder whose lack of Christian faith, inherent deviant tendencies, and unchecked fecundity all threatened the nation's survival."[87] The expunging of explicitly racist categories from Canada's immigration regime with official state embrace of multiculturalism has co-existed with the persistence and even expansion of the exclusion, marginalization, and precaritization of racialized migrants.[88] This includes practices of pre-emption to intercept "undesirable" migrants long before they reach Canadian territory,[89] treaties such as the Canada–US Safe Third Country Agreement that restrict the right of asylum seekers to claim refuge at the border,[90] and programs enabling the exploitation of labour from the Global South without provision of secure citizenship status.[91]

As Sean Rehaag and Sharry Aiken pointed out in an op-ed in the *Toronto Star*, "Canada continues to do everything it can to prevent asylum seekers from reaching Canadian territory and thereby accessing all these rights . . .If [Trudeau's] apology is sincere, he should also explain why his government continues to implement policies to keep modern day asylum seekers out of the country—including those fleeing genocide and humanitarian disasters in places like Syria, Sudan, the Democratic Republic of Congo, Ethiopia, and Myanmar."[92] Indeed, Trudeau's apology for the rejection of the MS St Louis refugees coincided with his government's promise to increase deportations of migrants by 25 to 35 per cent.[93]

Such continuities in exclusionary state policies, however, disappeared into Trudeau's assertion of a radical disjuncture separating the admittedly racist past from the ostensibly post-racial present: "That's not the Canada we know today—a Canada far more generous, accepting and compassionate than it once was. A place where citizenship is first defined by principles and ideals. Not by race, nor by faith."[94] Trudeau disavowed the racism of the state while instead projecting racism onto supporters of Palestinian rights, insisting that the modern-day threat of anti-semitism emanates from, "BDS-related intimidation" that makes, "Jewish students still feel unwelcomed and uncomfortable on some of our college and university campuses," and lamenting that, "out of our entire community of nations, it is Israel whose right to exist is most widely—and wrongly—questioned."[95]

Trudeau reiterated and defended this position in a subsequent town hall at Brock University, citing the problematic "3 D's" definition of anti-semitism that identifies "demonization," "delegitimization," and "double-standards" with respect to Israel as the three aspects of the "new anti-Semitism"[96]—which, in contrast to the "old" anti-semitism, is claimed to target not Jewish people as such but rather the "Jewish state." In response to a question from the floor challenging his denigration of BDS, Trudeau maintained,

> When you have movements like BDS that single out Israel, that seek to delegitimize and in some cases demonize, when you have students on campus dealing with things like Israel apartheid weeks that make them fearful of actually attending campus events because of their religion in Canada, we have to recognize that there are things that aren't acceptable, not because of foreign policy concerns but because of Canadian values.[97]

Troublingly, Trudeau's attempt to discredit BDS relied on a definition of anti-semitism that has itself been discredited; the "3 D's" approach to anti-semitism was discarded by the Fundamental Rights Agency of the European Union in 2013, due to serious concerns about the definition's incompatibility with freedom of expression.[98] The untenability of the "3 D's" was sharply highlighted by Nathan Thrall in a recent *Guardian* column:

> According to this definition, virtually all Palestinians (and a large proportion of ultra-Orthodox Jews in Israel, who oppose Zionism for religious reasons) are guilty of antisemitism because they want Jews and Palestinians to continue living in Palestine but not within a Jewish state . . . The second D, demonization, includes "Drawing comparisons of contemporary Israeli policy to that of the Nazis"—as the Israeli army's deputy chief of staff did during a Holocaust remembrance day speech in 2016, likening the "revolting trends" in Europe and Germany in the 1930s and 40s to tendencies visible in Israel today. The last of the three Ds, applying double standards, holds that singling Israel out for criticism is "the new antisemitism." Yet practically every earlier divestment and boycott initiative around the world could be accused of double standards, including the campaign against apartheid South Africa, most of whose proponents ignored graver transgressions elsewhere, such as the concurrent genocides in Cambodia, Iraqi Kurdistan and East Timor.[99]

The irony—that the "3 D's" themselves contribute to the "demonization" of Palestinians, "delegitimization" of their rights claims, and application of "double standards" inuring Israel from critique according to international standards - is of a piece with the collection of hypocrisies, contradictions, and aporias embedded within the workings of the liberal multicultural settler-colonial state.

Conclusion

The remarkable consistency in Canadian government attitudes of suppression towards Palestine solidarity—across different levels of government (municipal, provincial, federal) and competing parties (Conservative, Liberal)—testifies to the liberatory limits of Canadian state politics, in which spectacles of political conflict and contestation occur within the tightly-circumscribed ideological parameters of colonial sovereignty. Multiculturalism discourse is one interface where the internal and external faces of Canada's colonial sovereignty meet, with the border separating the internal from the external itself a colonial artifact, a selectively permeable membrane mediating the flow of colonial power while restricting the mobility of those whom it subjects.[100]

Deepening our understanding of the interactions, intersections, and inter-articulations of structures of violence and control in Canada's projections of colonial and imperial power is crucial for building decolonial solidarity across colonial borders. As Sara Ahmed reminds us, "Solidarity does not assume that our struggles are the same struggles, or that our pain is the same pain, or that our hope is for the same future. Solidarity involves commitment, and work, as well as the recognition that even if we do not have the same feelings, or the same lives, or the same bodies, we do live on common ground."[101] For those of us located in the state currently called Canada, this ground on which we live, feel, struggle, hope, and resist is, despite persistent efforts to erase the fact, Indigenous land: Turtle Island.

Notes

1.   See, for example: Independent Jewish Voices, "Challenging Israel's and Canada's Global Pacification"; Canadian Press, "Canada–Israel 'Solidarity' Includes Defence Partnership"; Kilibarda, "Canadian and Israeli Defense."

2.   Salaita, *Inter/Nationalism*; Salaita, "Zionism and Native American Studies"; Lloyd and Wolfe, "Settler Colonial Logics and the Neoliberal Regime."

3. See, for example: Tabar and Desai, "Decolonization is a Global Project," i–xix; Krebs and Olwan, "'From Jerusalem to the Grand River'"; Jackman and Upadhyay, "Pinkwatching Israel, Whitewashing Canada"; Bhandar and Ziadah, "Acts and Omissions"; Salaita, "The Native American Model of Palestine's Future."

4. Wolfe, "Settler Colonialism and the Elimination of the Native." For an analysis of the material bases of this structure, see Coulthard, *Red Skin, White Masks*.

5. Coulthard, *Red Skin, White Masks*, 14.

6. Coulthard, 15.

7. See note 1.

8. Nadeau and Sears, "The Palestine Test: Countering the Silencing Campaign"; Sears and Nadeau, "This Is What Complicity Looks Like."

9. Salaita, *Inter/Nationalism*.

10. Ziadah, "Outside the Multicultural."

11. Cairns and Ferguson, "Human Rights Revisionism and the Canadian Parliamentary Coalition."

12. Perugini and Gordon, *The Human Right to Dominate*.

13. See, for example: Mackey, *The House of Difference: Cultural Politics and National Identity*; Bannerji, *The Dark Side of the Nation*; Thobani, *Exalted Subjects*.

14. Wolfe, *Traces of History*, 210.

15. Wolfe, 15.

16. Esmeir, *Juridical Humanity*; Anghie, "Francisco de Vitoria and the Colonial Origins of International Law."

17. Coulthard, *Red Skin, White Masks*; Povinelli, *The Cunning of Recognition*.

18. This also includes the transnational violence committed by Canada-based multinational corporations, particularly in the mining sector, to Indigenous communities in Latin America and Africa, on whose land corporate extractive activities occur. Imai, Gardner, and Weinberger, "The 'Canada Brand.'"

19. Said, *Orientalism*, 27.

20. Kalmar and Penslar, eds., *Orientalism and the Jews*.

21. Anidjar, *The Jew, The Arab*, 38.

22. Akbari, *Idols in the East*.

23. For example, both Muslims and Jews were represented as monstrous cannibals, who literally eat away at humanity—even though it was Christian soldiers who were revealed to have consumed the flesh of their adversaries during the Crusades. Popular calumnies denigrating Jews as well-poisoners and Christ-killers were also transferred to Muslims. Medieval and Renaissance paintings of the crucifixion of Christ anachronistically featured Muslim characters wearing turbans and waving the crescent flag alongside Jewish figures, while medieval English mystery plays described Jesus's natal enemy King Herod as a "Mahumetan." See Arjana, *Muslims in the Western Imagination*; Matar, "Britons and Muslims in the Early Modern Period."

24. Nirenberg, *Communities of Violence*; Heng, "The Invention of Race in the European Middle Ages."

25. Heng, "Jews, Saracens, 'Black Men,'" 255.

26. Heng; Nirenberg, *Communities of Violence*, 65.

27. Kalmar and Ramadan, "Anti-Semitism and Islamophobia," 361.

28. See, for example, the discussion of the Salamanca debate in Mastnak, "Western Hostility Toward Muslims," 37–38.

29. Maldonado-Torres, "AAR Centennial Roundtable."

30. Boyarin, *The Unconverted Self*; Matar, *Turks, Moors, and Englishmen*; Morgensen, "Settler Homonationalism"; Grosfoguel, "The Structure of Knowledge."

31. Borrows, "The Durability of Terra Nullius," 701.

32. Miller, "The Doctrine of Discovery."

33. Maldonado-Torres, "AAR Centennial Roundtable."

34. Trudeau, "Justin Trudeau on Apology to Jewish Refugees."

35. Dussel, "Anti-Cartesian Meditations"; see also Grosfoguel, "The Structure of Knowledge."

36. Kalmar, "Anti-Semitism and Islamophobia."

37. See, for example, Amadahy and Lawrence, "Indigenous Peoples and Black People in Canada."

38. Stampnitzky, *Disciplining Terror*; Brulin, "Evolution and Debates About the Concept of Terrorism."

39. Crosby and Monaghan, *Policing Indigenous Movements*.

40. As Bonita Lawrence has observed, "you have to consider the way that anti-racist struggle has been appropriated and I think it might have to do with the discourse of multiculturalism being used to control the movements of racialized peoples, to, in a sense, bind them to the state as Canadians. It can turn a fight against racism into a fight for racial equality within a settler-state." Rutherford, "Colonialism and the Indigenous Present," 12.

41. Wolfe, *Traces of History*, 2.

42. Wolfe, 2.

43. Lawrence and Dua, "Decolonizing Antiracism."

44. Mackey, *The House of Difference*.

45. Mills, *The Racial Contract*; Nichols, "Indigeneity and the Settler Contract Today"; Abu-Laban and Bakan, "The Racial Contract: Israel/Palestine and Canada."

46. Pasternak, "Administrative Inquiry Regarding Hate-Sponsored Rallies."

47. See, for example, Peña, "Shaming Racists When the Media Won't"; Lungen, "JDL Partners with Soldiers of Odin"; CBC News, "Violence Breaks Out As Protesters Clash in Nathan Phillips Square"; Csillag, "Nationalist Rally Planned in Toronto."

48. Dotan, "City Council Reaffirms Support for Pride Toronto."

49. Pasternak, "Administrative Inquiry"; see also Pasternak, "Statement: Councillor Pasternak Once Again Calls."

50. Thobani, *Exalted Subjects*; Razack, *Casting Out*.

51. Backhouse, *Colour-Coded*.

52. As Glen Coulthard notes, "Through gentrification, Native spaces in the city are now being treated as urbs nullius—urban space void of Indigenous sovereign presence." Coulthard, *Red Skin, White Masks*, 176. See Blight and King "Naming is a Good Start"; Chorley, "Disappearing into White Space"; Freeman, "'Toronto Has No History!' Indigeneity, Settler Colonialism."

53. Lascaris, "Toronto's City Council Takes Advice."

54. Lascaris.

55. City of Toronto, "Hate-Sponsored Rallies Such as Al Quds Day: Committee Decision."

56. Reevely, "Ford Promises to Ban Al-Quds Day Protests Somehow."

57. See, for example: Brake, "Ford Government's Intentions for Reconciliation"; Cohn, "On the Road to Indigenous Reconciliation; Desmarais, "Anger Grows Over Ontario Decision to End Update"; Simonpillai, "Ford Government's Cut to the Indigenous Culture Fund."

58. The author was a member of the Directorate's anti-Islamophobia subcommittee until it was disbanded in September 2018.

59. Government of Ontario, "Anti-Racism Directorate."

60. Government of Ontario.

61. Local and Regional Government Alliance on Race & Equity, "Ontario Launches Anti-Racism Strategic Plan."

62. Yang, "Advocates Fear for Future of Province's Anti-Racism Directorate"; Bueckert, "Ontario's Anti-Racism Directorate Cuts a Step Backwards"; Csillag, "Ontario Axes Anti-Racism Subcommittees."

63. Government of Ontario, "A Better Way Forward: Ontario's 3-Year Anti-Racism Strategic Plan."

64. Government of Ontario.

65. Government of Ontario.

66. Government of Ontario.

67. Government of Ontario.

68. Veracini, *The Settler Colonial Present*; Gregory, *The Colonial Present*.

69. Bruser and Poisson, "Ontario Knew About Grassy Narrows"; Star Editorial Board, "Rod Phillips—The Latest Government Minister to Betray Grassy Narrows."

70. Butler and Dubinski, "Chippewas of the Thames Vow to Continue Pipeline Fight"; Patterson, "The Ongoing Fight to Shut Down the Enbridge Line 9 Pipeline."

71. Government of Ontario, "A Better Way Forward."

72. Armstrong, "Police-Reported Hate Crime in Canada, 2017." However, as many as two-thirds of hate crimes are unreported to police, and the same police forces responsible for investigating the individualized racism of hate crimes are themselves deeply implicated in the perpetuation of systemic racism. Statistics Canada, "Police-Reported Hate Crime, 2017"; Ontario Human Rights Commission, *A Collective Impact.*

73. On file with author.

74. See note 1.
75. Epstein, "Why was a Pro-Palestinian Jewish Organization Denied a Seat"; Shannon, "Ontario Anti-Racism Directorate's Anti-Semitism Committee"; Erlichman, "Chairman of Ontario's Anti-Semitism Subcommittee."
76. Video originally at https://www.youtube.com/user/premierofontario; not currently available. For a report on the town hall, see Benzie, "Wynne gets an Earful in Ottawa Town Hall."
77. MacLeod, "Wynne Speaks Out Against BDS During Israel Trip."
78. Mastracci, "Thought Crimes in Trudeau's Canada."
79. Trudeau, "Apology to Jewish Refugees." See generally Abella and Troper, *None is Too Many*.
80. Thobani, *Exalted Subjects*.
81. These policies were the subject of another, previous apology by the Trudeau government, for the exclusion of the Komagata Maru ship bearing migrants from the British Raj in India in 1914. CBC News, "Justin Trudeau Apologizes in House."
82. See, for example, Thobani, *Exalted Subjects*; Stasiulis and Yuval-Davis, eds., *Unsettling Settler Societies*; Carey and McLisky, eds., *Creating White Australia*; Lake and Reynolds, *Drawing the Global Colour Line*.
83. See Simpson, *Mohawk Interruptus*; Walia, *Undoing Border Imperialism*.
84. McDonald, "History of Halifax, a Mi'kmaw Perspective."
85. Lagerquist, "Indigenous Community Erased."
86. "Their ancestors were ignored in the aftermath of the disaster. No records of their stories were kept. Those who survived were relocated to First Nations elsewhere in the province." Lagerquist, "Indigenous Community Erased."
87. Thobani, *Exalted Subjects*, 75.
88. See chapter 9 in this volume, by Assi and Abdelnour, discussing the struggle of working-class Palestinians to retain their identity in Canada.
89. Arbel, "Bordering the Constitution, Constituting the Border."
90. Arbel and Brenner, "Bordering on Failure: Canada-US Border Policy"; Wright, "Blair Mulling Ways to Close Loophole."
91. Faraday, "Made in Canada: How the Law Constructs Migrant Workers' Insecurity."
92. Rehaag and Aiken, "Canada a World Leader in Preventing Arrival of Refugees."
93. Ghabrial and Razlogova, "Justin Trudeau Conflating BDS with Anti-Semitism is Dangerous."
94. Trudeau, "Apology to Jewish Refugees."
95. Trudeau.
96. Maloney, "Trudeau Says He Will 'Continue to Condemn the BDS Movement.'"
97. Maloney.
98. Palestine Solidarity Legal Support, "FAQ: What to Know About Efforts to Re-define Anti-Semitism."
99. Thrall, "BDS: How a Controversial Non-Violent Movement."
100. Haiven, "The Corollary of the Derivative is the Border."

101. Ahmed, *The Cultural Politics of Emotion*, 189.

References

Abella, Irvin, and Harold Troper. *None is Too Many: Canada and the Jews of Europe 1933–1948*. Toronto: Key Porter Books, 2002.

Abu-Laban, Yasmeen, and Abigail B. Bakan. "The Racial Contract: Israel/Palestine and Canada." *Social Identities* 14, no. 5 (2008): 637–60.

Ahmed, Sara. *The Cultural Politics of Emotion*. Edinburgh: Edinburgh University Press, 2004.

Akbari, Suzanne Conklin. *Idols in the East: European Representations of Islam and the Orient, 1100–1450*. Ithaca, NY: Cornell University Press, 2009.

Amadahy, Zainab, and Bonita Lawrence. "Indigenous Peoples and Black People in Canada: Settlers or Allies?" In *Breaching the Colonial Contract: Exploration of Educational Purpose*, edited by Arlo Kempf, 105–36. Springer, 2009.

Anghie, Anthony. "Francisco de Vitoria and the Colonial Origins of International Law." *Social and Legal Studies* 5, no. 3 (1996): 321–36.

Anidjar, Gil. *The Jew, The Arab: A History of the Enemy*. Stanford, CA: Stanford University Press, 2003.

Arbel, Efrat. "Bordering the Constitution, Constituting the Border." *Osgoode Hall Law Journal* 52, no. 3 (2016): 824–52.

Arbel, Efrat, and Alletta Brenner. *Bordering on Failure: Canada–US Border Policy and the Politics of Refugee Exclusion*. Harvard Immigration and Refugee Law Clinical Program, November 2013. http://harvardimmigrationclinic.org/hirc/files/2013/12/bordering-on-failure-harvard-immigration-and-refugee-law-clinical-program1.pdf.

Arjana, Sophia Rose. *Muslims in the Western Imagination*. Oxford: Oxford University Press, 2015.

Armstrong, Amelia. "Police-Reported Hate Crime in Canada, 2017." *Statistics Canada*, April 30, 2019. https://www150.statcan.gc.ca/n1/pub/85-002-x/2019001/article/00008-eng.htm.

Backhouse, Constance. *Colour-Coded: A Legal History of Racism in Canada, 1900–1950*. Toronto: University of Toronto Press, 1999.

Bannerji, Himani. *The Dark Side of the Nation: Essays on Multiculturalism, Nationalism, and Gender*. Toronto: Canadian Scholars' Press, 2000.

Benzie, Robert. "Wynne gets an earful in Ottawa town hall." *Toronto Star*, January 18, 2018. https://www.thestar.com/news/queenspark/2018/01/18/wynne-gets-an-earful-in-ottawa-town-hall.html?utm_source=share-bar&utm_medium=user&utm_campaign=user-share.

Bhandar, Brenna, and Rafeef Ziadah. "Acts and Omissions: Framing Settler Colonialism in Palestine Studies." *Jadaliyya*, January 14, 2016. https://www.jadaliyya.com/Details/32857.

Blight, Susan, and Hayden King. "Naming is a Good Start—But We Need To Do More For Reconciliation." *The Globe and Mail*, April 6, 2017. https://www.theglobeandmail.com/.

Borrows, John. "The Durability of Terra Nullius: Tsilhqot'in Nation v British Columbia." *University of British Columbia Law Review* 48, no. 3 (2015): 701–43.

Boyarin, Jonathan. *The Unconverted Self: Jews, Indians, and the Identity of Christian Europe.* Chicago: University of Chicago Press, 2009.

Brake, Justin. "Ford Government's Intentions for Reconciliation Funding a Foregone Conclusion, Say Critics." *Aboriginal Peoples' Television Network*, January 6, 2019. https://www.aptnnews.ca/national-news/ford-governments-intentions-for-reconciliation-funding-a-foregone-conclusion-say-critics/.

Brulin, Remi. "Evolution and Debates About the Concept of Terrorism." *Jadaliyya*, January 15,2015.https://www.jadaliyya.com/Details/31675/Evolution-and-Debates-about-the-Concept-of-Terrorism.

Bruser, David, and Jayme Poisson. "Ontario Knew About Grassy Narrows Mercury Site for Decades, But Kept It Secret." *Toronto Star*, November 11, 2017. https://www.thestar.com/news/canada/2017/11/11/ontario-knew-about-mercury-site-near-grassy-narrows-for-decades-but-kept-it-secret.html /.

Bueckert, Kate. "Ontario's Anti-Racism Directorate Cuts a Step Backwards, NDP's Lindo Says." *CBC News*, September 18, 2018 https://www.cbc.ca/news/canada/kitchener-waterloo/anti-racism-directorate-cuts-lindo-tibollo-1.4827091.

Butler, Colin, and Kate Dubinski. "Chippewas of the Thames Vow to Continue Pipeline Fight." *CBC News*, July 26, 2017. https://www.cbc.ca/news/canada/london/chippewa-thames-supreme-court-line-9-pipeline-decision-1.4222090.

Cairns, James, and Susan Ferguson. "Human Rights Revisionism and the Canadian Parliamentary Coalition to Combat Antisemitism." *Canadian Journal of Communication* 36, no. 3 (2011): 415–34.

Canadian Press. "Canada-Israel 'Solidarity' Includes Defence Partnership." *CBC News*. Last updated June 20, 2012. https://www.cbc.ca/news/politics/canada-israel-solidarity-includes-defence-partnership-1.1141196.

Carey, Jane, and Claire McLisky, eds. *Creating White Australia.* Sydney: Sydney University Press, 2009.

CBC News. "Justin Trudeau Apologizes in House for 1914 Komagata Maru Incident." Last updated May 18, 2016. https://www.cbc.ca/news/politics/komagata-maru-live-apology-1.3587827.

CBC News. "Violence Breaks Out As Protesters Clash in Nathan Phillips Square." April 1, 2017.https://www.cbc.ca/news/canada/toronto/violence-breaks-out-as-protesters-clash-in-nathan-phillips-square-1.4051336.

Chorley, Jasmine. "Disappearing into White Space: Indigenous Toronto, 1900–1914." *Active History*. http://activehistory.ca/papers/disappearing-into-white-space-indigenous-toronto-1900-1914/.

City of Toronto. "Hate-Sponsored Rallies Such as Al Quds Day: Committee Decision." November 28, 2017. http://app.toronto.ca/tmmis/viewAgendaItemHistory.do?item=2017.EX29.42.

Cohn, Martin Regg. "On the Road to Indigenous Reconciliation, Doug Ford Takes a Detour." *Toronto Star*, July 13, 2019. ttps://www.thestar.com/politics/political-opinion/2019/07/13/on-the-road-to-indigenous-reconciliation-doug-ford-takes-a-detour.html.

Coulthard, Glen. *Red Skin, White Masks: Rejecting the Colonial Politics of Recognition*. Minneapolis: University of Minnesota Press, 2014.

Crosby, Andrew, and Jeffrey Monaghan. *Policing Indigenous Movements: Dissent and the Security State*. Halifax: Fernwood Publishing, 2018.

Csillag, Ron. "Nationalist Rally Planned in Toronto on the Anniversary of Charlottesville Attack." *Canadian Jewish News*, August 8, 2018. https://www.cjnews.com/news/canada/nationalist-rally-planned-in-toronto-on-the-anniversary-of-the-charlottesville-attack.

Csillag, Ron. "Ontario Axes Anti-Racism Subcommittees." *Canadian Jewish News*, September 20, 2018. https://www.cjnews.com/news/canada/ontario-axes-anti-racism-subcommittees.

Desmarais, Anna. "Anger Grows Over Ontario Decision to End Update of Curriculum with Indigenous Content." *iPolitics*, July 9, 2018. https://ipolitics.ca/2018/07/09/doug-ford-scraps-reconciliation-curriculum-writing-sessions/.

Dotan, Hamutal. "City Council Reaffirms Support for Pride Toronto, Condemns Term 'Israeli Apartheid.'" *Torontoist*, June 7, 2012. https://torontoist.com/2012/06/city-council-reaffirms-support-for-pride-toronto-condemns-term-israeli-apartheid/.

Dussel, Enrique. "Anti-Cartesian Meditations: On the Origin of the Philosophical Anti-Discourse of Modernity." *Journal for Cultural and Religious Theory* 13, no. 1 (2014): 11–53.

Epstein, Rachel. "Why was a Pro-Palestinian Jewish Organization Denied a Seat on Ontario Government's Anti-Semitism Committee?" *Now Toronto*, November 28, 2017. https://nowtoronto.com/news/why-was-pro-palestinian-jewish-organization-denied-a-seat-on-ontario-governments-anti-semitism-committee/.

Erlichman, Wolfe. "Chairman of Ontario's Anti-Semitism Subcommittee Caught in Excuse to Exclude Groups Critical of Israel." *Rabble*, June 25, 2018. http://rabble.ca/blogs/bloggers/independent-jewish-voices-canada/2018/06/chairman-ontarios-anti-semitism-subcommittee.

Esmeir, Sameera. *Juridical Humanity: A Colonial History*. Stanford, CA: Stanford University Press, 2014.

Faraday, Fay. "Made in Canada: How the Law Constructs Migrant Workers' Insecurity." Metcalf Foundation, 2012. https://metcalffoundation.com/stories/publications/made-in-canada-how-the-law-constructs-migrant-workers-insecurity/.

Freeman, Victoria. "'Toronto Has No History!' Indigeneity, Settler Colonialism, and Historical Memory in Canada's Largest City." *Urban History Review* 38, no. 2 (2010): 21–35.

Ghabrial, Sarah, and Elena Razlogova. "Justin Trudeau Conflating BDS with Anti-Semitism is Dangerous." *Huffington Post*, November 15, 2018. https://www.huffingtonpost.ca/sarah-ghabrial/bds-anti-semitism-trudeau-holocaust_a_23590519/.

Government of Ontario. "A Better Way Forward: Ontario's 3-Year Anti-Racism Strategic Plan." https://www.ontario.ca/page/better-way-forward-ontarios-3-year-anti-racism-strategic-plan.

Government of Ontario. "Anti-Racism Directorate." https://www.ontario.ca/page/anti-racism-directorate.

Gregory, Derek. *The Colonial Present: Afghanistan, Palestine, Iraq.* London: Wiley-Blackwell, 2004.

Grosfoguel, Ramón. "The Structure of Knowledge in Westernized Universities Epistemic Racism/Sexism and the Four Genocides/Epistemicides of the Long 16th Century." *Human Architecture: Journal of the Sociology of Self-Knowledge* 11, no. 1 (Fall 2013): 73–90.

Haiven, Max. "The Corollary of the Derivative is the Border: Visions for the Democratic Control of Movement." *OpenDemocracy*, April 14, 2016. https://www.opendemocracy.net/.

Heng, Geraldine. "Jews, Saracens, 'Black Men,' Tartars: England in a World of Racial Difference." In *A Companion to Medieval English Literature and Culture c 1350–c 1500*, edited by Peter Brown, 247–69. London: Blackwell Publishing, 2007.

Heng, Geraldine. "The Invention of Race in the European Middle Ages 1: Race Studies, Modernity, and the Middle Ages." *Literature Compass* 8, no. 5 (2011): 258–74.

Imai, Shin, Leah Gardner, and Sarah Weinberger. "The 'Canada Brand': Violence and Canadian Mining Companies in Latin America." *Justice and Corporate Accountability Project*, 2017. https://justice-project.org/the-canada-brand-violence-and-canadian-mining-companies-in-latin-america/.

Independent Jewish Voices. "Challenging Israel's and Canada's Global Pacification: An Independent Jewish Voices Campaign Against the Military/Prison/Police/Surveillance Complex." 2015. https://ijvcanada.org/wp-content/uploads/2015/03/Challenging-Israeli-Canadian-Global-Pacification-no-Links.pdf.

Jackman, Michael Connors, and Nishant Upadhyay. "Pinkwatching Israel, Whitewashing Canada: Queer (Settler) Politics and Indigenous Colonization in Canada." *WSQ: Women's Studies Quarterly* 42, no. 3 (2014): 195–210.

Kalmar, Ivan Davidson. "Anti-Semitism and Islamophobia: The Formation of a Secret." *Human Architecture* 7, no. 2 (Spring 2009): 135–44.

Kalmar, Ivan Davidson, and Derek J. Penslar eds., *Orientalism and the Jews.* Waltham, MA: Brandeis University Press, 2004.

Kalmar, Ivan, and Tariq Ramadan. "Anti-Semitism and Islamophobia: Historical and Contemporary Connections and Parallels." In *The Routledge Handbook of Muslim-Jewish Relations*, edited by Josef Meri, 351–71. New York: Routledge, 2016.

Kilibarda, Kole. "Canadian and Israeli Defense—Industrial and Homeland Security Ties: An Analysis." The New Transparency Project, November 2008. https://www.sscqueens.org/.

Krebs, Mike, and Dana M. Olwan. "'From Jerusalem to the Grand River, Our Struggles are One': Challenging Canadian and Israeli Settler Colonialism." *Settler Colonial Studies* 2, no. 2 (2012): 138–64.

Lagerquist, Jeff. "Indigenous Community Erased by Halifax Explosion Looks to Return." *CTV News*, December 5, 2017. https://www.ctvnews.ca/canada/indigenous-community-erased-by-halifax-explosion-looks-to-return-1.3708979.

Lake, Marilyn, and Henry Reynolds. *Drawing the Global Colour Line: White Men's Countries and the International Challenge of Racial Equality*. Cambridge: Cambridge University Press, 2012.

Lascaris, Dimitri. "Toronto's City Council Takes Advice About Stopping Hate Speech from a Hate Monger—Part 1." December 1, 2017. https://dimitrilascaris.org/2017/12/01/torontos-city-council-takes-advice-about-hate-speech-from-a-hate-monger-part-1/.

Lawrence, Bonita, and Enakshi Dua. "Decolonizing Antiracism." *Social Justice* 32, no. 4 (2005): 120–43.

Lloyd, David, and Patrick Wolfe. "Settler Colonial Logics and the Neoliberal Regime," *Settler Colonial Studies* 6, no. 2 (2016): 109–18.

Local and Regional Government Alliance on Race & Equity. "Ontario launches anti-racism strategic plan." September 17, 2017. https://www.racialequityalliance.org/2017/09/08/ontario-launches-anti-racism-strategic-plan/.

Lungen, Paul. "JDL Partners with Soldiers of Odin on 'Ad Hoc' Basis." *Canadian Jewish News*, May 8, 2017. https://www.cjnews.com/news/canada/jdl-partners-soldiers-odin-ad-hoc.

Mackey, Eva. *The House of Difference: Cultural Politics and National Identity in Canada*. Toronto: University of Toronto Press, 2002.

MacLeod, Jennifer Tzivia. "Wynne Speaks Out Against BDS During Israel Trip." *Canadian Jewish News,* May 20, 2016. https://www.cjnews.com/news/israel/wynne-speaks-bds-israel-trip.

Maldonado-Torres, Nelson. "AAR Centennial Roundtable: Religion, Conquest, and Race in the Foundations of the Modern/Colonial World." *Journal of the American Academy of Religion* 82, no. 3 (2014): 636–65.

Maloney, Ryan. "Trudeau Says He Will 'Continue to Condemn the BDS Movement' at St Catharines Town Hall." *Huffington Post*, January 16, 2019. https://www.huffingtonpost.ca/2019/01/16/trudeau-bds-movement_a_23644306/.

Mastnak, Tomaz. "Western Hostility Toward Muslims: A History of the Present." In *Islamophobia/Islamophilia: Beyond the Politics of Enemy and Friend*, edited by Andrew Shyrock, 29–52. Bloomington, IN: Indiana University Press, 2010.

Mastracci, Davide. "Thought Crimes in Trudeau's Canada." *The Electronic Intifada*, March 8, 2016. https://electronicintifada.net/content/thought-crimes-trudeaus-canada/15926.

Matar, Nabil. *Turks, Moors, and Englishmen in the Age of Discovery*. New York: Columbia University Press, 2000.

Matar, Nabil. "Britons and Muslims in the Early Modern Period: From Prejudice to (a Theory of) Toleration." *Patterns of Prejudice* 43, no. 3–4 (2009): 213–31.

McDonald, Michael. "History of Halifax, a Mi'kmaw Perspective." *The Nova Scotia Advocate*, July 12, 2017. https://nsadvocate.org/2017/07/12/history-of-halifax-a-mikmaw-perspective/.

Miller, Robert J. "The Doctrine of Discovery: The International Law of Colonialism." *The Indigenous Peoples' Journal of Law, Culture & Resistance* 5, no. 1 (2019): 35–42.

Mills, Charles. *The Racial Contract*. Ithaca, NY: Cornell University Press, 2014.

Morgensen, Scott Lauria. "Settler Homonationalism Theorizing Settler Colonialism within Queer Modernities." *GLQ: A Journal of Lesbian and Gay Studies* 16, no. 1–2 (2010): 105–31.

Nadeau, Mary-Jo, and Alan Sears. "The Palestine Test: Countering the Silencing Campaign." *Studies in Political Economy* 85, no. 1 (2010): 7–33.

Nichols, Robert. "Indigeneity and the Settler Contract Today." *Philosophy and Social Criticism* 39, no. 2 (2013): 165–86.

Nirenberg, David. *Communities of Violence: Persecution of Minorities in the Middle Ages*. Princeton, NJ: Princeton University Press, 2015.

Ontario Human Rights Commission. *A Collective Impact: Interim Report on the Inquiry into Racial Profiling and Racial Discrimination of Black Persons by the Toronto Police Service*. November 2018 http://ohrc.on.ca/en/public-interest-inquiry-racial-profiling-and-discrimination-toronto-police-service/collective-impact-interim-report-inquiry-racial-profiling-and-racial-discrimination-black.

Palestine Solidarity Legal Support. "FAQ: What to Know About Efforts to Re-define Anti-Semitism to Silence Criticism of Israel." Accessed June 4, 2013. https://static1.squarespace.com/static/548748b1e4b083fc03ebf70e/t/556490f5e4b0658666cfe867/1432654069359/6.+FAQ-onDefinition-of-Anti-Semitism-3-9-15.pdf.

Pasternak, James. "Administrative Inquiry Regarding Hate-Sponsored Rallies Such as Al-Quds Day." City of Toronto, September 19, 2017. https://www.toronto.ca/legdocs/mmis/2017/ex/bgrd/backgroundfile-109011.pdf.

Pasternak, James. "Statement: Councillor Pasternak Once Again Calls for the Al Quds Day Hate Rally to be Banned from Queens Park." June 22, 2017. http://www.jamespasternak.ca/.

Patterson, Brent. "The Ongoing Fight to Shut Down the Enbridge Line 9 Pipeline." *Rabble*, December 2, 2018. http://rabble.ca/blogs/bloggers/brent-patterson/2018/12/ongoing-fight-shut-down-enbridge-line-9-pipeline.

Peña, Christian. "Shaming Racists When the Media Won't." *Now Toronto*, May 4, 2019. https://nowtoronto.com/news/shaming-racists-when-the-media-wont/.

Perugini, Nicola, and Neve Gordon. *The Human Right to Dominate*. New York: Oxford University Press, 2015.

Povinelli, Elizabeth. *The Cunning of Recognition: Indigenous Alterities and the Making of Australian Multiculturalism*. Durham, NC: Duke University Press, 2002.

Razack, Sherene. *Casting Out: The Eviction of Muslims from Western Law and Politics*. Toronto: University of Toronto Press, 2008.

Reevely, David. "Ford Promises to Ban Al-Quds Day Protests Somehow." *Ottawa Citizen*, June 11, 2018. https://ottawacitizen.com/news/local-news/reevely-ford-promises-to-ban-al-quds-day-protests-somehow.

Rehaag, Sean, and Sharry Aiken. "Canada a World Leader in Preventing Arrival of Refugees." *Toronto Star*, May 25, 2018. https://www.thestar.com/.

Rutherford, Scott. "Colonialism and the Indigenous Present: An Interview with Bonita Lawrence." *Race and Class* 52, no. 1 (July 2010): 9–18.

Said, Edward. *Orientalism*. New York: Random House, 1979.

Salaita, Steven. *Inter/Nationalism*. Minneapolis: University of Minnesota Press, 2016.

Salaita, Steven. "The Native American Model of Palestine's Future." *The Electronic Intifada*, March 10, 2016. https://electronicintifada.net/blogs/steven-salaita/native-american-model-palestines-future.

Salaita, Steven. "Zionism and Native American Studies." *Abolition Journal*, June 6, 2017. https://abolitionjournal.org/zionism-native-american-studies-steven-salaita/.

Sears, Alan, and Mary-Jo Nadeau. "This Is What Complicity Looks Like: Palestine and the Silencing Campaign on Campus." *The Bullet*, March 5, 2011. https://socialistproject.ca/2011/03/b475/.

Shannon, Harry. "Ontario Anti-Racism Directorate's Anti-Semitism Committee Stuck on Israel." *Now Toronto*, March 6, 2018. https://nowtoronto.com/news/ontario-anti-racism-directorate-anti-semitism/.

Simonpillai, Radheyan. "Ford Government's Cut to the Indigenous Culture Fund 'An Attack on Reconciliation.'" *Now Toronto*, December 15, 2018. https://nowtoronto.com/.

Simpson, Audra. *Mohawk Interruptus: Political Life Across the Borders of Settler States*. Durham and London: Duke University Press, 2014.

Stampnitzky, Lisa. *Disciplining Terror: How Experts Invented 'Terrorism*. Cambridge; New York: Cambridge University Press, 2013.

Star Editorial Board. "Rod Phillips—The Latest Government Minister to Betray Grassy Narrows." *Toronto Star*, March 5, 2019. https://www.thestar.com/.

Stasiulis, Daiva, and Nira Yuval-Davis, eds. *Unsettling Settler Societies: Articulations of Gender, Race, Ethnicity and Class*. London: Sage, 1995.

Statistics Canada. "Police-Reported Hate Crime, 2017." November 29, 2018. https://www150.statcan.gc.ca/n1/daily-quotidien/181129/dq181129a-eng.htm.

Tabar, Linda, and Chandni Desai. "Decolonization is a Global Project: From Palestine to the Americas." *Decolonization: Indigeneity, Education & Society* 6, no. 1 (2017): i-xix.

Thobani, Sunera. *Exalted Subjects: Studies in the Making of Race and Nation in Canada.* Toronto: University of Toronto Press, 2007.

Thrall, Nathan. "BDS: How a Controversial Non-Violent Movement Has Transformed the Israeli-Palestinian Debate." *The Guardian*, August 14, 2018. https://www.theguardian.com/news/2018/aug/14/bds-boycott-divestment-sanctions-movement-transformed-israeli-palestinian-debate.

Trudeau, Justin. "Justin Trudeau on Apology to Jewish Refugees." November 7, 2018. https://openparliament.ca/debates/2018/11/7/justin-trudeau-41/only/.

Veracini, Lorenzo. *The Settler Colonial Present.* London: Palgrave Macmillan, 2015.

Walia, Harsha. *Undoing Border Imperialism.* Oakland, CA: AK Press, 2013.

Wolfe, Patrick. "Settler Colonialism and the Elimination of the Native." *Journal of Genocide Research* 8, no. 4 (2006): 387–409.

Wolfe, Patrick. *Traces of History: Elementary Structures of Race.* London: Verso, 2016.

Wright, Teresa. "Blair Mulling Ways to Close Loophole in Safe Third Country Agreement." *National Observer*, March 17, 2019. https://www.nationalobserver.com/2019/03/17/news/blair-mulling-ways-close-loophole-safe-third-country-agreement.

Yang, Jennifer. "Advocates Fear for Future of Province's Anti-Racism Directorate." *Toronto Star*, September 14, 2018. https://www.thestar.com/news/gta/2018/09/07/advocates-fear-for-future-of-provinces-anti-racism-directorate.html.

Ziadah, Rafeef. "Outside the Multicultural: Solidarity and the Silencing of Palestinian Narratives." PHD diss., York University, 2014.

III

CANADA'S POLICIES AND THE PERPETUATION OF SETTLER-COLONIAL DOMINATION

5

CANADA'S ROLE IN THE PEOPLE-TO-PEOPLE PROGRAMME

A Critical Assessment

NADIA NASER-NAJJAB

Introduction

The People-to-People Programme (P2PP) is a second-track form of diplomacy established by Oslo II with the aim of bringing Palestinians and Israelis together and removing psychological barriers, prejudices and stereotypes. It continues to be funded by international donors, including the Canada Fund, European Aid, and the United States Agency for International Development (USAID). In this chapter, I argue it systematically distorts the underlying causes and objective dimensions of the conflict, most notably by diverting attention from the ongoing colonization of Palestinian land and perpetuating both dispossession and violence.

Although donors acknowledged these criticisms, they tended to work within a "problem-solving" paradigm,[1] which is explicitly devoid of context, limiting their ability to respond.[2] In 2005, the then Canadian International Development Agency (CIDA) invited Palestinians, Israelis, and international actors to a conference that would discuss the possibility of continued cooperation under the P2PP rubric. This chapter examines the subsequent conference proceedings more closely with the aim of providing further insight into the P2PP and the wider peace process, before then demonstrating how it contributed to the perpetuation of colonial relations. The axiom that holds cooperation and dialogue have the potential to transform material realities resonates in the outlines and content of the two-state solution. In highlighting its internal and practical limitations, I instead assert approaches and strategies that directly engage with the colonial realities of the conflict, with the intention of helping to establish a more sustainable, just and meaningful peace.

The Contribution of Colonial Theory

My experiences as a Palestinian have helped me to grasp the value of colonial theory. This is particularly true from a research perspective, as it helped me to appreciate how the preponderance of Western and Israeli research perspectives in this area has skewed perspectives and perpetuated misunderstanding.[3] It is first essential to acknowledge that these accounts stress neutrality and objectivity and, as a consequence, mitigate Palestinian experiences of injustice and the importance of power relations. The dangers that arise when concepts of "neutrality" and "objectivity" are applied to the Palestinian–Israeli conflict have been previously recognized by Abu Saad, who observes, "how skewed the discourse can become when neutrality is determined from the perspective of the dominant standpoint alone, in absence of an analysis of the power relations it is used to describe or disguise."[4]

Neutrality therefore denies the political realities of the conflict, while reconciliation requires Palestinian participation in contrived performances with tragicomic overtones. The expectations that Palestinians had invested in "contact" initiatives were bitterly frustrated when it became apparent that the P2PP was not intended to function as a tool of political education that would help educate Israelis about the realities of life in the OPT. Edward Said, in setting his more general suspicion of "reconciliation" initiatives aside, similarly recognizes the potential of encounters that note the existence of a "victim and victimizer," increasing the likelihood that Israelis will pressure their government to end occupation, expropriation, and settlement activity.[5]

Recognition of the extent to which the P2PP fell short of these expectations has however been inhibited by the dominance of Western and Israeli perspectives. In breaking with this predisposition to research through "imperial eyes,"[6] I instead propose to offer a critical assessment of the P2PP. As a Palestinian researcher, I have a clear advantage in this regard, as I have personally experienced the influence of unequal power relations,[7] and this informs my endorsement of resistance as a research commitment.[8] I take decolonization to be the ultimate objective, and therefore resist efforts to gloss over the underlying causes of conflict that include control and domination. All of this predisposes me to view the P2PP as a "metaphor" that "invades decolonization, [kills] the very possibility of decolonization; [recenters] whiteness; [resettles] theory, [extends] innocence to the settler; [and] entertains a settler future."[9]

The P2PP's ostensible appearance of neutrality effectively denied this colonial reality. The designers and administrators of the P2PP were required to adhere to the principle of equality, and this was reflected both in the number of participants and the distribution of funding. But these internal arrangements failed to acknowledge the wider political reality of occupation. Just before the Oslo Agreement was signed in 1993, the occupation authorities closed Jerusalem and imposed a permit system. In subsequent years, dependency by the Palestinian Authority (PA) on external donor funding meant that the "peace process" was advanced through elite cooperation, in pronounced absence of public oversight or accountability.[10] The peace process did not confront but actually reproduced the dynamics of colonialism, as Hanieh recognizes when he renders the incorporat[ion of] Israeli colonialism into the very practice of development itself.[11] Selby similarly notes that a substantial part of "co-operation" is actually a "repackaging" of patron-client relations that developed during the occupation.[12]

In failing to acknowledge the colonial reality, donors have become complicit in its reproduction. After the Second *Intifada* broke out in late September 2000, donors repeatedly failed to recognize the pervasive reality of fragmentation and the accompanying destruction of Palestinian self-governance, continuing to fund peace/state-building work.[13] This again underlines how international intervention operated alongside, rather than in opposition to, the colonial context. Badarin confirms that, "the overall institution-building and capacity-building arrangements coexisted with the operative colonial structure instead of bringing it to a close."[14]

The 1995 Oslo II Accord divided the West Bank and Gaza Strip into three administrative zones (A, B, and C). When the peace process stalled and lost momentum, Israel continued to refuse to commit to so-called "Final Status" issues such as Jerusalem and the right of return for Palestinian refugees.[15] The construction of the so-called "Separation Wall,"[16] the acceleration of settlement building, and the construction of bypass roads helped to consolidate this pervasive condition of fragmentation and pushed Palestinians into enclaves.[17] These developments, in addition to Hamas's 2007 seizure of the Gaza Strip,[18] negatively impacted the Palestinian economy.[19] Growing divisions that originated in both endogenous and external sources contributed to the classification of different categories of Palestinians.

Palestinian community and solidarity organizations, which once might have resisted these developments, have been unable to do so, in large part because they have been co-opted into a neo-liberal project of economic, political and social reform.[20] During the "Oslo years,"[21] a Palestinian "civil society" emerged that was in many respects defined by its dependence on international funding. Hammami clarifies, "By 1991, many of these formerly popularly-based grassroots initiatives had become professionally-based, foreign-funded development centres which targeted clients as opposed to working with a constituency."[22]

In this context, civil society was predisposed to reproduce and reinforce the neoliberal agenda rather than challenge or subvert it.[23] This recalls the Gramscian concept of hegemony, in which power and domination are maintained through the consent of the ruled.[24] It similarly invokes Foucauldian framings of "discipline" and "power."[25] Foucault observes that, "governing people is not a way to force people to do what the governor wants; it is always a versatile equilibrium, with complementarity and conflicts between techniques which assure coercion and processes through which the self is constructed or modified by himself [sic]."[26]

The peace discourse exemplifies Foucault's rendering of subtle and insidious power.[27] It is simultaneously illusionary and exclusionary. In the first respect, it renders enticing fictions of "development" and "reconciliation"; in the second, it aligns with Israel's strategic priorities by excluding Palestinian refugees from participation. Upon encountering its various deceptions and occlusions, the observer is reminded of Khalidi's striking

130   *Canada's Role in the People-to-People Programme*

indictment of "a veil of deceitful, Orwellian verbiage."[28] But it is clearly insufficient to denigrate this discourse as an external imposition, for the reason that it sketches the parameters of Palestinian struggle and resistance. In the words of Foucault, "discourse is the thing for which and by which there is struggle, discourse is the power [that] is to be seized."[29]

Robert Cox recalls this characterization of power when he renders international institutions as "rules" that assist the expansion of dominant economic and social forces, but which enable, "adjustments to be made by subordinated interests with a minimum of pain."[30] In both accounts, power is defined by its limitation rather than its maximization or completion. Similarly, Settler Colonial Theory renders the "logic of elimination" as falling short of the "maximal" act of genocide.[31] In the P2PP, discourses of "peace" and "reconciliation" nonetheless invoked this "logic" when they were invoked to "eliminate" Palestinian narratives of struggle and resistance.[32] Coulthard, in referring to the Canadian example, similarly presents this "logic" as extending through accommodation and consent rather than direct coercion. He observes,

> *In the Canadian context, colonial relations of power are no longer reproduced primarily through overtly coercive means, but rather through the asymmetrical exchange of mediated forms of state recognition and accommodation.*[33]

In drawing on this perspective, it is possible to reimagine the "peace process" as a colonial tactic that Israel exploits to achieve its own ends. Fanon, in precisely these terms, evokes, "a diplomacy which leaps ahead, in strange contrast to the motionless, petrified world of colonization."[34]

The P2PP

People-to-People (P2P) diplomacy has an intuitive appeal and attraction, which can perhaps be attributed to the simplicity of its underlying premise. It renders the expectation that meetings in a neutral setting will remove social and political constraints and enable former "antagonists" to engage and relate on a personal basis. The accumulated impact of their personal encounters will, over time, help to establish an alternative "track" and add a "micro-level" dimension to the broader political process.

In 1995, the "international community" decided to apply the principles of P2P diplomacy to the Israeli–Palestinian conflict. The relevant section (Annex VI, Article VIII) of Oslo II, also known as the Interim Agreement on the West Bank and the Gaza Strip· established the basis for the P2PP. Annex VI states,

1. The two sides shall co-operate in enhancing the dialogue and relations between their peoples in accordance with the concepts developed in co-operation with the Kingdom of Norway.
2. The two sides shall cooperate in enhancing dialogue relations between their peoples, as well as in gaining a wider exposure of the two publics to the peace process, its current situation and predicted results.
3. The two sides shall take steps to foster public debate and involvement, to remove barriers to interaction, and to increase the people to people exchange and interaction within all areas of cooperation.[35]

P2PP principles can be traced back to contact theories that originate in the field of social psychology, which examine how knowledge produced through intergroup interaction can change negative stereotypes about the "Other," reduce prejudice and encourage optimal contact.[36]

The P2PP guidelines are mainly drawn from the classical "Contact Hypothesis" that Allport developed.[37] He suggests positive and successful contact is possible if certain conditions, specifically equal status, intimate relations, common goals, and institutional support, are present in a contact situation.[38] The P2PP was a Norwegian initiative, and the country took the lead in establishing and funding the P2PP from the outset (other donors, including the European Union, USAID, and the Canada Fund, also supported similar activities).[39] The P2PP established working groups and a Standing Cooperation Committee (SCC) made up of Palestinian and Israeli representatives, and they were tasked with coordinating all joint projects.

The committee also included representatives from the Israeli Foreign Ministry and the Palestinian National Authority (PNA). This level of official involvement distinguished the P2PP from other joint activities funded by other countries. Lena Endresen, a P2P coordinator between 1996 and 1997, explains the SCC structure,

[The SCC] would combine governmental control and popular civic activities. One tier consisted of the governmental steering committee, made up of representatives from the Palestinian, Israeli and Norwegian authorities. On the other was the non-governmental body, which consisted of planning groups from the two parties, and a Norwegian Programme Secretariat.[40]

The P2PP was originally funded by the Norwegian Ministry of Foreign Affairs. The Fafo Institute for Applied Social Science, part of the Centre for International Studies in Oslo, was delegated managerial responsibilities. Palestinian and Israeli planning groups assisted Palestinian and Israeli organizations with project implementation, and Fafo provided administrative support.[41]

The Palestinian planning group was the "Palestinian Centre for Peace-Ramallah" (PCP); the Israeli counterpart group was the Andrea and Charles Bronfman Philanthropist Foundation, which was also known as Karen Karev and the CRB Foundation (this name will henceforth be used).[42] The Montreal-based CRB, which coordinated closely with the Israeli Foreign Ministry, provided full funding for Israeli NGOs involved in P2P projects. Palestinian project costs, meanwhile, were met by the Norwegian government. There was no Palestinian foreign ministry at the time, and this is why Mahmoud Abbas, the incumbent PA President, was appointed to the PCP board of directors.

After P2PP implementation began in 1995, many Palestinians and Israeli NGOs began to submit joint funding applications. Fafo guidelines stated that joint projects would need to have a minimum budget of $US 20,000 and operate in accordance with P2P goals set out in the Oslo agreement. From the outset, there was a clear intention to involve NGOs from different regions who would contribute new ideas.[43] Project categories were: (1) Youth; (2) Adult Dialogue and Seminars; (3) Culture; (4) Environment; and (5) School Twinning and Education.

The Limitations of the P2PP

Although many Palestinians came to the P2PP with the expectation of political engagement, this was directly opposed to the vision of donors and Israelis, which instead privileged personal and professional cooperation.[44] The relatively prescriptive character of the programme left little room for

Palestinian experiences of occupation or the expectation that Israelis should enter in a spirit of accommodation, let alone solidarity. One Israeli participant entered into the spirit of the P2PP by complaining that, "Palestinians are so busy showing us their misery and expecting us to be one-sided, on their side."[45] Abu Saad specifically observed that, "the dominant group tended to know only its own understanding of reality and social relations because it had ignored, rejected, and silenced the differing perspectives of those over whom it had power."[46]

Similar to Kanji's description of the flaws in the anti-racism work of the ARD in Ontario, Canada,[47] the P2PP had no comprehension of decolonization and was therefore incompatible with the aims of Palestinian participants who sought solidarity with Israelis in their struggle against the occupation and colonization of their land. It was therefore significant that Palestinians sought to challenge "colonial relations of power" in all P2PP evaluation workshops. This openly conflicted with the P2PP's emphasis on reconciliation. Sium et al. observe,

> The decolonizing project seeks to reimagine and rearticulate power, change, and knowledge through a multiplicity of epistemologies, ontologies and axiologies. Decolonization cannot take place without contestation. It must necessarily push back against the colonial relations of power that threaten Indigenous ways of being.[48]

But the P2PP failed to acknowledge the imperative of decolonization, which is why Palestinian participants voiced strong criticisms of donor guidelines that claimed to uphold neutrality while having little or nothing to say about displacement, dispossession, and fragmentation. It is hardly surprising that Palestinian participants came to view the P2PP as serving Israel's interests, not least by enabling it to project a "liberal" image while exerting control over the OPT through force,[49] and ultimately sought to resist its depoliticized framing of P2PP.[50]

Contact Theory is also diametrically opposed to the history of contact between Palestinians and Israelis. It is therefore perhaps surprising to note that contact actually occurred in the clear absence of a number of preconditions, and that Palestinians and Israelis participated in joint activities against the occupation.[51] This was clearly shown during the First *Intifada*, when the existence of a common goal was the *only* contact precondition that was met.[52]

134   *Canada's Role in the People-to-People Programme*

In June 1995, in my capacity as an Al-Jiser (a Jerusalem-based Palestinian NGO) coordinator, I arranged an internal P2PP meeting that was attended by directors and participants from 20 Palestinian NGOS. The meeting again reiterated the clear consensus on using the P2PP to educate Israelis about the occupation,[53] stressed the need to develop a unified strategy for donor engagement,[54] and raised concerns that donors were ignoring Palestinian concerns about the P2PP. In 2000, the Palestinian Ministry of NGO Affairs (which was established in 1999) arranged a meeting that arrived at similar conclusions.[55]

Donors acknowledged Palestinian concerns by arranging a series of evaluative workshops. In 1999, the Finnish Citizens' Security Council (KATU), the Palestinian Centre for Peace (PCP), and the Economic Co-operation Foundation arranged a conference (entitled "Israeli-Palestinian Civil Society-Cooperative Activities") in Helsinki. This again reiterated the political rationale for P2PP and the importance of capacity-building work that would narrow disparities between Palestinian and Israeli NGOs.

In 2006, Norway's Representative Office to the PA organized a public debate on P2PP that was coordinated by the Jerusalem Media & Communications Center (JMCC).[56] Palestinians criticized the apolitical character of P2PP because they believed it detracted from their efforts to influence Israeli public opinion. The asymmetry of Palestinian and Israeli NGOs was again a topic of discussion.[57] These interactions, in addition to engagements within the P2PP framework, could not be divorced from the wider political context. Astonishingly, donors continued to insist on implementing joint projects even after the Second *Intifada* broke out, when Palestinian NGOs had begun to call for a boycott of the P2PP.

The position of the General Assembly of the Palestinian NGO Network (PNGO) is particularly instructive in this respect. One of its press releases calls on Palestinian NGOs to disengage from Israeli NGOs and expresses particular opposition to the P2PP. It maintains that contact will only be justifiable when Israeli NGOs recognize "the right of the Palestinians to establish a state in the West Bank and Gaza Strip, with Jerusalem as its capital, and the right of return for the Palestinian refugees."[58] It further clarifies,

> [T]hese decisions do not conflict with the principle of cooperation with
> any activity held by the Israeli Human Rights Associations to support
> the Palestinian nation in its struggle for liberation and the establishment

of a Palestinian state, and to declare their support for a fair and durable peace.[59]

The PNGO's stance was not sympathetically received by most Israeli NGOs, including the Peres Center for Peace,[60] and Givat Haviva.[61] Bat Shalom, the Israeli feminist organization, was an exception to this general rule. On March 25, 2001, it published an open letter in *Al-Quds* newspaper that accepted the Palestinian conditions for cooperation. The letter stated, "Israel's recognition of its responsibility in the creation of the Palestinian refugees in 1948 is a pre-requisite to finding a just and lasting resolution of the refugee problem in accordance with relevant UN resolutions."[62]

In the Second *Intifada*, movement between the separate Areas of the West Bank became increasingly difficult, and the Gaza Strip was cut off from the West Bank.[63] The construction of the so-called "Separation Wall," which began in 2002, further complicated internal travel, including to Jerusalem.[64] Accelerated settlement construction also displaced growing numbers of Palestinians.[65] In 2005, 170 Palestinian civil society organizations established the Boycott, Divestment and Sanctions (BDS) Movement,[66] which strongly criticized apolitical contact and professional cooperation and maintained they were both forms of normalization.[67] BDS did however remain open to political cooperation that sought to change the status quo by asserting Palestinian national political rights.

Donors, in apparent defiance of the Second *Intifada*, continued to insist that P2P diplomacy was viable. From 2013 onwards, the European Union allocated an annual total of between €5–10 million to P2P-related activities, which it dispersed through the Partnership for Peace Program (PFP) and the Peacebuilding Initiative.[68] Donors also sought to "rebrand" P2P by incorporating it into economic development programs. For example, USAID's Conflict Management and Mitigation Program allocates an annual total of around US$10 million to P2P activities,[69] supporting projects that address prejudice and help to develop relationships between conflict parties.[70]

Instead of addressing Palestinian grievances with the P2PP, donors more frequently evidenced a preference to work around them. For example, parallel meetings were established in response to the prohibition on Israeli travel to Palestinian areas. When meetings were held in Jerusalem, only "successful" Palestinian applicants were permitted to attend. Some Palestinians, in recognizing that any application through the system would be a form of indirect recognition and even legitimization, instead sought to access the city through a series of side-roads.

The Canadian Government and P2PP

The Canadian International Development Agency (CIDA), which was established in 1996, is part of the Canadian Peacebuilding Initiative.[71] Both its aims and the P2PP guidelines focus on the psychological barriers that impede peace. In this section, I will not provide a general assessment or evaluation of CIDA's peace programme; rather, I instead propose to examine its claim to clearly understand Palestinian needs.[72] I will argue that this "understanding" is limited for the reason that it fails to transition beyond donor priorities and conceptual/theoretical framings.

After the outbreak of the Second *Intifada*, the number of Palestinian participants in joint projects continued to fall. In 2001, CIDA responded by establishing a new programme, which was entitled "Networking for Peace." Dominique Rossetti, who in 2005 was Deputy Representative and Head of Aid at the Canadian Representative Office in Ramallah, clarifies that the title and focus reflect a prior expectation that, "networking activities on issues related to peace in the region [will] create sustainable mechanisms for the exchange of information and experience."[73] But closer inspection revealed that it was in fact a repackaging of the P2P programme that remained beholden to Allport's "Contact Hypothesis" and other theories from the field of Social Psychology. Its inclusion of a capacity-building dimension did however make a partial, albeit somewhat belated, concession to Palestinian demands. Rossetti also claimed to have arrived at a fuller understanding of Palestinian needs and priorities. He observes,

> *what Palestinians wanted to achieve through P2P and other cooperative projects was to advocate their cause, affect Israeli public opinion and create a qualitative change in the understanding of the Israeli street at large, all with the intention of gaining support for Palestinian rights.*[74]

The value of this explicit acknowledgement was somewhat mitigated by the fact that "reconciliation" and "peace" continued to be refracted through the lens of Western donor priorities. This clearly recalled Richmond's warning that, "top-level actors will instil in the system their own biases and interests, while arguing that they are constructing a universal system. Any universal peace system is therefore open to being hijacked by hegemonic actors."[75]

Richmond's critique also evokes Foucault's claim that power is produced through and within the condition of freedom.[76] Rosetti similarly renders Palestinians as free, autonomous agents who are engaged in the production of "peace." But he fails to acknowledge the significance of Palestinian resistance, and this is indicated by the timidity and conservatism of his proposed reforms, which include the incorporation of historical narratives and the participation of Palestinian refugees.[77] Far from enabling the P2PP to overcome its contradictions, it is more likely that dialogue conducted under these circumstances will produce little more than, "apologies for one-sided robbery and murder."[78]

In order to explain Palestinian and Israeli positions during these projects, I will now consider the conference that Canadian Networking for Peace and other donors organized to evaluate and revive the P2PP. The conference, entitled "Assessing and Evaluating P2P Activities" was held in Jerusalem in April 2005. It was initiated by the Canadian Representative Office to the Palestinian Authority, who invited the Norwegian Representative Office and the European Commission to participate and make financial contributions. The Conference's conclusion echoes Palestinian concerns voiced at an early stage of the programme. It observes,

> *Palestinians were more concerned with raising Israeli public awareness about the Israeli occupation of the Palestinian territories and the injustice and difficulties Palestinians face in their daily lives. Some Israelis shared this view, but most thought that communication with Palestinians should focus on social and interpersonal relations, without a political dimension.*[79]

The conference focused on the Second *Intifada* because it had caused the suspension of most P2P projects. But this failed to acknowledge that a wide number of issues, including narrative, power relations, the occupation, and the permit system existed before the uprising. Some contributors blithely ignored the Palestinian consensus and even claimed the wider political situation should be ignored. Basel Jabir, a former advisor to the Palestinian minister of foreign affairs, takes a diametrically opposed position. He argues,

One cannot divorce the political context from the p2p process, especially taking into account the new facts on the ground created by the Israeli occupation. The Wall and new Israeli settlement construction cannot be ignored in P2P meetings. We have to change the concept and the philosophy of P2P as there will be no Palestinian public support for this kind of cooperation at a time when Israel's measures work towards an unjust and one-sided separation.[80]

The conference also discussed "facts on the ground" and relative inequalities between Palestinian and Israeli NGOs. It appeared doomed from the outset, as the decision to hold the event in Jerusalem meant many OPT Palestinians would be unable to attend. Donors and Israeli representatives then steadfastly resisted a deluge of Palestinian complaints by insisting that the P2PP should continue.

Palestinian participants in turn reiterated the importance of "Final Status" issues and argued that personal or professional engagement could not be separated from a reality of closures, control and fragmentation. When donors offered the partial ameliorative of capacity-building in response, Palestinians rejected it on the grounds that it did not acknowledge this wider context. Equally significantly, the conference also failed to engage the PNGO and BDS consensus, despite the fact that both had been recently clarified (in 2000 and 2004 respectively). Similar complaints were also rendered in a 2006 evaluation workshop organized by Norway's Representative Office to the PA. A Palestinian woman, in reflecting on her experience of the P2PP, observes,

One time, we were in one of the villages, and they were distributing a publication on how to use water and economize the use of water. One woman asked me a question: I cannot imagine how an Israeli is coming here to educate me on how to use water while I still use the bucket and close to me there is a settlement where they have swimming pools. So how it that an Israeli comes to educate me on how to use water when they are occupying our land? The Israeli institution working with you should work inside the Israeli society and not to educate me.[81]

Her contribution demonstrates how the P2PP became detached from reality and also illustrates how donors sought to impose their own vision of reconciliation through cooperation.[82] In 2005, Palestinian health sector workers published an open letter that provided an equally damning indictment of P2P. It states,

[conditions] are imposed largely from the outside, either luring professionals and academics with funds, facilities and opportunities for personal advancement in a resource starved environment, or bringing them solutions to individual medical and systemic problems that the Israeli military occupation of Palestinian land has created and maintained.[83]

The signatories did not reject reconciliation per se, but rather the form of "reconciliation" that had been rendered. Their position can be clearly distinguished from Coulthard's more principled rejection. He observes, "What is treated in the Canadian discourse of reconciliation as an unhealthy and debilitating incapacity to forgive and move on is actually a sign of our *critical consciousness*, [original emphasis] of our sense of justice and injustice."[84] Tamari adds,

as all colonial conflicts have shown, reconciliation is a slow process that comes much later than the ending of the conflict. To impose reconciliation while the wounds of domination are fresh would be contrived and could undermine the agreement itself. Better to leave healing as consequence of concord than a condition for it.[85]

A decade passed before the Government of Canada suspended the programme and gave up on joint cooperation.[86] But the Canadian government continues to fund neoliberal development projects in the expectation this will help to support Palestinian state-building.[87]

The Networking Peace Program and its vision of peace and reconciliation exemplifies the Canadian government's Palestinian foreign policy. Although Canada rhetorically upholds Palestinian rights (including the Right of Return) and rejects Trump's recognition of Jerusalem as Israel's capital,[88] it has failed to condemn Israel's closure of Jerusalem. As Wildeman notes, Canada's rejection of one-sided resolutions and the more general tendency of "pollicization" is, in actual fact, a resolute denial of the essentially political character of this conflict, and of conflicts more generally.[89] In any case, the Canadian government's position is quite clearly contradicted by Justin Trudeau's—quite transparently "political"—claim that BDS and even criticism of Israel are forms of anti-Semitism.[90]

Conclusion

Canada's attempt to retrieve the P2PP from its internal and external contradictions provides insight into the challenges associated with neo-liberal peacebuilding in Palestine. This chapter argues that the P2PP, in furthering the illusion that the "conflict" can be reduced to its psychological dimensions, effectively denies the objective realities of the conflict and the material factors that perpetuate it.

This chapter engages with the question of context on two levels. In the first instance, it highlights how designers failed to incorporate context into the programme activities. This was not accidental but was instead attributable to the way that the P2PP had been conceptualized and theorized. Palestinians who complained about the "detachment" of the P2PP therefore failed to appreciate that this was an embedded design feature. In the second instance, however, the designers failed to appreciate the extent to which the occlusion of context could impact on programme implementation.

While donors ostensibly recognized the contradictions and tensions that arose from the problematic incorporation of context, they repeatedly and systematically failed to address them. For example, while Dominique Rossetti acknowledged the reality of occupation and Palestinian grievances, he still remained beholden to the donor agenda.[91]

The Canadian government similarly demonstrated this cognitive dissonance. Despite being fully aware of the internal and external limitations of the P2PP, it still saw fit to propose capacity-building as a suitable reform, despite the fact that it was quite clearly incommensurate with the scale of the challenges that had been previously encountered. I would be predisposed to attribute this to an ideological commitment to "dialogue" and "contact," although institutional constraints should clearly not be discounted either.

In summary, while the Canadian government and other donors have ostensibly acknowledged Palestinian complaints, they have done so on terms that are deeply conditional and contingent. My own account, in contrast, has not been limited by these inhibitions, and this has enabled me to underline the importance of context, and reiterate the (actual and potential) contribution of colonial theory. A number of the contributions that I have made can be expanded to the peace process more generally. Perhaps most significantly, I present Palestine as the point where "dialogue" and "cooperation" encounter their logical and practical limitations, rendering the P2PP as a mechanism that perpetuates colonial relations.

Notes

1. Wildeman, "Either You're With Us or Against Us."
2. Pappé, "Historiophobia or the Enslavement of History."
3. Chaitin, *Peace-building in Israel and Palestine*; Hanssen-Bauer, "The Israeli-Palestinian People-to-People Program"; Gawerc, *Prefiguring Peace*; Hermann, *The Israeli Peace Movement*; Hirschfield and Roling, "The Oslo Process and the People-to-People Strategy"; Katz, *Connecting with the Enemy*; Ma'oz, "The Oslo Agreement."
4. Abu-Saad, "Where Inquiry Ends," 1914.
5. Said, "The Morning After," 20.
6. Smith, *Decolonizing Methodologies*, 58.
7. Al-Hardan, "Decolonizing Research on Palestinians," 67. This chapter is strongly influenced by my own personal experience of the P2PP, both as a coordinator and participant. It also draws on PHD research interviews that were conducted with Palestinian and Israeli participants in 2001–2004. Additional influences and reference points include several P2P projects, Palestinian evaluation workshops and evaluation conferences focused on the work of donors (most notably Canadian and Norwegian agencies) and a special issue of *Palestine-Israel Journal of Politics, Economics and Culture*, that I co-coordinated, which was entitled "People-to-People What Went Wrong & How to Fix It?" This chapter is also indirectly influenced by my work as a consultant for the Canadian Networking for Peace programme in 2004–2005.
8. Smith, *Decolonizing Methodologies*, 151.
9. Tuck and Yang, "Decolonization is not a Metaphor," 3.
10. Haddad, *Palestine Ltd: Neoliberalism and Nationalism*; Hanieh, "Development as Struggle"; Richmond, "Critical Research Agendas for Peace"; Shehadeh, *Language of War, Language of Peace*.
11. Hanieh, "Development as Struggle," 35.
12. Selby, "Dressing up Domination as 'Cooperation," 123.
13. Haddad, *Palestine Ltd.*
14. Badarin, "Settler-Colonialist Management of Entrances," 159.
15. Bishara, *Palestine/Israel: Peace or Apartheid*, 56.
16. B'Tselem, *By Hook and By Crook*, 5; World Bank, *Coping with Conflict*.
17. Badarin, "Settler Colonial Management," 4; Weizman, *Hollow Land*; Halper, *War Against the People*.
18. Haddad, *Palestine Ltd.*
19. Roy, "The Palestinian-Israeli Conflict."

20. Nakhleh, *The Myth of Palestinian Development*.

21. Roughly understood to be the period in the 1990s of peace negotiations between the signing of the Oslo I Accord in 1993 up to the outbreak of the Second *Intifada* in 2000.

22. Hammami, "NGOs: The Professionalization of Politics," 55.

23. Haddad, *Palestine Ltd*, 199.

24. Hoare and Nowell-Smith, eds., *Selections from the Prison Notebooks of Antonio Gramsci*, 244.

25. Shalhoub-Kevorkian, *Security Theology, Surveillance and the Politics of Fear*, 6.

26. Foucault, "About the Beginning of the Hermeneutics of the Self," 204.

27. Foucault, *Discipline and Punish*.

28. Khalidi, *Brokers of Deceit*, 28. This "dishonest language" also featured in the 1917 Balfour Declaration, most notably in its designation of Palestinians as members of a "non-Jewish" community.

29. Foucault, "The Order of Discourse," 110.

30. Cox, "Gramsci, Hegemony, and International Relations," 138.

31. Wolfe, "Settler Colonialism and the Elimination of the Native," 387.

32. Veracini, *Settler Colonialism*.

33. Coulthard, *Red Skin, White Masks*, 15.

34. Fanon, *The Wretched of the Earth*, 78.

35. Jerusalem Media & Communication Center (JMCC), *Palestinian-Israeli Public Debate*, 227.

36. Allport, *The Nature of Prejudice*; Pettigrew, *Racially Separate or Together?*; Tajfel, "Social Identity and Intergroup Behavior"; Tajfel and Turner, "An Integrative Theory of Intergroup Conflict," 33–37.

37. Allport, *The Nature of Prejudice*.

38. Allport, *The Nature of Prejudice*; Amir, "The Contact Hypothesis in Ethnic Relations"; Cook, "The Systematic Analysis of Socially Significant Events; Pettigrew, *Racially Separate or Together?*

39. After these projects, "P2P" was used as a general term for joint projects. When Israelis and Palestinians worked together prior to Oslo II (1995), the term "Israeli-Palestinian meetings" was most frequently used to describe their interactions.

40. Endersen, *Contact and Cooperation*, 10–11.

41. The Joint Planning Group responded to requests from Palestinian and Israeli organizations for logistical and administrative assistance. It is also a repository of P2P-related records and information.

42. Charles Bronfman is co-founder of Birthright Israel, which elicits controversy for funding free ten-day heritage trips to Israel for young adults of Jewish heritage between the ages of eighteen and twenty-eight, over its portrayal of Palestinians and erasure of their history. The CRB puts its official birth date as December 11, 1986. At that time, the two principles that would guide the Foundation were, "The enhancement of Canadianism; and the unity of the Jewish people whose soul is in Jerusalem."

"About Us /History," The Andrea and Charles Bronfman Philanthropies, accessed November 22, 2020, http://www.acbp.net/history.php.

43. Endersen, *Contact and Cooperation*, 13; Hanssen-Bauer, "The Israeli-Palestinian People-to-People Program," 38.

44. Said, "The Morning After," 20; Naser-Najjab, *Dialogue in Palestine*.

45. Naser-Najjab, "Palestinian-Israeli People-to-People Contact Experience."

46. Abu-Saad, "Where Inquiry Ends," 1906.

47. See Kanji, chapter 4, in this volume.

48. Sium, Desai, and Ritskes, "Towards the 'Tangible Unknown,'" III.

49. Mu'allem, "Palestinian Israeli Civil Society Co-operative Activities."

50. Hanafi, "Dancing Tango During Peacebuilding; Naser-Najjab, "The Oslo People-to-People Program and the Limits of Hegemony."

51. Hermann, *The Israeli Peace Movement*.

52. Bar-On, *In Pursuit of Peace*, 237; Kaminer, *Politics of Protest*, 72; Warschawski, "The Long March," 94.

53. Al-Jiser. Unpublished Paper from the Palestinian Meeting for People Concerned with Joint Activities with Israelis, Jerusalem, June 1995. Copies were distributed to all workshop participants.

54. Al-Jiser.

55. Palestinian Ministry of NGOs, "The Basic Concept in Dealing with Israeli NGOs, 24 January 2000," unpublished paper.

56. JMCC is a media centre established in 1988 by a group of Palestinian journalists and researchers. Its services, which include research and opinion poll analysis, are used by journalists, researchers, and international agencies. The Evans Program for Conflict Resolution and Mediation, which is based at Tel Aviv University, conducted the Israeli evaluation.

57. Jerusalem Media & Communication Center (JMCC), *Palestinian-Israeli Public Debate*; Maoz, "Issues in Grassroot Israeli-Palestinian," 63–67.

58. Palestinian NGO Network (PNGO). "PNGO Press Release: 23 October 2000," accessed January 7, 2020, https://www.pngo.net.

59. PNGO.

60. Peres Center for Peace and Innovation, "Who We Are," accessed December 28, 2019, https://www.peres-center.org/en/the-organization/about-us/

61. Givat Haviva, "Homepage," accessed December 28, 2019, http://www.givathaviva.org/index.php.

62. Bat Shalom, "Homepage," accessed February 25, 2004, https://www.batshalom.org.

63. Shehadeh, *From Occupation to Interim Accords*, 71.

64. Office for the Coordination of Humanitarian Affairs (OCHA), *Closure Update*, 4–5.

65. World Bank, *Coping with Conflict*; B'Tselem, *By Hook and By Crook*; OCHA, "Displacement and Insecurity in Area C of the West Bank, Executive Summary"; World Bank, *Movement and Access Restrictions in the West Bank*.

66. Qumsiyeh, "A Critical and Historical Assessment of Boycott."

67. BDS, "PACBI Statement, Israel's Exceptionalism."

68. 2015 guidelines issued by the European Union Partnership for Peace Programme set out a number of clear aims, which establish that P2P initiatives should: 1) Promote civil society peacebuilding and conflict transformation actions through initiatives that are likely to impact on everyday lives and attitudes: 2) Support practical actions that aim to build capacity for non-violent approaches to conflict resolution, combat incitement to violence, construct mutual trust through reconciliation, empower marginalized parties, promote tolerance and launch joint development actions and strategies; 3) Bring Palestinians and Israelis together, further enhance forms of co-operation grounded within equality and reciprocity and strengthen direct civil society relationships. The full guidelines can be viewed at "EU Partnership for Peace Programme: Guidelines for grant applications," European Commission, accessed November 22, 2018, https://webgate.ec.europa.eu/europeaid/online-services/index.cfm?ADSSChck=1476223366800&do=publi.getDoc&documentId=146786&pubID=136549.

69. The Congressional Research Service (CRS) Report, "U.S. Annual People-to-People Funding."

70. United States Agency for International Development (USAID), *People-to-People Peace Building*.

71. Canadian International Development Agency (CIDA), *CIDA Peacebuilding Fund Program Evaluation*.

72. Canadian Representative Office, *Networking for Peace*, 1.

73. Rosetti, "Peacebuilding Programmes," 64–66.

74. Canadian Representative Office, "Networking for Peace," 2.

75. Richmond, "Critical Research Agendas for Peace," 258.

76. Foucault, *Discipline and Punish*, 194.

77. Canadian Representative Office, *Networking for Peace*, 1.

78. Dunbar-Ortiz, *An Indigenous Peoples' History of the United States*, 5.

79. Canadian Representative Office, *Networking for Peace*, 2.

80. Canadian Representative Office, *Networking for Peace*, 6.

81. JMCC, *Palestinian-Israeli Public Debate*, 21.

82. Health Sector Signatories, Occupied Palestine, "An Open Letter to the Palestinian and International Community."

83. Health Sector Signatories, Occupied Palestine.

84. Coulthard, *Red Skin, White Masks*, 126.

85. Salim Tamari, "The Case for Geneva." *The Guardian*, January 6, 2004, https://www.theguardian.com/world/2004/jan/06/comment.

86. See "History," Peacebuild: The Canadian Peacebuilding Network, accessed December 17, 2018, https://www.peacebuild.ca/en/about/history.

87. Haddad, *Palestine Ltd*; Wildeman, "Either You're with us or Against us"; Government of Canada, "Canadian International Assistance in the West Bank and Gaza" Government of Canada, last modified July 21, 2017, https://international.gc.ca/

world-monde/issues_development-enjeux_developpement/priorities-priorites/
where-ou/west_bank_gaza-cisjordanie_gaza.aspx?lang=eng.

88. "Canadian Policy on Key Issues in the Israeli-Palestinian Conflict." Government of
     Canada, last modified March 19, 2019, https://www.international.gc.ca/world-
     monde/international_relations-relations_internationales/mena-moan/
     israeli-palistinian_policy-politique_israelo-palestinien.aspx?lang=eng.

89. Wildeman, "Either You're With Us or Against Us."

90. "Canada's Trudeau Condemns BDS in Apology to Jewish WWII Refugees,"*Middle
     East Eye,* November 8, 2018, https://www.middleeasteye.net/news/
     canadas-trudeau-condemns-bds-apology-jewish-wwii-refugees.

91. Rossetti, "Peacebuilding Programmes: A Canadian View."

References

Abu-Saad, Ismael. "Where Inquiry Ends: The Peer Review Process and Indigenous
     Standpoints." *American Behavioral Scientist* 51, no. 12 (2008): 1902–18.

Al-Hardan, Anaheed. "Decolonizing Research on Palestinians: Towards Critical
     Epistemologies and Research Practices." *Qualitative Inquiry* 20, no. 1 (2014): 61–71.

Al-Jiser. Unpublished Paper from the Palestinian Meeting for People Concerned with Joint
     Activities with Israelis. Jerusalem, June 1995.

Allport, Gordon W. *The Nature of Prejudice.* Reading, MA: Addison-Wesley, 1954.

Amir, Yehuda. "The Contact Hypothesis in Ethnic Relations." *Psychological Bulletin* 71, no.
     5 (1969): 319–42.

Badarin, Emile. "Settler-Colonialist Management of Entrances to the Native Urban Space in
     Palestine." *Settler Colonial Studies* 5, no. 3 (2015): 226–35.

Bar-On, Mordechai. *In Pursuit of Peace: A History of the Israeli Peace Movement.*
     Washington, DC: United States Institute of Peace Press, 1996.

BDS. "PACBI Statement, Israel's Exceptionalism: Normalizing the Abnormal." October 31,
     2011. https://bdsmovement.net/news/israel%E2%80%99s-exceptionalism-
     normalizing-abnormal.

Bishara, Marwan. *Palestine/Israel: Peace or Apartheid: Prospects for Resolving the Conflict.*
     London: Zed Books, 2001.

B'Tselem. *By Hook and By Crook: Israel's Settlement Policy in the West Bank: Summary.*
     Jerusalem: B'Tselem, 2010.

Canadian Representative Office. *Networking for Peace. Assessing and Evaluating P2P.*
     Activities Workshop. Unpublished proceedings. April 5, 2005.

Chaitin, Julia. *Peace-building in Israel and Palestine: Social Psychology and Grassroots
     Initiatives.* New York: Palgrave Macmillan US, 2011.

Canadian International Development Agency (CIDA). *CIDA Peacebuilding Fund Program
     Evaluation: Evaluation Report.* Gatineau, QC: CIDA, 2000.

The Congressional Research Service (CRS) Report. "U.S Annual People-to-People
     Funding." November 2, 2018. https://www.everycrsreport.com/files/20181102_
     RS22967_d79381d2efee828cba7a4af517182c1ea2e9f960.html.

Cook, S.W. "The Systematic Analysis of Socially Significant Events: A Strategy of Social Research." *Journal of Social Issues* 18 (1962): 66–84.

Coulthard, Glen S. *Red Skin, White Masks: Rejecting the Colonial Politics of Recognition.* Minneapolis: University of Minnesota Press, 2014.

Cox, Robert W. "Gramsci, Hegemony, and International Relations: An Essay in Method." In *Approaches to World Order*, edited by Robert Cox, 162–75. Cambridge: Cambridge University Press, 1996.

CRB Foundation. "About Us /History." The Andrea and Charles Bronfman Philanthropies. Accessed November 22, 2020. http://www.acbp.net/history.php.

Dunbar-Ortiz, Roxanne. *An Indigenous Peoples' History of the United States.* Boston: Beacon Press, 2015.

Endersen, Lena. *Contact and Cooperation: The Israeli-Palestinian People-to-People Program.* Oslo: Institute for Applied Social Science, 2001.

Fanon, Frantz. *The Wretched of the Earth.* New York: Grove Press, 1963.

Foucault, Michel. "The Order of Discourse." In *Language and Politics*, edited by Michael Shapiro, 108–38. New York: The New York University Press, 1984.

Foucault, Michel. "About the Beginning of the Hermeneutics of the Self." *Political Theory* 21, no. 2 (1993): 198–227.

Foucault, Michel. *Discipline and Punish.* New York: Vintage Books, 1995.

Gawerc, Michelle I. *Prefiguring Peace: Israeli-Palestinian Peacebuilding Partnerships.* Lanham: Lexington Books, 2012.

Government of Canada. "Canadian Policy on Key Issues in the Israeli-Palestinian Conflict," Last modified March 19, 2019. https://international.gc.ca/world-monde/ international_relations-relations_internationales/mena-moan/israeli-palistinian_ policy-politique_israelo-palestinien.aspx?lang=eng.

Haddad, Toufic. *Palestine Ltd: Neoliberalism and Nationalism in the Occupied Territories.* London: IB Taurus, 2016.

Halper, J. *War Against the People: Israel, the Palestinians and Global Pacification.* London: Pluto Press, 2015.

Hammami, Rema. "NGOs: The Professionalization of Politics." *Race & Class* 37, no. 2 (1995): 51–63.

Hanafi, Sari. "Dancing Tango During Peacebuilding: Palestinian-Israeli People-to-People Programs for Conflict Resolution." In *Beyond Bullets & Bombs. Grassroots Peacebuilding between Israelis and Palestinians*, edited by Judy Kuriansky, 69–80. Westport, CT: Praeger, 2007.

Hanieh, Adam. "Development as Struggle: Confronting the Reality of Power in Palestine." *Journal of Palestine Studies* 45, no. 4 (2016): 32–47.

Hanssen-Bauer, Jon. "The Israeli-Palestinian People-to-People Program: The Fafo Model of People-to-People." Paper presented at the Helsinki Workshop on Evaluating Israeli-Palestinian Civil Society Cooperative Activities, Helsinki, Finland, November 27–28, 1999.

Health Sector Signatories, Occupied Palestine, "An Open Letter to the Palestinian and International Community Regarding Palestinian-Israeli Cooperation in Health." Palestinian Committee for the Academic and Cultural Boycott of Israel, 2005. http://www.monabaker.com/pMachine/more.php?id=2903_0_1_84_M5.

Hermann, Tamar S. *The Israeli Peace Movement: A Shattered Dream*. Cambridge: Cambridge University Press, 2009.

Hirschfield, Yair. "The Oslo Process and the People-to-People Strategy." *Development* 43, no. 3 (2000): 23–28.

Hoare, Quintin, and Nowell-Smith, Geoffrey, eds. *Selections from the Prison Notebooks of Antonio Gramsci*. New York: International Publishers, 1971.

Jerusalem Media & Communication Center (JMCC). *Palestinian-Israeli Public Debate on People-to-People Program: An Evaluation*. Jerusalem: JMCC, 2006.

Kaminer, Reuven. *Politics of Protest: The Israeli Peace Movement and the Palestinian Intifada*. Brighton: Sussex Academic Press, 1996.

Katz, Sheila H. *Connecting with the Enemy: A Century of Palestinian-Israeli Joint Nonviolence*. Austin: University of Texas Press, 2016.

Khalidi, Rashid. *Brokers of Deceit: How the US has Undermined Peace in the Middle East*. Boston: Beacon Press, 2013.

Maoz, Ifat. "Issues in Grassroot Israeli-Palestinian Cooperation: A Report on the NGO Discussion Panels." In *The Role of Non-Governmental Organizations in Peace-Building Between Palestinians and Israelis*, edited by Sami Adwan and Dan Baron, 63–67. Beit Jala: PRIME Publications, 2000.

Ma'oz, Moshe. "The Oslo Agreement: Toward Arab-Jewish Reconciliation." In *After the Peace: Resistance and Reconciliation*, edited by Robert L. Rothstein, 67–83. London: Lynne Rienner Publisher, 1999.

Middle East Eye. "Canada's Trudeau condemns BDS in apology to Jewish WWII refugees." November 8, 2018. https://www.middleeasteye.net/news/canadas-trudeau-condemns-bds-apology-jewish-wwii-refugees.

Mu'allem, Naseef. "Palestinian Israeli civil society co-operative activities." Paper presented at workshop focused on Palestinian-Israeli Civil Society Co-operative Activities, Helsinki, Finland, November 27–28, 1999.

Nakhleh, Khalil. *The Myth of Palestinian Development: Political Aid and Sustainable Deceit*. PASSIA, 2004.

Naser-Najjab, Nadia. "Palestinian-Israeli People-to-People Contact Experience, 1993–2004: An Evaluation." PHD diss., University of Exeter, 2004.

Naser-Najjab, Nadia. "The Oslo People-to-People Program and the Limits of Hegemony." *Middle East Critique* 28, no. 4 (2019): 425–43.

Naser-Najjab, Nadia. *Dialogue in Palestine: The People-to-People Diplomacy Programme and the Israeli-Palestinian Conflict*. New York: Bloomsbury Publishing, 2020.

Office for the Coordination of Humanitarian Affairs (OCHA). *Closure Update: Main Findings and Analysis (30 April–11 September 2008)*. Jerusalem: OCHA, 2008.

Palestinian Ministry of NGOs. "The Basic Concept in Dealing with Israeli NGOs." Unpublished paper. January 24, 2000.

Pappé, Ilan. "Historiophobia or the Enslavement of History: The Role of the 1948 Ethnic Cleansing in the Contemporary Peace Process." *Arab Studies Quarterly* 38, no. 1 (2016): 402–17.

Pettigrew, Thomas F. *Racially Separate or Together?* New York: McGraw-Hill, 1971.

Qumsiyeh, Mazin B. "A Critical and Historical Assessment of Boycott, Divestment, and Sanctions (BDS) in Palestine." In *Conflict Transformation and the Palestinians*, edited by Alpaslan Ozerdem, Chuck Thiessen, and Mufid Qassoum, 89–113. Florence: Taylor and Francis, 2016.

Richmond, Oliver P. "Critical Research Agendas for Peace: The Missing Link in the Study of International Relations." *Alternatives* 32, no. 2 (2007): 247–74.

Roy, Sara. "The Palestinian-Israeli Conflict and Palestinian Socioeconomic Decline: A Place Denied." *International Journal of Politics, Culture, and Society* 17, no. 3 (Spring 2004): 365–403.

Selby, Jan. "Dressing up Domination as 'Cooperation': The Case of Israeli-Palestinian Water Relations." *Review of International Studies* 29, no. 1 (2003): 121–38.

Shalhoub-Kevorkian, Nadera. *Security Theology, Surveillance and the Politics of Fear.* Cambridge: Cambridge University Press, 2015.

Shehadeh Raja. *From Occupation to Interim Accords: Israeli and the Palestinian Territories.* London: Kluwer Law International, 1997.

Shehadeh, Raja. *Language of War, Language of Peace.* London: Profile Books, 2015.

Sium, Aman, Chandni Desai and Eric Ritskes. "Towards the 'Tangible Unknown': Decolonization and the Indigenous Future." *Decolonization: Indigeneity, Education & Society* 1, no. 1 (2012): i–xiii.

Smith, Linda Tuhiwai. *Decolonizing Methodologies.* London: Zed Books, 2012.

Tajfel, Henri. "Social Identity and Intergroup Behavior." *Social Science Information* 13 (1974): 65–93.

Tajfel, Henri, and John C. Turner. "An Integrative Theory of Intergroup Conflict." In *Social Psychology of Intergroup Relations*, edited by William G. Austin and Stephen Worchel, 33–37. Monterey, California: Brook/Cole, 1979.

Tamari, Salim. "The Case for Geneva." *The Guardian*, January 6, 2004. https://www.theguardian.com/world/2004/jan/06/comment.

Tuck, Eve, and K. Yayne Yang. "Decolonization is not a Metaphor." *Decolonization: Indigeneity, Education & Society* 1, no. 1 (2012): 1–40.

United States Agency for International Development (USAID). *People-to-People Peace Building: A Program Guide.* Washington: USAID, 2011.

Veracini, Lorenzo. *Settler Colonialism: A Theoretical Overview.* Basingstoke: Palgrave Macmillan, 2010.

Warschawski, Michel (Mikado) "The Long March Towards Israeli-Palestinian Cooperation." In *Walking the Red Line: Israelis in Search of Justice for Palestine*, edited by Deena Hurwitz, 164–71. Philadelphia, PA: New Society Publishers, 1992.

Weizman, Eyal. *Hollow Land: Israel's Architecture of Occupation*. London: Verso Books, 2007.

Wildeman, Jeremy Donald. "Either You're with Us or Against Us: Illiberal Canadian Foreign Aid in the Occupied Palestinian Territories, 2001–2012." PHD diss., University of Exeter, 2015.

Wolfe, Patrick. "Settler Colonialism and the Elimination of the Native." *Journal of Genocide Research* 8, no. 4 (2006): 387–409.

World Bank. *Movement and Access Restrictions in the West Bank: Uncertainty and Inefficiency in the Palestinian Economy*. New York: World Bank, 2007.

World Bank. *Coping with Conflict: Poverty and Inclusion in the West Bank and Gaza*, Washington: The World Bank Group, 2011.

6

AID FOR PEACE REVISITED

A New Paradigm for Understanding Conflict and Development

NADIA ABU-ZAHRA

Coexistence and Canada

On Canada's national public radio, the Canadian Broadcasting Corporation (CBC), the radio host is gushing over a bright new idea. He is talking with representatives from Project Rozana, which brings together Palestinian and Israeli medical professionals, as well as serving patients in need of medical services.[1] Surely, the radio host exclaims, the Canadian government should fund this project. The lengthy interview ends and a question lingers in the air: who could possibly disagree?

For many years, an insistence has persisted that, in the interests of building peace, initiatives be funded that "bring the two sides together." Instances of these initiatives abound, ranging from psychosocial interventions to ecological cooperation. These are some random examples: Mosaica is a Jewish center that aims for religious conflict transformation through its

"Adam Centers" situated in areas where Palestinians live; Heart to Heart invites Palestinians with Israeli citizenship to join socialist Zionist "sleep-away camps" in Canada; and the Abraham Fund aims for, "coexistence [as] the minimal, least demanding way for people to relate to one another positively."[2] Numerous medical initiatives exist alongside Project Rozana, like Save a Child's Heart, the Canada International Scientific Exchange Program (CISEPO), the Peres Centre for Peace and Innovation's programs in health, and Road to Recovery. Like Project Rozana, these promote themselves as saving lives while building peace.

Beyond Canada, these "coexistence" projects are funded by, among others, the European Union and the United States. The United States State Department Middle East Partnership Initiative, begun in 2002, funds the Abraham Fund, as does the United States Agency for International Development and the European Union.[3] The European Union Peacebuilding Initiative (formerly the European Union Partnership for Peace programme, 2002–2013, and the European Union's People to People programme, 1998–2001), funds Save a Child's Heart and many others, to a total of five million Euros (over seven million Canadian dollars) per year.[4] The European Union Peacebuilding Initiative has channelled $176,125,777.00 of public funds over the course of twenty-three years. Canada has joined this pattern in recent years, sending $816,614.29 of public funds to EcoPeace and the Peres Center for Peace and Innovation, and allocating over ten times that amount in each of two phases ($9,324,867.43 in Phase 2 alone) to a coexistence program run out of McGill University.[5] Private, tax-deductible donations likely surpass these numbers.

The logic behind these funding decisions is simple and can be summarized in three principles. First, conflict is the most pressing problem in need of resolution. Second, to resolve conflict, the conflicting parties must be brought together. Thus, projects that "bring them together" outbid others that do not. Third, it is the role of the international community, including Canada— a country that prides itself as the origin of United Nations peacekeeping—to bring them together. This role was meant for Canada, and Canada was meant for this role.

Some years ago, I wrote about the problems of "aid-for-peace," also known as "peacebuilding aid,"

The finding is that peacebuilding aid favours traditional development interventions, which serve to substitute for social and political justice, hinder grassroots planning, and extend donor, state and interstate control.[6]

I asked why aid-for-peace did not bring peace, and what the prospects were for an alternative. In answer to the first question, I found that aid-for-peace delegitimized and thereby increased pressure to avoid advocacy, protection, and restoration of human rights—all prerequisites for a just peace. "Suppressing advocacy and protection," I concluded, "not only fails to bring peace, but works against efforts to bring peace." In answer, therefore, to the second question about an alternative to the highly ineffective aid-for-peace model, I wrote about rights-based aid, and offered working examples of what was making positive change on the ground.

In this chapter, I take this earlier research a step further. Using the Canadian case study, I examine the relations implicit in the two models of aid-for-peace and rights-based aid. I argue that focusing on relations allows us to better understand why aid-for-peace fails so we can reassess current aid models. I propose a mechanism for envisioning these relations and clarifying the choices before the international community. Finally, I suggest a seven-part classification system as a possible tool for reconsidering forms of aid and making explicit their underlying assumptions or logics. Ultimately, this answers the lingering question above, "who could possibly disagree?" and deepens our understanding of the grave real-life consequences of peace-building and conditional aid practices to date.

The Nature of Relations

Israel is a settler colony. . . .[A]ll settler colonies constitute a continuous process of land annexation, whereby native inhabitants are removed and settlers from elsewhere are brought to occupy the land. [Among Israel's settler colonial] policies are the long-held policy of annexing East Jerusalem; the building of the apartheid wall; the siege on Gaza, separating Palestinian land into non-contiguous units; the constant imprisonment of Palestinians under the charge of being political; the occupation and the checkpoints that make life impossible for ordinary Palestinians, hence encouraging their emigration; the de-development of the Palestinian economy; the policy of home demolitions; the discriminatory policies against Palestinian citizens of Israel that deny them the ability to purchase and lease land; and the non-ending stream of Israeli government permits to build more settlements and expand existing ones.[7]

In 1922, a census of Palestine—excluding many Palestinians in the South—"revealed over three-quarters of a million Palestinians in the country... including a small minority of Jewish Palestinians concentrated in Jerusalem (34,431) and Jaffa (24,000)."[8] In that year alone, 7,844 colonists had arrived, mostly from Eastern Europe. Over the following quarter century, the Zionist movement would build up a paramilitary force named the *Haganah*,[9] while bringing in over 132,000 people from Poland, Germany, Romania, then-Czechoslovakia, and elsewhere.[10]

By the time Zionist paramilitary forces were prepared to expel Palestinians from their lands and waters, 1.4 million Palestinians were living in Palestine.[11] Of these, only 69,000 were counted in the Zionist census of 1948.[12] Tens of thousands of Palestinians were present but excluded, and hundreds of thousands were forcibly expelled to prevent them from being counted.[13] Despite international law that not only recognizes Palestinian sovereignty, but also specifies that any "successor state" must automatically extend citizenship to those of its predecessor state,[14] the vast majority of Palestinians are excluded from Israeli citizenship. They are instead—as detailed in the list of policies quoted above—controlled by a state that systematically excludes, discriminates against, and oppresses them. Systematic oppression is by definition routine; practices like the knee-on-neck were commonplace in Palestine but given little attention until the killing of George Floyd in 2020 in the United States.[15]

If we look, then, at the *nature* of relations between Palestine and Israel, between Palestinians and the Zionist movement historically and today, we can ask whether these relations are healthy or unhealthy, and we can look at the state of *relational accountability*—to what extent do people practice respect and fulfil their responsibilities toward one another and the world around us?[16] Peacebuilding aid looks not at the nature of these relations, but rather only at whether relations exist. Peacebuilding aid, at its worst, is about "bringing the parties together" without questioning the nature of the relations between those parties. Moving genuinely toward health and well-being is not about unrelated entities "developing"—through aid or otherwise—but rather about interconnections, "all our relations,"[17] and maintaining health in and through those.

154   *Aid for Peace Revisited*

Peacebuilding aid is meant to be the stone that kills two birds: first, it brings conflicting parties together in coexistence, and second, it addresses the problem of "fragile," "weak" states or even weaker, "non-state" actors in a context of "asymmetric" (or an "imbalance of") power. These "underdeveloped" parties need aid to keep them going, to "develop," while that same peacebuilding aid also "helps" them by bringing them closer to the stronger parties (the other part of the "asymmetric" equation, those that are "strong" and the opposite of "weak," "fragile" and "non-state") so they can all live together in "peace."

In this worldview, aid that is not peacebuilding aid only kills one bird. It "chooses sides." It is "pro-" for the weak party and "anti-" against the stronger party. In the case of Palestine, aid that is not peacebuilding is denigrated for being simply "pro-Palestine," partisan and, by extension, anti-peace. This is not only problematic for the reasons I outline below; it is also an incorrect labelling of what true allyship looks like. True allyship is about being honest, akin to the saying, "friends don't let friends drink and drive." Allies do not let injustice continue.

The problem with focusing on one party or another, "pro" this or that, "anti" this or that, is failing to see the relationship, and "our"—in this case, the international community's and Canada's in particular—connection to it. This failure is symbolized in a popular image from a 1941 postcard promoting cooperation over conflict (two straining donkeys tied together),[18] which has been used in educational materials promoted by the international community in Palestine and neighbouring countries,[19] as well as being painted as a larger-than-life mural in Bethlehem.[20]

An infinite number of images would better depict reality in Palestine than this one, which shows ongoing stereotypes promoted by the "coexistence" initiatives listed above. The relationship between the Zionist movement and Palestinians who are indigenous to Palestine is not simply being in the same space at the same time, symbolized by being tied together. The relationship is one of attempted control for the purpose of expulsion and colonization.[21] The labelling of the Wall in Palestine as a "separation" or "border" is another example of failing to depict reality. First, Palestinians are on both sides of the Wall, as are their lands and waters (figure 6.1). Second, Palestinians are confined *by* Israel to make them supposedly "separate"; it is in fact a *very* controlling and invasive connection.

NADIA ABU-ZAHRA   155

FIGURE 6.1: Palestinian homes with a 26 ft. concrete wall blocking them from one another. *(Photograph by Gustaf Hansson, 2004.)*

CONTROLLER
(CONTROL)
⬇
Survivor ⬅ **Allies or ENABLERS** (CONTROL)

FIGURE 6.2: Our choice: ally of the survivor, or enabler of the controller.

The entire situation, with the international community included, is reminiscent of the deep critiques made by renowned scholar Mahmood Mamdani of the "responsibility to protect." The terminology in his book, *Saviors and Survivors*, is helpful here. Saviours fail to recognize relations of control and their own role (indeed complicity) in these relations. Survivors have more agency than the term "victims" can connote. While "survivors" is used in its intended meaning, "saviours" is heavy sarcasm—they save no one. For this latter reason, I will use the term "enablers" rather than saviours (figure 6.2).

I use the term "controller" instead of "colonizer" because this is a diagram of all controlling relations, not limited to colonization. In no situation of control is it acceptable to force the survivor into remaining in the controlling situation. In all situations of control, it is imperative to end the relationship of control and seek freedom and safety for the survivor. This diagram shows the alternative(s) to the harmful "aid" that forces Palestinians to "grin and bear it." The international community has not only a possibility but a *choice* of being an ally rather than an enabler, to choose allyship rather than the enabling of continued or redoubled control.

The Goal of Healthy Relations

Of course, many will deny that the situation is one of control. A prominent geographer once wrote to me,

> the Israeli worldview [is] that Israel "is not interested in control" of the Palestinian people. This is a very deep belief (in my view) and it means that the mission of the [Israeli military] and other bodies in Israel that are involved in the occupation is to "contain" the Palestinians, which is very different from "control."[22]

The Israeli military claim to have "disengaged" and avoided, "the burden associated with a civilian administration."[23]

Denial of control over Palestinians' lives from birth to death contradicts reality. The Israeli military wrote about controlling an "area" rather than its people, for purposes like "tranquility"[24] and "quiet,"[25] even while advocating and defining this "quiet" as entailing "large-scale violence" referring specifically to Israel's attacks on civilians in 2002, 2006 and 2008–2009, 2012 and 2014,[26] which killed thousands of unarmed men, women, and children, and wounded tens of thousands more. This "tranquility" and "disengagement" resulted in Israel killing at least 9,545 Palestinians, including 1,769 children, between September 2000 and July 2020, according to Israeli sources.[27]

Israel engages in widespread imprisonment of men, women and children, routine torture, and some of the most severe movement restrictions known in history. Palestinians in Gaza have suffered an excruciating siege—for a decade-and-a-half—that not only imprisons millions of people in an area scarcely 360 square kilometres, but also blocks access to reconstruction materials and anything resembling a normal life: foods, books, blankets, shoes, medical supplies, utensils, toiletries, tea, coffee…[28] But still, the denial of control continues.

In situations of "conflict," we are told, what is needed is "order," "stability" and "containment," which is described above. Yet, nothing about the above is or even sounds humane. But the problem is not "conflict" and is, in fact, control. The proposed "solutions" are actually just increased amount and intensity of control; they are even more of the problem, as if saying the antidote to poison is more poison. In pushing or acceding to "peacebuilding" aid, the international community is suggesting to the survivor that overcoming the problem requires spending more time together; the onus is on the survivor to prove that the situation is indeed one of control. Unless and until the survivor proves this—and Palestinians have been appealing to international legal mechanisms since the early twentieth century before many such mechanisms even existed—the survivor will have no protection.

For Palestinians, the burden is put on the survivor to address or cope with the effects of the control on them. Moreover, instead of supporting the survivor, efforts are made to restrict them. Resistance from the survivor must be met by the survivor being "contained," restrained, and constrained. The international community offers the enabling environment for the controller to intensify control and repress resistance.

Even as these unhealthy relations continue and are enabled, another different dynamic toward healthy relations is taking place. Using the term "survivor" —rather than "victims" of colonialism or of structural inequality— reflects agency, a strength that is healthy and not made of "power over,"[29] but instead is resilience (and not the kind of "resilience" critiqued as learning to live with, and under, ongoing harmful control). Survivors rebuild—themselves and community. In the face of de-struction—hyphenated to emphasize the act of breaking down, breaking to pieces—survivors practice con-struction and re-con-struction, hyphenated to emphasize the struggles to scramble back together the pieces of self and community.

This act of putting back together is described in a book entitled, *Living Palestine*.[30] The terms "living" and "survivor" are deeply connected; "survivor" is from the Latin *supervivere* where "super" refers to "over or beyond" and "vivere" is "to live."[31] In the book, life stories are told where people put themselves and their families back together not once, but twice, three times, and again and again...after incisions of violence like a checkpoint encounter, a demeaning comment from an unexpected quarter, an assault on dignity.

Structural violence—control—is an assault on dignity,[32] and the logistical barriers it brings to everyday life and needs are inhumane. The violence of control, especially bureaucratic violence, kills children and adults unable to reach medical care[33] and erodes dignity until, "Everything inside you is wilting; your taste for life,...wishing to die, wishing the night would come so you can sleep."[34] Yet this violence—like psychological/emotional, surveillance, financial, spiritual, verbal, cyber, environmental, and other violence—is not seen as such. Even human rights organizations omit killings by bureaucratic violence in their death counts.[35] This is the "tranquillity" and "quiet"—the resounding but smothered anguish and suffering—of the continuation of control that results from both control and the refusal to admit to its existence.

Analysis of Forms of International Involvement

What would international action look like if its goal were justice and healthy relations, if it ceased to be labelled "pro" this party or "anti" that party, and instead entailed real community building, relational accountability, and "power with,"[36] not just "power over"? To envision a form of international cooperation that acknowledges and addresses the relations of control, and that positions members of the international community as allies rather than enablers of violent control, we first need to analyze aid from the perspective of its connection to the controlling relationship.

Does a given form of international involvement fuel control, and if so, to whom, and is that control direct or indirect? Does this form of international involvement acknowledge the controlling relationship, or ignore or deny it? Does it actively force the relationship, or does it seek to end it? Finally, if it seeks to end the controlling relationship, does this particular form of international involvement rebuild healthy relations? Using these questions as a framework, we can see perhaps seven kinds of international involvement with situations of controlling relations.

In the case of Palestine/Israel, the first kind could be active involvement or support to ongoing colonialism and military occupation, through military exports, military aid and subsidies, contracts, or funds to the Israeli military-industrial complex,[37] and related cooperation or coordination. The goal of this kind of international community involvement is aid to Israel, and it thus fuels control for the controller, maintaining explicit, direct control. This kind of international involvement acknowledges the controlling relationship, actively forces it and makes no effort to rebuild healthy relations.

The second kind of international community involvement is "blind" to colonialism and military occupation. It overlooks violations of international law and maintains complicity with colonial activities like the Wall (figure 6.3) and settlements through, for example, ties with settler institutions, "free trade" deals, inaccurate labelling of exports, and so on. As with the first kind of international involvement, this too has the goal of aid to Israel; it fuels control to the controller and upholds explicit, direct control. It differs from the first kind of international involvement in that it refuses to acknowledge the controlling relationship while nevertheless actively forcing it and making no effort to rebuild healthy relations.

The following three kinds of international community involvement purport to aid Palestine, but in fact aid Israel. For instance, Canada funds building prisons for Palestinians and "security coordination" with Israel, which has resulted in not only the arbitrary detention and torture, but also the killing of Palestinians.[38] Palestinians at the apex of operationalizing this kind of aid are called "very important persons" (VIPs) and given privileges that other Palestinians do not receive. This kind of international

160   *Aid for Peace Revisited*

FIGURE 6.3: The Wall in Jerusalem. *(Photograph by Gustaf Hansson, 2004.)*

involvement, with its divide and rule strategies creating and exacerbating dangerous hierarchies, offers control to certain Palestinian institutions and individuals, using them to maintain explicit, indirect control over the general population. With this kind of involvement, the international community professes that "internal" Palestinian "factionalism" is not a direct result, first, of controls, constraints, and incentives put in place by Israel, and second, of the international community enabling this controlling relationship. Thus, although this kind of international involvement acknowledges the controlling relationship, it studiously ignores it.

Another example of aid to Israel masquerading as aid to Palestine is aid to sectors like health or education, funnelled through Israeli institutions that do not pursue justice and equality. Instead, they uphold colonial structures of domination and dispossession while seeking to band-aid some of its worst effects. This aid may also be given conditionally to Palestinian institutions who are required to mask and continue relations of control by asymmetrically "partnering" with such Israeli institutions from below. Of the seven kinds of international involvement, this kind has received the least critical attention and will be discussed in detail further below.

The last example under this category of fake or failed aid to Palestine, and the fifth kind of international involvement, is aid that makes the situation tolerable to the survivor, only for the survivor to continue enduring the abuse. This kind of aid is analogous to counselling on how to live or cope with—rather than end—control. It operates as if the controlling relationship does not exist and addresses only its effects (not seeing them as such). Examples in Palestine include the international community supporting localized births and maternity centres rather than working to end checkpoints and movement restrictions;[39] entrepreneurship programmes in lieu of the freedom of movement necessary to actually engage in commerce;[40] educational scholarships but no freedom of movement to study at the awarding institution,[41] or for Palestinian institutions to operate normally to provide that education locally. Like the "anti-politics machine" of all aid to colonial situations that feigns ignorance of colonialism,[42] this aid is needed, but always fails in its stated goals of better lives and livelihoods.[43]

"Partnership" in a Controlling Relationship

Before continuing to the sixth and seventh kinds of international involvement, it is worth pausing to reflect more intensely on the fourth kind, aid to Palestinian institutions being conditional on their having a "partnership" with Israeli institutions (that uphold colonialism), or aid directly to such Israeli institutions for work with their Palestinian "beneficiaries." Canadian or Canada-funded examples listed at the beginning of this chapter included: Mosaica and its Adam Centers, Heart to Heart, the Abraham Fund, Project Rozana, Save a Child's Heart, the Canada International Scientific Exchange Program (CISEPO), the Peres Centre for Peace and Innovation, Road to Recovery, EcoPeace, McGill University's International Community Action Network, and the Palestinian-Israeli Environmental Secretariat.

This kind of aid originated with an Israeli political party's internal think tank in 1991, founded and led by the later Deputy Foreign Minister Yossi Beilin.[44] Within a decade-and-a-half, initiatives could be seen across Israel/ Palestine and were literally mapped in atlases.[45] One joint Palestinian-Israeli organization, which predated (and outlasted) most others, said they

162   *Aid for Peace Revisited*

"sprouted like mushrooms after the rain."[46] According to the vision set out in 1991, aid to these organizations was to ensure Israel could connect the Palestinian economy to the Israeli one, and thus "mobilize external economic assistance" and remain free to "transfer resources" towards its priorities of, "mass immigration and the necessity of growth."[47]

In this model of international involvement, the "very idea that aid is for its recipients is questioned,"[48]

> . . .with so many vested historical, national, economic, commercial and political interests in this very high-profile hotspot, it is unrealistic to expect that donors will eventually cede the lead role solely to the Palestinians.[49]

Joint Palestinian-Israeli initiatives are, "identified mostly with their Israeli and international donors and partners," despite being physically located in Palestine and resulting from Palestinian organizations' stronger fundraising experience and capacity.[50] In many such initiatives, Palestinian labour goes unpaid and/or intellectual contributions unrecognized; McGill University's initiative, for example, has eleven "volunteer-based" centres.[51]

The outcome is to benefit not the Palestinian but the Israeli sector.[52] Israel holds Palestinian tax funds—to the tune of $US 222 million a month—and takes the liberty of paying itself vast amounts—like $US 141 million in 2012 and 2019—for any health or other services before transferring any of these funds to Palestine.[53]

> Israel benefits from propaganda as well as financially. Israeli services make money while Palestinian services are underresourced. . .I am always cautious of these so-called bilateral initiatives. Palestinians avoid these because of the imbalance of power in the way these organisations function and run, in their boards, how policy is developed; rarely does this involve people in Palestine.[54]

These are not partnerships of allyship or healthy relations, but rather of continued control, good "public relations," and isolation. These partnerships ignore the agency of the survivor, who is seen first as victim, then as beneficiary, aptly placing the controller-"partner" in the position of saviour.

Justice is a priority for few Israeli counterparts:

Few Israeli environmental NGOs [non-governmental organisations] concentrate on environmental justice. . .which limits their ability to find common ground with Palestinian colleagues. . .Impoverished rural Palestinian villages with inadequate water or sewage sit a few kilometers across the Green Line from well-tended, prosperous Israeli towns. Under such conditions, even the most well-meaning NGOs, wishing to cooperate to mutual benefit, are likely to reach profoundly different conclusions on. . .priorities.[55]

The focus is not on transforming the controlling relationship, but on finding commonalities while ignoring the relationship. Instead of the goal being to address and end the controlling relationship, it is seen as a pesky impediment. Projects to build a "culture of peace," for instance, are seen as hindered when Palestinians and Israelis cannot physically meet due to movement restrictions.[56] The real question in such projects is why the movement restrictions are not at the centre of efforts to make change rather than seen as mere peripheral hindrances.

Why is justice not the priority? Organizations for whom justice is not a priority are working in a particular context of control that often goes unmentioned.

The overwhelming majority of Israeli Jews (70–80 percent in recent [2012] polls), are those who clearly prefer a Jewish majority over Greater Israel.[57]

When asked what their most important value was in Israel National Election surveys conducted over a period of two decades, a third of Israelis answered, "a Jewish majority" (not even a fifth answered "democracy").[58] To secure this majority, "voluntary transfer" of Palestinians is advocated and Palestinians are cast as "risks" whose rights to vote, hold demonstrations, appear on television, be elected as Prime Minister or any other position, or participate "in fateful decisions" are popularly believed to be mutable and preferably violated.[59]

In defending joint initiatives following this model, one advocate explained that racism is real and that it is good to have projects address it.[60]

164   *Aid for Peace Revisited*

The problem with this model, however, is that the projects do not address racism. In the early 2000s, the wave of international involvement of the 1990s dried up, and desperate fundraising for food was unsuccessful, summarized by an aid worker commenting on the connection with the end of the "peace process": "Donors say they're here to fund the peace process, not the Palestinian people per se."[61] Not only did the projects never aim to address racism in a situation that more and more observers recognize as apartheid, they also never genuinely addressed people's needs. As envisioned in 1991, they were there to distract from the actual relations of control and colonialism, creating an aid fantasy world while Israel gained territory, population, and economic expansion at the cost of Palestinian lives and livelihoods.

Allyship and Survivor-Led Community Building

The sixth and seventh kinds of international involvement—allyship and survivor-led community building—are not aid, but rather allyship with the survivor in the controlling relationship, and with all those who support justice or healthy relations. These kinds of international involvement are a form of solidarity that represent "power with" rather than "power over" (described above in the section on the goal of healthy relations). They recognize and seek to end the controlling relationship and—in the latter case—rebuild healthy relations.

Examples of allyship include accompaniment (i.e., the International Solidarity Movement, International Women's Peace Service, Christian Peacemaker Teams, Peace Brigades International, Anarchists Against the Wall, and others); academic groups (Palestinian and United States Campaigns for the Academic and Cultural Boycott of Israel, Academics for Palestine, Students for Justice in Palestine, Students Against Israeli Apartheid, the Coalition Against Israeli Apartheid); cross-cutting movements (like the Palestine Solidarity Campaign, Independent Jewish Voices, Jewish Voice for Peace); and ex-soldiers' movements (like Breaking the Silence for veterans or Courage to Refuse for conscientious objectors).

Allyship can have its own drawbacks, such as: positioning international allies and some Palestinians as superior to other Palestinians who either do not resist or resist outside certain norms;[62] overshadowing and draining Palestinian individuals, families, groups and institutions;[63] and the negative impact of association with bold-actioned internationals who do not adhere to Israeli military controls (whereas Israeli military repression is primarily, but not exclusively directed against Palestinians) or Palestinian social norms.

The positive aspects arguably outweigh the negative. To reiterate, allyship acknowledges and seeks to end the controlling relationship. This has benefits for all, as described by Nazeeh Shalabi's explanation of the conscious collective intent to challenge the controlling relationship and build healthy relations among Palestinians, Israelis, and the international community,

> *We, the Mas'ha farmers and our supporters, knew from the beginning that we could not stop the Wall in Mas'ha or remove it. But we wanted to show that the Israeli people are not our enemies; to provide an opportunity for Israelis to cooperate with us as good neighbors and support our struggle; to show that the Wall is condemned by the international community; to expose that the Wall is not for security, but is about confiscating land; and to focus the mass media's attention on this issue.*[64]

Allyship is not fettered by conditionality. Palestinians can choose with whom to have relations and the nature of those relations, and the principles of healthy relations apply.

Examples of the final category—survivor-led community building—include the Palestinian Center for Rapprochement Between People, Ta'ayush (literally, "life in common"), the Canadian-Palestinian Educational Exchange (CEPAL), and the Palestine Museum of Natural History alongside its parent institution, the Palestine Institute for Biodiversity and Sustainability, "an oasis for people and wildlife in a place of conflict and rapid transformation."[65] These and other initiatives demonstrate that healthy relations based on justice and anti-oppression can be sought and achieved, but that such initiatives are very different from so-called coexistence efforts—and the international community's involvement in upholding or pushing for them—that enable the continuation of controlling relations.

To return to the question of "who could disagree" with Israeli-led charity efforts that make no move to end the controlling relationship, or often even to acknowledge it, the answer is: anyone could disagree who believes in justice and healthy relations. Just as few would imagine insisting on every Indigenous person on Turtle Island being forced to work with white Canadian settlers as the solution to salving their ailments, we should not expect the same of Palestinians. True "life in common" or coexistence is

166   *Aid for Peace Revisited*

not forcing the survivor to remain in the controlling relationship. It is not activities that benefit the controller in the name of the survivor. More importantly, the first priority is to end the controlling relationship, which does not always mean working more closely with those who advocate, support, or ignore its continuation. Instead, the international community's role needs to be the opposite if Palestinian lives are ever to be improved, lives saved, and a true peace to take hold. This requires acknowledging the existence of the controlling relationship—of colonialism—to advocate for its end and to support healthy relations for and among all.

These last two statements apply not only to international involvement in Palestine/Israel, but to all situations of controlling relationships (or the obfuscating terminology often used in colonial and other situations like "fragile states," "asymmetric conflict," and so on). Revisiting "aid for peace" is long overdue, and perhaps the framework offered here can help build a new paradigm for understanding so-called "conflict and development." In the case of Canada in particular, this may mean recognizing Canada's colonial position as a settler colony in Turtle Island, and how that has informed Canadian acceptance of colonialism elsewhere.[66] Again, the benefits of this acknowledgement—a step toward decolonization and healthy relations—will be felt by all, in Turtle Island and beyond.

Notes

1. Project Rozana, "Interview on Canada's CBC Radio Show 'All in a Day,'" last modified November 21, 2018, https://projectrozana.org/interview-on-canadas-cbc-radio-show-all-in-a-day/.

2. National Center for Family Philanthropy (NCFP), "Alan B. Slifka: One Man's Faith Based Mission," accessed June 15, 2020, https://www.ncfp.org/knowledge/alan-b-slifka-one-mans-faith-based-mission/.

3. Abraham Initiatives, "About the Abraham Initiatives: Supporters," accessed June 15, 2020, https://abrahaminitiatives.org/about-us/supporters/.

4. European External Action Service (EEAS), "European Union Peacebuilding Initiative," accessed June 15, 2020, http://eeas.europa.eu/archives/delegations/israel/documents/projects/20160216_eupi-eupfp_programme_at_a_glance_2016_en.pdf.

5. "Canada and the World: Project Browser," Government of Canada, accessed June 15, 2020, https://w05.international.gc.ca/projectbrowser-banqueprojets/filter-filtre.

6. Abu-Zahra, "No Advocacy, No Protection," 1.

7. Ayyash, "Israel Is a Settler Colony."

8. Abu-Zahra and Kay, *Unfree in Palestine*, 22.

9. Morris, *The Birth of the Palestinian Refugee*; Pappé, *The Ethnic Cleansing of Palestine*, 53, 56, 267.

10. Cattan, *Palestine and International Law*, 88.

11. Abu-Zahra and Kay, *Unfree in Palestine,* 29.

12. Robinson, "Occupied Citizens in a Liberal State," 52.

13. Robinson, 52.

14. Boling, "Palestinian Refugees and the Right of Return," 5–6.

15. *TRT World*, "The Knee-on-Neck, Long a Staple of Israel's Occupation of Palestine."

16. Wilson, *Research Is Ceremony*.

17. The phrase "all our relations," and meanings behind it, come from the languages and teachings of the Anishinaabe, Lakota, and other First Nations.

18. Sala, "How Does the Gaza-Israel War and Our Reactions to It Reflect in Our Own Conflicts?" last modified August 8, 2014, https://www.choiceconflictresolution.com/2014/08/15/gaza-israel-war-reactions-reflect-conflicts/.

19. Abu-Zahra and Price, "The Effects of Cabinet Shuffles on Development Projects."

20. Bukharan, "Vostok-Zapad: A Graffiti and Travel Blog." last modified August 2, 2010, https://vostokzapad.wordpress.com/2010/08/02/israeli-graffiti-3-banksys-art/.

21. Shafir and Peled, *The New Israel*, 245.

22. Quoted in Abu-Zahra, "Population Control for Resource Appropriation," 315.

23. Inbar and Shamir, "'Mowing the Grass': Israel's Strategy," 72.

24. Inbar and Shamir, 70, 84, 87.

25. Inbar and Shamir, 65, 68, 82, 87.

26. Inbar and Shamir, 68.

27. B'Tselem, "Statistics," accessed August 31, 2020, https://www.btselem.org/statistics.

28. Kotef, "Objects of Security," 187.

29. Starhawk, *Truth or Dare*.

30. Taraki, ed., *Living Palestine*.

31. Online Etymology Dictionary, "Survive (v.)." accessed August 31, 2020, https://www.etymonline.com/

32. Jamoul, "Palestine—In Search of Dignity"; Bourgois, *In Search of Respect*.

33. Algherbawi, "My Child Died Before My Eyes"; Abu-Zahra and Kay, "Unfree in Palestine," 122–41.

34. Quoted in Abu-Zahra, "Population Control," 321.

35. B'Tselem, "Statistics."

36. Starhawk, *Truth or Dare*.

37. Shafir and Peled, *The New Israel*.

38. Gostoli, "Basil al-Araj, Palestine Activist"; Burns, "Palestinians Speak Out About Torture in PA Prison"; Tartir, "The Palestinian Authority Security Forces."

39. Giacaman, Wick, Abdul-Rahim, and Wick, "The Politics of Childbirth," 136; Giacaman, Abdul-Rahim, and Wick, "Health Sector Reform in the Occupied Palestinian Territories (OPT)," 65.

40. Bahdi, Wildeman, Abu-Zahra, and Dagher, "Why Canadian Aid Won't Really Help."

41. Marcelo, "U.S. Turns Away Palestinian."

42. Ferguson, *The Anti-Politics Machine.*

43. Wildeman, "Palestinian State-building Denied"; Wildeman, "EU Development Aid in the Occupied Palestinian Territory"; Badarin, "Politics and Economy of Resilience."

44. Shafir and Peled, *The New Israel*, 250.

45. Gilbert, *The Routledge Atlas of the Arab-Israeli Conflict.*

46. Israel-Palestine Center for Research and Information (IPCRI), "A Vision for the Future of IPCRI: A Concept Paper for the Years 2000–2010," quoted in Zwirn, "Promise and Failure," 119.

47. Shafir and Peled, *The New Israel*, 250.

48. Abu-Zahra, "No Advocacy," 7.

49. Balaj and Wallich. "Aid Coordination and Post-Conflict Reconstruction: The West Bank and Gaza Experience," 3, cited in Giacaman, Abdul-Rahim, and Wick, "Health Sector Reform," 66, and in Abu-Zahra, "No Advocacy," 7.

50. Zwirn, "Promise and Failure," 117, 124.

51. McGill University, "International Community Action Network."

52. Wildeman, "Palestinian State-Building."

53. Ravid, "In Response to UN Vote"; *Middle East Monitor*, "Israel to Deduct a Further $198m."

54. Steve Sosebee, personal communication with Nadia Abu-Zahra, August 21, 2020.

55. Zwirn, "Promise and Failure," 123–24.

56. Coskun, "Analysing Desecuritisations," 407–08; Hershman, "Building Bridges in a Battle-Scarred Land," 303.

57. Uriel and Abulof, "Deep Securitization," 407.

58. Olesker, "National Identity and Securitization in Israel," 384.

59. Abulof, "Deep Securitization," 407, 409–10.

60. Choiniere, "Israel's Shared Society of Arabs and Jews."

61. Hockstader, "Sanctions Suffocating Gaza Fragile Economy," quoted in Zwirn "Promise and Failure," 117.

62. Pollock, "Using and Disputing Privilege."

63. Stohlman and Aladin, eds., *Live from Palestine.*

64. Quoted in Abu-Zahra, "Resisting the Wall," 40.

65. Palestine Museum of Natural History, "Palestine Institute for Biodiversity and Sustainability," accessed August 31, 2020, https://www.palestinenature.org/

66. Shipley, *Canada in the World.*

References

Abraham Initiatives. "About the Abraham Initiatives: Supporters." Accessed June 15, 2020. https://abrahaminitiatives.org/about-us/supporters/.

Abulof, Uriel. "Deep Securitization and Israel's 'Demographic Demon.'" *International Political Sociology* 8 (2014): 396–415.

Abu-Zahra, Nadia. "Population Control for Resource Appropriation." In *War, Citizenship, Territory*, edited by Deborah Cowen and Emily Gilbert, 303–26. Aldershot: Ashgate Publishing, 2008.

Abu-Zahra, Nadia. "Resisting the Wall: An Interview with Nazeeh Shalabi in the Village of Mas'ha, West Bank, Palestine." *Arab World Geographer* 10, no. 1 (2007): 38–56.

Abu-Zahra, Nadia. "No Advocacy, No Protection, No 'Politics': Why Aid-for-Peace Does Not Bring Peace." *Borderlands e-Journal* 4, no. 1 (2005): 1–21.

Abu-Zahra, Nadia, and Adah Kay. *Unfree in Palestine: Population Registration, Identity Documentation, and Movement Restriction*. London: Pluto Press, 2013.

Abu-Zahra, Nadia, and Hayley Price. "The Effects of Cabinet Shuffles on Development Projects: A Case Study on Global Education in Jordan." *The Arab World Geographer* 12, nos. 1–2 (2009): 19–35.

Algherbawi, Sarah. "My Child Died Before My Eyes." *The Electronic Intifada*, July 27, 2017. https://electronicintifada.net/content/my-child-died-my-eyes/21236.

Ayyash, M. Muhannad. "Israel Is a Settler Colony, Annexing Native Land Is What It Does." *Al Jazeera*, July 7, 2020. https://www.aljazeera.com/opinions/2020/7/7/israel-is-a-settler-colony-annexing-native-land-is-what-it-does.

Badarin, Emile. "Politics and Economy of Resilience: EU Resilience-Building in Palestine and Jordan and Its Disciplinary Governance." *European Security* 30, no. 1 (2021): 65–84.

Bahdi, Reem, Jeremy Wildeman, Nadia Abu-Zahra, and Ruby Dagher. "Why Canadian Aid Won't Really Help Palestinian Entrepreneurs." *The Conversation*, August 23, 2018. https://theconversation.com/why-canadian-aid-wont-really-help-palestinian-entrepreneurs-101731.

Balaj, Barbara, and Christine Wallich. "Aid Coordination and Post-Conflict Reconstruction: The West Bank and Gaza Experience." *OED Précis*, 185 (1999): 1–5.

Boling, Gail. "Palestinian Refugees and the Right of Return: An International Law Analysis (BADIL Information and Discussion Brief No. 8.)." Bethlehem: BADIL Resource Center for Palestinian Residency and Refugee Rights, 2001.

Bourgois, Philippe. *In Search of Respect: Selling Crack in El Barrio*. 2nd ed. Cambridge: Cambridge University Press, 2003.

B'Tselem. "Statistics." Accessed August 31, 2020. https://www.btselem.org/statistics.

Bukharan. "Vostok-Zapad: A Graffiti and Travel Blog." Last modified August 2, 2010. https://vostokzapad.wordpress.com/2010/08/02/israeli-graffiti-3-banksys-art/.

Burns, Jacob. "Palestinians Speak Out About Torture in PA Prison." *Al Jazeera*, September 27, 2017. https://www.aljazeera.com/indepth/features/2017/09/palestinians-speak-torture-pa-prison-170906092016102.html.

Cattan, Henry. *Palestine and International Law: The Legal Aspects of the Arab-Israeli Conflict*. London: Longman Group, 1973.

Choiniere, Paul. "Israel's Shared Society of Arabs and Jews: 'Racism in Israel...Is a Curable Disease.'" *The Day*, March 27, 2016. https://www.theday.com/article/20160327/OP03/160329399.

Coskun, Bezen B. "Analysing Desecuritisations: Prospects and Problems for Israeli–Palestinian Reconciliation." *Global Change, Peace & Security* 20, no. 3 (2008): 393–408.

European External Action Service (EEAS). "European Union Peacebuilding Initiative." Accessed June 15, 2020. http://eeas.europa.eu/archives/delegations/israel/documents/projects/20160216_eupi-eupfp_programme_at_a_glance_2016_en.pdf.

Ferguson, James. *The Anti-Politics Machine: "Development," Depoliticization and Bureaucratic Power in Lesotho.* Minneapolis: University of Minnesota Press, 1994.

Giacaman, Rita, Hanan F. Abdul-Rahim, and Laura Wick. "Health Sector Reform in the Occupied Palestinian Territories (OPT): Targeting the Forest or the Trees?" *Health Policy and Planning* 18, no. 1 (2003): 59–67.

Giacaman, Rita, Laura Wick, Hanan Abdul-Rahim, and Livia Wick. "The Politics of Childbirth in the Context of Conflict: Policies or de facto Practices?" *Health Policy* 72, no. 2 (2005): 129–39.

Gilbert, Martin. *The Routledge Atlas of the Arab-Israeli Conflict,* 10th ed. London: Routledge, 2012.

Gostoli, Ylenia. "Basil al-Araj, Palestine Activist, Buried in West Bank." *Al Jazeera,* March 18, 2017. https://www.aljazeera.com/news/2017/03/palestinians-bury-activist-basil-al-araj-170317225908329.html.

Government of Canada. "Canada and the World: Project Browser." Accessed June 15, 2020. https://w05.international.gc.ca/projectbrowser-banqueprojets/filter-filtre.

Hershman, Tania. "Building Bridges in a Battle-Scarred Land." *Science* 301, no. 5631 (2003): 303.

Hockstader, Lee. "Sanctions Suffocating Gaza Fragile Economy." *Washington Post,* December 6, 2000.

Inbar, Efraim, and Eitan Shamir. "'Mowing the Grass': Israel's Strategy for Protracted Intractable Conflict." *Journal of Strategic Studies* 37, no. 1 (2014): 65–90.

Israel-Palestine Center for Research and Information (IPCRI). "A Vision for the Future of IPCRI: A Concept Paper for the Years 2000-2010." Jerusalem: IPCRI, 2000.

Jamoul, Lina. "Palestine—In Search of Dignity." *Antipode* 36, no. 4 (2004): 581–95.

Kotef, Hagar. "Objects of Security: Gendered Violence and Securitized Humanitarianism in Occupied Gaza." *Comparative Studies of South Asia, Africa and the Middle East* 30, no. 2 (2010): 179–91.

Marcelo, Philip. "U.S. Turns Away Palestinian Who Was an Incoming Freshman at Harvard." *PBS Newshour,* August 28, 2019. https://www.pbs.org/newshour/nation/u-s-turns-away-palestinian-who-was-an-incoming-freshman-at-harvard.

McGill University. "International Community Action Network." Accessed June 15, 2020. https://mcgill.ca/ican/.

Middle East Monitor. "Israel to Deduct a Further $198m from PA Tax Revenue." July 22, 2019. https://www.middleeastmonitor.com/20190722-israel-to-deduct-a-further-198m-from-pa-tax-revenue/

Morris, Benny. *The Birth of the Palestinian Refugee Problem Revisited*. Cambridge: Cambridge University Press, 2004.

National Center for Family Philanthropy (NCFP). "Alan B. Slifka: One Man's Faith Based Mission." Accessed June 15, 2020. https://www.ncfp.org/knowledge/alan-b-slifka-one-mans-faith-based-mission/.

Olesker, Ronnie. "National Identity and Securitization in Israel." *Ethnicities* 14, no. 3 (2014): 371–91.

Online Etymology Dictionary. "Survive (v.)." Accessed August 31, 2020. https://www.etymonline.com/word/survive.

Palestine Museum of Natural History. "Palestine Institute for Biodiversity and Sustainability." Accessed August 31, 2020. https://www.palestinenature.org/.

Pappé, Ilan. *The Ethnic Cleansing of Palestine*. Oxford: One World Publications, 2006.

Pollock, Mica. "Using and Disputing Privilege: Young U.S. Activists Struggling to Wield 'International Privilege' in Solidarity." *Race/Ethnicity: Multidisciplinary Global Contexts* 1, no. 2 (2008): 227–51.

Project Rozana. "Interview on Canada's CBC Radio Show 'All in a Day.'" Last modified November 21, 2018. https://projectrozana.org/interview-on-canadas-cbc-radio-show-all-in-a-day/.

Ravid, Barak. "In Response to UN Vote, Israel Confiscates NIS 460 Million in Palestinian Authority Tax Funds." *Haaretz*, December 2, 2012. https://www.haaretz.com/2012-12-02/ty-article/.premium/israel-confiscates-pa-tax-funds/0000017f-e9e1-dc91-a17f-fded02900000.

Robinson, Shira. "Occupied Citizens in a Liberal State: Palestinians Under Military Rule and the Colonial Formation of Israeli Society, 1948–1966." PHD diss., Stanford University, 2005.

Sala, Marina. "How Does the Gaza-Israel War and Our Reactions to It Reflect in Our Own Conflicts?" Last modified August 8, 2014. https://www.choiceconflictresolution.com/2014/08/15/gaza-israel-war-reactions-reflect-conflicts/.

Shafir, Gershon. and Yoav Peled. *The New Israel: Peacemaking and Liberalization*. London: Routledge, 2000.

Shipley, Tyler A. *Canada in the World: Settler Capitalism and the Colonial Imagination*. Black Point, NS: Fernwood Publishing, 2020.

Starhawk. *Truth or Dare: Encounters with Power, Authority, and Mystery*. San Francisco: HarperSanFrancisco, 1990.

Stohlman, Nancy. and Laurieann Aladin, eds. *Live from Palestine: International and Palestinian Direct Action Against the Israeli Occupation*. Boston, MA: South End Press, 2003.

Taraki, Lisa, ed. *Living Palestine: Family Survival, Resistance, and Mobility under Occupation*. Syracuse, NY: Syracuse University Press, 2006.

Tartir, Alaa. "The Palestinian Authority Security Forces: Whose Security?" Al-Shabaka, May 16, 2017. https://al-shabaka.org/briefs/palestinian-authority-security-forces-whose-security/.

TRT World. "The Knee-on-Neck, Long a Staple of Israel's Occupation of Palestine." May 30, 2020. https://www.trtworld.com/magazine/
the-knee-on-neck-long-a-staple-of-israel-s-occupation-of-palestine-36787.

Wildeman, Jeremy. "Palestinian State-building Denied and the Failure of Western Liberal Idealism." in *Democratisation of Palestinian Politics as a Basis to Rebuilding the National Project.* Birzeit: Muwatin Institute, 2020.

Wildeman, Jeremy. "EU Development Aid in the Occupied Palestinian Territory, Between Aid Effectiveness and World Bank Guidance." *Global Affairs* 4, no. 1 (2018): 115–28.

Wilson, Shawn. *Research Is Ceremony: Indigenous Research Methods.* Black Point, NS: Fernwood Publishing, 2008.

Zwirn, Michael J. "Promise and Failure: Environmental NGOs and Palestinian-Israeli Cooperation." *Middle East Review of International Affairs* 5, no. 4 (2001): 116–26.

IV

RESTRICTING THE PUBLIC DEBATE ON PALESTINE

7

PALESTINIAN IMAGES, ISRAELI NARRATIVES

Radio-Canada Coverage of the 2014 War on Gaza

RACHAD ANTONIUS

Introduction

The war on Gaza started in early July 2014 and ended officially on August 26, 2014, with a ceasefire agreement. The "spiral of violence," to use a common term that is, as we will see, not adequate, was re-activated with the abduction by a group of Palestinians from the West Bank of three teenaged Israeli settlers followed by their killing.[1] Soon after, a young Palestinian was burned alive by Israeli settlers. This was followed by a number of operations in the West Bank by the Israeli army, which imprisoned numerous Palestinians, including some who had previously been released from Israeli prisons. The war broke out in this context, and it lasted close to two months.

During this period, the news bulletins of Radio-Canada, the French sector of Canadian Broadcasting Corporation (CBC), like most important news networks, covered it almost every single day. The purpose of the present research was to find out to what

177

extent this coverage was in line with the journalistic standards of the CBC, which aim at representing what happens on the ground without bias or distortion. In its "journalistic standards and practices" section on its website, the CBC announces the following principles: accuracy, fairness, balance, impartiality, and integrity. We will see in the course of this study to what extent these principles have been respected in the coverage of the war on Gaza.

Objectivity in News Coverage

The notion of objectivity is the subject of much theoretical debate in journalism studies. While some dispute the relevance of defining it as "sticking to the facts,"[2] others maintain that it remains a horizon to be reached as well as an operating principle that guides the daily work of journalists.[3] Even when that sense of objectivity is challenged, it is not entirely abandoned; but rather is reduced to a weaker principle of impartiality in assessing the different or opposing views of social actors, which must be equally presented as part of an effort to make the journalists appear neutral.

Among the many aspects of objectivity listed by Michael Ryan, two of them seem particularly relevant to our present discussion:

- "accuracy, completeness, precision, and clarity in information collection and dissemination";[4] and,
- "fairness, impartiality, and disinterestedness, in that no social–political agenda is served and the tenets of objectivity are observed."[5]

These two aspects are another formulation of the principles mentioned in the *Journalistic standards and practices* of Radio-Canada.[6] I will designate the first one as *objectivity as concordance with what happens on the ground*, and the second one as *objectivity as impartiality*. Let us see what these two conceptions really mean in the case of the Israeli–Palestinian conflict.

Objectivity as Concordance with Empirical Facts

The coverage of a war includes coverage of empirical facts, interpretation of what they mean, and sometimes value judgments about their justifications. In the first category, objectivity is easier to define: if a bombing happens, it is possible to describe with a good degree of objectivity what was bombed, the power of the bombs, and the extent of damages measured in human lives and properties. Sometimes this information is not readily available, but eventually it does become available. In the case of a military occupation, it is also possible to determine, for instance, whether new settlements are established, on what land, and how many people they can accommodate.

Giving a balanced representation of the empirical acts of war does not consist in giving equal importance to the military initiatives, number of victims, or extent of destruction of the two sides, independently of the magnitude of these effects. On the contrary, when there is an enormous differential of power among the actors, objectivity consists in showing the actual imbalance of military power and capacity to destroy. In other words, treating two parties who are very unequal as being in a symmetrical position of power is not a sign of objectivity.

The interpretation of what political actions mean can, in some cases, be treated with a certain degree of objectivity, but there are more grey areas. For instance, we can say with a high degree of objectivity whether a settlement in an occupied territory is in violation of international law or not. There are usually very clear criteria to determine conformity with international law, and in the case of Palestine, there is a very broad consensus on this issue. For instance, in spite of its strong support for Israel, Canada does consider, officially, that Israeli settlements in the West Bank are in violation of international law (The Fourth Geneva Convention of 1949, in this case).

Objectivity is harder to achieve when reporting the *meaning* of certain actions because it depends on the interpretation of the various political actors. For instance, does a specific military action constitute an aggression or an act of legitimate self-defence? International law does provide broad criteria, but it needs to be interpreted in a given context. In this case, news coverage has to rely on a weaker definition of objectivity, that of impartiality towards the various political actors.

Objectivity as Impartiality

Impartiality means that political actors in a conflict situation should be given an equal opportunity to express their specific reading of the situation. Here, the notion of symmetry comes into play again, and it should be properly understood. The symmetry we are talking about is the symmetric representation of the *narratives* of the various political actors in conflict, not the symmetry of their actions.

A division of labour is then possible: in a situation where there is an observable and important differential in power, the journalists can (and must) document the asymmetry in power and in means between the actors. By doing so, they would not violate the principle of impartiality. But they must give an equal voice to the actors, in a symmetric way, to explain their point of view. Or more briefly, symmetric representation of *perspectives*, not symmetric representation of *actual power*, would better match the principles extolled by the CBC.

With these remarks in mind, we can examine more closely the coverage of the war by the Téléjournal.

We examined the 10 p.m. news bulletin of Radio-Canada, the *Téléjournal de 22 h*. This covered almost the entire months of July and August of 2014. CBC-Radio Canada defines the concept of this news bulletin as follows:

> *More than a simple summary of the events of the day, the* Téléjournal *de 22 h has the ambition to be the news bulletin "that goes the furthest," by the presence of its network of correspondents abroad, by its outreach, as it is broadcast in all of Canada and re-broadcast by TV5 at the international level, by the expertise of its craftsmen who come to supplement the news of the day with their explanations, analyses and contextualization; by more detailed reports on the major issues facing society; and finally, by the desire to present concrete solutions to the problems of our time.*[7]

In spite of these objectives, there is a very strong feeling on the part of many observers of the conflict over Palestine that media coverage of the issue, including at Radio-Canada, is heavily biased in favour of Israel.

We wanted to determine whether or not this impression corresponds to empirical reality (i.e., whether or not there is a pro-Israeli bias in the news coverage of the 10 p.m. *Téléjournal*, and what are the journalistic processes that produce this bias, if there is one). Our hypothesis was that there was such a bias, but it was not clear to us what elements of the news coverage expressed it, and through which communication processes. Over the last few decades, a number of studies have addressed similar issues, mostly for American media, rarely for Canadian media.[8] This study aims at filling partly this gap, as it focuses on a flagship program of Radio-Canada. Formulated differently, the question of our study becomes, "What are the journalistic

Palestinian Images, Israeli Narratives

and discursive processes that produce biases in spite of a stated intention to be fair?"

Theoretical Approach

Two concepts will help us name the processes at work: framing and narrative. The concept of framing is fundamental in news analysis. A frame is "a central organizing idea…for making sense of relevant events, suggesting what is at issue."[9] We are not interested in the question of how journalist frames are produced, a question that D'Angelo raises in the text referred to. We are trying, rather, to determine the processes through which the frames that are used produce a biased representation of the war. The frames that are at work in the news coverage will be determined inductively and not a priori. They will emerge from the analysis. Moreover, the question of the production of the journalistic frames will not be addressed in this paper. It can only be raised once we have identified what these frames are and how, specifically, they introduce biases in the representation.

In order to answer that general question, we will try to identify the framing of the war through two sub-questions,

a. The representation of empirical facts. Were they reported adequately in an objective and equitable way?
b. The representation of the narratives of the two main protagonists. Were these narratives reported in a fair and equitable way?

The notion of narrative is very important. A narrative is the overall representation of a given situation by a social or political agent. It includes the perspective of agents on the conflict, their justifications, their understanding of what is at stake, and their subjective perceptions of the conflict (emotions, fears, attitudes). Graef et al. identify three modes in which a narrative may be conceived: as a lens to view the social world; as data that provide insights into that world; and as a tool for analyzing this data in a systematic and coherent manner.[10]

The meaning we will adopt here is the third one, as it is more general, and it necessarily refers to the other two. A narrative allows an actor to sort out the information about a given issue and to structure it in such a way as to produce meaning. It allows the agent to build a more or less coherent overall picture of all the empirical information, to attribute to each of its elements a degree of relevance, to identify other agents, to identify what is at stake, to identify causal relationships between the various factors, and finally to determine the priorities about the actions to be taken. A central element of a narrative is the determination of what is at stake in a situation, in this case the asymmetric conflict between the Israelis and the Palestinians. Political narratives, in particular, are a way of ordering elements of the political reality, in such a way as to orient action, and they are not to be dismissed as a constructed "relative" truth, but as a rational organization of empirical reality that reflects a perspective and specific interests.[11] The notion of narrative as we use it is a little more complex than that of "perspective" used by Philo and Berry in their *Bad News from Israel*.[12]

In order to see how these elements play out let us first analyze specific excerpts of the news bulletin. We chose the dates of August 3rd and 4th, but many other excerpts could have been used as well. The news bulletins of these two days illustrate the way the journalistic processes, including the way issues are framed, allow the narratives of *some* of the political actors to shape the representation of the conflict in the *Téléjournal*. We will analyze them in some detail to show the underlying—probably not conscious—logic of the argument, then present some statistics compiled over the word-for-word transcription of the bulletin over the two-month period of the war.

This is how the segment on the war on Gaza starts on August 3, 2014,

> *Good evening, ladies and gentlemen. Israel has announced a seven-hour truce that will take effect tomorrow in the Gaza Strip except in the Rafah region in the south where fighting continues. It is precisely in Rafah that a new Israeli strike has aroused indignation; a United Nations school housing Palestinian refugees was hit, killing at least 10 people. This is the third school to be bombed in ten days.*[13]

In this first segment, an Israeli move away from violence is first announced: Israel announces a seven-hour unilateral truce. Then a single Israeli strike is announced, without mentioning the target of the strike. The indignation it has aroused is mentioned. The target is then disclosed, but in the passive tense: a United Nations school was hit. Paralleling the sentence where the Israeli strike had no target, the verb that announces that the school was hit has no actor that did the hitting. Similarly, the verb "to be bombed"

182   *Palestinian Images, Israeli Narratives*

has no subject either. It is in the passive tense. A reporter, Nathalie Cloutier, based in Montreal then steps in,

> *The Israeli army says the shooting was aimed at three members of the Islamic Jihad who were riding their motorcycles near the school. The projectile hit the courtyard where the children were playing. This new tragedy has raised outrage in the world; the United States is talking about an outrageous bombing. For the UN, it is a criminal and amoral act that violates international humanitarian law.*

The Israeli army's interpretation of the strike against the school is thus immediately communicated to viewers, with the word "projectile" used to talk about the bomb that was dropped. This explanation is adopted by the reporter who says, "This new *tragedy* has sparked outrage around the world," adopting the word "tragedy" to describe the bombing, without attributing it to some outside source. The harsher words, such as "an outrageous bombing" are not adopted by the reporter but attributed to their source (the American government), and the words "criminal and amoral act" are also attributed to their source, the United Nations, and not incorporated in the reporter's brief. The reporter says that the courtyard was hit, but visuals of destroyed school buildings are shown. The visuals also show Palestinian adults carrying the dead or praying, and later on, a Palestinian girl crying. The words used by the reporter are much softer than the images that are shown to illustrate them.

The next couple of minutes are devoted to communicating the difficult humanitarian conditions of the Palestinians in Gaza, and they include a declaration of the United Nations representative in the Palestinian territories, James Rawley, to the effect that there is no safe place for Palestinians in Gaza. The reporter continues,

> *To add to the tragedy, because of what he described as appalling health conditions, diseases that have been missing from Gaza for decades are reappearing. Cases of typhoid fever and cholera are reported in the shelters.*

It is interesting to note here that the difficult humanitarian conditions are highlighted by the reporter, but not their cause. They are presented as elements that "add to the tragedy," not as the context of the tragedy and a fundamental aspect of the situation in Gaza. The cause of diseases that reappear cannot be war because these health conditions develop over longer periods of time. Their cause is the blockade imposed on Gaza since 2006 that severely restricts the entry of medical equipment and food into Gaza. Lifting the blockade is a demand by Hamas and by all political actors in Gaza, but neither the blockade nor the demands to lift it are mentioned by the reporter when presenting the difficult humanitarian conditions that the Palestinians undergo. The blockade is the elephant in the room, but being absent from the framing of the "tragedy," it becomes invisible or irrelevant to the viewers. Reporter Nathalie Cloutier then continues,

> *While the civilian population suffers, Hamas continues to fire on Israel, which continues to respond: 55 rockets have been fired from Gaza in 24 hours, and the army says it has neutralized a Palestinian cache containing 150 mortar shells. The majority of Israeli victims are soldiers, including Hadar Golding, who was believed for a time to be a prisoner of Hamas before the army confirmed that he had died in combat. He was buried in his native village in Israel. This is Nathalie Cloutier for Radio-Canada, Montreal. (August 3, 2014)*

This excerpt is a digest of the discursive strategies used, consciously or unconsciously, that structure the bulletin's coverage of the war. The main elements of this discursive strategy are the following:

- Hamas is the initiator of the violence, and this is a pattern communicated by the use of the word "continues," while Israel only "responds" to the violence.
- The rockets fired by Hamas are counted: 55. But the actual destructive potential of the 55 rockets and of the mortar shells is not mentioned, and viewers could not be faulted if they assumed these are similar to the bombs Israel drops on Gaza. The number of bombs Israel dropped on the school is not mentioned, and neither is their power or destructive capacity. The magnitude of the "response" is not provided: only the fact that it is a "response."

184   *Palestinian Images, Israeli Narratives*

- Moreover, Hamas is presented as ignoring, or even betraying, the interests of its own population ("While the civilian population suffers"), which is one of the elements of the Israeli narrative. This narrative claims that, in spite of the fact that Israel worries about the Palestinian civilian population, it accidentally hurts Palestinian civilians while targeting "terrorists," but it is the Palestinian leadership that does not care about its own population. Hamas is firing on Israel, which leaves no choice for Israel but to "respond."
- Right after mentioning that Hamas is firing rockets and stocking mortar shells and counting them, the reporter says that the majority of Israeli victims are soldiers, and she cites the name of one of them. She then says that he was thought to be a prisoner of Hamas, but that Israel admitted he died in combat, probably in Gaza since there was a fear he was abducted. Therefore, although he is presented as a victim of the rockets, the rest of the paragraph allows us to understand that he was not...

The presence of mortar shells on Palestinian territory is also mentioned as part of the military actions by Hamas, thus providing an implicit justification of the initiative of the Israeli army. The following excerpt, from the August 4 *Téléjournal*, is also worth analyzing. From Montreal, André Gariépy files the following report,

A strange truce was declared unilaterally by Israel. The 7-hour ceasefire allowed the passage of humanitarian convoys carrying food, fuel and medicine to Gaza. At the same time, the Israeli army continues its raids on other parts of the Gaza Strip. In Rafah, an 8-year-old Palestinian girl was killed during the bombings. In this hospital in the Palestinian enclave, dozens of wounded were coming in. (Visual: a Palestinian man holding a wounded child.) "He's a child, he doesn't carry a gun. What did he do to deserve to be shot?" asked the man. The city of Jerusalem was shaken by two attacks on Israelis. First, near the Hebrew University in Jerusalem, an Israeli soldier and passers-by were wounded by a gunman riding a motorcycle. Then, in an ultra-Orthodox Jewish neighbourhood, an Israeli youth was killed and five others were injured when the driver of an excavator ran into a bus. The perpetrator of the attack, who according to the authorities was of Palestinian origin, was shot dead by the police. The destruction of the tunnels used by Palestinian fighters to carry out attacks on Israeli territories is almost complete according to the Israeli army. This was one of the main objectives of the attack on the Gaza Strip, which has been going on for 28 days. "The Gaza campaign continues and will not end until the Israelis regain prolonged calm and security," said Israeli Prime Minister Benyamin Netanyahu. (August 4, 2014)

The structure of this segment is as follows. First, the unilateral truce declared by Israel is put forward. It is labelled "strange" because simultaneously, there are attacks on other parts of the Gaza Strip. The impact of these attacks is mentioned and illustrated by a man carrying a wounded child and pleading that the child does not deserve to be shot. Then the bulletin focuses on attacks by Palestinian individuals in Jerusalem, giving them more airtime than the various Israeli bombings of the day. There is a double discursive process here:

- An apparent symmetry of the violence from the two sides is established, whereas in reality, there is no common measure in the magnitude of the violence and no comparison in the type of violence (systematic warfare by a state versus two individuals attacking whom they consider "the enemy" with the tools at hand). This differential in the magnitude of violence is not put forward.
- The logic of the Israeli army is presented by the reporter and attributed to the army: its actions aim at destroying tunnels used by the Palestinians to carry out attacks. And then, the Israeli prime minister himself is shown explaining that Israel is seeking "prolonged calm and security." No similar platform is given to the Palestinian side to explain its perspective.

The two news bulletins of August 3 and 4, 2014, and especially the last excerpt, illustrate the pattern that gives this chapter its title: In the excerpts where Palestinians talk, they tend to talk about their suffering. In the excerpts where Israelis talk, they tend to explain why there is a war.

Is this pattern verified statistically? We will see that it is indeed verified. Even if there are many images of Palestinians suffering, the narrative of the conflict is essentially the Israeli narrative. It should be noted that both André

Gariépy and Nathalie Cloutier were reporting from Montreal and not from Israel or Palestine.

The Palestinian perspective is not totally absent, however. Reporter Marie-Ève Bédard, who had just returned from a visit in Gaza, does present it twice before getting to the excerpt we are discussing below; she says that hundreds of families have taken refuge in the United Nations schools because they are unsafe in their own homes; information that was not linked to the bombing by Israeli missiles of the United Nations school a few days later. The news anchor then asks a question,

> *Anchor: . . .The population of Gaza, they are certainly angry with Israel, no doubt about that, but one could also wonder if they would be angry with the people of Hamas. It is Hamas after all that was the first to launch rockets. They are the ones who started the ball rolling. Do you sense a movement of revolt, the word may be a bit strong, but of discontent towards Hamas itself?*

Here we see again the same pattern at work. Palestinian suffering is acknowledged, but it is understood through the framework supplied by Israel. The anchor adopts the Israeli explanations uncritically and places the responsibility for starting the conflict on Hamas. A fundamental aspect of the journalist framing at work here consists in:

- trying to explain military violence as a response to earlier military violence, not to the structural conditions of the occupation and the blockade; and
- establishing a symmetry between the violence of Hamas and that of Israel.

In response, the reporter challenges the anchor's views,

> *Marie-Ève Bédard: No. Hardly. This is surprising. One could blame them for their intransigence, but most of the people we met, we talked to, told us: even if we do not necessarily support Hamas for all its very harsh policies towards Israel, in the conflict we are currently involved in, we are behind them, we are with them, we support them, we agree with their demands for a lasting ceasefire, in other words, we want*

much more than to put an end to the military operation under way, we want to find a solution to all the problems we have been suffering from for decades now; the blockade that has been imposed since 2006, the opening of borders, the free movement of people. Most Gazans are not allowed to leave the territory of the Gaza Strip. . .People are asking to live in dignity. . . (July 29, 2014)

This kind of framing of the issue by Marie-Ève Bédard seemed to us to be exceptional during the period of the war on Gaza. The reporter does not challenge the idea that Hamas is intransigent, but she does correct the perception of the anchor, and she gives an explanation of the situation of the Palestinians that expresses their perspectives and their concerns. The reporter communicates what "most people [she] met" told her. They are supporting Hamas in this war, they agree with their demand for a lasting ceasefire, for an end to the blockade and for the opening of borders. We must point out the fact that it is a Canadian reporter and not a Palestinian spokesperson who has articulated these views, because Palestinians are not asked to explain their perspective.

The question we then asked was whether these two patterns of presenting the Palestinian narrative and the Israeli narrative were equally present in the *Téléjournal* throughout the duration of the conflict. The answer is no. In order to arrive at that conclusion, we systematically analyzed the text of the news bulletin from the beginning of the coverage of the conflict (July 6, 2014) to its official end (August 26, 2014).

The Method

The method used is a classical method of computer-assisted content analysis and theme extraction as developed by Paillé and Mucchielli, Jodelet, and others.[14] We started by making a word-by-word transcription of the news bulletin. Based on a first, direct reading of the transcriptions, we identified two broad categories of elements that would constitute an a priori grid through which the content analysis of the transcripts was conducted,

a. Who is speaking, and
b. What are they talking about.

The "speakers" grid (*locuteurs*) included, for example, the following subcategories: witness, reporter, demonstrator, anchor, Israeli spokesperson, Palestinian spokesperson, etc. The issues that were discussed included: violence, aggressors, victims, responsibility attributed to…, actions taken, interests/justifications, support for…, critique of…, etc. We also coded the discursive strategies used: symmetry in violence, symmetry among the aggressors, Israeli action presented as being "in response to…", Palestinian action presented as being "in response to…", symmetry among victims, etc.

Our grid also distinguishes some subcategories of actors within each side. On the Israeli side, for example, we distinguished between the government spokesperson, the army, civilians, etc. On the Palestinian side, we distinguished Hamas, civilians, the Palestinian Authority, various militias, etc. Some of the statistics we have compiled lump together all the actors on each side. This is because the material of the news bulletin is not appropriate for a very detailed analysis, as the news is brief, and the overall size of the text to be analyzed does not always permit such distinctions. In order to carry out the analysis, we used the textual analysis software QDA *Miner*. The transcribed speech of the news bulletin was coded in QDA *Miner* with this grid. We have first compiled simple frequencies (i.e., how often destruction is the main issue, or how often Israeli or Palestinian spokespersons are interviewed), and we have then cross-tabulated some of the categories.

In particular, we have contrasted the frequency with which the Israeli understanding of the war was presented. That is, what is at stake for Israel, compared to what is at stake for the Palestinians. These are fundamental elements of the narrative of a political actor. We have also examined whether the triggers or the motivations of a given action were mentioned equally for Israel and Hamas, and to what extent the notion of "symmetry," and symmetry of what (of rights? or of means?) played out in these representations. Attention has been given to semantics (i.e., to the terms used to describe the protagonists, mainly Hamas, Israel, and the Israeli army).

One methodological point requires discussion. We will be counting below the occurrences of a given theme, not just the actual content of what was said. For instance, if Israeli security concerns are mentioned twenty times, and the demands to end the blockade on Gaza are mentioned ten times, we will conclude that the Israeli perspective is given twice as much coverage as the Palestinian perspective, which constitutes a bias. This is a standard approach in the field of computer-assisted content analysis. It has to be completed by a complementary qualitative examination of what is said and how it is said.

The conclusions one can draw from counting the occurrences must be dealt with differently when it comes to quantitative content. Consider the two sentences: "2000 Palestinians were killed" and "67 Israelis were killed." Each is counted as one occurrence of a mention of violence, but of course the content of the two sentences does convey a different impact. Nevertheless, we believe it is still meaningful to count the occurrences. From a viewer's perspective, hearing twenty times that there were victims on each side leaves a sense of symmetry that may have more impact than the sense of imbalance in the magnitude of the suffering. It will not change the fact that there are many more victims on the Palestinian side, but it may reduce the intuitive perception of the differential between the two situations. The situation is still different when counting bombs, raids, and rockets. Launching one air strike on Gaza is much more destructive than sending one hundred rockets on Israel, as the cumulative destructive impact of the rockets is minimal when compared to one single air strike that can destroy whole buildings and kill hundreds. In this case, simple counting can be misleading because the units that are counted are not comparable. Therefore, treating one air strike and one rocket as symmetric military actions is misleading, and it does constitute a bias.

We will take these limits into account when contrasting the representation of the suffering and the representation of the narratives.

Results
Representations of What is at Stake

This is perhaps the most important aspect of the biases in the representation of a political conflict. In the Israeli-Palestinian conflict, each of the two parties considers some issues to be much more fundamental than others, and each gives its own reasons for starting the war or for refusing a ceasefire. A fair coverage of the war would consist in making sure that both sides are allowed to express what is fundamental for each of them, and in making sure that reporters and anchors do not adopt the justifications of one of the parties as their own. Given the strong asymmetry of the conflict that results from the enormous differential of power (political and military) between the two main parties in the war, transmitting the specific narrative of the weaker of the two parties, whose narrative is rarely heard, in addition to that of the

190   *Palestinian Images, Israeli Narratives*

dominant party, which has been adopted by the political elites in Canada and the United States, is an important criterion of objectivity. Generally speaking, the *Téléjournal* fails on this criterion of objectivity. It mentions the Israeli perspective, including justifications for its overall offensive, much more often than the perspective of Hamas or other Palestinian actors.

The Israeli perspective is illustrated by comments such as: concerns for security; reasons given to destroy the tunnels dug by Palestinians; concern for an abducted soldier; the description of Hamas as a terrorist organization; and retaliation for an action by Hamas or by one of the Palestinian militias. The Palestinian perspective is illustrated by concerns such as the desire to see Israeli aggression stopped, or the desire to get an overall peace agreement (not just a ceasefire), the desire to end the blockade. More importantly, Palestinian perspectives are centered around the history of their dispossession that has resulted in the fact that former residents of present-day Israel and their descendants are now refugees, deprived of their legal rights and crowded in Gaza. That part of the story is completely absent from the narrative of the war on Gaza.

It turns out that 81 per cent of the times a perspective is communicated, or the motive of an action is mentioned, it is the Israeli perspective that is communicated to the audience, whereas the perspective of the various Palestinian actors or the motives given for Palestinian actions (offensive or defensive) are mentioned only 19 per cent of the time. Moreover, it often happens that the motivations given by the Israeli actors are incorporated in the reporter's account of what is happening. This means that sometimes, it is the reporter who says something like, "today Israeli war planes bombed… in retaliation for…" adopting as their own the justification given by Israeli spokespersons for Israeli actions. Table 7.1 illustrates this statistic.

TABLE 7.1: Mentions of Palestinian motives vs Israeli motives.

Palestinian motives	19% (n=30)
Israeli motives	81% (n=125)

The discursive strategies used to communicate the reasons of the various parties is illustrated in the following example. On August 4, 2014, reporter André Gariépy said the following,

The destruction of the tunnels used by Palestinian fighters to carry out attacks in Israeli territory is practically completed, according to the Israeli army. This was one of the principal objectives of the attack on Gaza strip, which has been going on for 28 days. "The Gaza offensive is going on and it will not be over until the Israelis can find again calm and security in a permanent way," said the Israeli Prime Minister, Benyamin Netanyahu. (August 4, 2014)

Here, we can see the following discursive strategy at work:

- The Israeli army is mentioned as the source of the news.
- The justifications given by Israel for targeting the tunnels is incorporated in the journalist's report without quotes: that the Palestinians are using the tunnels to carry out attacks against Israel.
- The principal objective of the attack on Gaza is incorporated in the news, without quotes.
- The Israeli Prime Minister is quoted.

Another example is illustrated by the following excerpt from a news anchor, in which the disappearance of an Israeli soldier is first attributed to his kidnapping by Hamas, but the information is immediately corrected to say that the soldier died in combat,

Good evening ladies and gentlemen. The alleged kidnapping of an Israeli soldier by Hamas triggered a bloody assault yesterday in the southern part of the Gaza Strip. However, the Israeli army confirmed tonight that Hadar Goldin, 23, died in action, rather. It remains to be seen whether this latest development will make it possible to accelerate the withdrawal of Israeli troops from Palestinian territory, while the destruction of the tunnels is being completed. (August 2, 2014)

The first statement, before being corrected, has a function: it explains the bloody offensive by Israel, by the use of the word "triggered." The information is structured by an underlying logic: the Israeli assumption about the kidnapping provides the excuse for the assault. Then the information is corrected. In other words, the anchor presents the information in such a way as to incorporate the Israeli logic in the presentation of an empirical

192   *Palestinian Images, Israeli Narratives*

fact, even when the excuse turns out to be erroneous. There is no equivalent treatment when reporting on Palestinian attacks.

Some comments must be added about the reference to the blockade of Gaza by Israel, given the importance of this issue for the Palestinians. Globally, the issue was explained in more or less adequate terms, but not by the Palestinians themselves. The term was used a total of twenty-five times, on twelve different days. On three occasions, the consequences of the blockade were explained on the *Téléjournal*, the first by a Canadian interviewee on July 18,[15] then on two other occasions by reporters Marie-Ève Bédard and Raymond St-Pierre. The rest of the occurrences were reports about Palestinian demands that the blockade be lifted.

The clip of Raymond St-Pierre on July 24, 2014, is interesting in that it does explain the destructive impact of the blockade on the residents of Gaza, but it looks at it through an Israeli narrative: Israel imposed it in 2007,[16] because Hamas came to real political power that year, and Hamas, "wants to destroy Israel." "And you can imagine," he says, "this is not very pleasant for the neighbourhood, so the blockade was imposed." When reporting about the conditions demanded by Khaled Mishaal, the head of the political bureau of Hamas, that the blockade be lifted, he reports, "But when it comes to a lasting ceasefire, they are unwilling to compromise. They say that we have come this far in these battles—we have fought—and there will have to be an outright lifting of the blockade of Israel and also of Egypt." And he adds: "These are already enormous demands."

Who is Talking, and What are They Talking About?

This overemphasis on the Israeli reasons or motives for military action, as opposed to Palestinian reasons or motives, is paralleled by the selection of interviewees who bring their points of view to the bulletin.

We looked at Palestinian and Israeli interviewees. Some were interviewed as spokespersons, others as witnesses. A total of forty-five Israelis and forty-one Palestinians were interviewed during the period of the war. Most Israelis who were interviewed were resource persons, or people in an official position, explaining their perspective. Three Israelis were asked to testify about their personal experience. On the Palestinian side, only fourteen Palestinians were asked to explain their position or that of Hamas, and twenty-seven were interviewed as witnesses, talking essentially about their suffering. We wondered whether, overall, these interviewees were providing an explanation of the situation or testimonies about what they were going through. We obtained data as shown in table 7.2.

TABLE 7.2: Who is talking about what?

	Israelis	Palestinians
Explanation or analysis	42 (75%)	14 (25%)
Testimony	3 (10%)	27 (90%)
Total	45	41

An essential characteristic of the news bulletin coverage is illustrated here. In general, Palestinians talk mostly about their suffering, and this is enhanced by the visuals of destruction that were shown day after day, triggering no doubt a certain empathy towards them. Israelis, on the other hand, mostly explain why there is a war and why the Palestinians are suffering. This division of labour basically reinforces the Israeli narrative: Yes, the Palestinians suffer, but it is their own fault. This mantra is often repeated by American, Canadian, and Israeli spokespersons, thus giving a specific, pro-Israeli interpretation of *why* there is suffering on the Palestinian side.

Explaining Israeli Assaults as Being "In Retaliation" or "In Response" to a Palestinian Assault

The trends explained above are reinforced by the use of the concept of "retaliation" to explain Israeli military actions, mostly by the anchor and reporters. For instance, on July 8, 2014, reporter A. Gariépy said,

> *The Israeli raids are a response to the hundreds of rockets launched by Hamas on southern Israel in the last 24 hours.*

This means that the Israeli justification for that military action is adopted by the reporter or the anchor, and is incorporated in the news itself, thus acquiring the status of "fact." Is this a pattern or an exception?

On twenty different occasions during the coverage of the war on Gaza, a reporter or the anchor herself explained an Israeli bombing as being in retaliation for some Palestinian action. On seven additional occasions, it was the interviewee that explained the Israeli action as being in retaliation to a

Palestinian action. But the converse *never occurs*. Never during this coverage, not a single time, was a Palestinian attack (usually firing rockets) presented as being in retaliation for some Israeli action, neither by the reporters nor by interviewees. It thus seems that the firing of rockets by Hamas is motivated by an irrational hatred—this is the dominant discourse on Hamas—since no rational reason is mentioned. The theme of irrationality is a fundamental aspect of the stereotyped and racist representation of Arabs and Muslims, and it has been documented and analyzed in many publications,[17] and is described in other chapters in this volume, as well.

Beyond the issue of the motives, including that of retaliation, the way daily operations are reported is also problematic. There are three other ways in which the apparently objective reporting tends to reproduce the Israeli narrative about the war:

- By the way military attacks are reported.
- By allowing Israelis to present their perspectives and analysis more than Palestinians do.
- By addressing direct moral blame to one political actor in a disproportionate way.

Let us now examine how these discursive elements play out in the news bulletins.

Counting Military Assaults

Military assaults are not counted in the same way for the Palestinian and the Israeli sides. When talking about Israeli assaults, four terms are used: offensive, strikes, raids, and bombings. The term "offensive" (*offensive*, in French) is generally used to describe the global Israeli initiative in this war. It was used on thirty-seven occasions. The word "strike" (*frappe* in French) was used twenty-eight times, mostly in the plural form, without mentioning the number of strikes (except once, where it was said that thirty Israeli air strikes had been conducted that day). The word "raids" was used to describe war plane sorties, and it was used eleven times, but the number of raids was never counted. The word "bombings" was used on thirty-seven different occasions. So, overall, Israeli assaults were talked about in 113 phrases over the period, without any quantification of the amount of firepower used. Rockets launched from Israeli tanks were never mentioned or counted. It was mentioned once that two warning rockets were fired by Israel, to inform residents of a building that an air strike was imminent.

In contrast, Palestinian assaults were described by counting—almost scrupulously—the rockets that were fired. On sixty-six different occasions, it was said that Hamas had fired rockets on Israeli targets. Most of the time, the statement did not indicate the number of rockets that had been fired. But on five occasions, on the dates indicated in table 7.3, numbers were provided, usually by the anchor or by the reporter. On three other occasions, an order of magnitude was given: "hundreds of rockets" or "a rocket every 10 minutes." On seven other occasions, a description was given. This is summarized in table 7.3 below.

TABLE 7.3: Counting the number of rockets fired by Hamas.

Description of the fire power of rockets or their numbers	Date
11 launching sites	July 7
Numerous rockets fired	July 7
Series of rocket attacks	July 7
Powerful rockets	July 8
Salvas of rockets	July 11
Rockets by the hundreds	July 14
Launching sites	July 14
95 rocket launchers	July 21
Hundreds of rockets	July 21
A rocket every 10 minutes	August 1
Numbers mentioned	
1500 rockets	July 7
40 rockets	July 7
100 rockets	July 8
22 rockets	July 17
55 rockets	August 3

No such numbers were given about Israeli air strikes (except twice: thirty strikes and fifty strikes were mentioned out of a total of 6,000 raids over the two-month period) or about Israeli tank shells, and no mention was made about the huge difference in destructive power between a rocket and a missile, or a rocket fired from a portable launcher and a rocket fired from a tank, thus giving a false impression of strong firepower in Hamas' hands, even symmetry.

A potential explanation for this coverage is the reliance on the Israeli army as a source of information, which means that every rocket launched by Hamas is accounted for, whereas the number of air strikes by Israel are rarely counted. We have not investigated this issue.

One has a completely different sense of the differential in firing power when seeing the actual figures, as shown in table 7.4, compiled by the United Nations Office of Coordination of Humanitarian Affairs (OCHA) and published in 2015.[18]

TABLE 7.4: Comparison of firepower between Israel and Hamas by the UN OCHA.

Israeli Firepower	Palestinian Firepower
The IDF carried out more than 6,000 airstrikes in Gaza, many of which hit residential buildings.	No air force.
The IDF reported that they supplied 5,000 tons of munitions to the Israeli fighting forces.	
The IDF reported that they had fired 14,500 tank shells and around 35,000 artillery shells	Palestinian armed groups fired 4,881 rockets and 1,753 mortars

While the detailed figures were not available at the time of the war, one can nevertheless see the discrepancy between what was reported and what was actually happening on the ground. The insistence on the detailed counting of the rockets fired by Hamas, while any detailed account of the Israeli firepower is ignored, does constitute a bias. This may be due to the fact that reporters ultimately get their information from Israeli sources eager to disclose the number of rockets fired by Hamas, but not the number of bombs they drop on Gaza, or the number of rockets fired on Gaza from their tanks.

Symmetry

The notion of symmetrical representation has to do with the notion of objectivity. But we claim that if a symmetric representation of dignity or of humanity is indeed a sign of fair treatment, symmetric representation of firepower is not a sign of objectivity if it does not correspond to empirical reality on the ground. From that point of view, symmetric representation of firepower or the number of victims is indeed misleading and biased. Statements such as the following have been constant during the coverage of the war, to the point that we can say that the notion of symmetry has played a structuring role in the representation of the war. Here are examples of the statements we are talking about:

- Tension in the Middle East becomes explosive. Israelis and Palestinians bomb each other with air raids and rockets. (July 7, 2014)
- On the international scene now, in the Middle East, the escalation of violence is accelerating between Israel and Hamas. (July 7, 2014)
- Israel strikes hundreds of targets in Palestine. Hamas launches hundreds of rockets into Israel. (July 10, 2014)
- While the international community condemns this violence, the exchange of missiles and rockets on the ground continues unabated. (July 10, 2014)
- ...despite some rocket and missile exchanges in recent hours. (August 13, 2014)
- ...the Israeli ground offensive in Gaza and the Hamas rocket launches against Israel. (July 21, 2014)
- And meanwhile, one fears that all this diplomatic pressure may push both sides to redouble their mutual aggression to perhaps maximize their respective gains before finally agreeing to lay down their arms. (July 21, 2014)
- We know who the losers are. The losers are the Israeli people and the Palestinian people especially, who are the victims and the prey of this war machine. The winners, surely, are the radicals on both sides. (Canadian expert, July 10, 2014)
- On the international scene, it has now been 6 days since missiles and rockets have rained down on Gaza and Israel. (Anchor, July 14, 2014)

- The truce between Israel and Hamas has been extended for five days, and it is still holding despite some rocket and missile exchanges in recent hours. (Anchor, August 13, 2014)

The equivalence between missiles and rockets is reaffirmed in all these statements. The overall representation viewers could reasonably have is that Hamas and Israel are equally hitting at each other, but for some unexplained reason, there are twenty times more victims on the Palestinian side than on the Israeli side, and more than a thousand more times civilian victims.

Indeed, apparent symmetry in firepower does not mean symmetry of damage inflicted or symmetry of the number of victims. The *Téléjournal* does mention the disproportionate number of victims on the Palestinian side. But this does not contradict the Israeli narrative, as we will see further down.

The "Moral High Ground": Information, Narrative, and Blame

In the course of the coverage of the war on Gaza, anchors and reporters have never addressed a direct moral blame at the warring parties. On one occasion (July 17, 2014), Anchor Maxence Bilodeau challenged a statement by the Consul General of Israel in Montréal, a posture that could be interpreted as an indirect blame. Direct blames were also addressed to Israel by the United Nations, especially after the bombing of the United Nations school on July 29, 2014, and they were reported by the *Téléjournal*.

But what interests us here is the link between the representations of empirical facts, narratives, and the moral positioning of the Canadian government. This link gives relevance to the processes we have outlined in the previous sections in the course of the war on Gaza.

The harshest indictments were addressed to Hamas, and they were coming from, besides Israel, the Canadian government. These are closely linked to the adoption of the Israeli narrative. In order to hold, they require this narrative to be validated. This link is seen in the comments of Mr. John Baird, then Minister of Foreign Affairs. On July 15, reporter Luc Chartrand said, "In Canada, Minister Baird reiterated his unwavering support for Israel," and he showed a clip of the Minister declaring, "For the Government of Canada," he said, "This is not a war between Israel and the Palestinians, but between the Jewish state and a terrorist organization." The clip by Reporter Manon Globensky on July 14, 2014, is also telling,

*John Baird said that Hamas and its allies are alone responsible for the
death and suffering of innocent civilians in Gaza. The Prime Minister
said that it is obvious that Hamas is using human shields. So it is these
two positions that recall exactly what is being said in Israel, and which
Prime Minister Netanyahu himself evokes. And John Baird even adds
that there can be no moral equivalence between what Hamas is doing—
which is a terrorist organization—and what Israel is doing, which is
trying to protect its citizens.*

We see in these two quotes the intertwining between the narrative, the
moral posture, and the blame. Minister Baird considers the conflict to be
between "the Jewish State" and a "terrorist organization." The identity of
the protagonists determines the position he adopts. And the characterization
of the two protagonists is precisely the one adopted by the present government of Israel: One party is the Jewish State, not the State of Israel; and the
other party is a terrorist organization. In the second clip, Baird reiterates
the Israeli view of the conflict, a point that is underscored by the reporter:
Hamas is responsible for the death of its "innocent civilians"; it is taking its
own population as human shields; Israel is trying to protect its citizens. And
the conclusion follows: there can be "no moral equivalence" between Israel
and Hamas.

On July 23, 2014, reporter Manon Globensky discusses the tweets of the
Canadian Ambassador to Israel, Ms. Viviane Berkowitz,

*It's mostly the bias in her tweets that's surprising. Because Mr. Berkowitz
is simply taking a single point of view, the point of view of Israel. She
gives her impressions but also retweets messages from the Canadian
government and the Israeli government. So look at what it comes down
to, she denounces activists who refuse to say that it is Israeli civilians
who are being targeted by Hamas rockets. Or she says that the cement
destined for the infrastructure in Gaza is destined to build tunnels rather
than shelters for the population.*

The importance of the Israeli narrative is highlighted by Ambassador
Berkowitz, who adopts it fully and uncritically, as pointed out by the
reporter. The fact that the Ambassador denounces activists who question
the Israeli narrative highlights the importance of spreading that narrative.

200   *Palestinian Images, Israeli Narratives*

The link between selecting empirical facts that support a given narrative, and supporting a moral and a political position is illustrated by these comments. We will draw further consequences from that link, and from the critical attitudes of the reporter, in the conclusion of this chapter.

Conclusion

Two broad conclusions emerge from the preceding analysis. The first is that the suffering of the Palestinian population of Gaza is communicated adequately and illustrated with strong visuals, even with some degree of empathy. The second is that this suffering is interpreted globally through an Israeli narrative, thus neutralizing the political impact and meaning of the wholesale destruction of Gaza and of the bombing of its population. This validates the Israeli position on the conflict and ultimately undermines any serious claim of objectivity in covering the war on Gaza.

This is achieved through the cumulative impact of a series of communication processes centred around:

- the unequal transmission of the narratives of both sides,
- a de facto division of labour between Palestinian and Israeli interviewees, the former mostly expressing what they undergo and the latter mostly explaining why this happens,
- an incorporation by reporters of Israeli motives into their own description of events on the ground, in particular the one-sided concept of "retaliation,"
- a detailed account of rockets sent by Hamas but no counting of Israeli air strikes or of Israeli tank shells,
- and a false understanding of the link between "objectivity" and "symmetry."

This coverage takes place in a context where both the Canadian government and the official opposition in Ottawa give their full support to the Israeli narrative, casting blame on Hamas and only on them, and fully endorsing the Israeli narrative. Thus, the Israeli narrative becomes the Canadian official narrative, as it has largely been adopted by the Canadian political elite in general, including in Quebec. This political context has a deep impact on the very definition of objectivity as abstaining to challenge the official narrative.

But how to cover the war with any pretense of objectivity, without challenging the official Israeli and Canadian narrative? That narrative is centred around two elements: the threat Hamas constitutes for Israel, and the position of Israel as acting in self-defence. These two elements can be taken care of by an insistence on the firepower of Hamas, on its representation as the initiator of military action, and on its intransigence when it comes to accepting a ceasefire. These three discursive processes are found in the coverage of the *Téléjournal*. Some of the reporters have incorporated in their discourse the notion of retaliation, and they evaluate the conditions for a ceasefire as "enormous demands," failing to mention that Hamas has been excluded from the discussion about the ceasefire brokered by Egypt.

These elements of information have been given a central place in the discourse on the war on Gaza. The conclusion follows: Israel is in a position of self-defence, and Hamas is to blame. This representation of the conflict is not in contradiction with the extreme positions taken by the Canadian government and by the opposition, and it does not challenge such representations. Israel is only reacting, only retaliating. A little too harshly, maybe, but it is just retaliating. In my discussions (and occasional conflicts) with the journalists and administration of Radio-Canada, they insist on the fact that they are extremely professional and objective, and that any challenge to the official narrative is a sign of "militancy" and lack of objectivity. Where does this feeling of objectivity come from?

My conjecture is that it comes from two factors. The first is the representation in the *Téléjournal* of the magnitude of the human suffering in Gaza. This allows even feelings of empathy toward the Palestinians. The second factor is the critical attitude of several journalists to Israeli policies, and to the uncritical support of Israel by right-wing Canadian politicians. This is what gives the reporters and the Corporation an assurance that the coverage is objective. It does show the harshness of the Israeli "response." But it presents it as a response, and this is precisely the problem. Presenting Israeli actions as a response reinforces the empirical elements of the Israeli narrative of self-defence, which is precisely what justifies the uncritical pro-Israeli positions they also challenge.

Thus, in spite of the fact that Palestinian suffering is amply represented, it is the Israeli narrative that frames the perception of Palestinian suffering and that allows to interpret its meaning and its causes. The effect of this representation is to legitimize the position of Israel in the diplomatic processes

202   *Palestinian Images, Israeli Narratives*

that take place at the international level, and to legitimize the Canadian position, which supports the Israeli occupation. The "moral high ground" that Israel claims to occupy in this conflict is not challenged by the narrative of self-defence: only its lack of restraint is. Israel does not deny this suffering, and on the contrary, it wants to highlight that the Palestinians will suffer even more if they continue to be defiant. Israel wants the viewer to see the suffering but to attribute it to the actions of Hamas...Israeli spokespersons themselves may even express some empathy for the Palestinian victims, as did the Consul General of Israel, and they invite them at the same time to get rid of Hamas, who is the cause of their suffering.

The Missing Elements

What is missing then? What are the elements that would allow for a better understanding of what is at stake, for taking into account the narrative of the colonized, not only that of the colonizer? The answer is hinted at by the way we formulated the question: colonization, and the violence that comes with it. The very recent history of Palestinians being colonized, a history whose consequences are still experienced in their bodies and in their lives and deaths, is hidden, concealed, and suppressed. Only acknowledging this history as a fundamental aspect of every war on Palestinians can help include their narrative in media representations, a condition without which objectivity is not possible.

We assert that any serious attempt at objectivity in this conflict requires a radical challenge of the official Canadian narrative towards Israel. This would put the CBC and its journalists on a collision course with its funders, the Canadian government, and with the Canadian political elite. It is not likely that CBC will do that in the foreseeable future.

Notes

1. The Associated Press, "3 Missing Israeli Teens Found Dead near Hebron."
2. See for example Muñoz-Torres, "Truth and Objectivity in Journalism."
3. Ryan, "Journalistic Ethics."
4. Ryan, "Journalistic Ethics," 4.
5. Ryan, "Journalistic Ethics."
6. CBC/Radio-Canada, "Journalistic Standards and Practices (JSP)."
7. Radio Canada, "Le Téléjournal: Concept." Translated from French. Unless otherwise stated, all translations are ours.

8. For example, Greg Philo and Mike Berry's *Bad News from Israel* which covers the BBC. The website *If Americans Knew* deserves a place apart. It specializes in the analysis of United States media coverage of Israel/Palestine. It does systematic comparisons of how an issue (for instance the number of Palestinians and Israelis children killed) is represented in major American news outlets, and it contrasts this representation with the actual figures. Several reports covering a specific aspect of the coverage are also produced by the group (ifamericansknew.org). There is nothing similar done for Canada. Greg Shupak's *The Wrong Story: Palestine, Israel and the Media* partly covers this gap.

9. Gamson and Modigliani, "Media Discourse and Public Opinion," 3, cited by Paul D'Angelo, "Framing Theory and Journalism."

10. Graef, Silva, and Lemay-Hebert, "Narrative, Political Violence, and Social Change."

11. Shenhav, "Political Narratives and Political Reality."

12. Philo and Berry, *Bad News from Israel*, 95–96.

13. All the excerpts in this chapter were in French and are verifiable on the website of Radio-Canada. This is the author's translation.

14. Jodelet, ed., *Les Représentations Sociales*; Paillé and Mucchielli, *L'Analyse Qualitative en Sciences Humaines et Sociales*, 4e éd.

15. The author of this chapter.

16. With support from most Western countries, including Canada. Here we see that the journalist framing is in tune with the dominant view of the conflict among Canadian political elites.

17. See, among many others, Antonius, "Un Racisme 'Respectable'"; Said, *Covering Islam*; Shaheen, *The TV Arab*.

18. Office for the Coordination of Humanitarian Affairs (OCHA), "Key Figures on the 2014 Hostilities."

References

Adams, Tony E. "A Review of Narrative Ethics." *Qualitative Inquiry* 14 (2008): 175–84.

Antonius, Rachad. "Un racisme 'respectable.'" In *Les relations ethniques en question: Ce qui a changé depuis le 11 septembre 2001*, edited by J. Renaud, L. Pietrantonio, and G. Bourgeault, 253–71. Montreal: Les Presses de l'Université de Montréal, 2002.

Associated Press. "3 Missing Israeli Teens Found Dead near Hebron." *CBC*. June 30, 2014. https://www.cbc.ca/news/world/3-missing-israeli-teens-found-dead-near-hebron-1.2692115.

CBC / Radio-Canada. "Journalistic Standards and Practices (JSP)." Accessed October 31, 2021. https://cbc.radio-canada.ca/en/vision/governance/journalistic-standards-and-practices.

D'Angelo, Paul. "Framing Theory and Journalism." In *The International Encyclopedia of Journalism Studies*, edited by Tim P. Vos and Folker Hanusch (General Editors), Dimitra Dimitrakopoulou, Margaretha Geertsema-Sligh and Annika Sehl (Associate

Editors), 1–10. Chichester: JohnWiley & Sons, 2019. doi: 10.1002/9781118841570. iejs0021.

Gamson, W.A., and A. Modigliani. "Media Discourse and Public Opinion on Nuclear Power: A Constructionist Approach." *American Journal of Sociology* 95, no. 1 (1989): 1–37.

Graef, Josefin, Raquel da Silva, and Nicolas Lemay-Hebert. "Narrative, Political Violence, and Social Change." *Studies in Conflict & Terrorism* 43, no. 6 (2020): 431–43.

Herman, David. "Introduction." In *The Cambridge Companion to Narrative*, edited by David Herman, 3–21. Cambridge: Cambridge University Press, 2007.

If Americans Knew. "If Americans Knew: What Every American Needs to Know about Israel-Palestine." Last updated March 26, 2020. https://ifamericansknew.org.

Jodelet, Denise, ed. *Les Représentations Sociales*. Paris: PUF, 2003.

Muñoz-Torres, Juan Ramón. "Truth and Objectivity in Journalism." *Journalism Studies* 13, no. 4 (2012): 566–82.

Office for the Coordination of Humanitarian Affairs (OCHA). "Key Figures on the 2014 Hostilities." https://www.ochaopt.org/content/key-figures-2014-hostilities.

Paillé, Pierre, and Alex Mucchielli. *L'analyse qualitative en sciences humaines et sociales*, 4e éd. Malakoff: Armand Colin, 2016.

Philo, Greg, and Mike Berry. *Bad News from Israel*. London: Pluto Press, 2004.

Radio Canada. "Le Téléjournal: Concept." https://ici.radio-canada.ca/tele/le-telejournal-22h/2016-2017/emission/concept.

Ryan, Michael. "Journalistic Ethics, Objectivity, Existential Journalism, Standpoint Epistemology, and Public Journalism." *Journal of Mass Media Ethics* 16, no. 1 (2001): 3–22.

Said, Edward. W. *Covering Islam: How the Media and the Experts Determine How We See the Rest of the World*. New York: Random House, 1997.

Shaheen, Jack. *The TV Arab*. Ohio: Bowling Green State University Popular Press, 1984.

Shenhav, Shaul R. "Political Narratives and Political Reality." *International Political Science Review* 27, no. 3 (2006): 245–62.

Shupak, Greg. *The Wrong Story: Palestine, Israel and the Media*. New York: OR Books, 2018.

8

CANADA'S ISRAEL LOBBY AND THE PALESTINIANS

MIRA SUCHAROV

ONE OF THE KEY ENGINES OF INFLUENCE shaping Canada's approach to the question of Palestine is the workings of the Israel lobby. This cluster of organizations, including the Centre for Israel and Jewish Affairs (CIJA) at the helm, and backed to greater or lesser degrees by a host of other organizations, attempts to shape Canadian policy directions in ways that prioritize Israeli security and prosperity as they perceive it. This perception typically accords with the Israeli government's general positions, as when CIJA situates its activities in a belief that Canada and Israel have a set of "shared values and shared interests."[1] Whether Israeli security and prosperity exist in a way that is at odds with Palestinian security and prosperity depends on one's political vantage point. So those who advocate some sort of compromise position tend to couch their policy proposals in terms that attempt to maximize the well-being of both sides.

Introduction

Since the signing of the Oslo Accords between Israel and the Palestine Liberation Organization (PLO) in 1993, a tacit international consensus has emerged that points to a two-state solution as the optimal outcome. Lack of agreement on the scope of refugee return, though, as well as Israel's continued building of West Bank settlements, among other developments, have cast this endgame into doubt.

In all this, the identities and preferences of diaspora communities are germane in framing these policy conversations. To understand the impact and activities of the Israel lobby in Canada, it is necessary to shine a light on the dynamics of mainstream Jewish community discourse, from which the Israel lobby derives much of its funding and its main policy directions. In this essay, I will argue that a sometimes tacit and sometimes explicit adherence to the two-state solution as the only feasible option has meant that rather than work towards change and rather than press to bring such a solution about, the Israel lobby in Canada has ended up shoring up the status quo. In other words, as long as that solution remains remote given Israeli intransigence coupled with Palestinian Authority (PA) impotence, these Israel-oriented organizations can claim to want change, but not do anything concrete to bring that change about.

Before I proceed, a note about terminology: Many scholars have urged the abandonment of the term "Jewish lobby" with its potentially antisemitic connotations, connotations that imply that Jews carry "dual loyalties."[2] While that critique has much merit, mainstream Jewish community messaging—as does the discourse emanating from any network of grassroots and organized institutions—carries its own tenor of values and preferences, including suggested policy directions for the country in which it operates.[3] The Jewish community in Canada is no exception, and thus looking at how the organized Jewish community operates in reflecting and shaping attitudes around Israel is relevant to understanding the flow of domestic ideas upwards towards government policymaking.

The Israel Lobby, the Mainstream Jewish Community, and its Canadian Jewish Critics

In Canada, the formal Israel lobby is embodied by CIJA, and less prominently by B'nai Brith Canada and Friends of Simon Wiesenthal Center for Holocaust Studies, as well as the informal network of groups representing a

208   *Canada's Israel Lobby and the Palestinians*

mainstream approach to Israel advocacy. These groups include the network of Jewish Federations, Jewish National Fund-Canada (JNF-Canada), the network of Jewish summer camps, (most) synagogues and Jewish Community Centres (JCCs), and the campus-based Hillel International, with the Toronto-based Hillel Ontario being the largest of these. On the far right is the Jewish Defense League which exerts some informal, grassroots pressure but does not represent the mainstream. On the non-Zionist, Jewish left, and thus in most ways serving as a hard check on Zionist activism, is Independent Jewish Voices (IJV). IfNotNow does not take a stand on Zionism or the Boycott, Divestment, and Sanctions (BDS) movement, but pressures Jewish institutions to end their support for the occupation. JSpace Canada calls itself a progressive Jewish voice; it is arguably situated on the centre-left, which is to say it supports the existence of Israel as a Jewish State and opposes BDS but seeks a two-state solution and an end to the occupation.[4] Similar to JSpace are Canadian Friends of Peace Now, the New Israel Fund-Canada (which includes within its agenda social justice and civil rights issues in Israel), and the smaller Ameinu.[5]

So, while all ethnic communities naturally care about collective well-being and self-preservation, there are important intra-communal divisions within the Jewish community around the issue of Israel. However, despite the existence of a plethora of groups representing different opinions, it remains difficult for Jewish groups outside of the Zionist consensus to mount dissent from within a Jewish community context and gain much traction.[6]

In CIJA, the mainstream policy consensus is represented most starkly. While small in scope compared to AIPAC (American Israel Public Affairs Committee), CIJA provides a uniquely apt indicator for assessing insti-tutionalized Canadian Jewish attitudes. This is because a portion of funds raised during the Jewish Federation's annual campaign in each Canadian city are funnelled directly to CIJA for their array of activities, including Israel lobby efforts; these monies, as CIJA itself describes them, represent its "core funding."[7] There is no such automatic funnelling in the United States between ordinary Jewish-community philanthropic efforts and Israel lobbying.

But CIJA's perceived Jewish legitimacy means that it is incumbent on researchers and writers—particularly those who identify as part of the Jewish community—to continue to check whether CIJA's positions accord with the community they claim to represent. CIJA's platform states that

Canada can continue demonstrating that Middle East Peace is not a zero-sum proposal by supporting bilateral and multilateral peace initiatives; assisting the building of accountable, liberal democratic institutions in the Palestinian Authority; and simultaneously opposing efforts to isolate or denigrate Israel.[8]

Notice that nowhere is pressure around settlement construction mentioned, and the focus remains on protecting Israel from mass protest efforts and on spotlighting where the PA falls short in its governance structures (which, given the continued delay of Palestinian elections, is not inconsiderable). While this is not surprising for an Israel lobby, it underscores how the rhetorical nod to "peace" does not necessarily have any teeth behind it. Any meaningful change in political relations between Israel and the PA will have to entail, at minimum, a curb on settlement construction and, in the event of a two-state solution, some meaningful land swaps. And it will have to recognize how the occupation constrains Palestinian governmental freedom of maneuver, on top of the curtailing of daily freedoms of the Palestinian people.

At the other end of Jewish communal activity is the anti-Zionist group IJV. Here, its recent campaign launched to strip JNF-Canada of its charitable status is instructive. Moves like this can serve to shed light on the implications of certain taken-for-granted policy commitments within Canada's landscape. But tipping sacred cows is a delicate business and, to be successful in shifting Jewish community attitudes, one needs to possess a degree of social and political capital that IJV arguably does not yet enjoy in the Jewish community landscape.[9] The question remains how much groups like IJV need to garner Jewish community sympathy in order to advance a more critical message about Israel and support for human rights in the Palestinian context, or whether they can bypass mainstream Jewish community sentiment and effectively shape Canadian government policy directly.

Canadian Jewish Attitudes to Israel/Palestine

The relationship between the formal cluster of Israel-lobby organizations (whether on the right, centre or left) and Jewish community attitudes is multi-layered. On one hand, the lobby claims to represent domestic community attitudes. On the other hand, some Canadian Jewish community organizations seek to challenge the views of the formal Israel lobby.

210   *Canada's Israel Lobby and the Palestinians*

Finally, the positions that the formal organizations take can in turn influence domestic Jewish political attitudes, particularly among those who believe that the community should speak with a united voice. For these Jews, institutions hold particular moral legitimacy.

In March 2019, a landmark survey of Canadian Jewish attitudes was released, confirming much of what researchers already knew from smaller-scale studies over the years, but it was significant nonetheless in its scope. Conducted by the Environics Institute and designed by Robert Brym at University of Toronto and Rhonda Lenton of York University, the survey paints a picture of a highly engaged Canadian Jewish community, one with high emotional attachment to Israel. But the survey also revealed significant divisions regarding attitudes toward Israeli policy.[10]

While American Judaism arguably represents the apex of Diaspora Jewish institutional life—and indeed American Jewish numbers (both in absolute terms and as a proportion of the total United States population) predict this, it is Canadian Jews who on every major indicator represent a tighter and more traditionally engaged community compared to Jewish Americans.[11]

These high levels of Jewish identification have resulted in a more Israel-attached community as well. According to the survey, more Canadian Jews (48 per cent) than American Jews (30 per cent) say they are "very emotionally attached" to Israel. (When "very attached" is pooled with "somewhat attached," the numbers are 79 per cent for Canadian Jews and 69 per cent for United States Jews.)

But opinions are divided on Israeli policy and the Israeli government. Some 35 per cent of Canadian Jews believe that "the current Israeli leadership is making a sincere effort to bring about a peace settlement," while 44 per cent disagree. But nearly all Canadian Jews are suspicious of the PA: only a tiny minority—7 per cent—believe that the Palestinian leadership is sincere in its peacemaking efforts. This roughly echoes American Jewish opinion.

On West Bank settlements, opinion is also divided. Among the approximately 50 per cent of Canadian Jews who feel the settlements have an impact on Israeli security, three times as many believe the settlements are having a negative impact. But regarding legality, many more (43 per cent) believe that the settlements are *not* illegal under international law compared to only (23 per cent) who believe they *are* illegal. The scholarly consensus—notwithstanding some outlying voices—is that they are illegal.[12]

American Jews are even more critical of settlements with "17 percent of American Jews think[ing] the continued building of settlements in the West Bank is helpful to Israel's security," and 44 per cent disagreeing.[13]

On perceived Canadian government support for Israel, "A plurality (45 per cent) consider the relationship between Canada and Israel to be about right, but a significant minority (36 per cent) say Canada is not supportive enough." This nearly echoes American Jews' view of their own government's policies in 2013, with, according to Pew, 54 per cent seeing the level of United States support for Israel (under the Obama administration, when the Pew survey was conducted) as being about right. The Canadian survey was conducted during the tenure of Liberal Prime Minister Justin Trudeau.

Not surprisingly, given past–Prime Minister Harper's attempts to position himself as Israel's best friend, one's view on the question of whether Canadian support for Israel is sufficient generally mirrors party identification.[14] While Harper did not change Canadian policies towards the region, he expressed solidarity with Israel in his United Nations votes—a pattern that diverged from his predecessors—and his rhetoric was effusively one-sided, calling Israel in a speech to the 2013 Jewish National Fund dinner in Toronto "a light of freedom and democracy in what otherwise is a region of darkness."[15]

All this suggests that while the Israel lobby in each country would like to portray the Jewish community as largely united regarding Israel, the report suggests that there is room for the many dissenters to make themselves more known if they would like to sever the assumed link between tacit support for the Israeli-Palestinian status quo and Jewish identity.[16] It will be a delicate balancing act, though, since there remains much suspicion around whether dissenting Jewish groups are committed to the maintenance of a Jewish state. Perhaps the best hope for change from within the Jewish community lies not in IJV, but in New Israel Fund-Canada and JSpace Canada. NIF-Canada succeeds in bringing together progressive Canadian Jews committed to a more just and equitable Israel/Palestine. (Disclosure: I am on the Advisory Council of NIF-Canada.) JSpace Canada has succeeded in carving out a centre-left position that angers some to the right, but whose biannual conference manages to bring establishment representatives—such as those from CIJA and even diplomatic representation from the Israeli consulate in Toronto—with progressive Zionists. Nevertheless, one should not underestimate the degree to which more fully dissenting groups—ones outside the Zionist consensus, such as IJV—can sow the seeds of indirect change. This can come about through a sense of solidarity with other Palestine solidarity groups—and with other social movement groups more broadly—which can then have an effect on elected officials, though it is a message that is more likely to be read by those officials as emanating from outside the Jewish community, however imagined.[17]

These recommendations are based on the role of Zionism and Zionist commitments in animating a broad swatch of Jewish community activities. So, while critique is certainly present, the boundaries of what is deemed acceptable so far almost totally exclude anti-Zionism. So it is not surprising to see some dissatisfaction on the part of North American Jews towards the current Israeli government. While there is an overall broad, affective relationship between American Jews and Israel it is not uncommon to see that relationship nuanced by critiques of the Israeli government. This was particularly the case during the long tenure of Israeli Prime Minister Benjamin Netanyahu, whose final years in government were dogged by domestic corruption scandals.[18] But whatever criticisms one hears in mainstream Diaspora discourse about Israel's government rarely extend to the Zionist project itself, including Israel's core demands of maintaining a Jewish demographic majority and thus barring major Palestinian refugee return. Moreover, mainstream Diaspora Jewish discourse frequently points to corruption within the PA (including the problematic postponement of elections by Mahmoud Abbas); the fact that the Palestinian territories are split between the PA, which rules parts of the West Bank, and Hamas, which rules Gaza; and a perception that there is "no partner" for peace. Even progressive Zionist Karen Mock, a founder of the centre-left JSpace, was quoted in September 2018 as saying that it "will likely require another generation of Palestinian leadership to arise before the two sides can begin serious negotiations."[19] Of course, one never knows whether a statement like this is simply meant to describe the current Israeli governmental thinking and thus to offer a prediction of the conditions necessary for change to come about—and in this, Mock is probably correct—or whether the statement is intended to endorse a certain Israeli government view that Israel should not be expected to negotiate with a divided Palestinian government. Readers may interpret it in different ways.

The sense of attachment by Canadian Jews to Israel that the survey captured no doubt motivates the official Canadian Jewish lobby organizations to feel emboldened to act in ways that appear to prop up Israel's perceived security in the face of perceived threats. However, the fact that many Canadian Jews—as the survey revealed—do not see the current Israeli government as making a sincere effort at peacemaking, and many oppose settlements, suggests that an Israel lobby that better reflects societal Jewish interests could nudge the Canadian government to push Israel harder on settlements and on negotiating a peace agreement and still be in accordance with community views.

The Occupation: A Dirty Word in Mainstream Canadian Jewish Discourse?

In addition to the refugee issue, where the two sides seem as far as they have ever been—though there had been some notable narrowing of positions at the Taba talks of 2001—the core issue of Israel-Palestine remains the occupation.[20] Canadian policy officially acknowledges the occupation, but officials seem to refrain from making any urgent demands that Israel end it. From the Global Affairs Canada policy statement:

> Canada does not recognize permanent Israeli control over territories occupied in 1967 (the Golan Heights, the West Bank, East Jerusalem and the Gaza Strip). The Fourth Geneva Convention applies in the occupied territories and establishes Israel's obligations as an occupying power, in particular with respect to the humane treatment of the inhabitants of the occupied territories.[21]

On the other hand, central within the Israel lobby's rhetoric—and, by extension, mainstream Jewish community discourse—is to avoid much mention of the occupation. A search for the word "occupation" on the CIJA website reveals the following articles:

> "Palestinians hold the key to ending the 'occupation'"
> "Is the 'Occupation' The Roadblock to Peace? History Says No"
> "Israelis cannot 'end the occupation' on their own"
> "Preoccupation with Israel"
> "Why Are the Palestinians Opposed to Ending the Occupation?"
> "Why Is Israel's Presence in the Territories Still Called 'Occupation'?"

and, most notably,

"Occupation, Shmoccupation."[22]

A personal anecdote reveals the extent to which the term occupation has become a lightning rod in mainstream Jewish community discourse. After nearly two years of writing a regular column for the Canadian Jewish News, in 2017, I wrote a column marking fifty years of occupation. While I had written about the occupation before, this time the editors chose to include the word (occupation) in the headline. Perhaps because of this, the reaction was swift. There is nothing terribly remarkable about letters to the editor, but in this case, reaction was so intense that the editor did something rare: he wrote an editorial defending his decision to run my piece.[23] "To some of our readers," he wrote, "invoking the term 'occupation' was deeply offensive, triggering very real concerns about Israel's security, highlighting the moral and intellectual bias the Jewish state faces, and questioning the ultimate viability of a Jewish homeland." (He acknowledged that for "other readers, occupation is a struggle that Israel, and by extension the Jewish Diaspora, must wrestle with. It is not an exercise in anti-Zionism, let alone antisemitism, but a matter of articulating that the State of Israel is not perfect and should strive to be better, however difficult the task.")

Canadian Policy on Israel

Canada's relationship to Israel and, by extension, to the Palestinian issue can be characterized by a longstanding friendship (to Israel) and an attempt, with some notable exceptions, to exhibit an approach of fair-mindedness when it comes to Israel's relationship with the Palestinians. Canada has served as an important global leader at particular points in the Middle East peace process, namely when it served as "gavel-holder" of the Refugee Working Group at the multilateral peace talks of the early 1990s, the ones that emerged from the 1991 Madrid peace summit.[24]

Under then–Prime Minister Paul Martin, Canada's votes in the United Nations shifted toward a stance more sympathetic to Israel than what it had been earlier; Harper continued this trend, leading some observers to contend that Canada's bid for a United Nations Security Council seat in 2010 was stymied because of a perception that Canada was too supportive of Israel at the United Nations.[25]

The Jewish community has been eager to retain broad Canadian support for Israel. As such, it is in the Jewish community's perceived interests to prevent policy towards Israel and the Palestinians from becoming a wedge issue in Canadian elections. Whether through successful lobbying, through a desire to remain competitive in three or four ridings with a concentrated Jewish population, or through sheer inertia, Canadian policy has coalesced around a basic commitment to securing Israel's existence as a Jewish state (which is to say no radical demands around large-scale refugee return) while concurrently opposing settlement building. However, Canada has been able to use a degree of constructive ambiguity in expressing its support for a "negotiated" solution to the refugee issue while still mentioning "the rights of the refugees, in accordance with international law."[26]

This has not stopped politicians from trying to edge each other out, occasionally, while trying to portray themselves as the superior ally to Israel. When then–Prime Minister Harper tried to position his party as the best friend of Israel in the leaders' debates in the run-up to the 2015 elections, Trudeau responded deftly. Harper said,

> *This government has been perhaps the most unequivocal in the world on the fact that when it comes to the Middle East, we are not going to single out Israel. It is the one western democratic ally. Threats that are directed at that state is on the frontline of the threats directed at us. We are not going to single out the Jewish state for attack and criticism. We recognize unequivocally the right of Israel to be a Jewish state and to defend itself.*

Trudeau replied,

> *The issue of Israel where we most disagree as Liberals with Mr. Harper is that he has made support for Israel a domestic political football when all three of us support Israel and any Canadian government will.*[27]

And while Prime Minister Harper was widely viewed as Israel's best friend—Israeli Prime Minister Netanyahu famously referred to him as "Stephen" in public, and the Jewish National Fund honoured Harper with a bird sanctuary built in his name in the Hula Valley in northern Israel—his actual policies on Israel-Palestine did not differ from those of his predecessor. As Bernie Farber, former head of the now-defunct Canadian Jewish

216   *Canada's Israel Lobby and the Palestinians*

Congress (CJC), put it, "Harper changed not one comma" on Canada's Middle East policy.[28] But tone matters, and for this, the Jewish community rewarded him at the polls, until they no longer did.

When Trudeau took the helm, he implied that Canada would return to its strong tradition of fair-mindedness when it comes to Canada's approach to the Middle East. In 2016, he stated, "Israel is a friend, Israel is an ally, Israel is a country that has values and an approach on many, many issues that are very much aligned with Canadian values," also adding, "But, at the same time we won't hesitate from talking about unhelpful steps like the continued illegal settlements. We will point that out. We will continue to engage in a forthright and open way because that's what people expect of Canada."[29]

The question remains as to what extent strong support of Israel must or does come at the expense of support for the Palestinians. Many so-called liberal or progressive Zionists see no conflict between the two: these groups—embodied in Canada by JSpace and the Israel wing of the Reform Judaism movement, for example, hold fast to a two-state solution. Under this solution, both Zionism and Palestinian nationalism could thrive under a side-by-side sovereign arrangement, whereby Israel would withdraw from all or most of the West Bank, dismantling the settlements (or leaving what are known as "settlement blocs" and swapping land on the other side of the Green Line in exchange). The mainstream Israel lobby has suggested that a "two-state solution" would be in accordance with its views as well.[30]

But the Palestine solidarity discourse has been shifting away from a two-state solution toward a conversation that acknowledges that calling for two states may be a way of both prolonging the status quo—especially in light of the current land distribution situation in the West Bank—and avoiding tough conversations about refugee return.

Canadian Jews and BDS

One of the most useful fulcrum points for examining Jewish and Canadian attitudes more broadly to the Israel-Palestine nexus is the debate around BDS. Calling for a broad-based consumer, cultural, and academic boycott—as well as divestment from companies that are perceived to be implicated in the occupation, and, least likely but potentially most powerful, the imposition of international sanctions against Israel, the BDS movement arose in 2005 from a call from Palestinian civil society. The mainstream Jewish community, not surprisingly, has vigorously opposed BDS, sometimes likening it to boycotts against Jewish businesses in Nazi Germany.[31] Relations between many organs of the organized Jewish community and mainstream Canadian church groups reached a low point in 2013 when the United Church of Canada adopted a limited boycott resolution—one targeting products produced in Israeli settlements in the West Bank. The Friends of the Simon Wiesenthal Center in Toronto called the move "nothing less than an assault on the Jewish people."[32] The Mennonite Church followed suit in 2016, including undertaking a "commitment to avoid economic investment that supports settlements on Palestinian lands and the Israeli Defense Forces," and to "urge Canada's federal government to support measures that put pressure on Israel (including through economic sanctions) to end the occupation and work for a just peace, in accordance with international law."[33] CIJA roundly condemned the resolution, noting that they had

> ...reached out to the Mennonite Church's leadership to urge the Assembly to adopt a positive, peace-building approach rather than destructive and discriminatory BDS measures. Frankly, its decision to join the toxic ranks of the BDS movement is a slap in the face to those of us in the Jewish community who have been building bridges with our Christian neighbours, particularly given our proactive efforts to create opportunities for interfaith partners to support projects that help foster Israeli-Palestinian peace.[34]

Once the domain of intra-campus, internal Jewish community, and insider Palestine solidarity community disputes, discourse over BDS has now reached the highest public bodies in Canada. On December 1, 2016, the Ontario legislature passed Motion 36, affirming its opposition to BDS.[35] And then, on November 7, 2018, in a parliamentary speech laying out Canada's apology for turning away 900 German Jewish refugees aboard the M.S. St. Louis, in which they were sent back to Europe where many of them perished in the Nazi Holocaust, Prime Minster Justin Trudeau stated that,

> During this Holocaust Education Week, it is all the more impossible to ignore the challenges and injustices still facing Jews in this country.
> According to the most recent figures, 17 percent of all hate crimes in Canada target Jewish people. Far higher per capita than any other group.
> Holocaust deniers still exist. Anti-Semitism is still far too present.

Jewish institutions and neighbourhoods are still being vandalized with swastikas.

Jewish students still feel unwelcomed and uncomfortable on some of our college and university campuses because of BDS-related intimidation.

And out of our entire community of nations, it is Israel whose right to exist is most widely—and wrongly—questioned.

Discrimination and violence against Jewish people in Canada and around the world continues at an alarming rate. [36]

(Emphasis added)

Back-channel accounts suggest that CIJA had lobbied for the inclusion of the mention of BDS.[37] It was a natural continuation from Trudeau's tweet in March 2015, seven months before taking office as prime minister, that "the BDS movement...has no place on Canadian campuses."[38]

It has become an article of faith that mainstream Jewish community organizations vigorously reject BDS and count its defeat as an automatic communal victory. Jewish Federation of Ottawa CEO Andrea Freedman has stated that BDS "denigrates the very identity of Jewish students."[39] In November 2018, in response to the Canadian Federation of Students (CFS) passing a resolution endorsing BDS, campus Hillels across Canada stated that "this latest call for a boycott of Israel is anti-academic, fuelled by hatred, and is counterproductive to peace. The motion is rife with factual inaccuracies and historical distortions. In its obsessive campaign against exclusively one country and one community, the CFS has further marginalized the thousands of Jewish students whom it is tasked with representing."[40]

Two months later, in a town hall at Brock University, Trudeau again equated anti-Zionism with antisemitism, invoking what are known in Israel advocacy circles as the "3-D's"—demonization, double-standards, and delegitimization. Trudeau said, "when you have movements like BDS that singles out Israel, that seeks to delegitimize and in some cases demonize, when you have students on campus dealing with things like Israel apartheid weeks that makes them fearful from attending campus events because of their religion—in Canada..." He continued, "unfortunately, the BDS movement is often linked to those kinds of frames. So yes, I will continue to condemn the BDS movement." He concluded by emphasizing that Canada's position is a negotiated two-state solution and stated that "unilateral actions" (including "settlements" and "unilateral declarations of statehood") are not helpful.[41]

Any widespread opposition to Israel is likely to engender opposition from mainstream Jews, including in Canada. After all, the State of Israel—and by extension, Zionism—has become a primary way for world Jewry to experience and express contemporary ethno-communal solidarity. Jewish communal events in major cities typically include an annual Israel parade, and most Jewish communities publicly celebrate Israel's annual Independence Day. Singing Hatikvah, the Israeli national anthem, is common at Jewish communal events. Thousands of young-adult Jews worldwide attend the annual free ten-day Birthright trips.[42] This, despite the internal Jewish community conflicts about Israel that scholars like Dov Waxman have examined.[43]

But it is the particular demands of BDS that also engender fear and cynicism among the mainstream Jewish community, especially the pillar calling for refugee return. After all, if many or most Palestinians were to return to Israel, the state might cease to have a Jewish majority. And this prospect frightens those who believe that there should be at least one state in the world governed by Jewish sovereignty—both as a way of expressing agency on the world stage and as a way of ensuring safety and security from global antisemitism. Demanding refugee return is, in the eyes of the mainstream Jewish community, both unrealistic and unfair.

In this essay, I do not offer my own moral assessment of this resistance—though readers who are curious about my views can read my co-authored short piece considering how refugee return could be accommodated within a desire to uphold Israeli-Jewish culture and identity.[44]

Anti-Zionism and Antisemitism

Related to the mainstream Jewish community stance on BDS is the degree to which anti-Zionism is seen in many quarters as equivalent to antisemitism. While there remains some healthy debate around this contention, the fact that the current antisemitism definition embraced by various countries, including the United States, the United Kingdom, and Israel, and by CIJA implicitly, links the two reveals that the issue remains a continued point of tension. CIJA head Shimon Koffler Fogel writes in the *National Post* that "relevant government agencies" should adopt the definition.[45] (The Canadian government, as a whole, has adopted the definition.[46])

220   *Canada's Israel Lobby and the Palestinians*

The International Holocaust Remembrance Alliance (IHRA) definition includes, among its many indicators of antisemitism, "Denying the Jewish people their right to self-determination, i.e., by claiming that the existence of a State of Israel is a racist endeavor," and "Applying double standards by requiring of it a behavior not expected or demanded of any other democratic nation."[47] The charge of double standards is one often levied by staunch Israel advocates, and it is indeed a tricky endeavour to fault a particular individual or group for not actively calling out every other human rights violator in the same breath that they call out Israel. The former claim is even more squarely about Zionism; Zionism's harshest critics of course do see fault with the existence of the State of Israel, but this fault does not occur in a vacuum. The state was founded on the backs of the Palestinian people, something even ardent (though liberal) Zionists admit, as when Ari Shavit writes, "And when I try to be honest about it, I see that the choice is stark: either reject Zionism because of [the massacre of Palestinians by Israeli state forces at] Lydda or accept Zionism along with Lydda."[48] It is therefore no surprise that Palestinians view Zionism's successes as a grave national and human rights defeat.

Fogel is clear. In an article in *Haaretz* penned in response to a column I had written in the same pages, Fogel argues that "[t]hough an anti-Zionist may not consider their views to be anti-Semitic in *intent*, to single out the Jewish state for dissolution while upholding the right of other nations to statehood—including the Palestinians—is unavoidably anti-Semitic in *effect*."

And to my claim in my op-ed that the charge of antisemitism directed at the BDS demand for refugee return, an outcome that would threaten the maintenance of Israel's Jewish majority, is "hyperbolic and misleading," Fogel is concise: "Really, Mira?!"[49] In a sense, we were talking past one another. His view assumes that Israel must maintain a demographic Jewish majority at all costs. Mine assumes that Jewish identity is well entrenched enough to allow a relaxation of demographic concerns for a redefined binational state to possibly one day emerge.[50]

Conclusion

This essay has attempted to situate Canadian policy in the context of mainstream Jewish community attitudes in concert with the official organ of the Israel lobby in Canada, the Centre for Israel and Jewish Affairs, along with its institutional supporters. With the rough concert of preferences between the mainstream Jewish community, CIJA, and the current Israeli government, it is unlikely we will see much Israel lobby activity pushing for any meaningful political change. However, Canadian foreign policy does not only respond to lobbying efforts—and there is the Arab and Muslim lobby to account for too, the effects of which are beyond the scope of this essay.[51] Plus, quiet diplomacy has its place, and Canada could conceivably draw on its legacy of being seen as fair-minded in the region to continue to look for diplomatic openings. Given that the occupation continues apace with few apparent costs for Israel, however, it is unlikely we will see any significant change soon. And if some elements of the Jewish community do demand change towards peace, justice, and equality, it is likely that they will be heard by Canadian officials to be operating as individual Canadian voters—or as elements operating in concert with other Palestine solidarity organizations and social justice movements—rather than as representatives of the Jewish community.

Notes

1. Centre for Israel and Jewish Affairs (CIJA), "Canada and Israel: Shared Values and Shared Interests."
2. See, for example, Stephen Walt, "How (and How Not) to Talk About the Israel Lobby," who rightly notes that given that many Jews in the United States (and, by extension, in Canada and elsewhere) oppose Israeli policies, that "using terms such as 'Jewish lobby' to talk about pro-Israel groups is both inaccurate and inevitably conjures up dangerous stereotypes." Walt, "How (and How Not) to Talk About the Israel Lobby," *Foreign Policy*, February 15, 2019, https://foreignpolicy. com/2019/02/15/how-and-how-not-to-talk-about-the-israel-lobby/.
3. See Sucharov, "Values, Identity, and Israel Advocacy."
4. JSpaceCanada, "Where We Stand."
5. For a concise view of the Israel lobby in Canada a decade ago, see Sasley, "Who Calls the Shots?"
6. Sucharov, "Israel and Canadian Jews."
7. CIJA, "How is CIJA funded?"
8. CIJA, "Advancing a Constructive Middle East Policy."
9. Csillag, "More Politicians Pledge Support." On the mainstream community perception of IJV, consider, for example, the Canadian Jewish News having turned away one of my regular column submissions when the editor deemed the piece too heavily sympathetic to IJV's position. This is an incident I wrote about here: Sucharov, "Is it Time to End IJV Herem [Excommunication]?"
10. Neuman, "2018 Survey of Jews in Canada."

11. These indicators include Hebrew literacy, intermarriage rates, visits to Israel, (not) having a Christmas tree, attachment to Israel, likelihood of belonging to a synagogue or another Jewish organization, choice of Jewish denomination—with Conservative, followed by Orthodox and then Reform, being the most popular Jewish denomination in Canada, scope (though probably not absolute dollars) of Jewish philanthropic donations, preponderance of Jewish friends, and formal Jewish education.

12. Lynk, "International Law and the Israeli-Palestinian Conflict."

13. Pew, "A Portrait of Jewish Americans."

14. On Harper, see Sucharov, "The Jewish Specter Haunting Canada's Elections."; and Sucharov, "What Principle?"

15. Sucharov, "Canadian PM Stephen Harper Displays Lockstep Friendship." On Harper's UN voting, see Yakabuski, "On Israel, Trudeau is Harper's Pupil."

16. Sucharov, "Canadian Jews Love Israel."

17. On anti-Zionist Jewish groups and anti-racist social movements in a United States context, see Ayoub, "Black-Palestinian Solidarity."

18. Underwood, "Israeli PM Benjamin Netanyahu could be indicted."

19. Quoted in Csillag, "Is the Two-State Solution Just a Pipe Dream?"

20. On Taba, see Eldar, "'Moratinos Document'—The peace that nearly was at Taba."

21. Government of Canada, "Canadian Policy on Key Issues in the Israeli-Palestinian Conflict."

22. CIJA, "Results: Occupation."

23. Goldstein, "A Response to a Controversial Column."

24. See, for example, El-Rifai, "Navigating the Palestinian Refugee Issue."

25. For a brief overview, see Sucharov, "A Brief History of Canada-Israel Relations."

26. Government of Canada, "Canadian Policy on Key Issues in the Israeli-Palestinian Conflict."

27. *Maclean's*, "Tale of the Tape."

28. Sucharov, "Canada's Israel Policy on the Day After the Elections."

29. *Haaretz*, "Canada Won't Hesitate to Criticize Israel."

30. Csillag, "Is the Two-State Solution Just a Pipe Dream?"

31. Weinthal and Romirowsky, "When a Nazi Comparison Makes Sense."

32. Hopper, "United Church of Canada's Israeli Boycott Campaign."

33. Dyck, "Action Seeks Solution for Israelis and Palestinians."

34. CIJA, "CIJA Condemns Mennonite BDS Resolution."

35. CIJA, "Press Release: CIJA Applauds Ontario Legislature Motion Rejecting BDS."

36. Trudeau, "Statement of Apology on Behalf of the Government of Canada."

37. Interview with an anonymous source who was told this by insiders.

38. Justin Trudeau (@JustinTrudeau), "The BDS movement, like Israeli Apartheid Week, has no place on Canadian campuses," Twitter, March 13, 2015, https://twitter.com/justintrudeau/status/576465632884981760?lang=en.

39. Shefa, "uOttawa Student Union Rejects BDS, Despite Plurality of Support."

40. CIJA, "Press Release: Hillels Across Canada Condemn Canadian Federation of Students' Endorsement of BDS."
41. CIJA, "Trudeau on BDS at Brock University Town Hall."
42. On Israel and the diaspora, see Sucharov, "Israel and the Jewish Diaspora." On birthright, see Kelner, *Tours That Bind*.
43. Waxman, *Trouble in the Tribe*.
44. Schreier and Sucharov, "If Israel Lets in Palestinian Refugees, Will it Lose its Jewish Character?"
45. Fogel, "A Global Rise in A-Semitism could Turn Back the Clock."
46. Government of Canada, "Freedom of Religion or Belief."
47. International Holocaust Remembrance Alliance, "Working Definition of Antisemitism."
48. Shavit, "Lydda, 1948."
49. Fogel, "How Anti-Zionism and Anti-Semitism Are Converging."
50. Schreier and Sucharov, "If Israel Lets in Palestinian Refugees, Will it Lose its Jewish Character?"
51. Wills offers insight into Palestinian community organizations in her chapter in this volume (chapter 10).

References

Ayoub, Joey. "Black-Palestinian Solidarity: Towards an Intersection of Struggles." In *Social Justice and Israel/Palestine: Foundational and Contemporary Issues*, eds. Aaron J. Hahn Tapper and Mira Sucharov, 204–13. Toronto: University of Toronto Press, 2019.

Centre for Israel and Jewish Affairs (CIJA). "Advancing a Constructive Middle East Policy." Last updated August 19, 2016. https://cija.ca/advancing-a-constructive-middle-east-policy/.

CIJA. "Canada and Israel: Shared Values and Shared Interests." Last updated July 30, 2015. https://cija.ca/resource/canada-israel-shared-values/.

CIJA. "CIJA Condemns Mennonite BDS Resolution." July 14, 2016. https://cija.ca/cija-condemns-mennonite-bds-resolution/.

CIJA. "Press Release: CIJA Applauds Ontario Legislature Motion Rejecting BDS." December 1, 2016. https://cija.ca/press-release-cija-applauds-ontario-legislature-motion-rejecting-bds/.

CIJA. "Press Release: Hillels Across Canada Condemn Canadian Federation of Students' Endorsement of BDS." November 19, 2018. https://cija.ca/pr_cfs_bds_20181119/.

CIJA. "Results: occupation." https://cija.ca/?s=occupation.

CIJA. "Trudeau on BDS at Brock University Town Hall." YouTube, January 16, 2019. https://www.youtube.com/watch?v=xvAGXxao5zo.

CIJA. "How is CIJA funded?" Last updated January 31, 2019. https://cija.ca/about-us/frequently-asked-questions/.

Csillag, Ron. "Is the Two-State Solution Just a Pipe Dream?" *Canadian Jewish News*, September 12, 2018. https://www.cjnews.com/news/israel/is-the-two-state-solution-just-a-pipe-dream.

Csillag, Ron. "More Politicians Pledge Support for Anti-JNF Petition." *Canadian Jewish News*, January 24, 2019. https://www.cjnews.com/news/canada/more-politicians-pledge-support-for-anti-jnf-petition.

Dyck, Dan. "Action Seeks Solution for Israelis and Palestinians." *Canadian Mennonite*, July 23, 2016. https://www.canadianmennonite.org/stories/action-seeks-solution-israelis-and-palestinians.

Eldar, Akiva. "'Moratinos Document'—The Peace that Nearly was at Taba," *Haaretz*, February 14, 2002. reprinted in https://prrn.mcgill.ca/research/papers/moratinos.htm.

El-Rifai, Roula. "Navigating the Palestinian Refugee Issue: An Insider's Guide." In *Social Justice and Israel/Palestine: Foundational and Contemporary Issues*, edited by Aaron J. Hahn Tapper and Mira Sucharov, 139–50. Toronto: University of Toronto Press, 2019.

Fogel, Shimon Koffler. "A Global Rise in Anti-Semitism Could Turn Back the Clock—Even in Canada." *National Post*, January 25, 2019. https://nationalpost.com/opinion/a-global-rise-in-anti-semitism-could-turn-back-the-clock-even-in-canada.

Fogel, Shimon Koffler. "How Anti-Zionism and Anti-Semitism Are Converging." *Haaretz*, March 24, 2016. https://www.haaretz.com/opinion/.premium-how-anti-zionism-and-anti-semitism-are-converging-1.5422096.

Goldstein, Yoni. "A Response to a Controversial Column." *Canadian Jewish News*, May 5, 2017. https://www.cjnews.com/perspectives/opinions/yonis-desk-response-controversial-column.

Government of Canada. "Canadian Policy on Key Issues in the Israeli-Palestinian Conflict," Last modified March 19, 2019. https://international.gc.ca/world-monde/international_relations-relations_internationales/mena-moan/israeli-palistinian_policy-politique_israelo-palestinien.aspx?lang=eng#a06.

Government of Canada. "Freedom of Religion or Belief." Last modified April 4, 2019. https://international.gc.ca/world-monde/issues_development-enjeux_developpement/human_rights-droits_homme/freedom_religion-liberte_religion.aspx?lang=eng.

Haaretz. "Canada Won't Hesitate to Criticize Israel, Says New Prime Minister Justin Trudeau," March 8, 2016. https://www.haaretz.com/israel-news/canada-won-t-hesitate-to-criticize-israel-1.5414970.

Hopper, Tristin. "United Church of Canada's Israeli Boycott Campaign an 'Assault on the Jewish People,' Toronto Group Says." *National Post*, December 5, 2013. https://nationalpost.com/news/canada/united-church-of-canadas-israeli-boycott-campaign-an-assault-on-the-jewish-people-toronto-group-says.

International Holocaust Remembrance Alliance. "Working Definition of Antisemitism." Last accessed June 8, 2020. https://www.holocaustremembrance.com/working-definition-antisemitism.

JSpaceCanada. "Where We Stand." Last accessed June 8, 2020. http://jspacecanada.ca/where-we-stand/.

Kelner, Shaul. *Tours That Bind: Diaspora, Pilgrimage, and Israeli Birthright Tourism.* New York: NYU Press, 2010.

Lynk, Michael, "International Law and the Israeli-Palestinian Conflict: Closer to Power than Justice." In *Social Justice and Israel/Palestine: Foundational and Contemporary Debates*, edited by Aaron J. Hahn Tapper and Mira Sucharov, 96–107. Toronto: University of Toronto Press, 2019.

Maclean's. "Tale of the Tape: Transcript of the Munk Debate." September 28, 2015. https://www.macleans.ca/politics/ottawa/tale-of-the-tape-transcript-of-the-munk-debate-on-the-refugee-crisis/.

Neuman, Keith. "2018 Survey of Jews in Canada," *Environics Institute*, March 11, 2019. https://www.environicsinstitute.org/projects/project-details/survey-of-jews-in-canada.

Pew Research Center. "A Portrait of Jewish Americans." October 1, 2013. https://www.pewforum.org/2013/10/01/jewish-american-beliefs-attitudes-culture-survey/.

Sasley, Brent. "Who Calls the Shots?" *Literary Review of Canada*, May 2011. https://reviewcanada.ca/magazine/2011/05/who-calls-the-shots/.

Schreier, Joshua, and Mira Sucharov. "If Israel Lets in Palestinian Refugees, Will it Lose its Jewish Character?" *The Forward*, October 17, 2016. https://forward.com/opinion/352075/if-israel-lets-in-palestinian-refugees-will-it-lose-its-jewish-character/.

Shavit, Ari. "Lydda, 1948: A City, a Massacre, and the Middle East Today." *The New Yorker*, October 21, 2013. https://www.newyorker.com/magazine/2013/10/21/lydda-1948.

Shefa, Sheri. "UOttawa Student Union Rejects BDS, Despite Plurality of Support." *Canadian Jewish News*, March 15, 2018. https://www.cjnews.com/news/canada/uottawa-student-union-rejects-bds-despite-plurality-of-support.

Sucharov, Mira. "A Brief History of Canada-Israel Relations." *Canadian Jewish News*, July 11, 2017. https://www.cjnews.com/culture/canada-150/brief-history-canada-israel-relations.

Sucharov, Mira. "Canada's Israel Policy on the Day After the Elections." *Haaretz*, October 21, 2015. https://www.haaretz.com/opinion/premium-canada-s-israel-policy-on-the-day-after-the-elections-1.5411571.

Sucharov, Mira. "Canadian Jews Love Israel. Out of Love, We Must Learn to Criticize It," *Haaretz*, April 22, 2019. https://www.haaretz.com/world-news/premium-canadian-jews-love-israel-out-of-love-they-must-learn-to-criticize-it-1.7105574.

Sucharov, Mira. "Canadian PM Stephen Harper Displays Lockstep Friendship with Israel at JNF Dinner." *Daily Beast*, June 11, 2013. https://www.thedailybeast.com/canadian-pm-stephen-harper-displays-lockstep-friendship-with-israel-at-jnf-dinner?ref=author?ref=author.

Sucharov, Mira. "Is it Time to End IJV Herem?" *Jewish Independent*, April 8, 2016. http://www.jewishindependent.ca/is-it-time-to-end-ijv-herem/.

Sucharov, Mira. "Israel and Canadian Jews: How the Mainstream Jewish Community Marginalizes Dissent." *Jewish Currents*, November 8, 2016. https://jewishcurrents. org/articles/israel-and-canadian-jews.

Sucharov, Mira. "Israel and the Jewish Diaspora." In *Oxford Handbook of Israeli Politics and Society*, edited by Reuven Y. Hazan, Alan Dowty, Menachem Hofnung, and Gideon Rahat, 515–29. Oxford University Press, 2018.

Sucharov, Mira. "The Jewish Specter Haunting Canada's Elections." September 25, 2015. https://www.haaretz.com/premium-the-jewish-specter-haunting-canada-s-elections-1.5402576.

Sucharov, Mira. "Values, Identity, and Israel Advocacy." *Foreign Policy Analysis* 7, 4 (October 2011): 361–80.

Sucharov, Mira. "What Principle?" *Policy Options*, December 1, 2012. https:// policyoptions.irpp.org/magazines/talking-science/sucharov/.

Trudeau, Justin. "Statement of Apology on Behalf of the Government of Canada to the passengers of the MS St. Louis," Office of the Prime Minister. November 7, 2018. https://pm.gc.ca/eng/news/2018/11/07/statement-apology-behalf-government-canada-passengers-ms-st-louis.

Trudeau, Justin. "The BDS Movement, like Israeli Apartheid Week, has no Place on Canadian Campuses." Twitter, March 13, 2015. https://twitter.com/justintrudeau/status/576465632884981760?lang=en.

Underwood, Alexia. "Israeli PM Benjamin Netanyahu Could be Indicted. Here's What You Need to Know." *Vox*, January 2, 2019. https://www.vox.com/world/2019/1/2/18125575/israel-pm-benjamin-netanyahu-corruption-charges.

Walt, Stephen M. "How (and How Not) to Talk About the Israel Lobby." *Foreign Policy*, February 15, 2019. https://foreignpolicy.com/2019/02/15/how-and-how-not-to-talk-about-the-israel-lobby/.

Waxman, Dov. *Trouble in the Tribe: The American Jewish Conflict Over Israel*. Princeton, NJ: Princeton University Press, 2016.

Weinthal, Benjamin, and Asaf Romirowsky. "When a Nazi Comparison Makes Sense: The BDS Movement Against Israel." *The Hill*, August 22, 2018. https://thehill.com/opinion/international/402887-when-a-nazi-comparison-makes-sense-the-bds-movement-against-israel.

Yakabuski, Konrad. "On Israel, Trudeau is Harper's Pupil." *The Globe and Mail*, May 10, 2018. https://www.theglobeandmail.com/opinion/article-on-israel-trudeau-is-harpers-pupil/.

V

PALESTINIAN LIFE AND ACTIVISM IN CANADA

9

EXCLUSION AND EXILE

The Identity of Working-class Palestinians in Canada

LINA ASSI AND SAMER ABDELNOUR

To our parents.

Introduction

Palestinians are in a constant state of articulating our identities, especially those of us in exile, or the *shatat* (scattered, spread), who embrace narratives of being and belonging that are distinct from yet deeply connected to shared grievances of dispossession and aspirations for return.[1]

Palestinians everywhere are forced to make sense of a national identity *in situ*. An example of this is the work of Randa Farah,[2] who unpacks the complex way in which the political identity-making of Palestinian refugees in Jordan is bound not only to our national grievances and political aspirations, but to regional political movements, processes, and societal structures that mediate our rights and privileges as stateless subjects. Farah's work importantly shows this is not unique to Palestinians alone. Hence, for Palestinians in exile our national Palestinian identity is but one means through which we express our "Palestinian-ness." Kathleen Fincham's *Learning The Nation in Exile*,[3] an ethnographic portrayal of identity-making among Palestinian refugees in South Lebanon, similarly suggests that Palestinian refugee youth articulate Palestinian-ness in relation to both exile and statelessness.

While Palestinians living in Occupied Palestine or in refugee camps are often subjects of study, a small body of work from Palestinians in the West has emerged that shows identity in a more individualistic, personal, and pluralistic way. Similar to the aforementioned works, this literature also seeks to understand Palestinian identity and belonging *in situ*. Yet it does so through more fundamental questioning of what it means to be Palestinian. A case in point is Suheir Hammad's *Born Palestinian, Born Black*,[4] which expresses identity sensemaking through poetry inspired by hip-hop, a powerful mode of expression empowering a generation of Palestinians, from Brooklyn to Bourj al-Barajneh, Toronto to Tulkarm, London to Lydd, Jerusalem to Jenin, and Ramallah to Gaza City. This globalization of Palestinian-ness reveals our identity/ies to be at the same time borderless, timeless, and situated; marked by our collective catastrophe and history, overlain with abstract notions of nationalism and liberation,[5] and awakened by shared culture and the trials of everyday lived experience.[6]

A recent work that has sought to capture the sheer diversity of how Palestinians in exile understand their identity is the edited volume by Yasir Suleiman, *Being Palestinian: Personal Reflections on Palestinian Identity in the Diaspora*. In this work, Suleiman brings together 102 Palestinians (the second author included) who neither live in Occupied Palestine nor in refugee camps (though many had), but who predominantly live in English-speaking countries (the United Kingdom, United States, Canada). They include academics, activists, artists, and professionals from a number of fields tasked to write about what being Palestinian means to them. Each provides a unique interpretation of the task. These chapters, though different, express shared pain and passion for, and gravitation towards, a deeper sense of collectivity. For Palestinians this is all too familiar. Or is it? An important critique of these works is that they are the reflections, experiences, and aspirations of a political and cultural class. This point was made by Sherif Almusa during a 2016 presentation of *Being Palestinian* at The Jerusalem Fund in Washington, DC,

232   *Exclusion and Exile*

All of them are accomplished, it seems, in their fields or are very promising. You have academic doctors, poets, writers, computer programmers, entrepreneurs, whatever, all kinds of people who seem to have the ability to write. Nonetheless, I still think the book is not representative because these are people who can write, and who can express themselves, part of the, you know, the elite. So, I hope the next book will be interviews with Palestinians who don't like to write or who are totally forgotten or who do not read or who do not have the privileges that a lot of these people have or have access to. So, I hope someone goes around and does this kind of book too. And we will see what it means.[7]

In considering how to approach this chapter, we took Almusa's critique to heart. On one hand we agree with Almusa. Having been raised in working-class Palestinian-Canadian families, we appreciate just how consuming the priorities of providing basic necessities are. Cutting coupons and focusing on other means to cope do not always lend themselves to celebrating or sharing a Palestinian political identity. Even more, for many Palestinians in exile, political identity making is associated with *politics*, and as such, is often perceived as a potential source of trouble and discouraged accordingly. This is particularly so when Palestine and Palestinians are routinely demonized in media and public discourse.[8] At least this reflects our experience in Canada. At the same time, we are hesitant to fully agree with Almusa. Though we come from working-class refugee backgrounds, something in how we were raised implicitly or even subconsciously encouraged us to explore and articulate our Palestinian political identities. Today, we embrace our Palestinian-ness to such an extent that it influences our everyday lives and work. Like many other Palestinians we know, our identity is redefined and regulated by family, community, peers, media, those struggles around us that spoke to us (Black and Indigenous movements, urban poverty), and of course, the political landscape of Canada and beyond.

Given our backgrounds and desire to address the oversight Almusa rightly points to, we focus our study on "everyday" Palestinians in Canada whose voices remain absent from contemporary discussions on political identity in exile: the working class. To do so, we utilize an inductive research approach involving narrative interviews and thematic analysis. The remainder of this chapter is structured to reflect this approach, hence we begin with research methods then introduce literature as part of our findings.

Finally, a note on semantics. In this chapter, we deliberately use the term "refugee" over "migrant" or "immigrant," and similarly, "exile" over "diaspora." Literary debates centred around contemporary diaspora studies highlight the importance of semantics when discussing Palestinian exile. Sari Hanafi and Isotalo, for instance, argue that the term "refugee" is used to describe the political-legal significance of the Palestinian case, and that the term "diaspora" and "migration" weaken the Palestinian cause for the Right of Return.[9] Terms like "diaspora," "immigrant" or even "migration" risk decentering the unique condition of statelessness that Palestinians experience. Peteet argues that while the term "diaspora" or "diaspora community" can account for the process of identity transformation in a host country, it risks dislodging the political-legal rights of the Palestinian struggle for liberation and return of all refugees.[10] Similarly, the term "migrant" is flexible to encompass the structural factors for displacement, and it can explain the similarities between the experiences of Palestinians and other migrant communities in Canada. However, Palestinian statelessness is unique. Most Palestinians in exile did not leave Palestine but were forced by circumstances that today prevent our return. Thus, statelessness is a condition that compels us to long for return. This is embodied within a collective aspiration for the liberation of and return to our homeland.

Research Methods

Our research design combines narrative interviews together with an inductive thematic analysis. We conducted six in-depth narrative interviews representing a small yet diverse group of Palestinian Canadians who self-identify as working-class refugees. Both authors were involved in identifying potential interviewees. Each interview lasted between forty-five and seventy minutes with participants ranging in age from mid-20s to late 60s. They were Muslim, Christian, agnostic, or atheist. They came from Palestine or via Syria, Jordan, the Gulf, and Europe, and settled in different cities across the country, mostly within Ontario and British Columbia. In terms of careers, they work (or worked, as some are now retired) in a variety of sectors, including office management, retail, graphic design, daycare, as well as tool and die machining. One was a university student at the time of the interview. They had attained different levels of education, from high school to technical education and professional certificates, both abroad and in Canada. Some came to Canada as early as the mid-1970s and as late

234   *Exclusion and Exile*

as the mid-2000s, most as adults and one as a young child. All identify as Palestinian refugees.

Like oral histories, narrative interviews are known to elicit rich and diverse information about the experiences and perspectives of participants.[11] We use the narrative interview protocol. Key to this approach is the "prime," which guides the participant to speak to a specific topic or set of topics.[12] After the prime is asked and understood, research participants spoke at length uninterrupted until finished. For our study, we developed the following prime, which was read to and if necessary, discussed with each participant at the outset of the interview,

> *In this study, we are speaking to Palestinians in Canada to understand their experience as working-class Palestinians. We want to listen to how you understand your work and what it was like for Palestinians to make a life in Canada, and in turn, how your experiences influence your views on being Palestinian. From your experience and perspective, could reflect on and provide an overview of your life and work in Canada, from the perspective of being Palestinian?*

General methodological protocols for conducting qualitative interviews, including informed consent, were followed.[13] All interviews were digitally recorded. The first author conducted and transcribed interviews, and both authors were involved with coding and analysis. The data were then analyzed using an inductive thematic analysis approach, a useful method to identify, organize, analyze, interpret, and report patterns or themes found in the empirical material.[14] The purpose of coding was to inductively capture semantic content as codes reflecting the words of participants, which would then be abstracted into themes. Thematic analysis procedures include familiarization with empirical materials, initial code generation, as well as the development (searching, reviewing, defining, naming) and reporting of themes.[15] Coding was done using Dedoose, an online coding platform. Upon saturation of codes, an iterative process of moving between codes and memos led to the grouping of codes into subthemes and eventually themes.[16] Themes were regularly checked for patterns, variability, consistency, and function.[17] Codes were collectively collated and carefully reviewed for each theme, and when necessary, rearranged, split, or re-coded. The final list of themes and subthemes are presented in table 9.1 and discussed in the Findings section to follow.

TABLE 9.1: Themes and subthemes of experiences of working-class Palestinians in Canada.

Subthemes	Themes
The paradox of Canadian credentials; Canadian experience as a key factor to secure employment; Underemployment due to foreign credentials and experience; Using personal connections to overcome exclusion; Education as a vehicle for upward social mobility; Parents sacrificing for child advancement	Liability of foreignness
Racial stereotypes and profiling during the hiring process; Discrimination and power dynamics in the workplace; Palestinian identity and political baggage; Limiting expression of identity at work to protect oneself	Racism, racialization, and work
Exile as lived experience; Intergenerational Palestinian storytelling; Articulation of class identity and experience	Conscientization of political identity

Findings

We present themes starting with newcomer perspectives (liability of foreignness), experiences of discrimination when attempting to enter into the workforce, and also once in it (racism and racialization at work), and identity-related reflexivity and sensemaking (conscientization of political identity). In this way, themes reflect the narratives of respondents as they share experiences from arrival, making sense of their belonging, and identity-related reflexivity.

Liability of Foreignness
This theme reflects the collective frustrations of participants concerning their capacity to enter into and progress within a racialized labour market favouring candidates with Canadian or Western/European experience and credentials over those without.

The Paradox of Canadian Credentials
Participants understand their exclusion from the labour market as a paradox: many positions require Canadian experience but being new to Canada,

236   *Exclusion and Exile*

they did not have any. For participants who immigrated more recently, the notion of having Canadian experience upon entry was simply beyond their imagination; as "skilled" immigrants, they expected to be integrated into the labour market in their respective fields. This paradox also appeared to participants as illogical, and as such, some felt it was strategically used as a tactic of exclusion. This was expressed by a participant from Gaza who migrated to Canada in 2016. According to him,

> Here, the Canadian experience is an umbrella, or a hidden word that the employer is using to convey lack of trusting the newcomer to this country. As I said, they always think that people who come to this country, particularly from a developing country, have a lower level of education or they don't speak English well. . .As I told you, I was hoping for a year, applying for jobs daily, writing cover letters daily, daily applying for jobs of different levels, upper jobs, down jobs, with the minimum job you can think of, and I wasn't called for a single interview. I was hoping only for one interview so that I can go and tell this employer that I am qualified for this job. I'm quite confident that if I go to an interview, I can impress.

Canadian Experience as a Key Factor to Secure Employment

Canadian experience is a determining factor in the ability of foreign-born participants to secure employment. Canadian experience in this way is a key criterion for or barrier to employment. Participants understood that their experience is not limited to Palestinian refugees, but something faced by other racialized people as well. For a participant from Gaza but with education obtained in Cairo, the lack of foreign credential recognition led to immense frustration. She explains,

> They don't actually try to see what your skills are, and where and how I can take advantage of these skills. . .Just sitting at home not doing anything, waiting for someone to recognize your experience. The first thing they say to you here is "You have no Canadian experience."

It is noteworthy that the interviews revealed a generational difference regarding how the participants relate to employment. A participant who is a machinist by trade and who migrated to Canada in 1974 immediately found a job in the trade. He recalls,

> I finished my training in 1974 or '73. And then we came to Canada in 1974. In order for me to work here, as you know, you need to have experience. But because of my technical background and my skills as a machinist, it was easy for me to find a job. In 1974, they were looking for people like me at that time, so it was easy to find a job. I found a job and started working.

His experience varied differently from other participants who have both substantial educational and work experience but found limited employment opportunities upon arriving in Canada. For instance, according to a participant who arrived more recently to Canada with a university degree, "So, this is the thing of course, after we studied, to come here and work as a sales associate or in a gas station, of course it's not easy."

This generational difference is supported in the literature. For instance, Fuller and Vosko argue that immigrants to Canada experience temporal differences in relation to securing employment, in that those who arrived earlier had less difficulty gaining meaningful employment than those arriving more recently.[18]

Underemployment Due to Foreign Credentials and Experience

Participants endure underemployment, frustration, and hardship resulting from the disconnect between their formal credentials and ability to enter into or progress within the Canadian labour market. That includes lack of recognition of credentials attained in Palestine or elsewhere, or simple dismissal that these might be equivalent to Canadian credentials and experience. Despite having extensive educational credentials and work experience, many participants had difficulty securing job interviews and employment within their respective fields. For a Palestinian participant born in Gaza, who immigrated to Canada after 2001, entry into the labour market was overrepresented in low-wage "low-skill" work, such as in retail sales and cashier positions. Not only was their foreign education and training a barrier to meaningful employment, but such credentials and skills were unrelated to jobs they could land,

With the help of a Palestinian friend I got to work as a cashier in one of the convenience stores to help with my income, which is not something related to what I do. At the beginning I found it humiliating for me because I used to do a very high-level job back in Palestine with a great salary, and here it wasn't matching what I was earning.

The understanding of the participant is that by immigrating to Canada, he might have been able to fulfill his ambitions relating to advancing his career with greater job and physical security. Despite constantly updating his resumé, networking, and applying for many positions, in his first two years in Canada he was not called for a single interview. On this topic, multiple participants expressed frustrations. Some were completely disillusioned with the lack of access to meaningful employment and career progression in line with their pre-Canada formal training and experience.

Using Personal Connections to Secure Employment

Participants who came to Canada alone, without existing support networks such as sponsoring family, relied heavily on establishing personal connections and networks to find and secure employment. For instance, a participant who recently came to Canada first contacted employment centres for support, yet some denied him services due to his immigration status,

I went to the employment centre, some of them they opened the door for me, some of them they didn't open the door for me because they classify me as #9, which is not a permanent resident. So some of the centres said we can't help you to find a job, the employment centres, as you're not a permanent resident.

Without permanent residency or Canadian citizenship, many government services were unavailable to him, including employment support. His foreign education credentials and non-profit sector experience were of little help securing employment in his field of choice. As such, and through a personal connection, he eventually took a position at a local convenience store. He recalls,

So I worked at a convenience store as a cashier for 5 to 6 months. At the same time, I kept freelancing, my tutoring. That wasn't the purpose

for me, to do tutoring or freelancing or even volunteering. It wasn't the purpose of getting money, as one of the keys when I came to this country is that you have to make connections.

Reliance on social networks is critical in establishing social capital to locate and secure employment.[19] Establishing social connections in the community allowed this participant to build a network for helping to secure employment as well as for social support. His priority at the time was to secure employment, be it temporary or within his field of expertise,

So I'm a social person, when I came here within a few months I managed to make a lot of friends from the community of Hamilton and out of Hamilton with people of different backgrounds—whether they were white, non-white, the Palestinian community. With every single party I was invited to, I was walking to everyone in the party, trying to make connection, get their contact information. After the party, I would message them and ask them to meet up to make connections to get a job.

Education as a Vehicle for Upward Social Mobility

Participants felt pressure to pursue education in Canada because their foreign qualifications were deemed less legitimate than those obtained in Canada. Every participant interviewed expressed they have either pursued or seriously considered pursuing further education in Canada to gain some advantage in the labour market. If meaningfully employed, the pursuit of further education was seen as a vehicle to advance their careers. A participant who immigrated to Canada from Gaza with a university degree and substantive work experience highlights how education, skills and job experience relate to income and labour mobility,

Sometimes we take that much education in order to validate ourselves to this society, like we need that self-defence. Like watch out, we are Palestinians, that we know things. Because no one wants us, everyone is trying to push us. So, this is the way you have to approach it. If you're being bullied, you want to be better than all of them.

In her experience, the education and experience she attained before coming to Canada was deemed to have little legitimacy in Canada. For this reason, she chose to pursue a certificate in graphic design as a route to demonstrate Canadian credentials and appear competitive to prospective employers. Her experiences reflect how beliefs about credentials and entitlements can discriminate against immigrants to Canada. This, in turn, pushes newcomers to pursue further credentials and/or education, even if they bring with them solid education and work experience. This issue is structural. For instance, while migrants to Canada have foreign credentials assessed on a point system during the immigration process, they find that their work experience and other dimensions of human capital are rarely transferable in the Canadian labour market.[20] Hence, while immigrants are deemed to have education worthy for entry, they can find themselves easily discriminated against upon entry. This is the case for both the participants from Gaza; despite studying for Canadian credentials, they experienced discrimination in the form of assumptions about their level of English fluency, lack of Canadian experience, and the quality of their foreign credentials.

Parents Sacrificing for Child Advancement

Participants sacrifice opportunities for themselves in order to provide a brighter, safer future for their children. Ambitions for children include education and financial security, and sacrifices include leaving their homeland and families, as well as financial and career-related opportunity costs.

For some participants, the idea of sacrificing for future generations reflects a confluence of concerns, including economic security and physical safety, as motivating factors for migrating to Canada. This is especially present in the responses of participants who experienced Israeli military violence and occupation and/or sought to avoid it. For instance, a participant born in Jerusalem but displaced as a child to Ramallah during the Nakba, opportunities outside of Palestine provided safety together with economic opportunity, and the ability to provide support to family from a distance,

> I got a scholarship to go to Sweden. It was in 1966. So I went to Sweden 1966 and was supposed to go back in August '67. But the Six Day War broke out in 1967 in June. So I couldn't go back. The Swedish authorities said to me they can arrange for me to go back, but if I'd like to stay they would issue a working permit. So I said I might as well do that, because

if I go back home there won't be work or anything. At least we can help our family this way.

Later, rather than returning to Occupied Palestine, he decided to migrate to Canada where he already had family and also where his Swedish credentials might be marketable (though he did continue technical education in Canada). His situation reflects the multiple layers of exile that many Palestinians as well as other dispossessed peoples endure (think Armenians who went to Palestine, the Kurdish people, and more recently, Palestinian refugees in Syria).

Moreover, for participants who lived in Occupied Palestine, "education" became an important aspiration given Israeli repression and targeting of Palestinian schools and universities. A mother compared the situation of her own children and those "back home" in Occupied Palestine,

Safety, security, bringing the boys here and to have the opportunity for them to have a good education and explore and grow. Because I see my nieces, they're all educated but it's not open for them. They can't travel, they're [the Israelis] are so strict. They can't even travel!

Participants consistently envisioned Canada as a country that would provide abundant economic and educational opportunity for their children. The priority for parents was for their children to attain a high standard of education, and to live in a safe and stable environment. However, in order to provide this "good life" for their children, participants were required to reskill and engage in temporary, low-wage work as a means to gain financial security and build an economic foundation for the family.[21] This experience is not unique to Palestinians, but reflects the experiences of other minority and racialized migrants.

It is important to emphasize just how gendered the notion of self-sacrifice was in relation to the betterment of children's lives is. Two participants, both mothers, spoke of the gendered dimensions of motherhood, work, and the family. One merged her family and work in the form of full-time home daycare work as a response to her need to secure childcare for her children and also provide income for the household. Upon having twins, she could no longer afford to keep her full-time day job at an insurance company. Instead, she began in-home daycare, allowing her to care for her own children whilst making an income, and also picked up a second job in the evenings for additional income, in the form of part-time retail work. In her words,

> *I started doing home daycare. I was taking kids during the day, and when my husband finishes work and comes home, I'll go work part-time in a department store, like an evening job, part-time. I did this for 4–5 years and then it was a bit too much. I decided to quit my part-time jobs and focus on full-time daycare.*

She also recalls how the daycare remained a constant and essential lifeline despite the sometimes precarious nature of her husband's work, "My husband would be laid on and off, on and off, on and off; so you know, I was stable, my work was stable."

This gendered dimension of social reproduction, of care work done inside the home, is usually unwaged but sometimes low-wage work. However, as a result of the home daycare, this participant could care for her own children while gaining income and building social capital within her community. In turn, this social capital provided a consistent flow of income through referrals, ultimately contributing significantly to household income, "I was always busy, I even had to say no to some people because I couldn't take them all."

For this participant, the sacrifice of her career outside the domestic sphere is caused by a combination of financial need, resulting from the inhibitive costs of childcare for her own children, the precarious nature of her husband's employment, and her central role in the family as mother and caretaker.

A second example is provided by a participant born in Gaza, educated in Egypt, and who migrated to Canada in 2000. Prior to coming to Canada, she was meaningfully employed with a stable position and financial security,

> *In Gaza, we were perfectly fine. Financially, we were actually doing much better than how much we make here. Because I had a full-time job, I was working for the government. So was my husband and they gave him a car, we had our own house. So* alhamdulillah, *everything was working fine. It wasn't that. It was always searching for more stability, more future for the kids, not having to worry about when things are going to start and when the war is going to start.*

She notes that despite maintaining employment in her respective field and achieving financial security, it did not bring physical security to her family due to the precarious situation of living under siege. She reflects that the overwhelming factor in the decision to migrate to Canada was physical security for her children, even though this came at a cost to her career and financial security,

> It's always there, a fight in your life, but safety is more important. Even now, they ask me, do you want security in your job or to feel insecure about your kids, or that when they leave the house you fear that they won't come back? No, I would rather choose here. I would choose their safety over my happiness. But did it come with a price? Yes.

Racism, Racialization and Work

This theme reflects the experiences of participants in relation to racism and racialization at the workplace, such as racial power dynamics, microaggressions and wage disparity.

Racial Stereotypes and Profiling During the Hiring Process

Foreign credentials and Arabic names are triggers for racial stereotyping and exclusion, especially for participants born outside Canada. These often materialized as so-called concerns about not having competency or fluency in the English language (even though many Palestinians studied English). Racialization in and around fluency in English is certainly not exclusive to Palestinians, but it did impact participants. According to a Palestinian born in Gaza, he felt regularly "othered" when attempting to secure employment,

> I guess these two things—the level of education and the English language—they assume before they even give a chance for the people to come for an interview...But in my case, they assumed, in my opinion, that I don't speak English, that I'm not qualified, without looking at my resume, or calling me for an interview.

Another participant, also born in Canada, recalls her experiences of exclusion while attempting to secure employment as a racial minority. She, too, felt that her racialized identity played a significant role in her inability to enter the workforce,

After 4 interviews, after an in-person meeting, after going back and forth because of how interested they are in me, and sitting with them and talking. . .I didn't get the job! I felt, yes, there is racism, of course there is, what else?

For others, being Palestinian led to racial profiling and microaggressions during the hiring process. A participant spoke of her mother's experience,

She tried to apply to places in the Jewish areas and I remember in one of her interviews, the person interviewing her was like, "Oh you know I'm Jewish, right?" And she was like "OK, I'm here for a job, what does that have to do with anything?" Even those microaggressions my mom definitely faced even before she put on the hijab. My mom was really racially ambiguous, but she still faced a lot of things when people learned she was a Palestinian.

Discrimination and Power Dynamics in the Workplace

Participants experienced racial power dynamics at work in ways that maintain racial hierarchy and structure in the workplace. For some, racial dynamics were centred around Canadian versus foreign experience. For others, they involved Islamophobic stereotypes surrounding the *hijab*, or headscarf. According to one participant who wears the hijab, she was exposed to microaggressions, blunt racist slurs, and workplace unease. For her, this discrimination was mostly a result of Islamophobic representations of Muslims in the media,

It was never a fair game and it was always harsh. Because people always assume, especially when I'm wearing a hijab, that it takes a lot of time and effort from my side to fit in. Because the minute they see you: 1) all they hear about you in the news is always something negative; and 2) they are always thinking maybe she doesn't know.

The racism is also manifested through the devaluation of skills. This is not only an issue of racialization, but also an issue of gender and power. For instance, a participant recalls experiences with her manager, who routinely devalues her work and non-Canadian experience,

*I've been doing this for 15 years. Every time I try to explain to him that
there's another way of doing this, I always feel that he tries to remind
me that he has more experience than I do. I say, I have 25 years of experience, I swear I wasn't born yesterday!...I don't want to tell him that I
have more experience than him, but the fact is that he just thinks I have
the 7 years of experience that I got here in Canada. That's what I feel.*

Palestinian Identity and Political Baggage

Participants experience anxieties in relation to being open about their
Palestinian identity and heritage, and fear hostility in the form of discrimination and other negative consequences. This is because being Palestinian
is inherently politicized; those who express it are racialized and targeted
with racist tropes, microaggression and hostility, even in the workplace. In
Canada, having a Palestinian identity is often considered taboo. This leads to
internalized anxiety and apprehension that Palestinians are made to endure.
A participant from Gaza shares her experience,

*During the 2014 war on Gaza, I was working at my employer in
Mississauga. We never shared. I wasn't even discussing things with them.
I was so upset, I wasn't eating or sleeping well. My mom is in Gaza, my
brother is in Gaza and they were forced outside of their home, and they
actually had rockets come in the middle of their house. So I couldn't
sleep, and I would come to work very stressed. The entire night I would
look at the news and wonder if the rockets would come down on them
and they would be safe or if something would happen to them?...I was
worried. But did I share this with my coworkers? No. Did they know that
I'm worried about my parents, my family? No they don't. Did they care
to ask? No.*

Like this participant, many Palestinians in exile have families that
continue to live in Occupied Palestine under military occupation and siege
or in refugee camps where they face hostility, poverty, and political marginalization. For this participant, media coverage of the 2014 bombardment
of Gaza amplified the very real threat to her family's safety. This blurred
into her work life. Yet she felt an inability to speak about this, even postu-
lating her coworker's indifference. Her story is supported by literature that

246   *Exclusion and Exile*

recognizes that for racialized people, the quality of social relations at work can foster or hinder positive emotions.[22]

Another participant, a university student working as a barista at a Toronto cafe, also spoke of her apprehension about sharing her Palestinian identity with coworkers,

At work, I remember when I first, at least in this job, I think it was after a couple of rallies this summer, or something, when I got my barista job. I was afraid of telling them where I was from, telling my coworkers. I was almost just cautious of it, like, should I be telling them? Because they seem very, you know, I don't know. You never know!

Such anxieties are indeed well-founded. For instance, Canadian universities are known to be unsafe for students seeking to raise awareness about Palestinian human rights. Students who do are routinely attacked by Zionist groups both on and off campuses. Moreover, university administrators and politicians also express hostility towards pro-Palestinian activities, adding to identity-related anxieties.[23] Still, Palestinian students do seek and locate support groups through community and campus coalitions and social justice events. Again, locating similar social support networks in the workplace can be more complicated, as racial stereotypes and discrimination in the workplace are known to create a negative work environment where racialized workers can experience social isolation.[24] In this instance, despite being empowered by sharing her Palestinian identity with like-minded students, the anxiety around confronting stereotypes at work remained a source of tension.

Limiting Expression of Identity at Work to Protect Oneself

Some participants expressed anxiety about expressing their Palestinian identity at work, and how their coworkers might react negatively or how doing so might impact their employment status. This led some respondents to minimize discussions about their cultural and political identity, as well as current events relating to Israeli military violence and occupation. According to a participant, a Palestinian man in his early 30s,

There's been a lot of jobs where politics are not on the table at all. . . Just because, I guess, the nature of it, you have to be able or neutral somehow

*as though the Palestinian liberation, to even mention it makes you on
the side of something. Like on the side of something that can be seen in
two different ways. To say anything like "Israeli Apartheid" is super
controversial.*

Hence, the very act of discussing issues important to Palestinians and
the Palestinian lived experience is problematic. This encourages many
Palestinians in Canada to minimize expressions of identity, which is a form
of self-silencing. This can also increase anxiety and the feeling of bearing
a burden alone, resonating with the notion of "landscapes of social exclusion."[25] For instance, the same participant also spoke of how the topic
of "Israel-Palestine" is strongly considered a taboo, especially when
mentioning Israeli human rights violations,

*So your politics are monitored more by supervisors, so that you don't
send a message that the organization can't stand behind. Not even that,
it's more that no one finds out...no Zionist finds out that someone who
works at this place or that place has said something about Palestine to
impressionable youth. Educating them about reality or even if you're
just sharing things in the news that are happening...When I first started
working in social services, there was a lot of news about when they were
first building the wall in Israel and how a lot of people are disgusted by
that. I got in trouble for talking about it.*

This perpetuates the (often self-imposed) regulation or silencing of
Palestinians in Canada, who might otherwise share their experiences or
identities but for the fear of retaliation. These exclusionary and silencing
pressures routinely occur at university campuses where there are active
Zionist student groups. However, in the workplace, the risks are even more
acute. In short, Palestinian refugees in Canada often feel they must make a
distinct separation between their personal and professional identities while
at work.[26]

Conscientization of Political Identity
This theme reflects how participants relate to their Palestinian *national* identity, not only individually but also collectively. This theme strongly evokes
the concept of *conscientization* (or "critical consciousness") as advanced

by Paulo Freire, involving notions of self-awareness, empowerment, and justice-seeking.[27]

Exile as Lived Experience

Participants relate their dispossession and exile from Palestine with their everyday lived experiences in Canada. For Palestinians, the Nakba is a defining "site of memory" informing personal and collective ideas about homeland and traditions. For all participants born outside Canada, recollection of their lives in Palestine is almost tangible, not imagined nor a memory. Even after physical displacement from Palestine and global movement, Palestinians seek to preserve customs and traditions, and most importantly, to connect with family "back home." For Canadian-born participants, their relationship to Palestine is influenced by a combination of intergenerational storytelling, and community and current affairs. This is supported by Ahmad Sa'di, who writes that Palestinians in exile, disconnected from their homeland, cannot help but engage with their national identity through "localized experiences and sentiments."[28] For participants, their Palestinian identities were informed by everyday experiences, with families, friends, and community, at school or in the workplace. Like other colonized peoples, Palestinians reconstruct their national identities through a "restoration of the individual's subjectivity" through life stories, artifacts, documents, memories and customs.[29] For instance, a Canadian-born participant from Toronto shared that social class was at the fore of her identity and material reality growing up. However, through her interaction with intergenerational storytelling, she began to understand the unique experiences of Palestinian displacement and its centrality to her articulation of a personal national identity,

> *I am Palestinian, which makes me sad because I wish I knew what that life was like. But then, as I get older, as I've been getting older, I've become more connected and understanding of these circumstances, because of all the displacement that we've faced in the past.*

This experience is shared by another participant who was born a refugee in Damascus but migrated to Canada in his youth,

> *By 16 is when I became more aware of the politics of it [Palestine] and started to talk about it. I realized very quickly that it was controversial,*

*and when I was younger that didn't matter at all because I didn't have
anything to lose. It was just you are who you are and if people don't like
it, they don't like it. . .Growing up, that shaped a lot of our perspectives—
remembering that we're Palestinians—but I didn't really think of it as
much in Syria; I became more aware of it in Canada.*

His story reflects how the Palestinian cause in the Arab world remains a
central theme in the Arab consciousness, despite the increased normalization between the Arab world and Israel.[30] However, the process of "Othering"
as a Palestinian is exacerbated in the West, namely in the United States and
Canada, where media and political rhetoric vilifies the Palestinian struggle
and identity.[31] This hostility reinforces our sense of exile and shapes our
understanding of what it means to be Palestinian.

Intergenerational Palestinian Storytelling

Participants expressed the centrality of storytelling for articulating and
preserving the Palestinian narrative, experience, and identity and for sharing
these across generations. For Palestinians, storytelling is an act of *sumud*, or
steadfastness in the face of cultural erasure and genocide. Storytelling can
thus do more than foster a sense of personal connection and community; it
can also reaffirm our history and national aspiration.[32] Each participant interviewed mentioned some form of storytelling as an important means for
exploring and sharing their identity, culture, and connections to Palestine.
For participants born outside of Canada, storytelling is a way to share with
their children and preserve culture.

For one participant who was born outside Canada, storytelling was a means
to recall and remember her mother's life in Bourj al-Barajneh, a Palestinian
refugee camp in Beirut, Lebanon. She imagined Palestine through her mother's
displacement together with her own exile. Doing so reinforced an emotional
attachment to her Palestinian identity and our collective struggle. She recalls
an assignment she did for high school, which prompted her to ask her mother
about her life in the camps. For her, this was a transformative moment,

*That's when I realized how important it was to learn about your roots
and not be so separated. I don't know, that's when I started asking
and getting these stories. I can say that was the moment that I started
exploring more.*

250   *Exclusion and Exile*

Listening to her mother's lived experience in the camp moved her to learn about her Palestinian roots and explore this narrative through creative writing, through schoolwork and poetry that she performs in the Toronto community. Born to a working-class Palestinian family, she articulates the intersections of her class and national identity through engaging in the arts in her local community,

> *Yeah so ever since I started to get more involved, since I started university, I've been more vocal and I've written some poetry and done more work around being Palestinian and the Palestinian cause.*

Intergenerational storytelling thus led this participant to explore her own political identity, which in turn caused her to engage with arts, culture, and activism. Sometimes this is motivated by a fear of assimilation or losing Palestinian cultural traditions and values. But more often than not, storytelling is a way for younger generations to channel intergenerational trauma and reaffirm new connections to Palestine. In the words of the same participant,

> *I think we definitely cling on [our Palestinian identity] in different ways and neglect in different ways, I think we do both. I think my mom always says, she doesn't talk about the news, she doesn't like to listen to the news. I think that's because of the trauma she's faced, that means she doesn't talk to me a lot about what's happening [to Palestinians] but now that I'm getting more vocal, I'm starting to cling on to the things that I want to learn and know. I don't want our culture to be wiped away. I don't want my Palestinian-ness to be wiped away, I don't want to be assimilated.*

Similar to the Armenians and other dispossessed communities who experienced genocide, Palestinian refugees were forced into a state of survival; refugees in exile had little choice but to adapt to new social, economic, political and legal realities in their host countries.[33] The preservation of language and cultural traditions thus remains central to the sustenance of the Palestinian cause and national identity.

For other participants, their Palestinian identity is something so integral to their personality, they feel compelled to share it whenever they can. As a participant from Gaza expressed,

My identity as a Palestinian is travelling with me everywhere I go, everywhere I socialize, everywhere I work. It's a part of me, I cannot separate it from my personality. So, whenever I have the chance to express my Palestinian identity and my Palestinian story, I would take it.

Articulation of Class Identity and Experience

Participants spoke of many issues relating to class identity, most often determined by financial insecurity. In this subtheme, we draw primarily from one participant whose experiences are strikingly similar to our own. For this participant, watching her single mother struggle to put food on the table and pay rent came to define her class identity, even more than being Palestinian,

It's definitely living a day-by-day mindset. You're going to go to work and you're going to come home and feed the kids. And for us kids it's like, you're going to go to school, come home and see what's on the table, you know? It's that kind of mindset, or we're going to go play with our friends outside, and I think I don't blame my mom and I don't say she's any less Palestinian or not connected.

Here, the participant speaks to how the precarious material conditions that impact her and her mother's lives weighed heavily on her identity, emphasizing the strength of class identity over the Palestinian identity. Coming from a single-parent working-class family meant she had limited opportunity to engage with or learn from her mother on Palestine-related issues, including culture and identity,

Because my mom wasn't always home at the time, she couldn't be there as a teacher or mother. I resented her for this as a kid because now I don't speak Arabic properly, I don't know my culture as much as I should, and I wish I did. I wasn't as connected as I could've been as a kid. I think it's because of those reasons, because my mom is balancing all of these things and unfortunately, culture and my "Palestinian-ness" didn't really have time for it, unfortunately. We were just like you know, building a life and trying to live. Trying to make ends meet, things like that.

For this participant, class identity is inseparable from her Palestinian identity. Her life has been defined by financial insecurity and struggle, which defined her family dynamics and responsibilities. She also notes that her Palestine activism also includes her class experience and analysis, which is often underrepresented in Palestinian student activism,

> Yeah so ever since I started to get more involved, since I started university I've been more vocal and I've written some poetry and done more work around being Palestinian and the Palestinian cause. It's early for me, but I've been vocal and my family sees that. I also talk about the class-stuff.

Moreover, her consciousness is so prevalent it determines with whom she chooses to form social bonds as, "Class came first for me, in terms of a connecting factor."

Conclusion

Our ambition to address the "gap" in the literature on Palestinian identity is personal. Coming from working-class Palestinian refugee families in Canada, we sought to better understand the structural and cultural conditions and experiences that shaped our families and ourselves. Indeed, we found ourselves in many of the participant's narratives; their stories, struggles and ambitions resonated with our own and those of our families. This project was an opportunity for us to listen to and learn from people within our community. To explore the intersectionality of class and national identity against the struggle to navigate a better life. To take stock of where we have come from, where we are as a community, and what may come next. This is part of our own conscientization, positionality, and sensemaking as Palestinians, as first-generation Canadians, as researchers, as organizers.[34] As Fanon articulates, we record and share our voices in the service of our perseverance and liberation.[35]

The Palestinian national identity was born from struggle and exile.[36] As the above-described themes and subthemes attest, it is also reflexively reproduced through struggle in exile. Participant narratives point us to the very real liabilities of foreignness and racialization that Palestinian refugees (and no doubt others) in Canada face. These reflect "landscapes of social exclusion" involving material, psychosocial and structural discrimination that shape and reinforce racialized identities.[37] We thus theorize that our working-class condition, together with the racialization and politicization inherent to being Palestinian, are contemporary forms of exclusion that influence our identity conscientization in ways that reproduce our understanding of self and exile, our Palestinian-ness.

Notes

1. Suleiman, *Being Palestinian*; Abdo and Masalha, eds., *An Oral History of the Palestinian Nakba*.
2. Farah, "Palestinian Refugees, the Nation," 41–47; Farah, "Refugee Camps in the Palestinian and Sahrawi National Liberation Movements."
3. Fincham, "Learning the Nation in Exile."
4. Hammad, *Born Palestinian*.
5. Sa'di, "Catastrophe, Memory and Identity."
6. Hammad, *Born Palestinian*; Farah, "Refugee Camps."
7. Almusa, "Being Palestinian."
8. Fourlas, "Being a Target," 101.
9. Hanafi, "Rethinking the Palestinians as a Diaspora"; Isotalo, *Interim Return and Palestine*, 9.
10. Peteet, "Problematizing a Palestinian Diaspora," 636.
11. Bauer and Aarts, "Corpus Construction."
12. Jovchelovitch and Bauer, "Narrative Interviewing."
13. Gaskell and Bauer, "Towards Public Accountability."
14. Braun and Clarke, "Using Thematic Analysis in Psychology."
15. Braun and Clarke.
16. Birks, Chapman, and Francis, "Memoing in Qualitative Research."
17. Braun and Clarke, "Using Thematic Analysis in Psychology."
18. Fuller and Vosko, "Temporary Employment and Social Inequality in Canada."
19. Creese, Dyck, and McLaren, "The Problem of 'Human Capital,'" 149.
20. Creese, Dyck, and McLaren, 145.
21. Creese, Dyck, and McLaren, 152.
22. Sloan, Newhouse, and Thompson, "Counting on Coworkers," 346.
23. Drummond, *Unthinkable Thoughts*.
24. Sloan, Newhouse, and Thompson, "Counting on Coworkers," 344.
25. Inwood and Yarbrough, "Racialized Places, Racialized Bodies," 300.
26. Ramarajan and Reid, "Shattering the Myth of Separate Worlds," 628.
27. Freire, *Education for Critical Consciousness*; Freire, *Pedagogy of the Oppressed*.
28. Sa'di, "Catastrophe, Memory and Identity," 176.
29. Sa'di, 176.
30. El-Kurd. 'What Do Ordinary Arabs Think."
31. See Antonius' chapter (chapter 7 in this volume) for an example of this process.
32. Sa'di, "Catastrophe, Memory and Identity."

33. Melkonian, *The Right to Struggle*, 183.
34. Abdelnour and Abu Moghli, "Researching Violent Contexts: A Call for Political Reflexivity."
35. Fanon, *Wretched of the Earth*.
36. Samidoun Palestinian Prisoner Solidarity Network, "Webinar: Palestinian Refugees and the Right of Return with Mohammed Khatib," Facebook, April 2, 2020, https://www.facebook.com/294670507233109/videos/232854514435753/.
37. Inwood and Yarbrough, "Racialized Places, Racialized Bodies," 300.

References

Abdelnour, Samer, and Mai Abu Moghli. "Researching Violent Contexts: A Call for Political Reflexivity." *Organization* (2021): 1–24.

Abdo, Nahla, and Nur Masalha, eds. *An Oral History of the Palestinian Nakba*. London: Zed Books, 2018.

Almusa, S. "Being Palestinian: Personal Reflections on Palestinian Identity in the Diaspora." *The Jerusalem Fund*, March 23, 2016. https://www.thejerusalemfund.org/8103/palestinian-personal-reflections-palestinian-identity-diaspora.

Aly, Ashraf El-Araby, and James F. Ragan. "Arab Immigrants in the United States: How and Why Do Returns to Education Vary by Country of Origin?" *Journal of Population Economics* 23, no. 2 (2010): 519–38.

Bauer, Martin W., and Bas Aarts. "Corpus Construction: A Principle for Qualitative Data Collection." In *Qualitative Researching with Text, Image and Sound: A Practical Handbook*, edited by Martin W. Bauer and George Gaskell, 131–51. London: Sage, 2000.

Birks, Melanie, Ysanne Chapman, and Karen Francis. "Memoing in Qualitative Research: Probing Data and Processes." *Journal of Research in Nursing* 13, no. 1 (2008): 68–75.

Braun, Virginia, and Victoria Clarke, "Using Thematic Analysis in Psychology." *Qualitative Research in Psychology* 3, no. 2 (2006): 77–101.

Creese, Gillian, Isabel Dyck, and Arlene Tiger McLaren. "The Problem of 'Human Capital': Gender, Place and Immigrant Household Strategies of Reskilling in Vancouver." In *Gender, Generations and the Family in International Migration*, edited by Albert Kraler, Eleonore Kofman, Martin Kohli, and Camille Schmoll, 141–62. Amsterdam: Amsterdam University Press, 2011.

Drummond, Susan G. *Unthinkable Thoughts: Academic Freedom and the One-State Model for Israel and Palestine*. Vancouver: UBC Press, 2013.

El Kurd, Dana. "What Do Ordinary Arabs Think about Normalizing Relations with Israel?" *Washington Post*, (26 October 2020). https://www.washingtonpost.com/politics/2020/10/26/what-do-ordinary-arabs-think-about-normalizing-relations-with-israel/.

Fanon, Frantz. *Wretched of the Earth*. New York: Grove Press, 1963.

Farah, Randa. "Palestinian Refugees, the Nation, and the Shifting Political Landscape." *Social Alternatives* 32, no. 3 (2013): 41–7.

Farah, Randa. "Refugee Camps in the Palestinian and Sahrawi National Liberation Movements: A Comparative Perspective." *Journal of Palestine Studies* 38, no. 2 (2009): 76–93.

Feagin, J., and McKinney, K. *The Many Costs of Racism*. New York: Rowman and Littlefield Publishers, 2013.

Fincham, Kathleen. "Learning the Nation in Exile: Constructing Youth Identities, Belonging and 'Citizenship' in Palestinian Refugee Camps in South Lebanon." *Comparative Education* 48, no. 1 (2012): 119–33.

Fourlas, George N. "Being a Target: On the Racialization of Middle Eastern Americans." *Critical Philosophy of Race* 3, no. 1 (2015): 101–23.

Freire, Paolo. *Education for Critical Consciousness*. New York: Continuum, 2005.

Freire, Paolo. *Pedagogy of the Oppressed*. New York: Continuum, 1970.

Fuller, Sylvia, and Leah F. Vosko. "Temporary Employment and Social Inequality in Canada: Exploring Intersections of Gender, Race and Immigration Status." *Social Indicators Research* 88, no. 1 (2008): 31–50.

Gaskell, George, and Martin W. Bauer. "Towards Public Accountability: Beyond Sampling, Reliability and Validity." In *Qualitative Researching with Text, Image and Sound: A Practical Handbook*, edited by Martin W. Bauer and George Gaskell, 336–50. London: Sage, 2000.

Hammad, Suheir. *Born Palestinian, Born Black*. New York: Harlem River Press, 1996.

Hanafi, Sari. "Rethinking the Palestinians as a Diaspora: The Relationships between the Diaspora and the Palestinian Territories." In *Homelands and Diasporas: Holy Lands and Other Places*, edited by André Levy and Alex Weingrod, 97–122. Redwood City: Stanford University Press, 2005. https://doi.org/10.1515/9781503624108-007.

Inwood, Joshua F., and Robert A. Yarbrough. "Racialized Places, Racialized Bodies: The Impact of Racialization on Individual and Place Identities." *GeoJournal* 75, no. 3 (2010): 299–301.

Isotalo, Riina. *Interim Return and Palestine: On Politics, Terminology and Structural Invisibility*. DIIS Working Paper no 2006/21. Copenhagen: Danish Institute for International Studies, 2006.

Jovchelovitch, Sandra, and Martin W. Bauer. "Narrative Interviewing." In *Qualitative Researching with Text, Image and Sound: A Practical Handbook*, edited by Martin Bauer and George Gaskell, 57–74. London: Sage, 2000.

Melkonian, Monte. *The Right to Struggle: Selected Writings of Monte Melkonian on the Armenian National Question*. San Francisco: Sardarabad Collective, 1990.

Peteet, Julie. "Problematizing a Palestinian Diaspora." *International Journal of Middle East Studies* 39, no. 4 (2007): 627–46.

Ramarajan, Lakshmi, and Erin Reid. "Shattering the Myth of Separate Worlds: Negotiating Nonwork Identities at Work." *Academy of Management Review* 38, no. 4 (2013): 621–44.

Sa'di, Ahmad H. "Catastrophe, Memory and Identity: Al-Nakbah as a Component of Palestinian Identity." *Israel Studies* 7, no. 2 (2002): 175–98.

Samidoun Palestinian Prisoner Solidarity Network. "Webinar: Palestinian Refugees and the Right of Return with Mohammed Khatib." Facebook, April 2, 2020. https://www.facebook.com/294670507233109/videos/232854514435753/.

Sloan, Melissa M., Ranae J. Evenson Newhouse, and Ashley B. Thompson. "Counting on Coworkers: Race, Social Support, and Emotional Experiences on the Job." *Social Psychology Quarterly* 76, no. 4 (2013): 343–72.

Suleiman, Yasir. *Being Palestinian: Personal Reflections on Palestinian Identity in the Diaspora*. Edinburgh: Edinburgh University Press, 2006.

10

PALESTINIAN ORGANIZATIONS IN OTTAWA

Understanding Communities in Practice

EMILY REGAN WILLS

Introduction

Every July, signs begin to appear on roadsides all over Ottawa announcing the Ottawa Palestinian Festival. The small roadside signs feature the festival's name in red, black, and green, the colours of the Palestinian flag, and a stylized olive branch. They invite the viewer to come to Marion Dewar Plaza, a public square located outside City Hall in the centre of downtown Ottawa, a few blocks from Parliament Hill. The Ottawa Palestinian Festival bills itself as the largest Palestinian community event in North America. It is held over the last weekend before Labour Day every August, featuring musical performers from the Arab world and the North American Arab diaspora, dabke (folk dance) performances and lessons, a Palestinian wedding show, a falafel-eating contest, and an Arabic spelling bee, as well as the sale of traditional Palestinian crafts and foods.

These signs stuck out to me as a relative newcomer to Ottawa in 2014, the year of the first festival. I had spent several years living alongside and writing about Arab diaspora communities in New York City, where Palestinians mobilized as Palestinians only as activists for Palestinian rights. Cultural and social events, on the other hand, were organized under the banner of Arab identity, rather than any specific national identity—even if Palestinians were at the forefront of organizing those events. What was particularly surprising to me was the public avowal of Palestinian identity, the placement of literal signs proclaiming a Palestinian celebration throughout the city. I imagined what would happen to those signs if they were placed anywhere in New York other than in the centre of Bay Ridge—the "Arab neighbourhood" in Brooklyn where I worked—and could only think that they would be torn down within a day. But in my new home, Ottawa, they stuck around.

Palestinians in the National Capital Region, consisting of the cities of Ottawa, Ontario and Gatineau, Quebec and their outlying areas, are a part of a vibrant local Arab diaspora community, where Arabic is the third most spoken mother tongue in the region (after English and French) and Arabs are the largest visible minority community. They are also part of the broad ethnic diversity of the city itself, where 22 per cent of the city's population was born abroad and a similar number are the children of immigrants, and 22 per cent identify as visible minorities. In addition, Ottawa's status as Canada's capital city provides unique proximity to political power and routine forms of integration into the public sector that are not available to Palestinians living elsewhere. In this chapter, I explore the ways that different Palestinian organizations in Ottawa envision and enact a Palestinian community in this unique context, as distinct but integrated into broader Arab, Palestinian, and Ottawan communities. These different organizations provide the social architecture for individuals to understand themselves as Palestinian and support the development of diverse Palestinian identities in ways that both reflect and influence people's social positions.

What is a Community in Practice?

It is commonplace to talk about a given group of people who share an ethnicity, religion, or other identifying feature as a "community." Because we think about communities as being made of people who share an attribute, we often assume that all the members of a community share the same experiences, traits, and perspectives. Of course, many people who share common identities do, in fact, share experiences, traits and perspectives—but not all of them will, and there will inevitably be many different ways of interpreting those experiences. Due to this complexity, speaking about a "community" can be a fraught experience, because, inevitably, not all people who one speaker might rule into their community will agree that they should be considered a member. Likewise, those left out might want to be included, and the voices chosen to speak "for" the community almost certainly do not reflect the position of all—or sometimes even most.[1] At its best, the concept of community should be considered a shorthand to refer to people who share an identity, not a determinant of how individuals will think or feel.

Because of the problems of overgeneralization, trying to study or describe a community is challenging. Where might a community be located? How can we understand the differences between community members? Where might we set the barriers between them? While we might think that the concept of "the Palestinian community" is straightforward, where could we go to look for that community? If we look for neighbourhoods where Palestinians live in given cities, does that mean that those who live elsewhere are not part of the community? If we look in religious congregations, does that mean we neglect nonreligious Palestinians, or the forms of community that include both Muslims and Christians? If we look for social service organizations serving newcomers, does that mean the second and third generations don't fit into our frameworks? If we look for political parties, what do we miss about other forms of social and political engagement?

In my own research on Palestinian and other Arab diaspora communities, I choose to focus in particular on organizations that aim to represent, unite, or serve a specific community.[2] These organizations serve an important purpose beyond whatever work they actually intend to do by creating what I call a community in practice. A community in practice is a group of people who understand themselves as connected to others who share an identity with them, and who engage collectively in activities with other people who act together under the banner of that identity. When people come together to join an organization that names itself as holding a particular identity, they acknowledge that they believe that identity applies to them—they recognize themselves as being called by that particular name. However, through

EMILY REGAN WILLS   261

engaging with other people who also recognize themselves as being called by that name, they develop an embedded concept of what holding that identity means that differs from the one they had before engaging. Through the practices of engaging in activities together, the identity that they hold becomes less of an assignment, and more of a lived experience. Organizations that function under the sign of an identity help to instantiate that identity in the lives of those who engage with them. This is the process of making a community in practice: not just a group of people with a common attribute, but a meaningful, embedded collectivity where people share assumptions, principles, and goals.

Communities in practice are no less diverse than communities that are invoked merely through a shared identity. But because they operate through practices, they have to find ways to manage those diversities—through making space for them to exist, through refocusing on what is shared or through disciplinary techniques to suppress them. Kimberlé Crenshaw uses the metaphor of a coalition to describe how all identities are constructed: through joining people who share one identity but have other variant identities simultaneously, choosing to work together collectively to achieve common goals.[3] Communities in practice are active coalitions, where all participants can withdraw if it no longer serves their interests.

A communities in practice framework makes it possible to study the different ways that organizations can facilitate different ideas of what an identity can mean, and what work that identity can do. As people develop different ideas about what it means to be a part of a group, they then *act* based on those different ideas—so people whose practices help them develop one specific notion of what it means to be what they are will then make choices about the world that will guide their political and social actions. It is not hard to understand that these differences will produce differences in political outcomes. What scholarship in this area tends to lack, however, is the tracing from cause to effect: how the identities instantiated in particular communities in practice end up concretely producing political behaviour. In looking at how Palestinian organizations in Ottawa build communities in practice, we can understand the different ways that Palestinians engage in their social and political milieu here in Canada's capital.

Palestinians in Canada and in Ottawa-Gatineau

The Palestinian diaspora numbers over six million, with the largest proportion still residing in the Arab world, especially Jordan and Lebanon (and, until recently, Syria).[4] North and South America, however, have been destinations for Palestinians looking to emigrate, especially for work, since before the Nakba. Although the United States appears larger in the Palestinian migratory imaginary, Canada is also a prime destination. Canada actively recruits migrants, particularly those with high human or financial capital, and has an international reputation as less hostile to newcomers than the United States or Europe. Arab migration to Canada parallels the broader global trends in Arab migratory patterns: a wave of mostly Syrian Lebanese people beginning in the late nineteenth century, Francophones from North Africa and Lebanon coming to Québec in parallel to those going to France, and then a larger wave from all countries in the region after the Second World War, including Palestinians displaced by the 1948 Nakba and then by the 1967 Six Days War.

Through the decennial census, Statistics Canada collects data on the ethnic origins of all Canadians, allowing Palestinians to identify themselves in federal data. Based on the 2016 Census, StatCan counts approximately 44,820 Palestinians in Canada, of whom 29,065 were born outside of Canada.[5] Palestinians in Canada are concentrated in Ontario, with approximately 63.5 per cent living in that province, mostly in Toronto (35 per cent of all Palestinians nationally), with large groups of Palestinians also in southern Ontario cities like London, Hamilton, and Windsor.[6] Compared to Lebanese Canadians, the largest Arab nationality in Canada, Palestinians are much more spatially concentrated, without large populations in the west or on the East Coast (although nearly a thousand Palestinians live in Nova Scotia) and only 6,870 Palestinians (15 per cent of the national total) living in Québec.[7]

StatCan identifies the National Capital Region (NCR), made up of the cities of Ottawa, Ontario and Gatineau, Québec and their outlying areas, as home to 4,265 Palestinians, almost all of whom live on the Ottawa side of the river.[8] Palestinians are actually one of the smaller Arab ethnicities in the region, which is also home to over 31,000 Lebanese, over 6,000 Egyptians, over 5,000 Syrians and 5,000 Iraqis, over 4,000 Moroccans and over 2,500 Algerians.[9] Palestinians in Ottawa-Gatineau are mostly immigrants, with 64 per cent of the population born abroad, and 33 per cent the children of

EMILY REGAN WILLS   263

immigrants.[10] Both older and younger populations are mostly born abroad (63 per cent of 15 to 24 year-olds, 91 per cent of 25 to 54 year-olds, and 92 per cent of those older than 55), and about 70 per cent speak Arabic as a first language.[11] The majority of immigrants came through economic immigration categories, either as primary immigrants or family members (72 per cent of all immigrants who landed between 1980 and 2016), with smaller numbers coming through family reunification (20 per cent) or with refugee status (7 per cent). Despite the high percentage born abroad, 85 per cent of all Palestinians in Ottawa have Canadian citizenship.[12] Anecdotally, Palestinians associated with the organizations profiled in this piece have told me that they believe there to be closer to 9,000 Palestinians living in Ottawa,[13] and that a large portion of them came to Canada from Kuwait after the 1990 Gulf War. At that time, in retaliation for Yasser Arafat's statement of support for Saddam Hussein's occupation of Kuwait, the Kuwaiti government revoked the residence of all Palestinians there, including those who had been born in Kuwait.[14]

Socioeconomically, the portrait of Palestinians in the NCR is complex. Of those over the age of 15, some 68 per cent have a postsecondary degree, with 50 per cent having a bachelor's degree or greater.[15] Only 3 per cent speak only Arabic; 62 per cent are Arabic/English bilinguals, and 20 per cent are English/French/Arabic trilingual.[16] However, their human capital does not always translate directly into economic success. The unemployment rate for Palestinians in the NCR is 13.2 per cent, while the citywide unemployment rate is 7 per cent and the national unemployment rate is 7.7 per cent.[17] The mean total income for all Palestinian workers over the age of 15 is $36,800, as opposed to $52,455 for all Ottawans and $47,487 for all Canadians; 40 per cent of Palestinians in Ottawa work part time, while 23 per cent work full time, which contrasts with an Ottawa average of 38 per cent working full time (33 per cent nationally) and 32 per cent working part time (34 per cent nationwide).[18] Meanwhile, 36 per cent of all Palestinians in Ottawa are classified as low income, while only 12 per cent of Ottawans and 14 per cent of Canadians are.[19] However, those who are able to obtain full-time work are generally doing well; the median salary for full-time, full-year Palestinian workers in Ottawa is $60,235, which is comparable to the citywide average of $62,792.[20] While 49 per cent of all Palestinians in Ottawa made less than $20,000 (as opposed to 27 per cent of Ottawans and 31 per cent of all Canadians), 12.6 per cent made over $80,000 (opposed to 19 per cent of Ottawans, but only 7.7 per cent of all Canadians).[21] This suggests a community with high levels of human capital on average, but with a strong bifurcation between those who have managed to convert that into material wealth and those who have not.

Because Palestinians are a numerically small community (only 0.3 per cent of the population of Ottawa-Gatineau),[22] there are no defined Palestinian neighbourhoods or areas, although observation suggests there is a concentration of Arabic speakers in general in Ottawa South and in the eastern suburbs such as Orleans and Gloucester. However, the lack of a physical neighbourhood where Palestinians in Ottawa live together does not mean that a Palestinian community in practice does not exist here. Instead, Palestinian communities in practice are formed through formal organizations that bring together Palestinians as Palestinians. While Ottawa is home to diverse activists organized around Palestinian causes, such as Independent Jewish Voices and the Canadians for Justice and Peace in the Middle East, Palestinian identity in Ottawa is represented more by organizations such as the Ottawa Palestinian Festival, the Ottawa Run for Palestine, and the Association of Palestinian Arab Canadians. Each of these organizations carries out a variety of activities and provides an opportunity for a particular variety of community in practice developed through its actions.

Palestinian Organizations in Ottawa

In a city with nearly 50,000 people who indicate their visible minority status as "Arab" on the census, based on my past observations of community events in New York, it would seem likely that organizing in Ottawa would orient itself around a collectively held Arab identity, bringing together the strengths of all Arab-identified people in the city. However, instead, much organizing takes place under national identities, with Lebanese, Syrian, Palestinian, and other Arab communities spawning organizations. This varies slightly from the pattern of historic organizing. Early organizations included both hometown associations and groups like the Canadian Arab Friendship League, which brought together all persons identifying as Arab.[23] It also varies from the case in Toronto, where national-origin level organizing takes place in parallel to pan-Arab organizing.[24]

For Palestinians, some of the organizations that take on this role include the Association of Palestinian Arab Canadians (APAC), the Run for Palestine, and the Ottawa Palestinian Festival. All of these organizations are relatively stable parts of Ottawa's current cultural landscape and promote visions of Palestinian community that are accessible to a broad range of people with Palestinian roots. None of them are exclusively political in their actions, although APAC does engage in political lobbying and position-taking; however, all of them do crucial work in helping to create Palestinian communities in practice in the National Capital Region.

APAC describes itself as "bring[ing] together Palestinians living in Canada's National Capital Region for cultural, educational, and fun activities."[25] It was founded in 1985 and has been continually active since that point. APAC seems to have two major sets of activities: those that focus on community building, and those that focus on engaging with the Canadian political system. Community-building events include Eid and Christmas parties, iftars, dabke lessons, events for Arab Mothers' Day (held in March rather than May), and educational lectures by community members. Events focused on the political system include the annual Palestine Day on the Hill, when members meet with Members of Parliament and hold a social event on Parliament Hill; candidate forums for federal, provincial, and municipal elections (all in Ottawa, none in Gatineau); and protests about Palestine-related issues, such as a 2017 protest titled "Rally in Solidarity with Al-Aqsa Mosque" held at the Human Rights Memorial near Parliament Hill, or a 2018 rally titled "Hands Off Jerusalem!" outside the United States Embassy.

The Ottawa Run for Palestine was founded in 2014. It is closely entwined with APAC, such that its president is a past APAC president, and both he and the leadership of APAC agree that the organizations are linked. The Run for Palestine fundraises for the United Nations Relief and Works Agency for Palestine Refugees in the Near East's (UNRWA) Community Mental Health Programme in Gaza. More recently, it has begun to also direct a portion of its fundraising to Youth Action Now, an Ottawa-based youth organization founded by the late Paul Dewar, former Member of Parliament for Ottawa-Centre and a long-time participant in the Run itself, as well as other Ottawa-based charities. The event includes a series of distances to run, along with festival-style activities for families to participate in, held on a fall weekend. The 2019 version of the Run, along with a gala banquet that followed it, raised over $24,000 for UNRWA, along with $4,000 for Youth Action Now and $1,000 for Children at Risk, an Ottawa-based service organization for autistic children and their families.

The Ottawa Palestinian Festival was also founded in 2014 and is independent from other organizations. The festival is a three-day event held every August at Marion Dewar Plaza at City Hall,[26] which features performers from the Middle East and across Canada, as well as dabke, fashion shows, a wedding show highlighting traditional practices; as well as many of the trappings of a summer fair with rides, games, food, and shopping. The festival receives regular coverage in Ottawa local media and is a part of the landscape of cultural festivals on most summer weekends across the city, including Lebanese, Ukrainian, and Greek festivals.

All three organizations describe themselves as "non-political" and "non-sectarian" in their activity. None carry out religious activities, apart from secular-in-content holiday parties, and all of them have members of diverse religious backgrounds. The leadership of APAC, for instance, all pointed out at their Christmas party that they were Muslims but ran the event anyway to build community. Indeed, in my conversation with leadership from both APAC and the Ottawa Palestinian Festival, they volunteered the opinion that religious conflict between Christians and Muslims in Palestine was uncommon, including between Christians, Muslims, and Palestinian Jews prior to Zionism. They felt that sectarian conflict was not a "natural" part of Palestinian culture.

However, the question of what it means to be "political" is more complex and is also a part of building a Palestinian community in practice. APAC has built strong ties to the Palestinian Authority, as represented in the General Delegation of Palestine in Canada, which serves the function of an embassy. This is not uncommon for diaspora organizations in Ottawa. For instance, the Lebanese Embassy hosts events for the Lebanese diaspora, and other embassies conduct outreach with their diasporas as well. APAC is able to use these connections to secure highly placed speakers, such as former ambassadors, and also uses them to support its activities like Palestine Day on the Hill (see below for more discussion). But for Palestinians who have a critical attitude towards the PA, these ties make APAC a less appealing site for engagement. Regardless of the ways in which these organizations build connections to the PA or avoid such connections, they still end up implicated in the everyday politics of Palestinian representation and misrecognition in the contemporary West. In other words, being perceived as political is unavoidable for Palestinian Canadians, though their organizations can choose different routes to respond to that politicization and which is part of how they construct their own community in practice.

In Baha Abu-Laban's pioneering work on the Arab community in Canada through the 1970s, he describes the model of the "friendship organization" (a name used by the first Canadian Arab organization and replicated in others throughout the twentieth century) as:

> tend[ing] to combine, in varying degrees, social, cultural, political, and, on occasion, charitable goals. Generally speaking, these associations attempt to foster better understanding between the Canadian and Arab peoples and to defend the Arab-Canadian community against attacks from the outside. Typically, this is accomplished through a variety of programmes and functions such as annual banquets, visiting speakers, picnics, cultural displays and/or folk dancing, Arabic classes for children, and immigrant assistance.[27]

Abu-Laban also describes pro-Palestinian organizing in most of the major cities of Ontario and Montréal (including a Canada-Palestine Committee in Ottawa), and describes those organizations as focused on, "provid[ing] information about and defend[ing] the national rights of the Palestinian people."[28] The three Palestinian organizations in Ottawa described in this chapter bridge this gap; they carry that mixture of social, cultural, political, and charitable goals, and work to foster "better understanding" and "defend rights," both of Palestinians in Canada and those in Palestine. Their activities serve to build forms of Palestinian community in practice available to all Palestinians in Ottawa, as well as space for non-Palestinians to interact with them. The differences in how they carry out this work demonstrate the diversity in the forms of community that different actors want and how practices can create substantively different experiences for similarly positioned people.

Constructing a Community

One major project that ethnic organizations engage in is making a shared identity meaningful, giving it substantive content and creating reasons for people to want to share it.[29] After all, if everyone shares an identity, but no one can agree on what that means, the substance of that identity is very limited. All three of the organizations have different ways of building

268   *Palestinian Organizations in Ottawa*

Palestinian community and giving substance to that identity for their members and their participants.

Many of APAC's activities are focused on literally bringing Palestinians in Ottawa together and providing them with opportunities to interact and come to know each other. Annually, some of their key events are holiday gatherings, such as the annual Christmas Party, Eid al-Fitr Barbecue, the evocatively named "Eid on Boat" held for Eid al-Adha, and the Arab Mothers' Day celebration held in March (as opposed to May, when North American Mothers' Day is held). Other activities include social events of various types, such as a "couples night" at a Lebanese restaurant, or the educational events that the women's committee hosts on matters related to children's well-being. Anecdotally, a friend who is on their email list says that most of the emails she gets from them are announcing funerals; these sorts of emails assume that everyone who is a member would want to attend the funerals of other members or the parents or kin of members, because they are meaningfully connected to each other. The actual "Palestinian" content of these events is mostly a side effect of bringing Palestinians together. For instance, the APAC Christmas Party I attended featured a Christmas tree wrapped in a kuffiyeh-print garland and a dabke remix of *Jingle Bells*, and plenty of spoken Arabic, but there was no emphasis on Palestinian Christmas traditions or practices. It was also held around the time of Western Christmas, not Orthodox Christmas.

The Ottawa Palestinian Festival and the Ottawa Run for Palestine provide a similar function in once-a-year format: a space for Palestinians to come together and exist as a collectivity. However, they approach it differently. At the Run for Palestine, the focus is on bringing together people *for* Palestine; many are Palestinian, but others are not, and what brings them together is a commitment to charitable support for Palestinians. This particular stance links participants, particularly Palestinians in diaspora, to the well-being of Palestinians in the homeland, and inscribes them as part of a continuous community. APAC also provides elements of this; one of the activities at the Christmas party was a trivia contest about Palestinian geography and economy, which served to pedagogically provide information about Palestine and build links between diaspora and homeland.

Organizers of the Festival told me that one of the major purposes of holding it in their minds, was to make it so people in the community knew each other and could reach out to each other when they were looking for,

for instance, contractors or vendors. As it takes over a major public space for an entire weekend, it presents a space for people to come together for days at a time, creating a place of *Palestinianness* that they can inhabit. But in addition to this, the festival also facilitates cultural reproduction by making literal space for Palestinian culture. The food vendors serve traditional Palestinian dishes—not just the easy-to-explain falafel, but more deeply culturally resonant dishes such as musakhan. The shopping area is called the Jerusalem Bazaar, and it focuses on Palestinian traditional crafts as well as tchotchkes, tiny decorative items that include Palestinian images such as the flag or the Dome of the Rock. There are dabke performances and lessons, various fashion shows, and, dominating the space, musical performances by Palestinian acts from the Middle East and North America. Here what makes a space Palestinian is not just Palestinians being in it, but there being substantive content that can be identified as Palestinian and making that Palestinianness the focus of activity. In some ways, this relies on an assumption that "Palestinianness" has content that can be pointed to—an assumption that can be undermined by the fluidity of cultural practice and the diversity of any community. In many ways, these forms of transmission of cultural practice can result in reification and in a static conception of a homeland that never changes.[30] But at the same time, they can serve to deepen affective attachment to the imagined homeland and help those in diaspora build empirical connection.

By providing a space for people to "be Palestinian" together, all three organizations help turn what could be an amorphous collection of individuals into a meaningful Palestinian community in practice. However, the organizations present different models for that engagement—emphasizing single large events or repeated small-scale events, and with a different balance between cultural reproduction, charitable action, social networking, physical activity, or celebration. Because of this diversity in activities and style, these different organizations provide Palestinians and their allies in Ottawa with the opportunity to select the kinds of practice that fit their needs. Brubaker describes diaspora as, "an idiom, a stance, a claim...As a category of practice, 'diaspora' is used to make claims, to articulate projects, to formulate expectations, to mobilize energies, to appeal to loyalties."[31] The "claims" inherent in Palestinian organizing in Ottawa echo each other—to make spaces of Palestinianness—but provide different routes to articulating that claim.

270   *Palestinian Organizations in Ottawa*

Addressing Outsiders

During our conversation, a leader in the Ottawa Palestinian Festival said that the community created through the festival is, "a big family, just like back home." This kind of work of building "a big family," a group of people who share a common identity and feel connected to each other, is a major part of the work that ethnic organizations do. But why is this worth the time and effort? One reason is the intrinsic feeling of shared membership, which, particularly for groups that feel marginalized or excluded for reasons of racialization or because their group is singled-out, can provide support against a broader context of exclusion or misrecognition. This is a common experience for Palestinians, particularly given the history of their homeland. But another reason is hinted at by the APAC member who told me that he belongs to the group in order to, "build community and tell the story of the plight of the Palestinian people to our brothers and sisters in Canada." That is, Palestinians in Ottawa want to engage with non-Palestinians in order to share their experiences, often with an explicit goal of social change. As other chapters in this volume can attest, Canada's government has often been explicitly hostile to Palestinian political interests, and in the recent political environment, has spent effort to marginalize voices in support of Palestinian rights.[32] Each organization works to address outsiders through its activities, but each takes a different strategic approach.

APAC takes advantage of Ottawa's status as Canada's capital to focus its attention on the federal government. It hosts annual "Palestine on the Hill" days, where members attend a lunchtime social event inside the Parliament building. Attendees have included Liberal, Conservative, NDP, and Green Members of Parliament, including Elizabeth May, former Leader of the Green Party. The 2019 iteration of the event (the most recent in six straight years of hosting) was sponsored by the Canada Palestine Parliamentary Friendship Group, including a suburban Ottawa Liberal MP, Chandra Arya, whose district includes many Arab Canadian residents. Other sponsors include Palestinian organizations from across Canada, as well as local Palestinian-owned businesses that also tend to support the Run for Palestine and other APAC events. At the event, the Chief Representative of the Palestinian General Delegation, the equivalent to a Palestinian Ambassador to Canada, gave a speech in which, according to APAC's press release, he "affirmed the official Palestinian position that there is no solution to the conflict in the Middle East except by establishing an independent Palestinian state with East Jerusalem as its capital."[33] This is a substantially more politically charged speech than is usually made at, for instance, the "national day" celebrations that some Gulf countries host for MPs and other relevant officials. The current chair of the United Nations Palestine Committee also came from New York to describe the work happening at the United Nations to support Palestinian rights. All of this occurred within the context of a well elaborated social event featuring cultural performances, Palestinian food, and the kind of business-suited civil servant, elected official, and business-leader hobnobbing that is a key part of Ottawa's daytime social scene.

At the same time as APAC invests time and energy in creating connections between Palestinian Canadians and their elected representatives, they also invest energy in expressing a pro-Palestinian position directly to government officials. Whenever a crisis occurs in Palestine, or when there is an opportunity for Canada to take a pro-Palestinian position— the frequent occasions where Canada fails to do so—APAC issues a press release or statement which makes clear its position on the issue. These statements are not cautious or delicate in their format; for instance, a December 14, 2018 press release, "calls on the Canadian government to use its influence internationally and utilize all means available to protect defenceless Palestinian civilians who are confronting the mighty and merciless Israeli military power," and states that, "The Palestinian people will never surrender to Israeli occupation, will continue to resist it, and will never give up their right to justice-based peace on their land."[34] The response statement to Trump's January 2020, "Deal of the Century" peace plan, which was authored by APAC and then co-signed by other Palestinian organizations across the country, states that "We reject Mr. Trump's plan and calls [sic] upon the Canadian government to uphold international law, all relevant United Nations resolutions, and the principles of justices [sic] by rejecting Mr. Trump's plan and calling on the international community to support the Palestinian people's struggle for justice-based peace and equal humanity."[35] These statements are not designed to gently nudge or negotiate a new position for Canadian policy; instead, they are blistering indictments of what APAC's leadership sees as failures of the Canadian government to meaningfully support Palestinian interests and rights. These two modes of interaction between APAC and the Canadian government seem to be contradictory—if the purpose of access is to change Canadian policy, the public press releases that APAC makes seem to be unlikely to meet that goal. At the same time, they take advantage of key allies within the government, many of whom would be happy if Canada's government took positions closer to those APAC is advocating, to find a platform from which to put forth an alternative position and find a route to political voice.

APAC's direct engagement with the federal government puts it closer to organizations like the Coalition for Justice and Peace in the Middle East than it does to other Palestinian organizations in Ottawa. But those other organizations also have a strong orientation towards building bridges with non-Palestinians. For the Ottawa Run for Palestine, this circles around being an event that is open to all, aiming to, "promote healthy lifestyles and charitable giving among Canadians of diverse backgrounds."[36] They have also made a choice to give not only to Palestine, but also to choose strategic local charitable recipients. Given that they fundraise for children's mental health support in Gaza, they chose local children's and youth charities, including those integrating mental health issues, which do not focus on the Arab or Palestinian community, or even more broadly immigrant or ethnic communities in the city. Despite this outreach element, in recent iterations of the run the majority of the organizers and participants, including nearly all of the participants whose names are publicly listed on the UNRWA fundraising page, are of Palestinian or other Arab origin. It is the Ottawa Palestinian Festival that is the most focused on bringing together Palestinians and non-Palestinians and fostering connections between them.

The organizers of the Palestinian Festival state that their goal is to allow people to "explore Palestine in Canada." "This is about us," one organizer said. The Palestinian Festival is a weekend-long exercise in self-representation for its organizers, an opportunity to put Palestine, as a location, front and centre in Ottawa's landscape. Its location at Marion Dewar Plaza in front of City Hall demonstrates this. By comparison, festivals such as the Lebanese, Greek, and Ukrainian ones are held at churches that serve those communities in the suburban areas of the city, while the Palestinian Festival puts itself two blocks from Parliament Hill and directly next to the Rideau Canal, where both Ottawans and tourists will encounter it even without setting out to do so. The festival's leadership has appeared on Ottawa media, such as CBC radio and the CTV morning show to promote the event, including using those opportunities to introduce viewers to information about Palestinian culture. And the festival conducts outreach with other ethnic communities in Ottawa, inviting other cultural groups to perform at

EMILY REGAN WILLS 273

various points, while engaging in activities such as announcing the Lebanese and Ukrainian festivals in their Instagram posts. In this way, the festival finds itself interwoven with the official multiculturalism and diversity of Ottawa—including in their ability to receive significant funding from the provincial government out of specific programs to support cultural festivals and tourist-attracting events. In my research on the festival, I found a telling quote on a Reddit page announcing the festival, "I thought it was pretty fun but when you really boil it down, it's kind of just the Lebanese Festival but with a different flag and hotter dudes."[37]

However, locating themselves in the context of multicultural Ottawa does not mean that the festival isolates itself from the almost-inevitable politicization of Palestine. The festival organizers, while intentionally framing the event as non-political and neutral on political issues, are clear on the fact that their self-articulation will inevitably have political consequences. In our meeting, they recounted a long and hilarious saga of trying to get permission to fly the Palestinian flag during the festival on City Hall grounds, as well as having to do repeated negotiations with City Hall in the earlier years to ensure they could run the event the way they wanted. They also use their public platform, where they can, to advance knowledge and understanding about Palestine in as delicate a way as possible. For instance, during a media interview, organizers discussed differences in *thobe* (a traditional women's dress) style between different Palestinian villages as varying based on whether a place is "closer to the ocean" or further inland. This both serves to point out that Palestinians come from the whole of historic Palestine, not just the West Bank and Gaza, and avoids having to use either the term "48 Palestine" or "Israel," both of which are contested terms. At another moment, an organizer said that, "we decided to bring artists from [momentary pause] back home, some of whom come from Palestine, others from neighbouring countries," a gesture which recognizes Palestinian dispersal, again avoids the Palestine versus Israel question, and is both accurate and nuanced.

All three of the organizations discussed in this chapter make an effort to extend beyond providing a space "just" for Palestinians into making broader connections with their fellow Canadians. The Run for Palestine tries to orient itself towards a general charitable attitude and chooses local beneficiaries along with their main goal of fundraising for Palestinians. APAC orients itself towards political action, trying to build bridges to the government for

274   *Palestinian Organizations in Ottawa*

political change. And the Ottawa Palestinian Festival reaches out to non-Arab and non-Palestinian Ottawans to share culture and mark their presence within the city. These dynamics together represent a wide variety of ways of using the community built through participation in an organization for broader political and social purposes.

Conclusion

Palestinians in the North American diaspora have a vibrant associational life, including political and advocacy organizations, and social and cultural associations. These organizations simplify and assist with the process of translating from identity to action, and in particular serve to instantiate a Palestinian identity in a particular context, whether in the broader framework of an Arab or religious community, the city in which they live, or a national Palestinian Canadian community as they imagine it. Without common practices, turning an identification as Palestinian into a social position from which to take action in the world is a lonely business and likely to be too challenging to maintain.

Often, studies of ethnic communities in North America tend to assume that "the community" is a homogenous entity, and that, despite the existence of a multiplicity of organizations rooted in that community, the members of the community share an orientation towards the world. The works in this volume, such as Abdelnour and Assi regarding class identity and Sucharov on differences within the Jewish community, add to the chorus of empirical research on communities that emphasizes their internal diversity. Even people who share a community differ from each other, not just in terms of specific identities or political ideology, but in their desires for how to articulate who they are, and their subtle orientations to social and cultural action. The diversity of practices within Palestinian organizations in Ottawa is a sign of their maturity in responding to these differences, as well as the opportunities available to Palestinians and other ethnic communities in the Canadian and Ottawa context. APAC orients itself towards making a space of assumed commonality, while using that to reach out and build connections to the federal government. The Ottawa Palestinian Festival, on the other hand, focuses on making space for cultural reproduction, using the discourses and tools of Canadian multiculturalism to engage in self-representation. A better understanding of how local Palestinian communities choose to organize themselves, and the conditions under which their organizations develop and diversify, helps us better understand the processes of collective organizing within ethnic communities, particularly those whose conditions of existence are as politicized as Palestinians.

Notes

1. We can see how this plays out for the Canadian Jewish community in Sucharov's chapter (chapter 8 in this volume).
2. Wills, *Arab New York: Politics and Community*.
3. Crenshaw, "Mapping the Margins."
4. Palestinian Central Bureau of Statistics, "Dr. Awad Presents a Brief on Palestinians at the End of 2019." December 31, 2019, http://www.pcbs.gov.ps/.
5. Statistics Canada, "2016 Census of Canada: Data Tables."
6. Statistics Canada.
7. Statistics Canada.
8. Statistics Canada.
9. Statistics Canada.
10. Statistics Canada.
11. Statistics Canada.
12. Statistics Canada.
13. In the study of Arab American demographics, most scholars and advocates are convinced that national statistical data includes a massive undercount of Arab Americans. Although I am not aware of similar arguments made systematically in Arab Canadian studies, the discrepancies between official statistics and community estimates suggests that there may be similar dynamics at work in Canada.
14. For an examination of this wave of migration in Toronto see Rothenberg, "Ties that Bind."
15. This is consistent with other data on Palestinians in Canada, including from Abu-Laban, *An Olive Branch on the Family Tree* and Rothenberg, "Ties that Bind."
16. Statistics Canada, "2016 Census of Canada: Data Tables."
17. Statistics Canada.
18. Statistics Canada.
19. Statistics Canada.
20. Statistics Canada.
21. Statistics Canada.
22. Statistics Canada.
23. Houda Asal, "Transnationalism, States' Influence, and the Political Mobilizations."
24. Abu-Laban, *An Olive Branch on the Family Tree*; Rothenberg, "Proximity and Distance"; Ziadeh, "Disciplining Dissent."
25. Association of Palestinian Arab Canadians (APAC), "Homepage," accessed November 23, 2020, http://www.apaccanada.org/.

276   *Palestinian Organizations in Ottawa*

26. This plaza is named for a former mayor of Ottawa, who also was the mother of the above-mentioned MP, Paul Dewar.

27. Abu-Laban, *An Olive Branch on the Family Tree*, 148–49.

28. Abu-Laban, 149.

29. See, for example, Wills, *Arab New York*, 15–16, 64–65.

30. For a good discussion of this process in Arab American communities see Naber, *Arab America: Gender, Cultural Politics, and Activism*.

31. Brubaker, "The 'Diaspora' Diaspora," 12.

32. See Ziadeh, "Disciplining Dissent."

33. APAC, "Media Release: The 6th Annual Palestine Day on The Hill," Facebook, April 4, 2019, https://www.facebook.com/APAC.CANADA/photos/a.448606948681188/1179127208962488.

34. APAC, "Press Release," Facebook, December 14, 2018, https://www.facebook.com/APAC.CANADA/.

35. APAC, "Press Release," Facebook, January 29, 2020, https://www.facebook.com/APAC.CANADA/.

36. Ottawa Run for Palestine, "About ORFP," accessed February 27, 2020, http://www.ottawarunforpalestine.com.

37. Unknown user. "Palestinian Festival Was Awesome (And the Only One in Canada)," Reddit, 2018, https://www.reddit.com/r/ottawa/comments/9all2h/palestinian_festival_was_awesome_and_the_only_one/

References

Abu-Laban, Baha. *An Olive Branch on the Family Tree: The Arabs in Canada*. Toronto: McClelland and Stewart, 1980.

Association of Palestinian Arab Canadians (APAC). "Home." Accessed November 23, 2020. http://www.apaccanada.org/.

APAC. "Press Release." December 14, 2018. https://www.facebook.com/APAC.CANADA/.

APAC. "Press Release." January 29, 2020. https://www.facebook.com/APAC.CANADA/.

APAC. "Media Release: The 6th Annual Palestine Day On The Hill." April 4, 2019. Accessed June 17, 2020. https://www.facebook.com/APAC.CANADA/photos/a.448606948681188/1179127208962488.

Asal, Houda. "Transnationalism, States' Influence, and the Political Mobilizations of the Arab Minority in Canada." In *A Century of Transnationalism: Immigrants and Their Homeland Connections*, edited by Nancy Gren and Roger Waldinger, 162–84. Urbana: University of Illinois Press, 2016.

Brubaker, Rogers. "The 'Diaspora' Diaspora." *Ethnic and Racial Studies* 28, no. 1 (2005): 1–19.

Crenshaw, Kimberlé. "Mapping the Margins: Intersectionality, Identity Politics, and Violence Against Women of Color." *Stanford Law Review* 43, no. 6 (1991): 1241–99.

Naber, Nadine. *Arab America: Gender, Cultural Politics, and Activism*. New York: New York University Press, 2012.

Ottawa Run for Palestine. "About ORFP." Accessed February 27, 2020. http://www.ottawarunforpalestine.com.

Palestinian Central Bureau of Statistics. "Dr. Awad Presents a Brief on Palestinians at the End of 2019." December 31, 2019. http://www.pcbs.gov.ps/.

Regan Wills, Emily. *Arab New York: Politics and Community in the Everyday Lives of Arab Americans*. New York: New York University Press, 2019.

Rothenberg, Celia E. "Proximity and Distance: Palestinian Women's Social Lives in Diaspora." *Diaspora: A Journal of Transnational Studies* 8, no. 1 (1999): 23–50.

Rothenberg, Celia E. "Ties that Bind: The Gulf Palestinian Community in Toronto." *Communal/Plural* 8, no. 2 (2000): 237–55.

Statistics Canada. "2016 Census of Canada: Data Tables—Ethnic Origin (101), Age (15A), Sex (3) and Selected Demographic, Cultural, Labour Force, Educational and Income Characteristics (651) for the Population in Private Households of Canada, Provinces and Territories, Census Metropolitan Areas and Census Agglomerations, 2016 Census—25% Sample Data." Government of Canada. Data tables, 2016 Census, May 30, 2018. https://www12.statcan.gc.ca/census-recensement/2016/dp-pd/dt-td/Rp-eng.cfm?TABID=2&LANG=E&APATH=3&DETAIL=0&DIM=0&FL=A&FREE=0&GC=0&GK=0&GRP=1&PID=112450&PRID=10&PTYPE=109445&S=0&SHOWALL=0&SUB=0&Temporal=2017&THEME=120&VID=0&VNAMEE=&VNAMEF=.

Ziadeh, Rafeef. "Disciplining Dissent: Multicultural Policy and the Silencing of Arab-Canadians." *Race and Class* 58, no. 4 (2017): 7–22.

11

RE-PRESENTING PALESTINE

Sami Hadawi and the Palestinian Revolution in Canada

MAURICE JR. LABELLE

Introduction

Sami Hadawi (1904–2004) was no stranger to Western misrepresentations of the land of Palestine and its Indigenous Arab population. In fact, he dedicated most of his life to re-orienting a global Zionist program and its imperial ways of seeing, perpetuated in the Canadian media and buttressed by Ottawa, that dehumanized Palestinians like himself. Standing before audiences in Edmonton and Calgary in early December 1981, Hadawi joked that his, "visit to Alberta is not to sell Arab oil or to invite Alberta to join OPEC." Instead, as he had done so often in the previous decade or so, he was there, "to tell the other side of the story about the Palestine problem."[1] He was there as a concerned Palestinian Canadian, renowned to like-minded folks as a rare "gold mine of information" on the interconnected Israeli–Palestinian and Arab–Israeli conflicts. The then seventy-seven-year-old retired intellectual and bureaucrat, who recently obtained his Canadian citizenship, was not alone in denouncing Canadian Orientalism and its Zionist shade or calling upon Canadians to empathize with Palestinians.[2] Yet, because of his particular life journey and accumulated knowledge, Hadawi's intervention was distinct in Canada.

To push Palestinian self-determination forward, Hadawi encouraged his Albertan audience "to imagine yourself *in my place*." His presence and place evidenced Palestinian existence in Canada and the world. Hadawi, alongside roughly four million innocent and lawful Palestinians, "were either ousted or dispossessed of all our earthly belonging" since the Nakba (disaster or catastrophe) of 1947–48, which destroyed Palestinian society and erected Israel in its place.[3] Zionists in the Middle East and the West, at the time and thereafter, justified this humanitarian tragedy, "to make room for total strangers to whom we own nothing[,] to satisfy the needs of a racist political movement[,] to establish a state of its own in homes and on lands belonging to us." How would exiled Canadians feel, he asked, if they were "stagnating in a refugee camp," while absolute, "strangers sleep in your beds, eat the fruit of your labors, and enjoy the life you had built for you and your family in your homeland"? How would they feel if, like the Palestinians that were able to stay, they instantaneously became, "the victims of oppression and persecution living under despotic Israeli rule"? He then asked his Canadian listeners, "Would you fight with all the means at your disposal to regain what legally and legitimately belong to you and your family, or just sit back, do nothing, brood, and blame others for your misfortune?"[4]

The essence of this very question, Hadawi explained, was in the heart of Palestinians and at the heart of their revolution in Israel, neighbouring Arab states, the United Nations (UN), Canada, and elsewhere.[5] The ongoing Palestinian revolution, contrary to Canadian popular belief, was not only a military and sociopolitical conflict over land, governance, and repatriation, fought mainly by *keffiyeh*-wearing *fedayeen* (commandos) and hijackers on behalf of destitute tent-refugees. For Hadawi and many other members of the Palestinian national movement, their revolution was equally a cultural struggle over the politics of self-representation. How the world perceived Palestinians and who represented them mattered, given the fact that many in the West did not or could not see Palestinians at all, let alone understand their plight, during the first two decades after the Nakba.[6] Palestinians, he insisted before his Albertan audience, had a right to exist. They were "no exception." Contrary to Zionist misrepresentations, Palestinians "are human too." In an attempt to shed the popular perception of Palestinians as destitute refugees, he explained, "What the Palestinians demand is understanding, not charity." Both politically and culturally, they wanted to represent themselves and, in turn, for everyone to rightfully recognize them, along with their decolonial cause.[7]

This essay tells the story of how the Palestinian revolution migrated to Canada in the 1970s. It does so by examining Sami Hadawi's efforts to re-present Palestinians in a Canadian public sphere that most often mis-represented the Palestinian national movement at a key point in the Israeli–Palestinian and Arab–Israeli conflicts—that is, when Palestinians asserted their revolutionary right of self-determination in the Middle East and everywhere else. The Canadian government, for its part, opposed the global politics of Palestinian recognition.[8] As Hadawi understood it then, and Moustafa Bayoumi explains it now, "Being present in the world is no longer enough. Being able to re-present something to others provides its 'proof of life.'"[9] For Palestinians, to be seen in Canada was one thing; being heard was another.

The globalization of Palestinian resistance in the 1970s made headline news. Canadian Zionist commentators and readers, however, quickly mis-represented the Palestine Liberation Organization (PLO) and its members as terrorists, silencing all Palestinians in the process. Sami Hadawi most often experienced such dehumanization and muting from the confines of his Willowdale apartment in the Greater Toronto Area, while sifting through the pages of the *Toronto Star*, a leading Canadian newspaper. Even though "age would not allow" the seventy-year-old retiree "to be more active," he stood at the forefront of, "the resistance, both cultural and political, to Zionist successes" in Canada. As one of the only world-renown intellectual and English-speaking members of the "Nakba generation" that vividly remembered his dispossession and forced relocation, Hadawi invoked his personal experience in ways that other Palestinian and Arab Canadians simply could not when confronting Zionist misrepresentations and their practitioners in the Canadian public sphere.[10]

Advocacy against Misrepresentation

Hadawi's journey from Palestine to Canada's largest metropolis was both tragic and remarkable. Born, "in a house immediately outside the Damascus Gate" in the Eastern section of Ottoman Jerusalem in 1904, the Anglican Christian grew up in a "middle-class family." He suddenly became "the sole provider for a family of seven" after Ottoman authorities conscripted his father, who never returned from World War I's No Man's Land in the Eastern Mediterranean. Having abandoned school, he became "a batman to a British military officer" when Britain began to establish its imperial authority in Palestine at the end of World War I. In 1920, Hadawi earned a clerical job in the office of the Governor of Jerusalem. From there, he "taught himself the profession of Land Valuation" and eventually took up that post under both the Rural and Urban Property Tax Ordinance. The British mandate government valued his work so much that, in 1943, it awarded the near forty-year-old Hadawi with the prestigious—albeit controversial—medal of the Member of the British Empire (MBE) "for 'Outstanding Service.'"[11]

Hadawi's extensive knowledge of land and property ownership in Palestine earned from working inside the mandate government for almost three decades was unparalleled by fellow Palestinian nationalists, British officials, or Ashkenazi Jews in Zionist ranks. When the United Nations General Assembly officially recommended the partition of British Palestine against the popular will of Palestinians in November 1947, he "had the foresight to recognize... that his knowledge of land and land taxation would be needed for the setting up of the proposed 'Arab State.'" Ahead of the expiration of the British mandate roughly sixth months thereafter, Hadawi "collected his records" and "had them transferred to the Old City of Jerusalem." Roughly two weeks before the official end of the British mandate in Palestine, Zionists dynamited "the steel door" of his home in western Jerusalem and emptied it "except for two steel bedframes."[12] He later recalled, "I found myself, overnight, homeless, penniless, my only worldly possession the suit I stood in."[13]

Following the creation of the state of Israel, a dispossessed Hadawi relocated to Jordanian-controlled "Arab" East Jerusalem. His records awaited him "as if ready for work to begin." Once the first Arab-Israeli war of 1947–49 officially ended, he started devising a tax collection system for the so-called Arab state in the West Bank, placed under the tutelage of the

Hashemite Kingdom of Jordan by the United Nations. In 1953, he left the Jordanian ministry of finance to accept a position as a land specialist with the United Nations Palestine Conciliation Commission in New York City in the hope that it would bring him, "closer to returning to my home in Jerusalem and regaining possession of my property if not my plundered belongings." He wanted "to help protect the property rights" of Palestinians. Soon disgruntled by United Nations stalemate, Hadawi resigned in 1956 and "became active in presenting and defending the Palestinian cause" in North America.[14]

Hadawi's shift from tax and land bureaucrat to public intellectual began with a three-year stint at the Palestine Arab Refugee Office, the first unofficial Palestinian-run information organization in the United States after the Nakba. As external funding for the tiny two-person Palestinian operation dwindled, he took on the post of Director of Public Relations for the Arab League Information Center in New York. Under the aegis of the Arab League, Hadawi established a branch of the Arab Information Office in Dallas, Texas, and briefly directed its Ottawa office.[15] During this period, he appeared in national newspapers of record, like the *New York Times* and *The Globe and Mail*, to denounce Zionist propaganda in North America and its grip on policymakers and the media. Moreover, in 1963, Hadawi authored *Palestine: Loss of a Heritage*, which provided a rare Palestinian perspective in English on the Nakba and the creation of the state of Israel. This book, along with his 1967 *Bitter Harvest*, immediately became one of few resources for anti-Zionists in North America, "who wanted to hear both sides of the Palestine story."[16]

The Palestinian's work in the West earned him much respect from the greater Arab community. Dr. Constantine Zurayk, "one of the great Arab intellectuals of the twentieth century," presented him with an opportunity in 1965 that he could not refuse: the inaugural directorship for the Institute for Palestine Studies (IPS).[17] Grateful, Hadawi left North America to run what is today the premier institution of research on Palestine in the world. From the Beirut neighbourhood of Verdun, he deepened his expertise and dedicated himself to the "cultural front" of the nascent Palestinian revolution, becoming globally renown as an "authority on Palestine" in the process.[18] Jean-Paul Sartre, for instance, invited Hadawi to pen an essay for a special issue on the Arab-Israeli conflict for his prestigious Paris-based periodical, *Les temps modernes*. In the end, the IPS director contributed two pieces.[19]

Hadawi ultimately spent almost three years in the intellectual heartland of the Palestinian national movement and in the near proximity of commandos before opting for retirement in 1968. Yet retirement did not thwart his lifelong dedication to the global politics of Palestinian self-representation, decolonization, and return. He left Beirut and, with his British passport, eventually applied for landed immigrant status in Canada in order to "settle" in Toronto to be near three of his siblings. Free of official affiliation and "paid service," he henceforth devoted, "all [his] time and energy to the Palestine question."[20]

Hadawi's initial retirement years were spent writing in English and travelling across North America, Europe, and the Middle East on speaking engagements. His writings focused on challenging misrepresentations of the Palestinian national movement and its revolution in English-speaking public spheres. While maintaining strong connections to IPS, he pamphleteered for the Arab Information Center in Washington, DC, and the Beirut-based Palestine Research Center (PRC), which had a more activist bent than the academic-minded IPS.[21] The image of the Palestinian *fedayeen* as a blood-thirsty and anti-Jewish terrorist in popular Western imaginations was defamatory, his writings asserted. This misrepresentation, moreover, occluded Israel's structural mistreatment of Palestinians inside its borders and beyond. Zionist representations failed to clarify that most revolutionaries, "avoid[ed] harming genuine civilians and direct[ed their] attacks against the Israeli military and para-military forces whether they [we]re in uniform or not."[22] "Zionist influence over the media of information suppressed any condemnation of official Zionist action," Hadawi contended.[23]

The Munich incident during the 1972 Olympics in Germany both exacerbated and globalized Zionist misrepresentations of the Palestinian national movement and its divided constituency. The abduction and killing of Israeli Olympians, along with a much-televised standoff and attempted hijacking by the Black September Organization, a fringe assemblage of Palestinian extremists, further delegitimized Palestinian decolonization in Western imaginations. Reporting and ensuing media conversations framed Canadian perceptions of the Palestinian revolution, as Palestinians embodied the nascent phenomenon of global terrorism. Israel, in relation, was its primary victim without full explanation of Palestinian reasoning and realities. The PLO, which corralled dispersed revolutionaries, commandos, activists, scholars, artists, and refugees and led efforts for Palestinian self-determination, condemned the incident. Its chairman Yasser Arafat went as far as to denounce all commando activities outside of Israel. Nonetheless, the words "Palestinian" and "terrorism" became synonymous in Western imaginations, Canada included.[24]

The prevalence of Zionist ways of misrepresenting and memories of Munich meant that Palestinians entered most ill- or under-informed Western imaginations as "terrorists." While problematic on myriad levels, such misrepresentations solidified a Palestinian presence in Canadian thinking that barely existed beforehand. They also exacerbated Ottawa's pro-Zionist bent. Following the fourth Arab–Israeli war of 1973, Canadian politicians and newspapers alike steadily began to refer to Palestinians as Palestinians, rather than mere "Arab refugees." Changes notwithstanding, the Toronto press was at the forefront of mis-representing Palestinian revolution, the PLO, and its divided constituencies.[25] Hadawi knew different. As such, he and like-minded others concluded that strictly being seen often led to misrepresentations by non-Palestinians. Being heard, therefore, was both integral to their humanization and the re-presentation of Palestinians in Canada.

Hostility toward Palestinians at the United Nations

The Palestinian revolution formally entered Canada via the PLO's global offensive at the United Nations after Munich. As PLO representative Shafiq al-Hout later put it, "the halls of the United Nations became a new alternative to the battlefield" for Palestinian nationalists.[26] In an effort to both politically represent and culturally re-present Palestinians in the international arena, Arafat's PLO adopted a radically new position toward Israel that supported a partitioned two-state solution, rather the wholesale destruction of the so-called Jewish state, with the establishment of a secular democratic Palestinian state in the Occupied Territories. Abu Ammar's unprecedented approach bore fruit. At the 1974 Arab League summit in Rabat, Morocco, Arab states unanimously declared the PLO to be the sole representative of the Palestinian people for the first time. From there, the PLO turned to the UN General Assembly. With a vote pending on the PLO's application for official observer status, the *Toronto Star*'s William Frye commented, "What the UN now has done is to tell Israel, by a massive majority, that the Palestinians do exist and must be dealt with."[27]

Increasing acknowledgements of Palestinian presence in the pages of the *Toronto Star* and the formation of a perception that the Palestinian national movement "must be heard" activated Canadian Zionists anxieties and, in turn, a fresh wave of Orientalist misrepresentations. For instance, a Duncan Macpherson political cartoon in the *Star* depicted nine well-armed "fictional Arab villains" huddled over a map that hinted at a pending "guerilla" attack on New York City. The desert-looking commandos appeared prepared for battle with grenades, Kalashnikov rifles, and ammunition belts excessively hanging over their shoulders. The apparent leader, who wore three watches, devilishly smiled, with his eyes clearly fixated on the master plan. Two *keffiyeh*-wearing men stood behind him: on the left, a blood-thirsty ghoul, and on the right, a thief holding an Arabian knife in his mouth.[28] Elsewhere, Executive Vice President of Toronto's B'nai B'rith chapter Herbert Levy penned a letter to the *Star*'s editor, which insinuated that the PLO should not be permitted to address the United Nations. Israel, he asserted, had not recognized the PLO as the representative of Palestinians because it was composed "of 10,000 would-be assassins" and "terrorists" that simply could not be trusted. The *Toronto Star*, both in its coverage and commentaries, maintained a general line that the mischievous PLO remained dedicated to "the destruction of the Jewish state of Israel."[29]

Arafat's infamous olive branch and freedom-fighter's gun speech before the United Nations General Assembly in mid-November 1974, which called for a "peaceful future" between Palestinians and Israelis, "proved to be a gateway through which Palestinian diplomacy" entered popular Canadian mindscapes.[30] Yet Palestinian self-representations, once again, became the object of Zionist misrepresentations. Abu Ammar's address landed him on the front page of the *Star*, albeit in a way that defamed the Palestinian revolution. Rather the focus on the PLO leader's historic message of peace, the Toronto newspaper zoomed in on his holster and whether it had a piece to discredit him, the Palestinian national movement, and the United Nations. Arafat, it declared, "really had a gun at the UN."[31]

Canadian Zionists responded en masse ahead of the General Assembly's pending vote on the right of Palestinian self-representation. The Canada–Israel Committee (CIC), "the principal representative of Jewish pro-Israel interests in Canada," organized a 6,000-person rally in Toronto's Nathan Phillips Square where Holly Blossom Temple Rabbi Gunther Plaut accused the PLO of encouraging Jews to take "a march of suicide into the sea."

286   *Re-Presenting Palestine*

Ensuing letters to the editor of the *Toronto Star* used its front-page coverage of Arafat's holster as evidence to support historical misrepresentations of Palestinian nationalism. Palestinians, many opined, were clearly "murdering lunatics." The PLO leader could not be trusted, a reader wrote, since he stood, "before the United Nations extending an olive branch, but under his cloak he totes a loaded gun."[32]

Canada, despite a recent willingness to tolerate Palestinian calls for self-representation at the United Nations, was amid a handful of states that did not vote in favour of UN resolutions 3236 and 3237, which respectively recognized the Palestinian right to self-determination and accorded permanent observer status to the PLO as the sole representative of Palestinians.[33] While Palestinians outside Canada celebrated the historic votes, those inside Canada grumbled at Ottawa's insistence that both resolutions "ignored the existence of the state of Israel" as if the latter negated the existence of Palestinians. Zionists, for their part, hailed Canada, "as a voice condemning all of the activities of those who irresponsibly continue their acts of terrorism."[34]

The Palestinian-recognized right to self-representation within the United Nations presented Ottawa with an intertwined set of Palestinian and Zionist problems. The PLO's permanent observer status automatically granted it a seat at all UN-sponsored conferences, including its forthcoming fifth Congress on the Prevention of Crime and Treatment of Offenders to be held in Toronto during the fall of 1975. The official entry of PLO representatives into Canada to attend the United Nations conference led myriad Canadians in and outside Parliament Hill to ask themselves, as *The Globe and Mail* did, "do we really want them here?" Was Ottawa prepared to sanction the travel of the Palestinian revolution and its "conspiracy of terror" into Canada? To the dismay of Zionists, Canada and the PLO were equal participants in the eyes of the international body.[35]

The CIC, in the months between UN Resolution 3237 and the crime conference, augmented misrepresentations of Palestinians and the Palestinian revolution. To address the perceived threat of the PLO's official visit to Toronto, the CIC oversaw the creation of Canadians Against PLO Terrorism (CAPLOT). Led by "key leaders of the Toronto Jewish community," CAPLOT's mandate was simple: lobby against the entry of official Palestinian representatives into Canada. Put differently, CAPLOT's goal was to exclude the PLO from Canada. The Zionist group convinced organizations, such as the International Association of Police Chiefs and the Law Society of Upper Canada, to support its anti-Palestinian cause.[36] CAPLOT also elicited the public support of Ontario Premier William Davis, who sent a letter to Canadian Prime Minister Pierre Trudeau that was subsequently released to the national press, which objected to the participation of "members of terrorist organizations" in the United Nations crime conference. Ontario NDP leader Stephen Lewis concurred, opining that the PLO was "an affront to civilized people and minority groups across Canada." Moreover, another Macpherson cartoon in the *Toronto Star* buttressed CAPLOT efforts by portraying a *keffiyeh*-wearing Arafat standing in front of a clown-looking Trudeau. Both men displayed large smiles, as Abu Ammar's left hand held a gun to the Canadian prime minister's chin, while his right hand held a branch with three maple leaves that resembled part of the provincial logo of Ontario. A word bubble above Trudeau's head read, "Who knows more about crime?" A caption in the bottom left-hand corner, meanwhile, announced, "United Nations has invited Palestinian terrorists to Canada for crime conference."[37]

The CIC initiated a letter-writing campaign to vilify the PLO, which was seconded by a handful of widely circulated supporting press releases from the Israeli Embassy in Ottawa. Over 1,500 letters and telegrams were sent to executive branch members of the federal government, Ontario MPPs, and prominent media outlets to protest the potential presence of PLO representatives in Canada.[38] Many of these questioned the PLO's legitimacy as the representative of the Palestinian people. Wrongfully speaking on behalf of Palestinians, Canadian Zionist letter-writers claimed that "these people did not consider the PLO their representative and spokesmen." PLO delegates, according to their generalized misrepresentations, were a "seedy serpentine pack of perverted psychotics" and "despicable cowards" that setup "'training camps' in the midst of settlements of women and children." In a letter to Trudeau that erased Palestinian Canadians and their allies, CIC member and CAPLOT leader Norman May proclaimed that, "the presence of any PLO members in Canada would accordingly be a profound affront and a provocation not only to Canadians of specific ethnic or religious groups, but to every Canadian who places value on human life and on the rule of law." The presence of PLO representatives at the Toronto crime conference, others assured, would gravely damage Canada's image in the world, as, "these blood-thirsty terrorists are only interested in planning crime, not preventing them."[39]

When Ottawa seemed unwilling to bar Palestinian participation at the international conference in Toronto, Canadian Zionists organized more protests and called on the Trudeau government to cancel the United Nations gathering altogether. CAPLOT and its allies grew more militant, threating to block the physical entry of Palestinian representatives into the conference. In an interview with *The Globe and Mail*, the chairman of Toronto's Jewish Defense League, Albert Applehaum, declared that PLO delegates, "may not make it back home... If Arafat came." The pharmacist told the national newspaper, "I wouldn't be afraid to go up and shoot him, even if it were to mean 20 years in prison." Following Applehaum's comments, CAPLOT co-directors Louis Silver and David Sadowski insisted that their organization did, "not condone threats of violence" and criticized Canadian newspapers for "irresponsible" reporting.[40]

Ottawa, in the end, caved to Zionist pressures and "reluctantly" asked the United Nations to postpone its crime conference. According to Canadian external affairs minister Allan McEachen, it "could not ignore the risk of public disorder," and, "the inevitable intrusion of unrelated political consideration into the proceedings of the congress." Whereas acting CIC chairman Rabbi Gunther Plaut and other Zionists applauded the "moral and politically courageous decision," Hassan Rahman, spokesman for the PLO observer mission in Canada, deemed it "regrettable" and "outrageous." Meanwhile, from the Syrian capital of Damascus, the PLO's secretary general of the executive committee Mohammed Zhudi Nashashibi issued an official statement that accused Canada of, "bowing to Zionist and imperialist pressures." Affirming his organization's determination to attend the United Nations crime conference notwithstanding its last-minute relocation to Geneva, Nashashibi insisted that, "the attitude of the Canadian government in support of Israel is of no use in covering up the crimes committed by Zionism against our people."[41]

Entering the Canadian Fray

Hadawi watched the Palestinian revolution's initial migration from the sidelines of the Canadian public sphere. Ultimately, the advent of a fresh United Nations controversy that centred on Israel's mistreatment of Palestinians and its legacy launched him into the Canadian fray. In the fall of 1975, an Arab-led resolution forwarded to the General Assembly that classified Zionism as a form of racism and racial discrimination engendered Canadian

Zionist angst and condemnations anew. The *Toronto Star*, Hadawi's reluctant newspaper at the time, defamed the resolution as an "anti-Israel gang-up" that delegitimized the United Nations. A *Star* editorial declared "the charge" that Israel was racist to be false. The so-called Jewish state did not mistreat "the Arabs within its borders," it claimed. To the contrary, "Israel gives the Arabs who are its citizens a kind of ethnic equality." Arab refugees in the West Bank, for their part, were mostly "citizens of Jordan" and, therefore, someone else's responsibility. As for exiled Palestinians like Hadawi, the *Star* adopted a Zionist stance that belied both Palestinian desires and the right of return outlined by UN Resolution 194 in December 1948.[42]

Such misrepresentations of Palestinian realities and their unequal relationship to Israel led Hadawi to re-present the Palestinian revolution in Canada. As he explained in a private 1969 report to the Arab League on "public information work" in North America, Palestinian self-representation was integral to revolutionizing Western misperceptions of the Israeli-Palestinian and Arab-Israeli conflicts. When Palestinians speak about their revolution, the retired Palestinian-Canadian intellectual reported, they, "do so out of deep conviction and personal experiences, and as such, [they] are in a better position to influence [their] audience." In the Canadian context, a mere handful of Palestinians occupied the front lines in the Greater Toronto Area and beyond during the mid-1970s. Palestinians likely represented less than three per cent of Arab immigrants in Canada, numbering under two thousand.[43] Khaled Mouammar, founding president of Toronto's Arab Palestine Association in 1966, as well as political scientist George Hajjar were often overpowered and overwhelmed, with little support from a "non-existent" Arab information office in Ottawa.[44] Mouammar, Hajjar and their non-Palestinian allies defended the Palestinian cause, but were not as experienced and informed as Hadawi at the time.

Based on his personal Nakba experience and unmatched knowledge, the retired Palestinian-Canadian penned a lengthy rebuke to the *Star*'s editorial on the proposed United Nations resolution on Zionism as racism, which he insisted "misses the point." Whereas Palestinians living in Israel, "lead a life of third-class citizens after Oriental Jews," the Arab-led anti-racism resolution presented before the General Assembly targeted two foundational Israeli laws that structured inequalities between Jews and, "those Moslems and Christians who were expelled and dispossessed because of their race and religion." Both the Law of Return of 1950 and the Nationality Law of 1952, he explained, prejudiced Indigenous Palestinian Arabs, such as himself. Such Israeli legislation prevented Hadawi, "to return to Jerusalem where I was born and lived and regain possession of my home and property only because I happen to be Christian." Canadian Jews, meanwhile, "can go there any time, occupy my home and immediately become a citizen of a country he has never seen. If this is not a form of racial and religious discrimination of the worst type, I don't know what is!" The Toronto newspaper only published Hadawi's letter eight days later, following reports that the Royal Canadian Mounted Police (RCMP) was investigating Palestinian and Arab Canadians allegedly involved in a Munich-style terrorist conspiracy that targeted the upcoming 1976 Olympics in Montreal.[45]

The Toronto press overflowed with Zionist objections to United Nations discussions over a Zionism as racism resolution, while Palestinian and Arab perspectives were essentially absent or lost amid the terrorism controversy; Hadawi's letter stagnated in the *Star*'s pipeline. The *Toronto Star* reported that the metropolitan Jewish community denounced the proposed United Nations resolution as "anti-Semitic." Prior to the publication of Hadawi's letter, renowned Toronto writer and rabbi Reuben Slonim editorialized in the *Star* that, "Saying Zionism is racism doesn't make it so." Worse yet, in his opinion, the anti-Zionist critique before the United Nations exacerbated "Arab-Jewish hatred." Rabbi Slonim openly asked, "How did Zionism become a dirty word?" The liberationist ideology of Zionism, he explained, engendered the establishment of Israel, "as a haven for persecuted Jews." To safeguard the newfound liberties of its Jewish citizenry and their livelihood in the Holy Land, the state of Israel needed to privilege the latter in relation to Palestinians. Israel and its supporters across the globe, he wrote, "have a right to be suspicious that Palestinians and other Arabs would like to see the Jewish state ultimately disappear." Slonim had "the same suspicion." As such, Israeli and Jewish securities trumped both accusations of racially discriminatory practices and its Palestinian casualties.[46]

Hadawi, upon reading Slonim's editorial, understood that he would do the Palestinian revolution a grave disservice if he did not make himself heard—and seen—in the *Toronto Star* once again. The retired Palestinian Canadian's unmatched experience as an information officer in North America and "authority on the Palestine Problem" convinced him that Palestinian perspectives needed to be in conversation with Zionist ones in the pages of one of Canada's most-read newspapers, for all to witness. His life, above all, evidenced that Zionism was indeed a form of racism and racial discrimination. "As one who was born in Jerusalem in the year of the official birth of the Zionist movement in 1904 and lived in Palestine to suffer its consequence," his lengthy letter to the *Toronto Star* read, "I feel I am in a position to comment" on the Toronto rabbi's latest editorial.[47]

Hadawi's letter to the editor of the *Toronto Star* represented a "counter-story of the myth of the birth of Israel."[48] Zionism, he explained, constructed "the Jewish people" as a distinctly superior and deserving nation. The creation of so-called Jewish state in 1948 codified a settler-colonial form of white privilege.[49] Henceforth, "the right of entry into Israel [was] automatically and unconditionally conferred upon a Jew, of whatever nationality, the moment he steps into Israel." Land-owning non-Jews that were indigenous to Palestine like himself, meanwhile, needed, "to be naturalized under the most difficult conditions and at the discretion of the Minister of the Interior." Zionism's success, therefore, hinged on the fortification of a European-Judaized racial structure that perpetuated his exiled status and prevented his return to his land.[50] Palestinians, Hadawi argued, "are a living example of Israeli discrimination." Unsettling Slonim and others, he warned that, "the stigma of discrimination will remain with the Israelis and Zionists abroad so long as the Palestinian Moslem and Christian remain outside of their homes and country."[51]

Contrary to Hadawi's desire, the *Toronto Star* did not treat him with the same courtesy as Rabbi Slonim. His extensive rejoinder, which was substantially shortened and the subject of much editing, was published roughly three weeks after being initially submitted and ten days after the United Nations General Assembly passed Resolution 3379, which officially condemned Zionism as a form of racism and racial discrimination.[52] Meanwhile, Hadawi's initial piece in the *Star*, which preceded Slonim's, fell prey to Zionist backlash. Zionist readers responded directly to Hadawi. H. Greenberg of Toronto negated the Palestinian Canadian's Nakba experience and prioritized Middle Eastern Jewish ones in the process by declaring that he was, "in favor of the Israeli government compensating reader Sami Hadawi for the house *he left* in Israel… just as soon as Egypt, Syria, Iraq, Libya, etc., return the hundreds of millions of dollars of property which they seized from the Jews *whom they expelled*." Don Mills' Esta Pomotov, for her part, slandered Hadawi's integrity by accusing him of hiding the fact that, "Israel has offered to repatriate Arabs and has been refused." Pomotov,

292   *Re-Presenting Palestine*

however, failed to contextualize such refusals and perpetuated the Zionist idea that the conflict was principally between Israelis and Arabs, thus suppressing Palestinians.[53]

The PLO officially entered Canada roughly a week after UN Resolution 3379. Zionists in Toronto amassed once word spread that the PLO's al-Hout was to speak at the University of Toronto. "Apalled that Canada was allowing PLO members into the country," CIC and CAPLOT members like Paul Godfrey demanded that al-Hout be silenced. In the end, al-Hout's voice was not heard at U of T; yet his actions were seen. As the PLO representative remembered it, Zionists "packed the hall." As per a *Star* report, chants of "Go Home PLO" and "Murderers" prevented organizers from introducing him. Al-Hout "never even approached the microphone." Before an audience of 600 or so, he nonetheless declared victory by, "giving the V-for-Victory sign as the press and TV cablers looked on."[54] *Post facto*, local CIC leader Rabbi Erwin Schild opined the fact that al-Hout, "had come to speak was incidental *to the provocation of his presence*."[55]

Like Hadawi had done via the publication of his Zionism as racism letter in the *Toronto Star*, which finally appeared amid the al-Hout protests, the PLO spokesperson understood the basic importance of being seen alongside Zionists in such a hostile public environment. Yet al-Hout refused to be muted and made his voice heard elsewhere at a Unitarian Church in Scarborough in the days that followed. Devoid of Zionist "cacophony" and protected by roughly fifty police officers, he justified his presence and explained that it took Palestinians roughly two decades to fully grasp "the games of the media" and the global politics of misrepresentation. The ongoing Palestinian revolution, however, ensured that it was, "now the PLO who are having the platform while the Zionists are picketing outside."[56]

Whereas al-Hout's "friendly mission" left town, Hadawi continued to face Zionist misrepresentations and their protagonists. Toronto's Channel 11 invited Hadawi to represent the Palestinian perspective on the United Nation's Zionism as racism resolution for its 10 p.m. show, *The Great Debate*. York University's Irving Layton opposed him. Prior to the debate, the producer asked the audience, "to indicate which side they were on." Attendees, as Hadawi remembered it in his privately published memoir, "were equally divided." Limited to four minutes, Hadawi opened the debate. Layton then had six minutes, leaving the Palestinian-Canadian with two minutes to respond. Questions from the audience then ensued.[57]

MAURICE JR. LABELLE 293

Hadawi wasted little time summarizing, "the basic policies, laws, and practices of Zionism which had all the ingredients of racism and racial and religious discrimination." Layton, in turn, deviated from the specifics of UN Resolution 3379 and "made no mention of Zionism." Instead, like recent Zionist letter-writers to the *Star* that belied Hadawi, he focused on Arab mistreatments of the Palestinian diaspora and Middle Eastern Jews. During his two-minute rebuttal, the retired Palestinian-Canadian stressed that his, "opponent had said nothing to prove that Zionism was not racist." He explained to those in attendance that this demonstrated, "that Zionism has no defense and that is in fact a racist movement as the UN had proclaimed," which received "great applause." After a final tally, the TV show declared Hadawi to be the clear winner by a vote of 69 to 45. In the aftermath, station employees informed him that his victory "was unexpected" because "a large part of the audience was Jewish."[58]

Hadawi's televised success did not mitigate Zionist efforts to disparage the PLO's presence in Canada and mute Palestinian points of view. The CIC amplified its campaign to prevent the PLO from participating in Vancouver's United Nations Conference on Human Settlements in early June 1976. Al-Hout, when in Toronto, insisted that the PLO would be present at Habitat, as the United Nations gathering was commonly referred to. Rabbi Plaut told *The Globe and Mail* that he objected to PLO participation at Habitat on the basis that, "The people who counsel the bomb throwers and the trigger pullers are just as responsible as the actual bomb throwers and trigger pullers." Zionists continued their assault on Hadawi. In a letter to the *Star*, Toronto resident Lori Slutzki insisted that the retired Palestinian Canadian was, "not familiar with the facts." In her perspective, "Arabs in Israel are treated as equal citizens, run their own businesses, and even have members in the Israeli parliament." Hadawi's implication that Israel was "uncivilized" unsettled her. Reifying Munich and the Zionist misrepresentation that all Palestinians were terrorists in a way that projected Israelis antithetically, Slutzki rhetorically asked, "Who are the uncivilized ones?"[59]

With Habitat looming, the CIC magnified its misrepresentations of the Arab-Israeli and Israeli-Palestinian conflicts. In a published letter to the *Star*, CIC leader Samuel Ross reified a founding Israeli-Zionist myth that Indigenous Palestinians were not forced to leave their homes during the first war of 1947 to 1949; rather, they "left on their own free will." According to Ross, it was, "unfortunate that they did not see fit to remain as did some

294   *Re-Presenting Palestine*

500,000 other Arabs who have and enjoy the same rights and privileges equally with all residents of Israel." Israel, he explained, had "no animosity to any Arab"; Israelis "wanted to live in peace with their Arab neighbors."[60]

Again, Hadawi keenly intercepted Zionist misrepresentations and re-presented the Palestinian revolution in Canada. A day after Ross's letter appeared, the Palestinian-Canadian impugned the CIC leader by invoking moral claims based on memories of his own Nakba experience. To suggest that Palestinians left on their own accord was libellous. "I," Hadawi expressed, "am a living 'fact' of expulsion and dispossession." The fact that refugees and exiles like him "can't return to homes," further dispelled the notion that Israel did not prejudice Palestinians and Arabs more broadly. His rejoinder openly asked, "why will they not allow us to return to our country and restore to us our usurped property as prescribed in numerous resolutions of the United Nations?" Unlike previously, the *Star* published Hadawi's letter four days after its reception. To the Palestinian Canadian's dismay, however, the newspaper omitted two paragraphs from his five-paragraph piece, including its one-sentence conclusion that read, "I trust these facts will help to open the eyes of Samuel Ross and his kind and instead of falsifying the 'facts' to begin to take the road to 'peace with justice' in the Holy Land."[61]

One more time, Hadawi became the direct object of Zionist attacks in the *Toronto Star*. M.F. Bochner challenged the former mandate official's factual knowledge on British Palestine and the core cause of Palestinian refugee-ness. Like Ross, Bochner invoked a Zionist myth that leading historians of Israel/Palestine have debunked since the late 1980s.[62] He insisted that, at the start of the 1947–49 war, "Arab leaders exhorted their cohorts in the Jewish areas to leave and join the Arab combatants in an organized attack on the Jews in order to drive them out of Palestine." Contrary to what Hadawi wrote and thought, Bochner affirmed that most Palestinians, "left volun-tarily, expecting to return as conquerors." Arab leaders, not Israel, were responsible for the dispossession of Palestinians.[63]

Elsewhere in the *Toronto Star*, Hadawi's letter merited the backlash of the CIC's top brass. Norman May wrote that, "Sami Hadawi's lament over his inability to return to his 'country' does not explain what forced him to leave, or prevented him from returning to" his "yearned-from" homeland. Palestine's existence was no more following "partition and the war of inde-pendence," May contended. If Hadawi wanted to return to his land and property, he needed to "pledge allegiance to Israel and its right to exist as an independent Jewish state in the Middle East."[64]

Upon reading May's letter, Hadawi concluded that the best way to respond to Zionist disavowals was to share his Nakba experience more explicitly and in greater detail, while not losing sight of Toronto newspaper's "editorial requirements" and space limitations. It was very important that he not be restricted or disregarded this time around. The Palestinian-Canadian did not stand down from May's challenge of proofing his Palestinian existence and its entanglement with Israel. Hadawi refused to "pledge allegiance to Israel," as doing so did not relate to, "principles of ownership of property as practiced in any other country." Referencing Article 13(2) of the Universal Declaration of Human Rights, which Israel signed, he affirmed that his rights, "to leave and return to my home and not be deprived of my property," were internationally protected. Hadawi then explained in the Toronto paper, "what forced [him] to leave":

> I fled on the night of April 29, 1948—16 days before the state of Israel was due to come into existence—during a Hagana attack on Katamon Quarter where I lived. Fourteen homes were destroyed and the entrance of my home was blown in before it was plundered of its contents. I made an attempt the next day to return but was fired at and a man walking near my car was hit.

> May did not comment on Hadawi's response.[65]

Palestinians Exist

The beginning of the Habitat meeting in Vancouver and Palestinian participation garnered Canadian Zionist energies, as the PLO went on Canadian public record as saying that it "would not shy away from politics." Al-Hout's delegation vowed to utilize the international forum on human settlements to decry Israel's role in Palestinian dispossession and homelessness—or, as the PLO's national report to Habitat called it, Israel's making of the "Arab-Palestinian Non-Person."[66] That moment came when Israeli Minister of the Interior Josef Burg took to the podium. PLO delegates and their Third Worldist allies walked out, a strategy often adopted by dissenting members at United Nations gatherings. As PLO delegate Abdullah Abduallah explained to The Globe and Mail, "The walkout came as a result of our belief

296   Re-Presenting Palestine

that the presence of Israel is illegal and inconsistent, because Israel has treated Palestinian settlements in an inhuman way, confiscating their lands." In his own address to Habitat participants the day after Burg's, al-Hout declared Palestinians to be, "a people whose habitat has been usurped." Israel, in turn, denounced such views as mere "anti-Israeli propaganda."[67]

Much to Hadawi's discontent, the *Toronto Star* followed in Israel's footsteps by mis-representing Palestinian self-representations at Habitat. Like most delegates, the PLO submitted a twenty-four-minute film that presented local settlement challenges ahead of the meeting. The Palestinian video, the *Star* reported, contrasted "refugees' plight with animals." Chickens, rabbits, horses, and birds had homes, whereas Palestinians did not, the PLO montage explained. "The houses and tents where the Palestinians live are no home." Reflecting on the PLO's "sideshow," the Toronto paper qualified the film as "Arab propaganda." Rebutting the accusation of Israel's sole responsibility for the continuing humanitarian plight of Palestinians, the *Star* inferred that the settlement of Palestinians outside Israel was a so-called Arab problem.[68]

Upon reading the *Star*'s last editorial, Hadawi protested anew. Speaking from his Nakba experience, the Palestinian-Canadian explained that Arab states did not fully support Palestinian resettlement due to, "the wishes of Palestinians themselves." The Nakba generation, "categorically reject all plans of resettlement outside their ancestral homeland." He then clarified that, although Palestinians were Arab, they, "are determined to retain their Palestinian personality, in the same way that a Canadian is part of the British Commonwealth in language and culture, and would resist any forcible resettlement in England, Australia or New Zealand." As Hadawi put it, "Love of home and country is a right not confined to the people of the West, and the Palestinians are no exception."[69]

As Habitat ended, a Zionist deluge overflowed the *Star* and drowned out Hadawi's letter, which appeared a week after being received. The Vancouver conference was an abysmal failure because of PLO machinations, concluded *Star* readers and editorialists alike. Letters branded Habitat a "farce" and "waste of taxpayer money," as it gave, "a voice for the Munich Olympics killers." The Palestinian-led walkout on Israel, they found, was "disgusting." The Toronto paper reported that Canadian officials were disillusioned, "grim-faced," and teary-eyed by the outcome of the United Nations meeting, spoiled by PLO shenanigans. The CIC's Samuel Ross chimed in on the Palestinian revolution's nefariousness again, opining that Habitat "degenerated into a witch-hunt against Israel." Much like the *Star*'s latest editorial that sparked Hadawi, Ross projected the Palestinian refugee problem onto neighbouring Arab states. Instead of accepting this humanitarian burden, the CIC leader asserted that non-Palestinian Arabs, "prefer to maintain these camps as a supposed example of the villainy of Israel." The lead editorial in the *Star*'s June 14, 1976 issue concurred, with its headline, "Habitat ruined by anti-Israel bias."[70]

However small, Hadawi's personified re-presentation of the Palestinian revolution gained recognition, albeit in the form of Zionist repudiation. Acton's M. Stasiuk complained to the *Star* that it printed "*the thousandth letter* from Sami Hadawi," whom he mis-represented as "defending his friends, the terrorists, who were given refuge in Lebanon." He then repeated a powerful Zionist myth that, in many ways, moved the Palestinian revolution: Palestinians "never exist[ed] in history." According to Stasiuk, "Hadawi is probably happy to live in Canada and so are immigrants from most countries." The Palestinian Canadian, therefore, should desist.[71]

Attacks like these notwithstanding, Hadawi refused to stop re-presenting Palestine in Canada. Instead, he became more involved in the broad domain of relations between the Arab Middle East, Israel, and Canada. Henceforth, the retired Palestinian Canadian did not limit his presence to the pages of the *Toronto Star*; he restarted pamphleteering for groups in Canada, like the Arab Palestine Association and the Arab Information Center, on controversial and misrepresented topics such as the Arab boycott of Israel.[72] Furthermore, he engaged extensively with Ottawa, Queen's Park, myriad political leaders, national and provincial parliamentarians, and the Arab Canadian community in ways that he had relented to do since becoming a landed immigrant. Hadawi, as a result, became a key voice in Canada that called for the recognition of the PLO. Canada, he felt, could no longer "ignore the existence of the Palestinians."[73]

Likewise, the retired Palestinian-Canadian refused to ignore ongoing Zionist misrepresentations in Canada and their mis-representers. Before an Ontario justice committee in 1978, Hadawi argued that "the Zionist Lobby" was so powerful that it harmed "the well-being of Canada"; it placed Israeli interests ahead of Canadian ones. He experienced the relentless strength of Canadian Zionist organizations first-hand. Above public dehumanizations, Toronto Zionists infringed upon Hadawi's private life to, "the unethical

298   *Re-Presenting Palestine*

state of intimidation." After making himself heard and seen, he frequently received threats against his family and "telephone calls of harassment at all hours of the day and night." Unbothered, Hadawi felt that such acts, "merely indicate the obnoxious character of Zionism which cannot flight a clean battle!" They had the adverse effect of animating him to advance the, "defence of my own just cause." As Hadawi confided to his long-time friend Elmer Berger, a leading anti-Zionist rabbi in the United States, "I often ask myself why don't I give up. I simply cannot as a Palestinian and one most concerned."[74]

Conclusion

Sami Hadawi's continuous re-presentation of Palestine in places like Edmonton, Calgary, Toronto, Ottawa, and elsewhere since his immigration in 1968, this essay argues, best represented the Palestinian revolution's coming to Canada. In fact, one cannot properly understand the beginnings of the Palestinian revolution in Canada without Hadawi. Whereas official PLO representatives like al-Hout left after concluding their diplomatic business at Habitat, he stayed. And, because of his deep engagement with the politics of representation, so did the Palestinian revolution. In the case of 1970s Canada, the PLO did not embody the Palestinian revolution; Hadawi did by steadfastly challenging, in peaceful ways, the popular misperceptions of Palestinians as either blood-thirsty terrorists or helpless refugees. Whereas he was not ultimately successful in returning to his Jerusalem home, he was integral to legitimizing Palestinian self-determination in Canada.

Upon invitation, the Palestinian-Canadian represented the Palestinian revolution during a handful of standings before a Canadian senate committee in the mid-1980s. Arab friends and Zionist foes alike, albeit in drastically different contexts, often mocked his dedication to "be heard" in Canada by sharing, "the discouraging unanimous remark that [he] was wasting [his] time." While acknowledging, "that the remark had a certain degree of truth in it," Hadawi shared with the Senatorial committee that he was, "a firm believer in the old adage: 'If you do not succeed the first time, try and try again." In his mind, contrary to Zionist mythmaking, Palestine did not imperil Canada. Likewise, his Palestinian identity did not contradict his Canadian citizenship. Rather, his Canadian citizenship allowed him to represent Palestine by re-presenting Palestinians in a humanizing way that had escaped myriad eyes and ears alike beforehand.[75]

Hadawi understood full well the difficulties of telling a Palestinian "side of the story" in Canada and beyond.[76] But that did not stop him from asserting political and moral claims to justice concerning Palestinian self-representation, self-determination, and decolonization. Nor did it prevent him from connecting Canadians to memories of his Nakba experience in unprecedented ways and surely that of myriad other Palestinians thereafter. His particular Palestinian-Canadian presence since the mid-1970s, alongside his re-presenting Palestine, evidenced Palestinian existence in Canada and the world, to all Canadians. By doing so, Hadawi better positioned other Palestinian and Arab Canadians, as well as their supporters, to stand in relation to Zionist misrepresentations and their protagonists in Canadian imaginations in ways that ensured that the Palestinian cause would not disappear or be disregarded as had essentially always been the case prior. As a result, Sami Hadawi was integral to two interconnected phenomena: the Canadianization of the Palestinian revolution and the re-orientation of Canadian perceptions of Palestinians and Palestine.

Notes

1. "The Camp David Accord versus the Fahed Peace Plan," Sami Hadawi Fonds, Vol. 1, File 64, Library and Archives Canada [LAC].

2. Conversation with Salman Abu-Sitta, December 20, 2018; and Sami Hadawi to John Rosley, June 23, 1980, Sami Hadawi Fonds, Vol. 1, File 18, LAC; Baha Abu-Laban, "Arab-Canadians and the Arab-Israeli Conflict"; Asal, *Se Dire Drabe au Canada*; and Hassan-Yari, *Le Canada et le Conflit Israélo-Arabe Depuis 1947*.

3. Sa'di and Abu-Lughod, eds., *Nakba: Palestine.*

4. "The Camp David Accord versus the Fahed Peace Plan."

5. Chamberlin, *The Global Offensive*; Rashid Khalidi, *Palestinian Identity*, 178–81.

6. Nassar, *Brothers Apart: Palestinian Citizens of Israel and the Arab World*, 157–58; Sayigh, *Armed Struggle and the Search for a State*, 91; Christison, *Perceptions of Palestine.*

7. "The Camp David Accord versus the Fahed Peace Plan."

8. Purves, *Canadian Reaction to Palestinian Self-Determination*; Ismael, *Canada and the Middle East*; Ismael, ed. *Canada and the Arab World.*

9. Bayoumi, *This Muslim American Life*, 241–42.

10. Said, "Introduction," 3; Conversation with Salman Abu-Sitta, December 20, 2018; "The Nakba Generation."

11. Hadawi, *The Story of My Life: Memories and Reflections* (Amman: n.p., 1996), 1; Letter, June 21, 1981, Sami Hadawi Fonds, Vol. 1, File 12, LAC; Summary of Positions Held, n.d., James Peters Fonds, Vol. 9, LAC.

12. Foreword, n.d., Sami Hadawi Fonds, Vol. 1, File 1, LAC; Hadawi, *The Story of My Life*, 247.

13. Hadawi, *Bitter Harvest*, 326.

14. Hadawi, *The Story of My Life*, 237, 248, 270, 284, and 298; and Foreword, n.d., Sami Hadawi Fonds, Vol. 1, File 1, LAC.

15. *Middle East News Digest and Newsletter*, 1.

16. Hadawi, "Zionist Sway Western Policy, Arab Charges," 5; Hadawi, "Israeli Law Protested," 30; Hadawi, *Bitter Harvest*, xix; Hadawi, *Palestine: Loss of a Heritage*; and Said in *Blaming Victims*, 14.

17. Rogan, *The Arabs: A History*, 269.

18. Nassar, *Brothers Apart*, 159; Conversation with Salman Abu-Sitta, December 20, 2018.

19. Di-Capua, *No Exit: Arab Existentialism*, 45; Hadawi, "Les Revendications 'Bibliques' et 'Historiques,'" 91–105 and 176–212.

20. Hadawi, *The Story of My Life*, 384 and 392; Summary of Positions Held, n.d., James Peters Fonds, Vol. 9, LAC.

21. Hadawi, *Palestine and the Bible*, 4; Conversation with Salman Abu-Sitta, December 20, 2018.

22. Hadawi *Palestine Occupied*, 5 and 24.

23. Hadawi, *The Holy Land Under Israeli Occupation 1967*, 10.

24. Christison, *Perceptions of Palestine*, 153; McAlister, *Epic Encounters: Culture, Media, and U.S. Interests*, 182.

25. Noble, "When the Angels Fear to Tread," 113–15; *Toronto Star* (TS), April 6, 1973, 25.

26. al-Hout, *My Life in the PLO*, 125.

27. Anziska, *Preventing Palestine*, 68; and TS, October 16, 1974, A16.

28. TS, October 16, 1974, B4; TS, November 4, 1974, C4; Yaqub, *Imperfect Strangers*, 92; and TS, November 5, 1974, B4.

29. TS, November 12, 1974, B4 and B5.

30. United Nations (UN), "UN General Assembly, 29th Session, Official Records: Agenda Item 108, Question of Palestine"; al-Hout, *My Life in the PLO*, 134.

31. TS, November 14, 1974, A1 and A4.

32. Goldberg, *Foreign Policy and Ethnic Interests Groups*, 31; TS, November 18, 1974, C1; and TS, November 22, 1974, B5.

33. Noble, "When the Angles Fear the Tread," 115; TS, June 19, 1974; Solicitor General Secretariat Fonds (SGSF), Vol 13, File N. 11-98-1, LAC.

34. TS, November 23, 1974, A10; TS, November 28, 1974, B5 and B15; and TS, December 9, 1974, C5.

35. *The Globe and Mail* (GM), February 20, 1975, 6 and 41.

36. Goldberg, *Foreign Policy and Ethnic Interest Groups*, 108 and 114; and TS, September 6, 1975, B6.

37. GM, May 30, 1975, 5; TS, May 30, 1975, A12; and TS, June 3, 1975, B4

38. Press Release, June 16, 1975, SGSF, Vol. 5, File N. 11-98-1, LAC; Press Release, June 23, 1975, SGSF, Vol. 10, File N. 11-98-1, LAC; Press Release, July 4, 1975, SGSF, Vol. 13,

File N. 11-98-1, LAC; *TS*, September 6, 1975, B6; *TS*, June 12, 1975, B5; *TS*, June 25, 1975, B5; *TS*, July 16, 1975, C5; and *TS*, July 18, 1975, A4.

39. Letter, June 4, 1975, SGSF, Vol. 5, File 11-98-1, LAC; May to Trudeau, June 5, 1975, SGSF, Vol. 5, File 11-98-1, LAC; Letter, July 16, 1975, SGSF, Vol. 12, File 11-98-1, LAC; Letter, June 5, 1975, SGSF, Vol. 4, File 11-98-1, LAC; Telegram, June 6, 1975, SGSF, Vol. 5, File 11-98-1, LAC; Letter, June 10, 1975, R1184, Vol. 5, File 11-98-1, LAC; Telegram, June 11, 1975, SGSF, Vol. 4, File 11-98-1, LAC; and Letter, June 13, 1975, SGSF, Vol. 8, File 11-98-1, LAC.

40. *GM*, July 11, 1975, 8; *GM*, July 17, 1975, 1; *GM*, July 18, 1975, 7; and *TS*, July 18, 1975, B5.

41. *Palestine in Struggle* 1, 1 (September 1975): 11; *TS*, July 22, 1975, A1 and A2; *TS*, July 25, 1975, B5; July 28, 1975, C5; *TS*, July 30, 1975, B5; *TS*, July 23, 1975, A1.

42. Letter, March 6, 1977, Sami Hadawi Fonds, Vol. 1, File 5, LAC; *TS*, October 21, 1975, B4.

43. Abu-Laban, "Arab-Canadians and the Arab-Israeli Conflict," 106.

44. Memorandum, July 1969, Sami Hadawi Fonds, Vol. 1, File 24, LAC; Asal, *Se Dire Arabe au Canada*, 146; *GM*, July 11, 1975, 8; Letter, July 16, 1975, SGSF, Vol. 13, File 11-98-1, LAC; Peters to Azzaria, February 5, 1969, James Peters Fonds, Vol. 4, LAC; and Joseph Lahoud, "Non-Information Center!!!," 1.

45. *TS*, October 30, 1975, B5; *GM*, October 27, 1975, 1; *GM*, October 28, 1975, 1; and *GM*, October 30, 1975, 5.

46. *TS*, November 4, 1975, B5; *TS*, November 11, 1975, A13; *TS*, October 29, 1975, B4.

47. Letter, November 1, 1975, Sami Hadawi Papers, Vol. 1, File 2, LAC.

48. Sa'di and Abu-Lughod, eds., *Nakba*, 6.

49. Feagin, *The White Racial Frame*; Erakat, "Whiteness as Property in Israel"; and Becke, "Dismantling the Villa in the Jungle."

50. See Farah and Desjarlais (chapter 3) and Wildeman (chapter 2) in this volume for more discussion of the nature of settler colonialism and the practice of erasure.

51. Robinson, *Citizen Strangers*, 29–112; and Letter, 1 November 1975, Sami Hadawi Papers, Vol. 1, File 2, LAC.

52. "Zionism-A Racist Movement," November 1975, James Peters Fonds, Vol. 9, LAC; *TS*, November 20, 1975, B3.

53. Emphasis added. *TS*, November 12, 1975, B4; *TS*, November 13, 1975, A14; *TS*, November 14, 1975, A1, B4, and B5.

54. *TS*, November 17, 1975, C1; *GM*, November 20, 1975, 5; al-Hout, *My Life in the PLO*, 135–36.

55. Emphasis added. *TS*, December 20, 1975, B3.

56. *TS*, November 20, 1975, B3; al-Hout, *My Life in the PLO*, 136; and *GM*, November 24, 1975, 5.

57. *GM*, November 24, 1975, 5.

58. Hadawi, *The Story of My Life*, 397–98.

59. *TS*, November 28, 1975, B5; *TS*, December 20, 1975, B3; *Palestine in Struggle* 1, 3 (January 1976): 8; *Canadian Middle East Digest* 1, 1 (n.d.): 1; *TS*, December 10, 1975, B5; *GM*, November 19, 1975, 9; *GM*, November 20, 1975, 1; and *TS*, December 9, 1975, B5.

60. Flapan, *The Birth of Israel*; TS, May 1, 1976, B3.

61. Letter, May 2, 1976, Sami Hadawi Fonds, Vol. 1, File 2, LAC; and TS, May 6, 1976, B5.

62. Khalidi, "Plan Dalet: Master Plan for the Conquest of Palestine"; Morris, *The Birth of the Palestinian Refugee Problem*; Rogan and Shlaim, eds., *The War for Palestine*.

63. TS, May 14, 1976, B5.

64. TS, May 19, 1976, B5.

65. TS, May 28, 1976, B5.

66. TS, May 28, 1976, A3; HABITAT Conferences Digital Archive, "National Report of Palestine."

67. TS, June 4, 1976, A3; GM, June 4, 1976, 10; GM, June 5, 1976, 11; HABITAT Conferences Digital Archive, "Press Release: Delegation of Israel to Habitat, June 7th. 1976."

68. HABITAT Conferences Digital Archive, "Palestine Liberation Organization—The Key (French Audio)." ; TS, June 4, 1976, A3; and TS, June 10, 1976, B4.

69. Letter, June 11, 1976, Sami Hadawi Fonds, Vol. 1, File 2, LAC; and TS, June 18, 1976, B5.

70. TS, June 12, 1976, A3; TS, June 11, 1976, B5; and TS, June 14, 1976, C4.

71. Emphasis added. TS, June 28, 1976, C5.

72. TS, March 19, 1977, B3; TS, April 6, 1977, B5; Hadawi, *Between the Olive Branch and the Battlefield*; Hadawi to El-Dali, December 7, 1976, Sami Hadawi Fonds, Vol. 1, File 4, LAC; Hadawi to El-Dali, February 13, 1977, Sami Hadawi Fonds, Vol. 1, File 4, LAC; Hadawi, *The Arab Boycott of Israel*; Hadawi, *The Palestinians: Victim of a Conspiracy*; Hadawi, *Christianity at the Crossroads*; Hadawi, *The Realities of Terrorism and Retaliation*.

73. "The Arab Boycott of Israel and Canada," n.d., Sami Hadawi Fonds, Vol. 1, File 15, LAC; Statement, September 19, 1978, Sami Hadawi Fonds, Vol. 1, File 15, LAC; Statement, September 20, 1978, Sami Hadawi Fonds, Vol. 1, File 15, LAC; Hadawi to Trudeau, March 4, 1980, Sami Hadawi Fonds, Vol. 1, File 9, LAC; and Memorandum, June 21, 1976, James Peters Fonds, Vol. 9, LAC.

74. Hadawi to Labadi, August 16, 1981, Sami Hadawi Fonds, Vol. 1, File 12, LAC; Statement, August 30, 1978, Sami Hadawi Fonds, Vol. 1, File 15, LAC; "Arab Boycott of Israel," May 1977, Sami Hadawi Fonds, Vol. 1, File 33, LAC; Hadawi, *The Story of My Life*, 403; "Zionist Racism and the Lands of Palestine," April 1977, Sami Hadawi Fonds, Vol. 1, File 37, LAC; Hadawi to Berger, September 11, 1981, Sami Hadawi Fonds, Vol. 1, File 12, LAC.

75. Hadawi, *The Story of My Life*, 410; Presentation, n.d., Sami Hadawi Fonds, Vol. 1, File 23, LAC.

76. Presentation, April 1977, Sami Hadawi Fonds, Vol. 1, File 37, LAC.

References

Abu-Laban, Baha. "Arab-Canadians and the Arab-Israeli Conflict." *Arab Studies Quarterly* 10, no. 1 (1988): 104–26.

Al-Hout, Shafiq. *My Life in the PLO: The Inside Story of the Palestinian Struggle.* New York: Pluto Press, 2011.

Anziska, Seth. *Preventing Palestine: A Political History from Camp David to Oslo.* Princeton: Princeton University Press, 2018.

Asal, Houda. *Se dire arabe au Canada : Un siècle d'histoire migratoire.* Montréal : Les Presses de l'Université de Montréal, 2016.

Bayoumi, Moustafa. *This Muslim American Life: Dispatches from the War on Terror.* New York: New York University Press, 2015.

Becke, Johannes. "Dismantling the Villa in the Jungle: Matzpen, Zochrot, and the Whitening of Israel." *Interventions* 21, no. 6 (December 14, 2018): 1–18.

Canadian Middle East Digest 1, no. 1 (n.d.).

Chamberlin, Paul. *The Global Offensive: The United States, the Palestine Liberation Organization, and the Making of the Post-Cold War Order.* New York: Oxford University Press, 2012.

Christison, Kathleen. *Perceptions of Palestine: Their Influence on U.S.-Middle East Policy.* Berkeley: University of California Press, 1999.

Di-Capua, Yoav. *No Exit: Arab Existentialism, Jean-Paul Sartre and Decolonization.* Chicago: University of Chicago Press, 2018.

Erakat, Noura. "Whiteness as Property in Israel: Revival, Rehabilitation, and Removal." *Harvard Journal on Racial and Ethnic Studies* 31 (2015): 69–103.

Feagin, Joe. *The White Racial Frame: Centuries of Racial Framing and Counter-Framing.* New York: Routledge, 2009.

Goldberg, David Howard. *Foreign Policy and Ethnic Interests Groups: American and Canadian Jews Lobby for Israel.* New York: Greenwood Press, 1990.

HABITAT Conferences Digital Archive. "National Report of Palestine." Accessed March 7, 2019. https://habitat.scarp.ubc.ca/wp-content/uploads/2018/04/Palestine_NationalReport.pdf.

HABITAT Conferences Digital Archive. "Palestine Liberation Organization—The Key (French Audio)." February 21, 2018. https://www.youtube.com/watch?v=1vFg_hmYFJo.

HABITAT Conferences Digital Archive. "Press Release: Delegation of Israel to Habitat, June 7th. 1976." Accessed March 7, 2019. https://habitat.scarp.ubc.ca/wp-content/uploads/2018/03/DelegationOfIsraelToHabitat_07061976.pdf.

Hadawi, Sami. *Between the Olive Branch and the Battlefield.* Ottawa: Canada-Palestine Committee, 1976.

Hadawi, Sami. *Bitter Harvest: Palestine Between 1914–1967.* New York: The New World Press, 1967.

Hadawi, Sami. *Christianity at the Crossroads.* Ottawa: Jerusalem International Publications, 1982.

Hadawi, Sami. "Israeli Law Protested," *New York Times,* April 2, 1958.

Hadawi, Sami. "Les revendications 'bibliques' et 'historiques' des sionistes sur la Palestine" and "Les réfugiés arabes." *Les temps modernes* 253 (1967): 91–105 and 176–212.

Hadawi, Sami. *Palestine and the Bible*. Beirut: Institute for Palestine Studies, 1970.

Hadawi, Sami. *Palestine: Loss of a Heritage*. San Antonio: Naylor, 1963.

Hadawi, Sami. *Palestine Occupied*. New York: The Arab Information Center, 1968.

Hadawi, Sami. *The Arab Boycott of Israel: Peaceful, Defensive, and Constructive*. Ottawa: Arab League Information Center, 1977.

Hadawi, Sami. *The Holy Land Under Israeli Occupation 1967: An Appeal to World Conscience*. Beirut: Palestine Research Center, 1969.

Hadawi, Sami. *The Palestinians: Victim of a Conspiracy*. Toronto: Arab Palestine Association, 1981.

Hadawi, Sami. *The Realities of Terrorism and Retaliation*. Toronto: Arab Palestine Association, 1987.

Hadawi, Sami. *The Story of My Life: Memories and Reflections*. Amman: n.p., 1996.

Hadawi, Sami. "Zionist Sway Western Policy, Arab Charges," *The Globe and Mail*, July 24, 1984.

Hassan-Yari, Houchang. *Le Canada et le conflit israélo-arabe depuis 1947 : Un demi-siècle de diplomatie engagée*. Montreal: L'Harmattan, 1997.

Ismael, Tareq. ed. *Canada and the Arab World*. Edmonton: University of Alberta Press, 1985.

Ismael, Tareq. ed. *Canada and the Middle East: The Policy of a Client State*. Calgary: Detselig Enterprises, 1994.

James Peters Fonds, Vol. 4 and 9, Library and Archives Canada.

Khalidi, Rashid. *Palestinian Identity: The Construction of Modern National Consciousness*. New York: Columbia University Press, 1997.

Khalidi, Walid. "Plan Dalet: Master Plan for the Conquest of Palestine." *Journal of Palestine Studies* 18, no. 1 (1988): 4–33.

Lahoud, Joseph. "Non-Information Center!!!" *Canadian Middle East Journal* 2, no. 40 (April 1, 1968): 1.

McAlister, Melani. *Epic Encounters: Culture, Media, and U.S. Interests in the Middle East since 1945*. Berkeley: University of California Press, 2001.

Middle East News Digest and Newsletter, no. 8 (December 1964): 1.

Morris, Benny. *The Birth of the Palestinian Refugee Problem, 1947–1949*. New York: Cambridge University Press, 1987.

"The Nakba Generation." The Palestinian Revolution. Accessed March 7, 2019. http://learnpalestine.politics.ox.ac.uk/teach/week/2.

Nassar, Maha. *Brothers Apart: Palestinian Citizens of Israel and the Arab World*. Stanford: Stanford University Press, 2017.

Noble, Paul. "When the Angels Fear to Tread": Canada and the Status of the Palestinian people 1973–1983." In *Canada and the Arab World*, edited by Tareq Y. Ismael, 113–15. Edmonton: University of Alberta Press, 1985.

Palestine in Struggle 1, no. 1 (September 1975).

Palestine in Struggle 1, no. 3 (January 1976).

Purves, Grant. *Canadian Reaction to Palestinian Self-Determination*. Ottawa: Library of Parliament Research Branch, 1987.

Rogan, Eugene. *The Arabs: A History*. New York: Basic Books, 2009.

Rogan, Eugene, and Avi Shlaim, eds. *The War for Palestine: Rewritting the History of 1948*. New York: Cambridge University Press, 2001.

Sa'di, Ahmad H., and Lila Abu-Lughod, eds. *Nakba: Palestine, 1948, and the Claims of Memory*. New York: Columbia University Press, 2007.

Said, Edward. "Introduction." In *Blaming the Victims: Spurious Scholarship and the Palestinian Question*, edited by Edward Said and Christopher Hitchens, 1–20. New York: Verso, 1998.

Sami Hadawi Fonds, Vol. 1, Library and Archives Canada.

Sayigh, Yezid. *Armed Struggle and the Search for a State: The Palestinian National Movement, 1949–1993*. Oxford: Clarendon Press, 1997.

Solicitor General Secretariat Fonds, Vol. 4, 5, 8, 10, 12, and 13. Library and Archives Canada.

United Nations (UN). "UN General Assembly, 29th Session, Official Records: Agenda Item 108, Question of Palestine." November 13, 1974. https://digitallibrary.un.org/record/743672?ln=en.

CONCLUSION

The Struggle for a Fairer Future

JEREMY WILDEMAN

The Struggle

Whether in Palestine or the diaspora, being Palestinian constitutes a daily struggle. In Canada, having a Palestinian identity is often considered taboo.[1] Many Palestinian immigrants to Canada enter a discursive setting where their identity has for some time been linked to in-civility, savagery, violence, and terrorism. This constructed image owes in no small part to deliberate Orientalist misrepresentations of Palestinians in the Canadian press, which became pointed in the 1970s,[2] a time when the international community was by contrast moving steadily toward the broader recognition of the Palestinians as a people with their own legitimate aspirations. This included among Canada's key G7 allies. The United States' Carter Administration was in search of a broader Middle East peace, which began with the Camp David Accords (1978) between Israel and Egypt,[3] but would eventually need to include Israel and the Palestinians. Eventually the European Community's Venice Declaration

(1980) called for, "recognition of the right to existence and to security of all countries in the Middle East including Israel, as well as the legitimate rights of the Palestinian people."[4]

The European Community's declaration also stressed the need for a comprehensive solution that would include the issues of Palestinian refugees and sovereignty over Jerusalem. That comprehensive solution was expected to be found through negotiations that would include the Palestine Liberation Organization (PLO), with an aim to end Israeli rule of the Occupied Palestinian Territory (OPT), which had begun with the 1967 Six Day War.[5] The declaration further cited Israeli settlements in the OPT as a serious obstacle to peace and called on Israel to refrain from unilateral actions in Jerusalem.[6]

Canadian public opinion was not immune to these international movements.[7] Yet, in that same era, a short-lived Joe Clark Progressive Conservative government would attempt to effectively recognize Israeli sovereignty over Jerusalem, including OPT East Jerusalem, by fulfilling a 1979 campaign pledge to move Canada's embassy in Israel from Tel Aviv to Jerusalem.[8] The Clark government eventually had to back down from the pledge due to intense international pressure. Meanwhile, the Government of Canada was loath to recognize the PLO as a legitimate representative of the Palestinian people. Not only was the Canadian government unwilling to recognize them, but it was unhappy to speak with an organization it typically labelled as a terrorist entity,[9] and even went so far as to cancel entire United Nations conferences to prevent PLO participants from passing through Canadian border control.[10]

This elite-driven discourse against the Palestinians (d-)evolved in Canada into a structural racism that has had a deleterious impact on Palestinians, which includes at the workplace. As we learned through Assi and Abdelnour's interviews with Palestinian-Canadians, those interviewees faced significant racial prejudice in Canada, including Islamophobic stereotyping and, especially when they embrace their identity as Palestinians, being targeted with racist tropes, microaggressions, and outright hostility. Assi and Abdelnour also described how economic insecurity interrupts the Palestinian-Canadian working class's ability to recognize and celebrate their identities, especially when combined with the racist, anti-Palestinian pressure heaped upon them.[11] They found that for many Palestinians in exile in Canada, political identity making is seen as a potential source of trouble

308 *Conclusion*

in an insecure and struggling community, and is accordingly discouraged. Thus, while researching the Palestinian diaspora in Canada, Wills found that a flourishing of distinctly Palestinian community organizing in Ottawa was at the same time centred on avoiding politics, with the lead organizations describing themselves as "non-political" in their activities.

Assi and Abdelnour also described how an important public space, Canadian universities, can be particularly unsafe for students who raise awareness about Palestinian human rights. Anti-Palestinian racism is rife there. Students who do engage in advocacy are routinely attacked by Zionist groups both on and off campus.[12] Moreover, university administrators and politicians, including Premiers and Prime Ministers,[13] regularly express hostility towards Palestine advocacy and research. This contributes to the silencing of countless Palestinians in Canada, contributes to a general anxiety among many Palestinians about expressing their identity and leads to a fear of engaging in political advocacy. It is something many of the writers in this collection have themselves grappled with in their lives.

The abuse is not to be taken lightly. It can transgress from threats to one's professional life toward one's personal security. Hadawi frequently received threats against his family, which Labelle recounts as, "telephone calls of harassment at all hours of the day and night." Such threats could extend to non-Palestinian allies in the cause of Palestinian rights. In the same era that Hadawi was active, the editor of the United Church's influential *Observer* magazine, Rev. A.C. Forrest (1955–1978),[14] was hit with a barrage of accusations of anti-semitism and regular telephone harassment over his attempt to offer fair-minded coverage of Israel and Palestine. This continued right up until his death in 1978.[15] Meanwhile, the widow and some former employees of the now defunct Canadian Crown-funded human rights agency, Rights and Democracy, blamed the 2010 premature death of their then President Remy Beauregard on a contentious fight over several small grants the agency made to well-regarded Palestinian and Israeli human rights organizations after the first Gaza War (2008/9).[16] The harassment from government-appointed, partisan pro-Israel advocates on the organization's Board of Directors was fierce,[17] and ultimately the entire agency was shuttered over the affair.[18]

As Sucharov outlines in her chapter, the silencing of narratives extends into the Jewish community. Sucharov has found that the dominant and most influential Jewish community organizations in Canada tend to parrot

Conclusion   309

the political line adopted by the Government of Israel, regardless of the plethora of different and often dissenting opinions being held by Canadian Jews.[19] One of the results is that the Jewish diaspora's discourse about the Government of Israel rarely extends into criticism of the nature of the Zionist project itself, such as Israel's core demands to maintain a Jewish demographic majority and bar Palestinian refugee return. It has proven difficult for Jewish groups outside of the Zionist consensus to mount dissent from within a Jewish community context, and especially to gain much traction in presenting alternative narratives.[20] The result is a Jewish community organizational discourse whose focus has become centred on protecting Israel from mass protest efforts. One strategy has been to deflect attention from Israel's shortcomings by spotlighting what the Palestinians are doing wrong.

Decontextualization

As a result of this hostile environment, in Canada, it is difficult to speak to the basic reality of Israel and Palestine. Sucharov discussed, for instance, how hard it is to come across accurate contextual terminology in Canada, owing in part to the main organizations in the Canadian Jewish community doing their utmost to avoid use of an essential descriptive word like "occupation,"[21] despite it being the internationally recognized term to describe Israel's rule over the OPT. This process of decontextualization is consistent with a trend we see among the Canadian government's and Canadian civil society organizations' peacemaking and development aid programming, spotlighted in the chapters by Naser-Najjab and Abu-Zahra, and of Canadian media coverage of Israel and Palestine, in the chapter by Antonius. I have also written extensively, either alone or with Palestinian colleagues, about the Canadian and international community's approach to Palestinian development aid.[22] I experienced it in person when funding and delivering support for communities in crisis in the OPT. In Palestine aid, decontextualization has been the norm, despite it being widely acknowledged in development studies that when interventions in a conflict situation are conducted based on poor analysis, they are likely to exacerbate and fuel the underlying conditions of conflict, rather than ameliorate them.[23]

Exploring how decontextualization and the process of misrepresenting Palestinians plays out in the Canadian media, Antonius uncovered a deeply ingrained bias against Palestinians, their narrative, and their lived

310   *Conclusion*

experiences. Antonius found in his case study that the Canadian media would describe the Israeli perspective in some detail, to the point of justifying Israel's actions in a devastating 2014 Gaza war, while often not bothering to present the Palestinian perspective. Worse yet, when the Canadian media did mention how Palestinians were suffering, Antonius found the information was conveyed in a way that presented a racist and one-sided narrative that only reinforced an Israeli talking point that, "Yes the Palestinians suffer, but it is their own fault." The bias was so strong that Canadian public broadcast reporters ended up incorporating Israeli motives into their own description of events on the ground, as part of a process whereby the Israeli narrative becomes the Canadian official approach. Altogether these acts of silencing, decontextualization, erasure and racism are indicative of a discursive environment familiar to scholars of colonization, or specifically settler colonization. Thus, many of the authors in this collection converged on the settler colonial paradigm as the best lens to understand the Israeli–Palestinian relationship, and Canada's ardent support for Israel.

A Colonial Context

European settler colonial states consider their own actions, and typically those of fellow European settler states,[24] to be on the vanguard of the enlightened spread of civilization. Fot them, this justifies to themselves any of their own actions.[25] Indigenous resistance to such "progress," in reality settler aggression, is almost always inverted and re-presented in such a way that the settler state's violence is legitimatized while indigenous resistance becomes an act of (barbaric) aggression that needs to be "defensively" contained. Thus, international donors from across the Occident, such as Canada, ended up perverting Israeli–Palestinian peacebuilding through a programme of "aid" to the Palestinians that consisted of building up security services for an unelected, Western-installed/reinforced Palestinian Authority, that then coordinates security for Israel in major West Bank population centres (in Area A).

This is one aspect of what Kanji describes as settler colonial collusion between Canada and Israel that exists across multiple modalities of government power, central to both states' projects of colonial erasure and replacement. Kanji describes less overt tools like the epistemological use of liberalism, and associated ideals like multiculturalism and anti-racism,

Conclusion 311

in the demonization of colonized peoples to warrant their ongoing dispossession and imprisonment onto bantustans/reservations. There, just as the Indigenous person may be *re*-presented as the aggressor toward their colonial oppressor, they are often in turn re-presented (in an act of "projection") as the racist party by a racist colonial enterprise. This is part of an attempt to align the settler colonial state with all that is "good," and thus render the eliminatory and genocidal violence of settler colonialism as ultimately a righteous violence. It is a colonial way of thinking as old as Hegel and Rousseau themselves, centred in European imperial and colonial thought,[26] which takes place in an unfettered manner on the northern section of Turtle Island as a result of the Canadian state so completely failing to address its own settler coloniality.[27]

In this context, the enlightened Occidental voice, be it Israeli or Canadian, or American and European, is always given greater weight over that of the colonized subaltern narrative. Naser-Najjab thus observed a preponderance of Western and Israeli research perspectives in peace research, which end up compounding skewed perspectives and misunderstandings of Israel and Palestine, contributing to ineffective and outright harmful programming. Worse, the Occidental standpoint is presented as the "neutral" and "objective" viewpoint, even though it is only a *re*-presentation of the dominant, colonial discourse and specifically discredits many of the key factors for conflict and humanitarian disaster in the Middle East. This has contributed to a persistent insistence that peacebuilding should be centred on "bringing together" and enjoining two (relatively equal) sides of a conflict, completely ignorant of the fact that Palestinians and Israelis are already intimately intertwined through a long-running and donor-funded process of settler-colonial annexation and colonization undertaken by the Government of Israel. The result is a fictitious and harmful forced conjoining of victim with victimizer, which Abu Zahra argues is reinforcing structures of dominance and abuse while delegitimizing and blocking necessary advocacy work in the protection of human rights. Indeed, Naser-Najjab found liberal peacebuilding concepts have been warped by Canada and other Occidental international actors to perpetuate colonial relations within the rubric of cooperation and dialogue. Thus, the Canadian state ultimately operates to silence and block Palestine's human rights advocacy, domestically and in the Middle East, even though human rights are intrinsic to any true positive peacebuilding taking

312   *Conclusion*

place. Thus, Canada is contributing to making Palestinian lives worse, much like it has done to Indigenous peoples on Turtle Island.

The Hope

Whether intentional or not, and despite the alarming context they are describing in their contributions, the scholars in this collection also offer a combined sense of hope for a better world. One is through Labelle's description of Sami Hadawi and his tireless advocacy efforts, challenging popular misperceptions projected about Palestinians in Canada. This reflected Hadawi's optimism that Canadians could be moved toward adopting a more just and conciliatory position on the issue of Palestine. Though he was unsuccessful in his personal quest to return to the home he fled from Jerusalem in the Nakba/foundation of Israel, his advocacy work played an integral role in legitimizing the call for Palestinian self-determination in Canada. This happened in spite of incredible counter-pressure by the Toronto media and harassment of his personal space.

Indeed, a similar path is being trodden by many of the scholars in this collection, as Palestinians, Jews, or other backgrounds, who choose to engage in polemics critical of the status quo that are grounded in reality, in a Canadian academic and professional environment that can be outright hostile to truth and the Palestinian perspective.[28] Palestinian Canadians may not even have a choice, as Wills found, because even when they are being "non-political," their identity is always hyperpoliticized. Or, as Ayyash wrote, Palestinian existence necessitates resistance.

Effecting change in Canada will not be easy given the predisposition of elite institutions to support Israel's colonial project and given the crackdown they have been part of against Palestine advocacy in Canada. Sucharov suggests it will be difficult for advocates of Palestinian rights to enter the political lobbying game and make an impact in it. So, change is likely only going to take place if pressure comes from the grassroots up. A successful action will need to consider and address Canada's settler colonialism. That will require Canadians to look into the proverbial mirror, as citizens of a settler state, to understand their own normative subjectivity and address the wrongs Canada perpetrates against Indigenous peoples. As Kanji wrote, understanding the structures of violence and control in Canada's projections of colonial and imperial power, on Turtle Island and in the Middle East,

Conclusion 313

is crucial to building solidarity against the crimes of coloniality across colonial borders. It is an arc my co-editor Ayyash found himself on, after his transmutation from the position of colonized to colonizer, following his immigration to Canada. Likewise, it is a journey I have been on as an (off-white) settler from the plains/Prairies, who was long blind to the process I was raised into, on a heavily segregated Battlefords / Treaty 6 region of Canada / Turtle Island. For, as Naser-Najjab found (and experienced) through the failure of the dialogue-for-peace programming in the early years of the Oslo Peace Process, any programme that does not acknowledge the imperative of decolonization will end up serving colonial interests, making the situation worse (again and again).

Meanwhile, even though Sucharov's chapter may offer a cautious and pessimistic outlook on change driven within the mainstream Canadian Jewish community, she hints at alternative paths for a just peace being pursued by a number of committed advocates for change, whose numbers are not insignificant. Likewise, though the Ottawa Palestinian organizations, such as the Ottawa Palestinian Festival, may actively describe themselves as *not* being engaged in political advocacy, they are organizing what may be among the largest Palestinian community events in North America.[29] In the process, they have helped to create a space for the continued affirmation of the Palestinian part of the Palestinian-Canadian identity,[30] which is no small act given the history of anti-Palestinian racism and coloniality that puts incredible pressure on Palestinian-Canadians to hide their identity.[31]

As I described in my chapter, being Indigenous under Canadian rule is very difficult, given the Canadian state's long history of genocidal erasure against them. Being Indigenous can still be taboo in many parts of Canada today, and that reality constitutes an exacting daily struggle. Thus, Indigenous existence on Turtle Island has always necessitated resistance and, as a result, those remarkable peoples, their communities and their nations have managed to endure (though not unscathed). So, while Hadawi appealed to progressive ideals in Canada to alter the state's approach to the Middle East, Ayyash is right to caution that is in and of itself not the best approach, unless one recognizes that "Canadian values" are a contested space, where the worst of them are centred on settler coloniality, and many of the best are rooted in a sense of collective freedom and well being that was never purely settler Canadian, but rather springs from Indigenous knowledges and worldviews, as well as the hybridity of settler–Indigenous interactions and exchanges. I also caution that there is a long-established propensity among settlers to share the ideals and accoutrements of liberalism among themselves, while explicitly denying those (Canadian values) to the colonized "Other." Kanji also adds a cautionary note about a Canadian government that labels itself as being on the vanguard of anti-racism, even when we have seen it doing the exact opposite throughout its colonized approach to Indigenous well-being. This attitude has almost certainly contributed to the Canadian state standing directly in the path of Palestinian freedom, contrary to the progressive image it projects of Canada to the international community.

Palestinian Canadians have much to learn from the struggle of Indigenous peoples on Turtle Island, and we, either Palestinian settler or non-Palestinian settler, have the moral and political obligation to stand shoulder-to-shoulder with them in this struggle. Certainly, some of us are already stepping onto this path, but much more needs to be done. Only a genuinely decolonial, anti-colonial approach can check, challenge, and possibly remedy the ravages of coloniality.

Notes

1. See Assi and Abdelnour's chapter 9 in this volume.
2. See Labelle's chapter 11 in this volume.
3. "Camp David Accords."
4. Economic Cooperation Foundation (ECF), "Venice Declaration (1980)."
5. ECF.
6. ECF.
7. Wildeman, "Assessing Canada's Foreign Policy."
8. Giniger, "Canada Abandons Plan."
9. Robinson, "Talking to the PLO."
10. See Labelle's chapter 11 in this volume.
11. Increasingly this racism is being referred to in Canada as anti-Palestinian racism. Al Masri, "Anti-Palestinian Racism Is Behind IHRA's Antisemitism Definition"; Paradkar, "Controversies at U of T Law."
12. Bandler, "Trudeau Condemns Protests"; Thompson, *No Debate*; Nathan-Kazis, "Anonymous Online Blacklist."
13. DPA and *Haaretz*, "Trudeau's Anti-BDS Message"; Times of Israel staff, "Trudeau Blasts BDS Movement"; The Canadian Press, "Premier Doug Ford Weighs in on Clash."
14. Forrest, *Unholy Land*.
15. Bradley-St-Cyr, "The Downfall of the Ryerson Press."

Conclusion   315

16. Cheadle, "The Staff of a Government-Funded Rights"; Roman, "Widow Calls for Rights & Democracy Inquiry."

17. voices-voix, "Rights & Democracy."

18. One of those board members, Jacques Gauthier, was honoured a decade later with the inaugural Canadian Antisemitism Education Foundation's "Advocate Award of Excellence" for his 1,100 page doctoral thesis arguing for Jewish sovereignty over all of Jerusalem. Arnold, "Scholar Honored for Work on 100th Anniversary of San Remo Conference."

19. Allen, "Canada Votes at the UN."

20. Sucharov herself has faced vitriol over her own positioning, which she touches upon in chapter 8 in this volume.

21. In my own analysis of Canadian government reporting on its significant Palestinian aid programming, I found a similar and long-standing approach of avoiding contextually relevant terminology, including words like occupation or settlements. Wildeman, "Donor Aid Effectiveness and Do No Harm."

22. Wildeman, "EU Development Aid in the Occupied Palestinian Territory"; Tartir and Wildeman, "Persistent Failure"; Tartir and Wildeman, "Can Oslo's Failed Aid Model Be Laid to Rest?"; Wildeman and Tartir, "Political Economy of Foreign Aid."

23. Anderson, "'Do No Harm': The Impact of International Assistance"; Karlstedt et al., "Effectiveness of Core Funding to CSOs"; Organisation for Economic Co-Operation and Development (OECD), "International Engagement."

24. Ayyash, "The IHRA Definition Will Not Help."

25. This is something I write about in detail in my own contribution in this book (chapter 2).

26. Alpert, "Racism Is Baked into the Structure of Dialectical Philosophy."

27. See the introduction in this volume by M. Muhannad Ayyash.

28. Friesen, "Canadian University Teachers Begin Process to Censure U of T."

29. Toronto has also been the centre of a large and robust Palestinian film festival, and a hub for overtly political campus-wide Israeli-apartheid week organizing that takes place across Canada every year.

30. See Wills' chapter in this volume (chapter 10).

31. See chapter 9 by Assi and Abdelnour in this volume.

References

Al Masri, Dalya. "Anti-Palestinian Racism Is Behind IHRA's Antisemitism Definition." *Passage*, November 18, 2020. https://readpassage.com/anti-palestinian-racism-is-behind-ihras-antisemitism-definition/.

Allen, Jon. "Canada Votes at the UN: A Response to the CIJA, B'nai Brith Canada and Friends of Simon Wiesenthal Center." *Canadian Jewish Record*, November 25, 2020. https://canadianjewishrecord.ca/2020/11/25/canada-votes-at-the-un-a-response-to-the-cija-bnai-brith-canada-and-friends-of-simon-wiesenthal-center/.

Alpert, Avram. "Racism Is Baked into the Structure of Dialectical Philosophy." *Aeon*, September 24, 2020. https://aeon.co/essays/racism-is-baked-into-the-structure-of-dialectical-philosophy.

Anderson, Mary B. "'Do No Harm': The Impact of International Assistance to the Occupied Palestinian Territory." In *Aid, Diplomacy and the Facts on the Ground: The Palestinian Experience of Disconnection*, edited by Michael Keating, Anne Le More, and Robert Lowe, 143–53. London: Royal Institute of International Affairs, 2005.

Arnold, Steve. "Scholar Honored for Work on 100th Anniversary of San Remo Conference." *Canadian Jewish Record*, December 2, 2020. https://canadianjewishrecord.ca/2020/12/02/scholar-honored-for-work-on-100th-anniversary-of-san-remo-conference/.

Ayyash, M. Muhannad. "The IHRA Definition Will Not Help Fight Anti-Semitism." *Al Jazeera*, November 23, 2020. https://www.aljazeera.com/opinions/2020/11/23/the-ihra-and-the-palestinian-struggle-for/.

Bandler, Aaron. "Trudeau Condemns Protests of Pro-Israel Event at York University." *Jewish Journal*, November 22, 2019. https://jewishjournal.com/news/world/307537/trudeau-condemns-protests-of-pro-israel-event-at-york-university/.

Bradley-St-Cyr, Ruth. "The Downfall of the Ryerson Press." PHD thesis, University of Ottawa, 2014. https://ruor.uottawa.ca/bitstream/10393/31080/3/Bradley-St-Cyr_Ruth_2014_thesis.pdf.

"Camp David Accords." The Avalon Project: Yale Law School, September 17, 1978. https://avalon.law.yale.edu/20th_century/campdav.asp.

Cheadle, Bruce. "The Staff of a Government-Funded Rights Advocacy Group Is Calling for the Resignation of Three Conservative Appointees from Its Board." *Toronto Star*, January 12, 2010. https://www.thestar.com/news/canada/2010/01/12/tory_appointees_unfit_for_rights_agency_board_staff_says.html.

DPA, and *Haaretz*. "Trudeau's Anti-BDS Message During Apology for Turning Away Jews During WWII Continues to Make Waves." *Haaretz*, November 11, 2018. https://www.haaretz.com/world-news/americas/trudeau-s-hard-line-anti-bds-stance-draws-attention-1.6639351?fbclid=IwAR3NbE3cF2zmCuCgsGqxn-pf8vMYeg86S9aOWSnG86ggwWT-if_Gmkbcacs.

Economic Cooperation Foundation (ECF). "Venice Declaration (1980)." The Israeli-Palestinian Conflict: An Interactive Database. Accessed December 2, 2020. https://ecf.org.il/issues/issue/11.

Forrest, A.C. *Unholy Land*. Toronto: Devin-Adair Pub, 1972.

Friesen, Joe. "Canadian University Teachers Begin Process to Censure U of T over the Azarova Law School Affair." *The Globe and Mail*, October 15, 2020. https://www.theglobeandmail.com/canada/article-canadian-university-teachers-begin-process-to-censure-u-of-t-over-the/.

Giniger, Henry. "Canada Abandons Plan to Move Its Israel Embassy to Jerusalem." *The New York Times*, October 30, 1979. https://www.nytimes.com/1979/10/30/archives/canada-abandons-plan-to-move-its-israel-embassy-to-jerusalem.html.

Karlstedt, Cecilia, Waddah Abdulsalam, Smadar Ben-Natan, and Haneen Rizik. "Effectiveness of Core Funding to CSOs in the Field of Human Rights and International Humanitarian Law in Occupied Palestine: Final Report." Stockholm: SIDA, 2015. https://www.sida.se/English/publications/139125/effectiveness-of-core-funding-to-csos-in-the-field-of-human-rights-and-international-humanitarian-law-in-occupied-palestine---f1/.

Nathan-Kazis, Josh. "Anonymous Online Blacklist Canary Mission Is Getting Scarier." *The Forward*, August 2, 2018. https://forward.com/news/national/407279/canary-mission-s-threat-grows-from-u-s-campuses-to-the-israeli-border/.

Organisation for Economic Co-Operation and Development (OECD). "International Engagement in Fragile States: Can't We Do Better?" Conflict and Fragility Series. OECD Publishing, 2011. https://www.oecd.org/countries/somalia/48697077.pdf.

Paradkar, Shree. "Controversies at U of T Law, York University Highlight Escalating Suppression of Moderate Voices Criticizing Israel." *Toronto Star*, October 25, 2020. https://www.thestar.com/opinion/star-columnists/2020/10/25/controversies-at-u-of-t-law-york-university-highlight-escalating-suppression-of-moderate-voices-criticizing-israel.html.

Robinson, Andrew. "Talking to the PLO: Overcoming Political Challenges." *Canadian Foreign Policy Journal* 27, no. 1 (January 2, 2021): 21–30.

Roman, Karina. "Widow Calls for Rights & Democracy Inquiry." *CBC*, April 13, 2010. https://www.cbc.ca/news/politics/widow-calls-for-rights-democracy-inquiry-1.917863.

Tartir, Alaa, and Jeremy Wildeman. "Can Oslo's Failed Aid Model Be Laid to Rest?" Al-Shabaka, September 19, 2013. http://al-shabaka.org/node/672.

Tartir, Alaa, and Jeremy Wildeman. "Persistent Failure: World Bank Policies for the Occupied Palestinian Territories." Al-Shabaka, October 9, 2012. http://al-shabaka.org/node/513.

The Canadian Press. "Premier Doug Ford Weighs in on Clash at York University Pro-Israel Event." *CBC*, November 21, 2019. https://www.cbc.ca/news/canada/toronto/york-university-israel-protest-ford-1.5368601.

Thompson, Jon. *No Debate: The Israel Lobby and Free Speech at Canadian Universities.* Toronto: Formac Lorimer, 2011.

Times of Israel Staff. "Trudeau Blasts BDS Movement as Anti-Semitic." *Times of Israel*, January 17, 2019. https://www.timesofisrael.com/trudeau-blasts-bds-movement-as-anti-semitic/.

voices-voix. "Rights & Democracy." Accessed September 9, 2014. http://voices-voix.ca/en/facts/profile/rights-democracy.

Wildeman, Jeremy. "Assessing Canada's Foreign Policy Approach to the Palestinians and Israeli-Palestinian Peacebuilding, 1979–2019." *Canadian Foreign Policy Journal* 27, no. 1 (January 2, 2021): 62–80.

Wildeman, Jeremy. "Donor Aid Effectiveness and Do No Harm in the Occupied Palestinian Territory." Aid Watch Palestine, December 10, 2018. http://www.aidwatch.ps/sites/

default/files/resource-field_media/Aid%20Effectiveness%20%26%20Do%20
No%20Harm%20in%20OPT-%20Final-compressed_1.pdf.

Wildeman, Jeremy. "EU Development Aid in the Occupied Palestinian Territory, Between
Aid Effectiveness and World Bank Guidance." *Global Affairs* 4, no. 1 (2018): 115–28.

Wildeman, Jeremy, and Alaa Tartir, "Political Economy of Foreign Aid in the Occupied
Palestinian Territory: A Conceptual Framing." In *Political Economy of Palestine:
Critical, Interdisciplinary, Decolonial Perspective*, edited by Alaa Tartir, Tariq Dana, and
Timothy Seidel, 223–48. Cham, Switzerland: MacMillan-Palgrave, 2021.

CONTRIBUTORS

SAMER ABDELNOUR, PHD (London School of Economics), is a senior lecturer (associate professor) at the University of Edinburgh Business School. In his research, he employs organization theory to study topics such as humanitarian technology, postwar enterprise intervention, and international standards. He also writes about research methods. His work has been published in leading organization studies and energy/environmental studies journals.

NADIA ABU-ZAHRA, DPHIL (Oxon), was raised in territory taken from First Nations, including the Wendat, that was covered by the Dish With One Spoon Wampum Belt Covenant, an agreement between the Confederacies of the Haudenosaunee and Ojibwe and allied nations. She is Associate Professor of International Development and Global Studies and the Joint Chair in Women's Studies at the University of Ottawa and Carleton University. She is co-author of *Unfree in Palestine* (Pluto Press 2012), co-editor of *Advocating for Palestine in Canada* (Fernwood Publishing 2022), and co-facilitator of Community Mobilization in Crisis (cmic-mobilize.org).

RACHAD ANTONIUS, born in Egypt, is an adjunct professor (retired full professor) of sociology at the Université du Québec à Montréal. His research deals with Arab societies and Arab immigrant groups in Canada. He is the author of *Interpreting Quantitative Data with* IBM-SPSS (Sage 2013) and "A Mediated Relationship: Media Representations of Muslims and Arabs as a Political Process," in *Targeted Transnationals: The State, the Media, and Arab Canadians,* edited by J. Hennebry and B. Momani (UBC Press 2013), as well as several other articles on the representations of Arabs and Muslims in mainstream media.

LINA ASSI earned her BA in Political Science and Labour Studies and an MA in Labour Studies at McMaster University. Her dissertation focused on the Palestinian labour movement in the post-Oslo era. She is currently the advocacy manager at Palestine Legal and a community organizer with the Palestinian Youth Movement.

M. MUHANNAD AYYASH was born and raised in Silwan, Al-Quds, before immigrating to Canada, where he is now full professor of sociology at Mount Royal University. He is the author of *A Hermeneutics of Violence* (University of Toronto Press 2019). He has published several articles in journals such as *Interventions*, the *European Journal of International Relations*, *Comparative Studies of South Asia, Africa and the Middle East*, and the *European Journal of Social Theory*. He has written opinion pieces for *Al-Jazeera*, *The Baffler*, *Middle East Eye*, *Mondoweiss*, *The Breach*, and *Middle East Monitor*.

VELDON COBURN, PHD (Queen's), is Anishinaabe and a member of the Algonquins of Pikwàkanagàn. He is currently an assistant professor of Indigenous Studies at the University of Ottawa. His research is focused on Indigenous politics and policy, particularly settler colonialism, anti- and decolonizing theories of society, state, and power. He has authored numerous articles and is the co-editor of *Capitalism and Dispossession: Corporate Canada at Home and Abroad* (Fernwood Publishing 2022).

PEIGE DESJARLAIS is a doctoral candidate in Social Anthropology at York University in Toronto, whose current research project explores the intersection of tree-planting and colonial dispossession. Her publications have addressed the way Israeli practices of archaeology and tree-planting have worked to make claim to the lands of occupied Palestine. Her work stems from involvement and commitment to movements to end settler colonialism, both in Palestine-Israel and at home.

RANDA FARAH was born and raised in Haifa and lived in different countries before migrating to Canada. She is an Associate Professor of Anthropology at the University of Western Ontario. Her research in refugee camps led to several publications that focus on refugees, memory/history and identity, nations and nationalism, and humanitarianism. Her articles appeared in several books and journals, including: *Journal of Palestine Studies*, *Jerusalem Quarterly*, *Interventions*, *Refuge*, *Refugee Survey Quarterly*, *Forced Migration Review*, *Mediterranean Journal of Human Rights*. She has written opinion pieces for al-Shabaka, *al-Majdal*, and *al-Akhbar*, among others.

AZEEZAH KANJI is a legal academic and journalist whose work focuses on issues relating to racism, colonialism, law, and social justice. She received her Juris Doctor from University of Toronto's Faculty of Law, and her Masters of Law specializing in Islamic Law from the School of Oriental and African Studies, University of London. Her writing appears regularly in Canadian and international media, including *Al Jazeera English*, *Haaretz*, the *Toronto Star*, and *TruthOut*, as well as academic anthologies and journals.

MAURICE JR. LABELLE was born and raised as a French-Canadian settler in the traditional territories of Ho-de-no-sau-nee-ga (Haudenosaunee), Kanien'kehá:ka (Mohawk), and Wendake-Nionwentsïo (Wendat), also known as the contemporary municipality of Cornwall, Ontario, Canada. An associate professor of history at the University of Saskatchewan, he currently lives and works on Treaty 6 Territory and the Homeland of the Michif/Métis. Labelle's research and teaching interests explore how discursive practices of decolonization become universalized modes of liberation and reparation. His latest publication is an edited volume, *The Boomerang Effect of Decolonization: Post-Orientalism and the Politics of Difference* (McGill-Queen's University Press, 2023).

NADIA NASER-NAJJAB holds a PHD in Middle East Studies from the University of Exeter. She is a senior lecturer in Palestine Studies at the European Centre for Palestine Studies, Institute of Arab and Islamic Studies, University of Exeter. Her research is based on first-hand experience and original data collection, focusing on the peace process, Palestinian education, and resistance. She regularly publishes newspaper and online magazine articles. Her recent book is entitled *Dialogue in Palestine: The People-to-People*

Diplomacy Programme and the Israeli-Palestinian Conflict (Bloomsbury Publishing 2020). Her recent academic articles include "Palestinian Education and the 'Logic of Elimination,'" in *Settler Colonial Studies* and "The Oslo People-to-People Program and the Limits of Hegemony" in *Middle East Critique*.

EMILY REGAN WILLS, PHD (The New School), is an associate professor of comparative and American politics in the School of Political Studies at the University of Ottawa, and co-director of the Community Mobilization in Crisis (cmic-mobilize.org). Her roots are in anti-war, feminist, and queer liberation movements. She is the author of *Arab New York: Politics and Community in the Everyday Lives of Arab Americans* (NYU Press 2019) and co-editor of *Advocating for Palestine in Canada* (Fernwood Publishing 2022).

MIRA SUCHAROV is Professor of Political Science at Carleton University in Ottawa, Canada. She has developed courses in Israeli-Palestinian relations, op-ed writing and social media engagement, Netflix and politics, and graphic novels and political identity. She is the founding co-chair of the Jewish Politics Division at the Association for Jewish Studies, and from 2018–2022 was co-editor (with Chaya Halberstam) of *AJS Perspectives*. She is the author of *Borders and Belonging: A Memoir* (Palgrave Macmillan 2021), and *The International Self: Psychoanalysis and the Search for Israeli-Palestinian Peace* (SUNY Press 2005). She is co-editor (with Aaron J. Hahn Tapper) of *Social Justice and Israel/Palestine: Foundational & Contemporary Debates* (University of Toronto Press 2019).

JEREMY WILDEMAN, PHD (Exeter), was raised in Treaty 6 / Saskatchewan. He is a Fellow at the Human Rights Research and Education Centre at the University of Ottawa and is an adjunct lecturer of Middle East politics. His research includes comparative analyses of Western donor development programming toward the Palestinians, and Canada's historical and contemporary relationship with the Middle East. He co-guest edited a special issue of the *Canadian Foreign Policy Journal*, "What Lies Ahead: Canada's Engagement with the Middle East Peace Process and the Palestinians" (2021), since republished as a book by Routledge (2021).